NIOBES

CLASSICAL MEMORIES/MODERN IDENTITIES
Paul Allen Miller and Richard H. Armstrong, Series Editors

NIOBES

Antiquity, Modernity, Critical Theory

∽

Edited by Mario Telò and Andrew Benjamin

THE OHIO STATE UNIVERSITY PRESS
COLUMBUS

Copyright © 2024 by The Ohio State University.
All rights reserved.

Library of Congress Cataloging-in-Publication Data
Names: Telò, Mario, 1977– editor. | Benjamin, Andrew E., editor.
Title: Niobes : antiquity, modernity, critical theory / edited by Mario Telò and Andrew Benjamin.
Other titles: Classical memories/modern identities.
Description: Columbus : The Ohio State University Press, [2024] | Series: Classical memories/modern identities | Includes bibliographical references and index. | Summary: "Reconstructing the dialogues of Phillis Wheatley, G. W. F. Hegel, Walter Benjamin, and Aby Warburg with Niobe as she appears in Aeschylus, Sophocles, Ovid, and the visual arts, contributors imagine new ways of connecting the classical tradition and ancient tragic discourse with crises and political questions relating to gender, race, and social justice"—Provided by publisher.
Identifiers: LCCN 2023046870 | ISBN 9780814215630 (hardback) | ISBN 0814215637 (hardback) | ISBN 9780814283349 (ebook) | ISBN 0814283349 (ebook)
Subjects: LCSH: Niobe (Greek mythological character)—In literature. | Niobe (Greek mythological character)—Art. | Wheatley, Phillis, 1753–1784—Criticism and interpretation. | Hegel, Georg Wilhelm Friedrich, 1770–1831—Criticism and interpretation. | Benjamin, Walter, 1892–1940—Criticism and interpretation. | Warburg, Aby, 1866–1929—Criticism and interpretation. | Mythology, Greek, in literature. | Mythology, Greek, in art.
Classification: LCC PN57.N56 N56 2024 | DDC 880.9—dc23/eng/20231220
LC record available at https://lccn.loc.gov/2023046870

Cover design by Susan Zucker
Text design by Juliet Williams
Type set in Adboe Minion Pro

∞ The paper used in this publication meets the minimum requirements of the American National Standard for Information Sciences—Permanence of Paper for Printed Library Materials. ANSI Z39.48-1992.

CONTENTS

Acknowledgments	vii
INTRODUCTION Critical Encounters with Niobe MARIO TELÒ	1

PART 1 · AN-ARCHIC BEGINNINGS

CHAPTER 1	Niobe's Hypermaternity ADRIANA CAVARERO	25
CHAPTER 2	*Nihil Est in Imagine Vivum* REBECCA COMAY	36
CHAPTER 3	Niobe's People: Ambiguous Violence and Interrupted Labor in *Iliad* 24 BEN RADCLIFFE	54

PART 2 · AROUND OVID

CHAPTER 4	Philosophers' Stone: Enduring Niobe VICTORIA RIMELL	69
CHAPTER 5	Niobe's Tragic Cryo-Ecology MARIO TELÒ	85
CHAPTER 6	Tears from Stone JOHN T. HAMILTON	98
CHAPTER 7	Shadow and Stone: Niobe between Platonism and Stoicism ANDRES MATLOCK	114

PART 3 · ART AND AESTHETICS

CHAPTER 8	The Weeping Rock: *Paragone, Pathosformel,* and Petrification	
	BARBARA BAERT	129
CHAPTER 9	Schelling's Niobe	
	MILDRED GALLAND-SZYMKOWIAK	145
CHAPTER 10	The More Loving One: On Postmelancholic Life	
	PAUL A. KOTTMAN	160
CHAPTER 11	Niobe's *Nomoi*	
	DANIEL VILLEGAS VÉLEZ	178

PART 4 · PHILOSOPHY, POETRY, SOCIAL JUSTICE

CHAPTER 12	Niobe between Benjamin and Arendt—and Beyond	
	MATHURA UMACHANDRAN	195
CHAPTER 13	Countering Injury: On the Deaths of the Niobids	
	ANDREW BENJAMIN	208
CHAPTER 14	*Lacrimae Rerum*: Institution of Grief	
	JACQUES LEZRA	223
CHAPTER 15	"How Strangely Changed": Finding Phillis Wheatley in Niobean Myth and Memory, an Essay in Verse	
	DREA BROWN	238

Bibliography	253
List of Contributors	267
Index	271

ACKNOWLEDGMENTS

Mario Telò expresses his deepest thanks to Andrew Benjamin, an unmatchable coeditor, the soul of this project, the alpha and the omega of Niobean philosophy, the most inspiring theoretical interlocutor. The project started with him, and I am profoundly honored to have been brought on board as coeditor. What I admired of the original project and sought to reproduce is its interdisciplinary force, its programmatic quest for encounters and proximities within, beyond, and on the edges of the classical tradition and critical theory. Alex Press is, as always, the sine qua non of everything.

A million thanks to all of our wonderful contributors; to the editors, Paul Allen Miller and Richard Armstrong, for welcoming the book in the fearless Classical Memories and Modern Identities series; to Ana Jimenez-Moreno, acquisitions editor at The Ohio State University Press, for her vision, as well as her constant support and patience; and to our three anonymous readers for their extremely helpful comments, which have enhanced the coherence of the book.

Translations are by the contributors unless otherwise indicated.

INTRODUCTION

Critical Encounters with Niobe

MARIO TELÒ

Despite Niobe's numerous epiphanies, her ancient and modern appearances-in-disappearance in Homer, Sappho, Aeschylus, and Ovid, as well as Hegel, Phillis Wheatley, and Walter Benjamin, not to mention visual artists, named or anonymous, there has yet to be a sustained engagement—intensely, creatively, rapturously interpretive—with this hauntological presence that has shaped art, literature, and critical theory. The goal of this collection is not to provide a history of Niobe's reception,[1] but to offer insights and impressions, suggestions for encountering and affectively bonding with her diachronic persistence, which is troped by her becoming stone. Niobe's human and posthuman living in and beyond time also amounts to a vital yet exhausting synchronicity after a serial (re)production of filial losses, wounds that solidify her melancholic immortality. The material insistence, liquid as well as solid, of her petrified survival as a weeping rock opens a possibility of construing the classical tradition as a monumentality disrupted by an exchange or confusion of states, which unsettles the very idea (physical and symbolic) of being in a *state*.[2]

---

1. For histories of Niobe, see Cook (1964), Kerényi (1979), and Stark (2022).
2. On liquid antiquity, see Holmes (2017), who asks: "What would happen if the ground began to shift? If antiquity, no longer carved stone, turned liquid?" Holmes observes that "liquidity haunts classicism" (20). (Monumental) classicism, one might say, can be replaced by Niobe. As she observes, "The liquid raises the specter of the loss of antiquity at its most foundational."

"Niobe is the image of the withdrawal of the image," as Rebecca Comay puts it. "Frozen in grief and yet overspilling," "shrinking into solitude yet expanding into the landscape, fixed in place but defying gravity, freezing-seething," "neither animate nor inanimate, neither living nor dead," "a stone that is not quite stony enough, a corpse that does not stay dead enough," Niobe embodies a narrative fragmentation, an off-centeredness, and a hermeneutic impossibility that seep into the discursive texture of the chapters presented here. This collection is an experiment in Niobean writing, an assemblage of serendipitous, affectively charged meditations on critical–theoretical potentialities.

In Antonietta Raphaël's 1939 sculpture of Niobe, which provides the cover of this book, we observe Niobe's mobile immobility, her flowing, agitated immanence, the kinetic force—even in the grip of the paralyzing contours of representation—of a maternal care that disrupts the bounds of individuation. In joining the child's head to her breast, welcoming a filial leg into a web of limbs, the sculpted Niobe shades deindividuation into melancholic introjection—an absorption whose impossibility, traced by a hole, protects the otherness of the other.[3] As in the tearful flow of Niobe's perennial lamentation, care in this sculpture appears to be the impetus of her forward projection, the ethical inclination inherent in maternal *towardness,* a relationality encompassing *justice to*[4] whose kinetic energy erodes representational boundaries, undoing the distribution of the sensible that births Niobe through a cutting, a chiseling of matter.[5]

The daughter of Tantalus, married to Amphion, Niobe boasted that she was more fecund than Leto/Latona, which caused Leto to engage her own children, Artemis/Diana and Apollo, to slaughter Niobe's. Inconsolable, turned to stone, she continues, in her petrified form, to weep. Though there is no original story, her most significant presence is in Ovid's *Metamorphoses*.[6] In his conciliatory encounter with Priam in the *Iliad,* Achilles, precariously

---

3. On deindividuation, see esp. Moten (2003; 2017). On melancholy as an ethical eating of the other that never results in absorption or digestion, see Derrida (1989; 1991). On Antonietta Raphaël, see Cavarero's chapter. Deuber-Mankowsky (2016, 259) aptly points out that "the very title of chapter 5 of [Judith Butler's] *The Psychic Life of Power: Theories in Subjection,* 'Melancholy Gender/Refused Identification,' recalls Niobe."

4. In the context of his discussion (and critique) of Hegel's comparison of Niobe with Mary ("while Mary has become love personified, Niobe must remain without love"), A. Benjamin (2015, 120–21) suggests that the foundational ethical question is "what would it mean to be just to Niobe?" As he puts it, "Being just on the one hand and either loving or befriending on the other are not simply radically different undertakings; rather, they bring importantly different senses of being a subject and as a result differing modes of being-in-relation into play." See also Schmidt (2017).

5. On Jacques Rancière's antimimetic Niobe, see Telò's chapter.

6. For analyses of the Ovidian narrative, see Hamilton's, Rimell's, and Telò's chapters.

reintegrated into the heroic Symbolic, uses Niobe as an *exemplum* of interrupted grief, of a return to life—perhaps a signal that his apparent healing is just a parenthesis in his self-marginalization, his detached life of grief, his constitutive, turbulent petrification.[7]

On the way to the cave that will be her own petrifying receptacle, Sophocles's Antigone sees herself as imprisoned, melting, in lamentation like Niobe (823-33)[8]—for Lacan, reading this passage, they are twin embodiments of the death drive. (And before Lacan, Hamlet assimilates Niobe's liquefaction to suicide but also the impossibility thereof.)[9] In the fragments of Aeschylus's eponymous tragedy, Niobe acquiesces to speech after a protracted silence referred to by Aristophanes's *Frogs* and visualized on many vases, where she merges into the medium, into the material substrate,[10] forced to switch to the side of *logos*, the interpellative imperative that calls itself reason. In his *De mulieribus claris*, Boccaccio (and many others before and after him) misogynistically casts her as "foolish" and guilty of an unforgivable act of hubris, which is nothing but the inescapable condition of guilt imposed by law as such, for Walter Benjamin and Judith Butler. Contrasting her with Mary, the symbol of love, Hegel sees Niobe as unlovable and incapable of love.[11] Our intention is to present Niobe as another Antigone—as a tragic figure, or a complex of figurations, who continues to exert a profound influence on various modes of modern thought, especially in aesthetics, ethics, psychoanalysis, and politics.[12] Benjamin, Butler, Cavarero (one of the contributors), Lacan,

---

7. *Iliad* 24.602-17. On this passage, see Radcliffe's chapter.

8. For a close reading of this passage, see Kornarou (2010).

9. See Hamlet's first soliloquy (act 1, scene 2), where the reference to Niobe ("Like Niobe, all tears") as a comparandum for his mother's (hypocritical) grief at the funeral of her husband is preceded by words that suggest his own identification with the ancient tragic mother: "O that this too solid flesh would melt, / thaw and resolve itself into a dew! / Or that the Everlasting had not fix'd / his canon 'gainst self-slaughter." Niobe's liquefaction, the condition of infinite mourning in which Hamlet finds himself, is initially assimilated to suicide; yet the subsequent reference to the divine prohibition of "self-slaughter" invites us to see Niobe's lifedeath as precisely forbidden suicide. This passage is part of Hamlet's "struggle to . . . free the masculine identity of both father and son from its origin in the contaminated maternal body" (Adelman 1992, 17).

10. On Aeschylus's *Niobe*, see Telò's chapter in this volume and ch. 8 in Telò (2023); for an analysis of the surviving fragments, see Seaford (2005) and Pennesi (2008). On Niobe in Sophocles, see Ozbek (2015). On the iconography of Niobe in vase painting, see esp. Sevieri (2010).

11. See A. Benjamin (2012; 2015). For Hegel (1975b, 817), Niobe conveys "a cold resignation in which the individual, without altogether collapsing, still sacrifices what [s]he had clung to." The painted or sculpted Niobe, like Laocoon, "does not display any wrath, contempt, or vexation, and yet the loftiness of [her] individuality is only a persistent self-consistency, an empty endurance of fate in which the nobility and grief of [her] soul still appear as not balanced."

12. The inspiration comes, of course, from Steiner's *Antigones* (1984).

Levinas, Rancière, Schelling, Warburg, and others have engaged with Niobe (Homer's, Sappho's, Aeschylus's, Sophocles's, Ovid's—or nobody's in particular) in ways that have informed their theorizations of art and the tensions between life and death, generation and destruction, trauma and survival, punishment and justice, silence and critical resistance, representation and sensation. Niobe invites us to think about the marginalization and silencing of the maternal and also about possibilities for unconventional, nonagentic agencies for subjectivities that are a priori denied recognition or even a subject position. Niobe thus also offers an opportunity to address questions central to contemporary intersectional feminisms and critical race theory.[13]

In what follows I propose four close readings—of Phillis Wheatley's, Michael Field's, Søren Kierkegaard's, and Alberto Savinio's Niobes—that supply glimpses of the Niobean discourses mobilized by the contributors. The epigraphs that open each section, drawn from the chapters, exemplify the thematic and theoretical clusters of the book—forms of the Niobean mode urgently relevant to our time of chronic crisis.

1. SLAVERY LOSS DISPOSSESSION

an impossible story to tell: being brought. bought. the ship on the child's head. her mother a briny venus, the sea conflicted with maritime prey. she saw their faces and blinking eyes the glory of black liquescent hands waving. mellifluent ocean calling her name. what a salve. (brown)

The incorporation of the daughter becomes petrification—not a return to the maternal sea of the organic life, to birth-giving flesh before the birth of the singular body through detachment, splitting, but a return to an exit, by means of mineral solidification, from the flux of life. (Cavarero)

As Niobe strives to remove herself from time, she immobilizes representational and thanato-political imperatives while mobilizing an icy virtuality before and after consciousness. (Telò)

---

[13]. See Spigner (2021, 321) on Phillis Wheatley's engagement with Niobe: "I named Wheatley's multilayered classical revision as 'Niobean Poetics,' the results of which respond to the intersectional conditions of race and power manifested in the historical conditions of black mothers during Atlantic slavery." Pinto (2020, 63) observes that "fantasies of Wheatley and her celebrity legacy can point to black intimacies and uncertainty as politically viable politics instead of focusing on the horizon of freedom as a litmus test for the use of and engagement with black women's history."

Niobe resonates with [Saidiya] Hartman's figuring of loss [in *Lose Your Mother*] by inverting our attention toward the mother as also a subject who must avow her losses (the mother who loses, always). What all of this "promises" remains open-ended: it may well be new political commitments, different ideas of self-integrity, alternatives patterns of relating individually or collectively to the world structured by histories of violent dispossession. (Umachandran)

As we read in drea brown's poignant poetic intervention in this book, the Ovidian Niobe of Phillis Wheatley—the first African American to publish a book of poetry, in 1773[14]—presents "an impossible story to tell," the drama of submerged faces in the Middle Passage, and the tragedy of survival, of being "brought" and "bought":

The queen of all her family bereft,
Without or husband, son, or daughter left,
Grew stupid at the shock. The passing air
Made no impression on her stiff'ning hair.
The blood forsook her face: amidst the flood
Pour'd from her cheeks, quite fix'ed her eye-balls stood.
Her tongue, her palate both obdurate grew,
Her curdled veins no longer motion knew;
The use of neck, and arms, and feet was gone,
And ev'n her bowels hard'ned into stone:
A marble statue now the queen appears,
But from the marble steal the silent tears.[15]

Rhyming with *bereft*, *left* suggests the overlap between, on the one hand, forced departure from the motherland, the journey of enslaved exile, a movement of brutal displacement, "of violent dispossession," and, on the other, the overdetermined loss of lives left behind in the Atlantic as well as on the African continent. A living death, Niobe's "stupor" translates the process of her stony frozenness (*deriguit malis*) into *matterphorical* (rather than metaphorical)[16]

---

14. Wheatley 2020. See Jeffers (2020, 186): "She was a little girl when she arrived in Boston, but she did have African birth parents. Her life did not begin in America or with slavery. She had a free lineage that did not include the Wheatleys. If nothing else, a treatment of that lineage would be an appropriate and respectful introduction to this poet's life in America."
15. Wheatley 1988, 112–13.
16. On matterphorics, see Gandorfer and Ayub (2020, 4): "What would it mean ... to slide between language and materiality ... to not limit life's 'speech' to communication but ... to acknowledge ... that concepts matter-forth, that some concepts are lethal?"

endurance, the exhausting forbearance inflicted on the slave, a self-dulling in the face of each new cutting blow.[17] In the image of *air* unable to make itself felt on *hair*, to lend its elemental motion to, and blend into, a supplemented, "aspirated," version of itself, Wheatley reads Niobe's petrification as an interruption of the contact with the nonhuman externality that we may call nature or environment, or with the human other that can allow a notional living self to recognize itself as such. Niobe's silence famously captured at the beginning of Aeschylus's play resonates with Saidiya Hartman's exploration of the legacy of slavery through the figure of the lost mother, a mother who, we might say, projects her own self-loss into generations facing an impossible future:

> I had grown weary of pleading our case and repeating our complaint. It seems to me that there is something innately servile about making an appeal to a deaf ear or praying for relief to an indifferent and hostile court or expecting remedy from a government unwilling even to acknowledge that slavery was a crime against humanity.[18]

Petrified, Niobe cries but does not vocalize her lament, does not verbalize the injustice, does not seek compassionate ears for her perennial injury, does not demand relief from her own inhabitation of loss—losslosslosslossloss (in drea brown's formation). Any relief would diminish the manifest cruelty of the crime—of divine law, of law as such—that enslaves her. Niobe's silence visualizes her acting as a rem(a)inder of an accreted loss, as the outcome, the offspring of repeated loss—the mute, mutilated-at-birth child of the multiple children whom she no longer has. Hartman says: "I am a reminder that twelve million crossed the Atlantic Ocean and the past is not yet over. I am the progeny of the captives. I am the vestige of the dead. . . . My pessimism was stronger than my longing. In my heart I knew my losses were irreparable."[19]

Even as, in the suffocation of slavery, the *air* slips away from the mother's *hair*, the material phonic surplus in *passing* and *stiff'ning* anticipates the life in death, the liquidity in solidity awaiting the petrified Niobe. The enhanced *if* in *st-iff-ening* emanates the verbal air of what Kevin Quashie calls "subjunctivity"—"the animating of being through the expressiveness of might-

---

17. On "stuplimity," see Ngai (2005, ch. 6).
18. Hartman 2007, 166.
19. Hartman 2007, 18, 54. See Spigner (2021, 320): "In reworking this myth, Wheatley speaks to the power of black motherhood, something that is otherwise, specifically in the Atlantic Slavery context, framed and experienced as denigration. By highlighting Niobe's rebellion against a totalizing power, Wheatley reclaims black motherhood as a site of resistance, not just one of vulnerability."

be,"[20] a conceptualization of "experience as a toggling between then (past), now (present), and what may come."[21] The current of *air* materialized as *iff* is like the tears that put a tear in Niobe's stony death. As Judith Butler observes, Niobe "would be fully deadened by guilt, if it were not for that sorrow, those tears."[22] Niobe's life is *"a state of suspension in the intensity of presence and possibility, a state of readiness and surrender."*[23] This suspension or subjunctivity makes Wheatley—the slave becoming poet—and the metamorphosed Niobe into participants in and embodiments of an "aesthetics of aliveness."[24] Such aesthetics are perceptible in the sonic triangulation of "blood . . . flood . . . stood," in which the phonetic variation introduces a motion of becoming into eyeballs that otherwise stood fixed, while the blood forsaking her neck is transubstantiated into tears. It is as though the flood of Niobe's tears percolates through the line and Wheatley draws a measure of self-liberation from the suspension between self-affirmation and dissolution, self-possession and dispossession. The reification or mortification of the enslaved person's corporeality seen in the commodifying list of bodily parts numbed, paralyzed, congealed (tongue, palate, veins, neck, arms, and feet) is obstructed by fugitive, furtive motion, by the silent sound of sibilant tears (*steal . . . silent*), by the swelling (the root meaning of *Phillis*)[25] of watery trauma or liquid life.[26]

2. RELATIONALITY QUEERNESS MOTHERHOOD

[A] sense of human "well-being" in Aristotle, and its connection to friendship, means that friendship is a particularized relation, as it can be seen as forming part of the general description of human being as *being-in-common*. (Andrew Benjamin)

To be a friend, Niobe cannot be a mother, and to be a mother means entering an actively antisocial relationality, destructive both within and outside of

---

20. Quashie 2021, 61.
21. Quashie 2021, 59.
22. J. Butler 2006, 208.
23. Quashie 2021, 66.
24. This phrase is inspired by the title of a chapter in Quashie's book (2021, ch. 3, "Aliveness and Aesthetics").
25. Phillis is cognate with Greek *phyllon* ("leaf"), Latin *flos* ("flower"), and English *bloom*, words that share the PIE root *bhel- ("to blow, swell").
26. *Steal . . . silent* replace the alliteration *liquitur . . . lacrimas* in Ovid, *Metamorphoses* 6.312.

her family. The loss of Leto as a friend foreshadows the loss of her children as a mother. (Matlock)

While self-sacrificing Mary has become love personified, Niobe—without her beloved children, her relationality excised—must remain without love. (Rimell)

Sappho's Niobe or a Sapphic Niobe appears in one of the poems of the collection *Long Ago* (1889), published under the name Michael Field by Katherine Harris Bradley and Edith Emma Cooper, an aunt and a niece who lived as a lesbian couple for forty years in Victorian England. Every poem in this collection opens with one or more lines from a Sappho fragment. Michael Field, that is, Bradley and Cooper, "turn to Sappho, whom they certainly understand to be Lesbian in more than the proper sense of the name," Yopie Prins observes, "in order to develop a model of lyric authorship in which voice is the effect of an eroticized textual mediation between the two of them rather than the representation of an unmediated solitary utterance."[27] Their expansion on Sappho fragment 142 Voigt, in which the apparent enemies Niobe and Leto/Latona are presented as originally friends (and lovers),[28] is a programmatic enactment of Bradley and Cooper's dual singularity, or singular duality, of "the mutual implication of each in the writing of the other":[29]

> Λάτω καὶ Νιόβα μάλα μὲν φίλαι ἦσαν ἔταιραι
> Leto and Niobe were friends full dear:
> Then were they foes
> As only those
> Can be who once were near
> Each to the other's heart,
> Who could not breathe apart,
> Nor shed a lonely tear.
>
> Leto and Niobe were virgins then,
> Nor knew the strange,
> Deep-severing change

---

27. Prins 1999, 76.
28. The most recent commentator on the Sappho fragment calls the line a commentary, "poisonously ironical or ironically tragic," on "the intense friendship, the *compagnonnage* (φίλαι . . . ἔταιραι) between Leto and Niobe" (Neri 2021, 822). On Sappho's fragment, see esp. A. Benjamin's chapter.
29. Prins 1999, 89.

That comes to women when
Elected, raised above
All else, they thrill with love,
The love of gods or men.
From forth seven-gated Thebes Amphion sped,
And by his side
Bore off as bride
Fair Niobe; more dread
The wooer who unknown
From thunder-guarded throne
Rose her shy friend to wed.

And when they met once more Leto had borne
With willing pain
To Zeus her twain
On Delos' beach, forlorn.
But Niobe, elate
With her more bounteous fate,
Heard of the two with scorn:
For she had nine fair sons, nine daughters fair,
And this she told
With comment bold,
And jeered at Leto's pair.
Ah, shameless were the taunts,
Unbearable her vaunts,
And over-weening air.

Apollo and his sister both divine,
Insulted, fierce,
With darts to pierce
The Theban brood combine;
Then girls and boys sink dead
As pitiless o'erhead
The vengeful archers shine.

And Niobe in anguish sees her own
Injurious friend
Aside commend
The deed—and makes no moan:
'Tis not her stricken flock,

Hate's violating shock
Turns her fond heart to stone.

Leto and Niobe—ah!—once were friends
Youth's tender way,
Together lay,
Quarrelled, and made amends;
Though clinging children fall
Around, this to recall
Maternal grief transcends.

The dyadic bond that produces Michael *Field* is a *philia* mirrored not just in the semantics, but also in the sound of φίλαι. The expansiveness of *field* goes along with the emotional energy of *philia*, also exuded by "Phillis," a name in which *philia* spreads into the organic vitality, the bloom and swell, of *phullon* ("leaf"). Prins observes that *Michael* emerges as "a third term that produces the interplay between identities, an 'I' that can shift to 'we' and 'you' and 'he' and 'she' and 'they,'"[30] while Wayne Koestenbaum suggests that "Michael Field frees the love lyric, long a genre of possession, into an ownerless, borderless 'field.'"[31] Field's translation of φίλαι as "*fully* dear" conveys the sense of the lesbian bond as a "fullness" that encompasses and transcends the distinct roles of "friend" and "enemy." This ontological "fullness" generated by feminine homoerotic intimacy is transferred to the motherhood of Niobe, who is introduced as "*elate* with her more *bounteous* fate," the extended plumpness of the Ovidian number fourteen (here eighteen), a sprawling excess expressed in the "over-weening air" of her vaunts. The Sapphic intimacy, the homoerotic idyll, that has been broken by Niobe's marriage lingers as hypermaternity, an expanded *field* of plural subjectivity,[32] the rem(a)inder of a bond whose deindividuating queerness is recast as a reproduction that, in the intensive excess of maternal care, troped by the sheer number of children, sabotages the notion of reproduction, the heterosexist Symbolic it is supposed to enforce.

---

30. Prins 1999, 83.

31. Koestenbaum 1989, 174. Elaborating on Koestenbaum's point, Prins (1999, 102) suggests that "literally and figuratively, [Bradley and Cooper's] Sapphic lyrics are located in the spaces between the Sapphic fragments . . . in order to open a textual field that [they] may enter together as Michael Field." "Is it the name of Michael Field, perhaps, metaphorically displaced into the Lesbian vales as well as the other meadows, groves, and fields, that we read about throughout this volume of Sapphic lyrics?" (104).

32. On Sappho's subjectivity expanding through choral projections and impressions, see Kurke (2019).

"The mother is hardly a subject, a human-faced being, but, instead, she is constructed relationally, not in regard to other women or others of her choosing, but in regard to a socially determined other," says Quashie.[33] At the same time, to quote Matlock, "To be a mother means entering an actively antisocial relationality," one that destines Niobe to "remain without love." Even after Latona and Niobe become enemies—as a consequence of mythology's misogynistic plotting—their bond persists as the nonsingularity, the rejection of an individuated "I" dramatized both in the plural oneness of Michael Field and by the mother's self-undoing as the other, by the vocalization of the name of Sapphic Latona in the apparently self-affirming inhabitation of Niobe's maternity ("But Niobe, e**la**te" continues the distribution of Latona's distinctive sound through the Sapphic line: Λατώ . . . μάλα . . . φίλαι).[34] The bond remains in Niobe's conflation of generation and (self-)loss, in her modeling of generation as (self-)loss.[35] Niobe may well be regarded as the embodiment of the queer disidentification, the self-exit, the ecstasy that motherhood is, "as a site of radical openness," as Jennifer Nash says, "a form of care that alters the self by linking it to an Other."[36]

3. TIME NEGATIVITY BIOPOLITICS

Nihil est in imagine vivum. Nothing, the Nothing, is alive in the image. In the depths of the image, nothingness itself is stirring. Nothing nominalizes itself, assumes grammatical density and dignity—it takes on a life of its own—in the secret inwardness of the image. (Comay)

The [Florentine] *Niobe* suggests that art realizes the exhibition of the absolute in the sensible only by negating at the same time the sensible as such. (Galland-Szymkowiak)

---

33. Quashie 2004, 67.

34. Latona thus becomes, in Michael Field's line, an embodiment of the *lalangue,* the nonlanguage that disrupts the Symbolic with the *jouissant* stutter of the Real: see Lacan (1998, 44, 138–39).

35. On queer motherhood as a recognition of a bond, see Musser (2018, 177–78), who says that Audre Lorde "marks herself and her mother as part of a multigenerational, diasporic selfhood and illuminates the contours of an intimacy that insists on the material." See Nash (2021, 146) on Black mothering as "*sister*ing, a recognition of the deep alliance between Black mothers and daughters."

36. Nash 2021, 151. See also Cavarero's chapter.

> Niobe's melancholic beauty persists, but whatever work of mourning art may have once afforded is closed off to us: beauty shines from a past in which we cannot take up residence. (Kottman)

> The paradox that Ovid condenses in the figure of the endlessly weeping Niobe, stone impervious to wear, expresses the fantasy of achieving a *poetical* expression both immortal *and* transient. (Lezra)

In the fifth section of *Either/Or*, entitled "The Unhappiest One," Kierkegaard assimilates the tragic to despair, in which one feels the disjointed temporality, the displaced, alienated feeling, of a future located in the past and a past lying in the future, the sensation of having "come to the world too soon and . . . constantly arriving too late," of being "quite close to the goal and at the same moment at a distance from it."[37] Before getting to Antigone, he ventures into an extemporaneous discussion of Niobe, presenting her achronic or melancholically synchronic (non)living, a frozen existence, as emblematic of the political pressure of the past, of a loss that shatters time through its material insistence:

> Is this a real being or is it an image, a living person who is dying or a dead one that lives? . . . She lost that to which she had given life; she lost that which gave her life. . . . She stands a little higher than the world, as a memorial stone on a burial mound. But no hope beckons her, no future moves her, no prospect tempts her, no hope disturbs her—hopeless she stands, petrified in memory.[38]

Niobe's melancholy is the expression of the lack of hope that stems from her reduction to "an eternal, mute bearer of guilt," as Walter Benjamin puts it in "Towards the Critique of Violence," in which Niobe's punishment marks the establishment of the law not as "an end that would be free of, and independent from, violence but, on the contrary, an end that, under the name of power, is necessarily and intimately bound up with it."[39] Commenting on Benjamin, Butler observes that Niobe is the illustration of the melancholy constitutive of life by which "to be a subject . . . is to take responsibility for a violence

---

37. Kierkegaard 1992, 216–17.
38. Kierkegaard 1992, 218.
39. W. Benjamin 2021, 56. Deuber-Mankowsky (2016, 257) compares Niobe to the characters in Kafka's *The Trial*, who "are antecedently condemned to guilt by the order in which they live." On the Benjamin passage, see, especially, the chapters by Comay, Lezra, Radcliffe, and Umachandran.

that precedes the subject and whose operation is occluded by the subject who comes to derive the violence she suffers from her own acts."[40] Can we say that, for Kierkegaard, it is the lack of hope that makes Niobe "happy" as well as "unhappy"? Is it the negativity of despair, a negativity "tak[ing] on a life of its own," that makes her mobile immobility, the flow of tears on her petrified cheeks, a gain—the impossibility of being perturbed, moved, "de-petrified" by the prospect or the illusion of a future? The end of chronological time sanctioned by her lithic metamorphosis, which is at the same time a radicalization and negation of the sensible, is a form of self-protection from what Lauren Berlant calls "cruel optimism"[41]—from the self-sabotaging expectation of a better future, from the promise of a fulfilling happiness engendered by the rhetoric of hope.[42] In connecting Niobe with the character of "the unhappiest one"—the one who "has no contemporaneity to attach himself to, no past he can long for . . . and no future he can hope for"[43]—Kierkegaard allows us to see her as a figure, whether human, posthuman, or inhuman, that locates itself beyond or above time, lending itself to possibilities of imagining nonchronological temporality. Like Kierkegaard's "unhappiest one," the petrified Niobe "cannot die, for [s]he has never lived" and "cannot live, for [s]he is already dead."[44] She thus literalizes or, more precisely, matterphorizes lifedeath, the condition of organic being, which, for Freud, is structured by the death drive.[45] While, for Lacan, the petrified Niobe, paired, just as in Kierkegaard, with Antigone, constitutes the destination of the Freudian *Todestrieb*—an inanimate origin—considering her "inclusive disjunction" (a never-resolved *either/or*)[46] of solidity *and* liquidity, paralysis *and* flow, immortality *and* transiency helps us see her as enacting not a telos, but an impetus of the Real, a perverse (or *jouissant*) projection toward impossibility.[47]

Niobe's living death—her matterphorization of lifedeath—is a form of despair that enables her to escape, ecstatically, from the despair of hope, from the illusion that comes with a life eagerly disavowing its entanglement with

---

40. J. Butler 2006, 208. On Butler's position in relation to Benjamin, see Lezra's chapter.
41. Berlant (2011, 14) assimilates "optimism" and "hope." For Berlant, "an optimistic attachment is cruel when the object/scene of desire is itself an obstacle to fulfilling the very wants that bring people to it."
42. For a different reading of the Kierkegaard passage, see A. Benjamin (2015).
43. Kierkegaard 1992, 217.
44. Kierkegaard 1992, 217.
45. On the matterphoric, see above.
46. On "inclusive disjunction," see Deleuze (1995).
47. On the Lacan passage from *The Ethics of Psychoanalysis* (1992), commenting on Freud (1920), see Telò's chapter.

death, its emergence as a movement toward death.[48] The disjunctive form of Kierkegaard's existentialist aesthetics invites us to see Niobe as neither dead nor fully alive,[49] the victim of the state's *right to maim*,[50] as suggested by a Banksy's image of her in Gaza discussed in the book. But if we fix our critical attention on the intensity of the flowing tears that rupture the rock, that disaggregate Niobe's petrified solidity, or, in Comay's words, on the "internal fissure between inside and outside," we may be able to replace hope's deceptive, fallacious affirmation, which she rebuffs, with a "dramatically vivid" glimpse of what Roberto Esposito calls "the continual suspending of the positive in the negative and of the negative in the positive," or of "the inactual that continues to disrupt our actuality."[51]

4. MATTER ARTIFACT PERFORMANCE

Niobe's transformation as the most radical conceivable form of "iconogenesis": the visual arts sprout from a paradoxical inertia and continue to be watered by Niobe's bitter tears. (Baert)

Like a goddess, [Niobe] believes she is free from time itself, immune to the vagaries of Fortune, of what might still happen. (Hamilton)

Petrification serves at once to institute a boundary and to punish Niobe for transgressing the same boundary, a semiotic murkiness redoubled by Niobe's enigmatic existence as a grieving stone. (Radcliffe)

How can we listen to Niobe if, as [Walter] Benjamin writes, she is the very figure of "that other who, in standing in stone on the outside, complicates assimilation insofar as she is positioned outside any structure of recognition"? (Villegas)

In a painting by Alberto Savinio, the brother of the famous Giorgio de Chirico, Niobe appears as a human-animal assemblage, a beaked mother seated

---

48. Derrida (2020, 1) observes that *lifedeath* expresses "the process by which one opposite passes into the other, the process of identification whereby the one is sublated into the other."
49. On Kierkegaard's foreshadowing of postmodern theorizations of biopolitics, see Brower (2021).
50. This is the title of Puar's book on necropolitics (2017).
51. Esposito 2019, 205, 207.

FIGURE 0.1. Reproduction of Alberto Savinio, *Niobe*, 1932. Private Collection. Photo: Archivio Alberto Savinio.

on a rock.[52] Stationed on a stony armchair shading into her figure,[53] she seems embedded in the rock itself, both a sedimented layer and an archaeological fragment,[54] raw matter and the sculptural rem(a)inder of an Ionic swirl, the before and the after of monumentality (see fig. 0.1). The lower body of this mother is her own indispensable nonfleshy support, an (in)organic, textured, overdetermined seat (rock, capital, tree stump) that attaches her to the ground, enables her presence, and dresses her, but that also immobilizes and paralyzes her. The tension in this painting between open and occluded existence connects with the multiple implications and contradictions of petrified Niobe as

---

52. *Niobe*, Collezione Ferdinando Ballo (1932). https://www.pinterest.com/pin/335729347200401931/.

53. See Cardano (2020).

54. As Cardano puts it, "The static pose of the mother, petrified and incorporated into the rock, seems to allude . . . to the hybrid of the motherly armchair in which Savinio, in the 1940s, will fix the autobiographic recollection of the severe figure of his mother, afflicted by excessive maternal love" (2020, 269).

a latent or recognizable work of art, as an image of art itself, as "iconogenesis" and "semiotic murkiness," which is discussed in various ways in this book.[55]

The hypermaternity of Savinio's Niobe is emblematized by her trans-species mobility—her avian nomadism, despite her paralysis, exceeding the well-worn idea of the *mamma chioccia* ("bird [hen] mother"), which is ironically subverted. This ontological errancy emerges from the poetic portrait of Niobe that Savinio supplies in his 1925 musical tragedy *La morte di Niobe* (*Niobe's Death*):[56]

> O madre solenne, feconda tacchina,
> Cantano le mammelle il canto profondo dell'umanità
> O cuppole galatee stillate la brina
> Sui labbri riarsi di cento città.

> O solemn mother, fecund hen, your breasts chant the profound chant of humanity. O Galatean [milky] cupolas, drip frost on the thirsty lips of one hundred cities.[57]

Language becomes liquid, a flow of tears—imagined as a dripping of milk—the cumulative effect of liquid sounds (*mammelle, galatee, stillate, labbri*) and labial intensities. Language is almost a stone sheltering or entrapping liquid sound, the percolating motion of pure life, a musical lactation.[58] Animality and humanity are combined in the architectural roundness, the formal fecundity of the cupolas (*cuppole*), anatomical upward protrusions, while the double *p*, a unity within the word, emphasizes Niobe's reduplicating power through self-splitting, but also the social solitude of maternity.[59] This humananimality of Niobe takes us back to Savinio's painting, in which petrification encompasses a bodily transition: the loss of her children leaves her, in the spatial orientation of the portrait, with one eye, with one strong arm enveloping her ruins. This masculine arm goes along with—complements and replicates—the phallic surrogacy of the beak. This is a Niobe who is no longer herself, a

---

55. See esp. Baert's chapter. Levinas (1998, 11) views Niobe as an exemplification of the fear of mortality intrinsic to art, that is, of the "uncertainty of time's continuation," of "the petrification of the instant in the heart of duration" or "of the insecurity of a being which has a presentiment of fate." On this passage, see Matlock's chapter. On Niobe in ancient art, see, e.g., Trendall (1972), Keuls (1978), Neils (2008), Sevieri (2010), and Rebaudo (2012).

56. See Curinga (2013) and Bernard (2021, 63–68). On another example of musical Niobe, see Villegas-Vélez's chapter.

57. For this quotation, see Curinga (2013, 10).

58. On the voice and maternity, see Dolar (2006); see also Nooter (2017) on Aeschylus.

59. On Niobe's self-splitting maternity, see Cavarero's chapter.

phallic mother, displaying, in her hypermaternal, trans-masculine appearance, the multiple accoutrements necessitated and produced by becoming mother.[60] When the children have been taken away, her arms are drawn into a conglomerate of desolate prostheses.

Niobe's hypermaternity, her multilayered becoming in spite of her petrified being, an ontological capaciousness, incarnates the convergence and conflation of multiple artistic practices that has been called *œuvre d'art totale*.[61] Savinio's various artistic roles and positionalities—as a poet, painter, and musician—congeal around Niobe, who can be construed as a version of an all-encompassing work of art.[62] If we contemplate the Weeping Rock of Niobe (Niobe Aglayan Kaya), a natural formation at the foot of Mount Sipylus in Turkey,[63] we get the sense of how Niobe manages to be both raw matter and quasi-artistic creation, a rem(a)inder of the former even when it has ostensibly become the latter. This Weeping Rock is a counter-monument—that is, an artifact that maintains itself unformed, even though it appears to have been hewn (by nature, time, or human nature), has acquired distinct boundaries, and has seemingly been subjected to the shaping violence of a representational design. Rather than being used to set the boundary that is *nomos,* as in Walter Benjamin's discussion of her, this emblematic Niobe revolts against representation's nomological force, expressing the boundary-crossing expansiveness of the artistic avant-garde; abolishing the notional division between natural and artificial, as well as inhuman and human; and unsettling the idea of a development, a chronological transition, from material to (finished) product. She is a space of artistic *chôra* that is not simply pre-Symbolic:[64] it folds the formed, the artificial, back into the domain of the unhewn, but through juxtaposition, dissonant coexistence, a synchronic deterritorialization. In this way, through

---

60. On object-oriented maternity, or postmaternity, see Baraitser (2009).

61. On the idea of the *œuvre d'art totale,* see Lista et al. (2003).

62. See Fagiolo dell'Arco (1983): "Alberto Savinio's life defines him as an argonaut—his life was a continuous voyage through the world. . . . First of all there was Savinio the painter. . . . Then there was Savinio the composer, who in the years prior to World War I stupefied Guillaume Apollinaire with his dodecaphonic blocks of sounds. Finally there was Savinio the man of letters, the contributor to Dada publications, who frequented Surrealist circles in Paris and who later became the disenchanted poet of black humor."

63. See Pausanias 1.21.3. See Comay's chapter.

64. "Amorphous and undifferentiated" is Burchill's (2006, 91; and 2017, 194) gloss of *a-morphon* in Plato's description of *chôra* in *Timaeus* as "something that is without the shape of all those forms that it is about to receive." *Chôra* can be seen as a space that is reluctant to become a receptacle and resists being marked by division, by the wounding partitions of meaning as well as social order. See J. Butler 1993, 41, on *chôra* as "a disfiguration that emerges at the boundaries of the human both as its very condition and as the insistent threat of its deformation."

Niobe, materiality as such also comes to coincide with the idea of the *œuvre totale*[65]—an antihierarchical notion of wholeness, which confuses the boundaries between artistic domains and sensory or perceptive spheres (visual, aural, haptic) so that one accesses or just feels the sublime opacity, saturation, no-sense[66] of a Real hyperobject. This opaque artistic totality brings us back to the performative scandal of Aeschylus's *Niobe*—a play (not) opened by its protagonist's prolonged, proto-avant-garde silence, a play boldly materializing as negativity, as a dramatic impossibility[67]—and then to the havoc wreaked by Savinio's own Niobic operatic experiment in its first production. One special spectator, Savinio's wife, reports:

> At least for me, the night that *The Death of Niobe* was put onstage was unforgettable, announced in the program as "A tragedy in one act, with music by Alberto Savinio." It was a tempestuous night: the majority of the audience clapped frantically, climbing on the seats, but trouble was not lacking. A fight arose. Savinio, who was the orchestra director, sought to calm the water. At a certain point he gave up and, disappointed, said to the audience: "But I didn't do anything bad."[68]

As violently experimental as Antonin Artaud and Alfred Jarry, Savinio is also like Aeschylus as depicted by Aristophanes: the initial performance of Aeschylus's *Niobe* upset, immobilized, or infuriated the audience. But, in giving up, in stopping, Savinio is also like Niobe herself. In saying, "I didn't do anything bad," he may even verbalize a Niobean response to punishment, to the angry act that makes her "permanently guilty," that establishes "her as the guilty subject"[69]—even though, as Benjamin implies, she "did not transgress any existing law."[70] In other words, he may enable us to regard her immobility not just before but after the petrification as a gesture of refusal, a willful act,[71]

---

65. "His painting emerged from literature and later returned to its literary origins; his music is a form of ballet which aspires to pure imagery in motion; his stage designs—which complete the cycle—can be viewed as painting, which in turn undergoes a metamorphosis into literary discourse" (Fagiolo dell'Arco 1983).
66. See Telò 2023, ch. 1.
67. On the beginning of Aeschylus's *Niobe*, see Telò (2023, ch. 8) and Telò's chapter.
68. M. Savinio 1987, 28.
69. J. Butler 2006, 208.
70. Deuber-Mankowsky 2019, 298.
71. On willfulness, see Ahmed (2014). In a commentary on Benjamin's discussion of Niobe, J. Butler (2006, 218) observes: "We can imagine her rising up again to question the brutality of the law, and we can imagine her shedding the guilt of her arrogance in an angry refusal of the violent authority wielded against her and an endless grief for the loss of those lives." On Niobe's revolutionary force, see Comay's chapter.

the survivor's protestation of innocence and the artist's demand for unconditional (pro)creative freedom. Niobe reclaims a liberating virtuality, the infinite range of imaginary possibilities afforded by the vital negativity of ever-moving tears as well as of silence itself.

•

While we believe that the connections, resonances, and subliminal links and dialogues among sections are more significant than any thematic partition, we have divided the book into four clusters. Yet Niobean writing, for us, signifies a nonlinear, nondevelopmental discourse, one that does not recoil from repetition and a continuing, melancholic back-and-forth insistence. For example, one notices, in all the sections, the overwhelming resonance of Walter Benjamin as well as Aeschylus and Sophocles, whose takes on Niobe have been most influential and generative. It is, to an extent, inevitable to hear these voices reverberating throughout the volume. The repetition, the circling back, again and again, a persistent background, is a textured mimetic effect that enacts, through writing and reading, Niobe's infinite mourning, the melancholic impossibility of working-through.

The first section ("An-Archic Beginnings") thematizes the fact that, especially in the case of Niobe, there is no original story by proposing three possible modes of conceiving the Niobean *archê*: first, gestation and generation, the acts that make Niobe; second, a synoptic view of Niobe in all of her duplicities and contradictions; third, her first mention in Greek literature. In the first chapter, Adriana Cavarero theorizes Niobe's hypermaternity as "the vibrating flesh that splits in the labor of procreation," an excess dramatized in Phillis Wheatley's "Niobe in Distress"—to whom drea brown returns in the last chapter—and in the sculptures of Antonietta Raphaël. In the second chapter, Rebecca Comay elaborates on Niobe's overdetermined excess emblematized by the stone: "No longer a hollow vessel into which meanings are poured and from which morals are extracted, no longer a tablet for the inscription or infliction of punishment, the stone presents an impenetrable thickness which nonetheless continues to secrete." Lastly, Ben Radcliffe places the first depiction of Niobe in Greek literature—book 24 of the *Iliad*—in dialogue with Walter Benjamin's discussion. For Radcliffe, the exchange between Achilles and Priam, within which the reference to Niobe is nested, is charged with the ambiguity that, for Benjamin, characterizes the threshold between gods and humans, a threshold constitutive, in Niobe's story, of the violent boundary of the law. Additionally, the context of the Iliadic episode, the suspension of war, "evokes Benjamin's conception of the general strike—

a mass, revolutionary suspension of labor that breaks the circular logic of violence."

Venturing deconstructively into psychoanalysis, ethics, and ecocriticism, the second section of the book focuses on the most extensive, nonfragmentary rendition of the Niobe myth, in Ovid's *Metamorphoses*. Victoria Rimell pushes against a solipsistic reading of Niobe with what she calls a "nonnarcissistic maternal relationality." Ovid invites us not just to look at her rocky mass, but also, as Rimell puts it, "to hear her speak, in this liquefaction-petrification, the wild language of the mother, or the child, or the mother-mirroring-the-child, echoing Narcissus's innovative other, Echo, as well as tongueless, expressive Philomela." Mario Telò focuses on Niobe's aesthetic coldness, observing the points of contact between depictions of Niobe in Aeschylus, Aristophanes, and Ovid. Staging an encounter between various thinkers (in particular, Lacan, Deleuze, and Meillassoux), Telò brings together the frozen Niobe, the Deleuzian mother of the steppe, and the inhuman Nature posited by dark ecology. Striving to remove herself from time, Niobe congeals the imperatives of representation, bio- and necropolitics. In a complementary fashion, John T. Hamilton sees Niobe's petrification as equivalent to the space of *mythos*—an alternative to the implacable restlessness of rational *logos*—which she inhabits, finding refuge in, and valorizing, an invisible and subjectless reality beyond mortal experience. Looking at the Latin background and aftermath of Ovid, Andres Matlock explores the Platonic and Stoic appropriations of Niobe in Cicero and Seneca. In these contexts, Niobe demonstrates above all that the nourishment of the mother, the equality of friendship, and the logic of the sensible are predicated on their dissolution. Between the Platonist sense of the insubstantiality of the image and the Stoic excavation of Niobe's mineralogy, a durable marker remains of the limits of human corporeality, sociality, and speech.

In the third section, Niobe is analyzed from the viewpoint of aesthetics, visual and nonvisual. Considering Aby Warburg's engagement with Niobe, Barbara Baert demonstrates how her assimilation to a weeping rock is emblematic of the visual artifact's alluring insistence; the liquid fertility, animate and inanimate, that generates the work of art; and "the brute matter in which art lies locked, the ur-form in which artistic eruption is already heralded." Comparing Hegel's view of Niobe with Schelling's, Mildred Galland-Szymkowiak suggests that for the latter Niobe is the emblem of symbolic art as such, of symbolism as artistic expression—an idea that invites us to regard Niobe's weeping rock as abstract art.

Paul A. Kottman's essay mines Kant's notion of disinterested pleasure alongside Hegel's less well-known notion of "passionless love" (*begierdelose*

Liebe) as resources for thinking about melancholic apprehensions of beauty, and the possibility of postmelancholic life. In treating Niobe, Kottman considers ethical and psychological implications of the contrast Hegel draws between Niobe's and Mary's responses to loss. As he suggests, "Niobe's independent and free beauty transcends the cycle of life and death, but only by 'working' in and through dead nature whose mere *appearance* of liveliness it persistently confronts."

In his chapter, Daniel Villegas Vélez explores how the use of the silent Niobe in Baroque opera illuminates the relationship between auditory aesthetics and sovereignty. In particular, Niobe illustrates the convergence between two senses of *nomos*—"as custom, law, land-appropriation (*Landnahme*) in the Schmittian sense" and "as a mimetic musical genre developed from the sixth century BCE onwards." Niobe also expresses the possibility that the latter sense of the word may open nomadic lines of flight in nomological sovereignty.

Mathura Umachandran's return to Benjamin opens the fourth section of the volume, which focuses on justice at the intersections of philosophy and poetry, considered as modes of Niobean writing. Using as a starting point Hannah Arendt's decision not to include "Critique of Violence" in *Illuminations,* her collection of Benjamin's essays, and the lack of references to it in her own "Reflections on Violence," Umachandran invites us to linger on Niobe's condition as a form of resistance and to rethink it in terms of a politics of refusal. In the wake of, but also going beyond Benjamin and Arendt, they also draw attention to Niobe's queer potentialities. In his chapter, Andrew Benjamin reconsiders the narrative of Niobe's punishment, in light of the conceptual nexus of relationality, ethics, and time. In this perspective, "care depends upon justice" and "the only possible response to the presence of injury/injury and the continual threat of immediacy is to maintain the conditions that allow for and sustain justice." Jacques Lezra uses Niobe to propose a comparison between the ethical positions of Walter Benjamin and Judith Butler. For Lezra, Benjamin's and Butler's different readings of Niobe urge us to pose the following questions: On what sort of foundation do claims concerning the relation between one or another position or disposition (social, political, ethical . . .) stand? One that stands by "dissolving" into mute historicity, or one that makes its disappearance—as "dissolving," as the wearing-into-water of stone—the condition of its effectiveness? As he observes, following Butler, justice "holds me to account without counting forward to or back from the event. Because I give way, I face justice rather than judgment based in 'moral causality.' Now the path of expiation opens before me, uncertain, endless, conjectural: it is the way of endless tears."

In her lyrical engagement with Wheatley, drea brown explores the connection between Niobe's mythical symbolism and the narratives of the Middle Passage, seeing Niobe both as an image of the slave ship and as the archetypal Black mother who lost her children (and herself) in the ocean. Wheatley's reading of Niobe speaks of and to the constant losses of enslaved Black mothers whose children were theirs and never theirs:

> this was the consequence of her loving, slaughter and unimaginable grief.
> should she become stone? jagged heart, soggy rock, salt watered
> each
> losslosslosslossloss
> losslosslossloss
> losslossloss
> a dank prayer.

PART 1

An-Archic Beginnings

CHAPTER 1

Niobe's Hypermaternity

ADRIANA CAVARERO

According to classical philologist and mythology scholar Karol Kerényi, the name Niobe comes from Asia Minor and can be related to the figure of the Great Mother, as suggested by its kinship with Cybele/Kybele, the Great Mother of the gods.[1] Worshipped since Neolithic times, this chthonic, archaic mother showcases the features of a plump, voluptuous female body whose fertility is played up by the size of her belly and breasts. The Great Mother, often identified with Mother Earth, is ultimately a pregnant female body that gives birth to the living—first and foremost, living human beings, but, to an extent, all living creatures, the world of the living. Her womb swells with fruits. Allied with the multifaceted process of the propagation of life itself, she is an icon of hypermaternity.

Punished for having boasted about her ability to give birth to multiple children, Niobe is one of the many mythological characters who commit hybris. This term is usually translated as "arrogance," "pride," "insolence," but its primary meaning is "excess." Usually, in Greek, the term marks an act of arrogance that violates cosmic and divine order, that is, an act through which a human being, defying the gods, oversteps the limits fixed for mortals; it *exceeds* them. It may also be seen as a rebellion. Since Antigone, in Sophocles's

---

Translated from the Italian by Mario Telò.
 1. See Kerényi (2010, 208–23).

eponymous play, claims to resemble Niobe (823–33), some interpreters have, in fact, cast Niobe as a rebel. But it is more correct, I argue, to speak of a knack for excess, for violating a behavioral code by claiming to surpass the gods in some skill or quality—a specific technical talent (weaving, singing), or physical force or, in the case of Niobe, a power, the capacity for procreation.

As we read in Ovid's *Metamorphoses* (6.182–83), Niobe gave birth to seven sons and seven daughters—and she is insolently proud of it.[2] Just in mere terms of quantity—a magical number, for she produces a double seven evenly distributed between sons and daughters—Niobe's maternity presents itself as a creative power that immediately evokes excess; still, this is an excess marked by an idea of perfection. It is a paradoxical completion inherent to excess itself, which, in this case, does not aim at the numberless, at infinite procreation, at maternity as an inexhaustible source of life, but, rather, at the perfect number as a symbol of exemplary childbearing and of beauty. Up to this point in the story, we seem to be in the presence of an excess that constrains itself, that amounts not to a lack of measure but to a hypermaternity held up as example.

In its essential kernel, the mythical icon of Niobe conjures, in fact, a figuration of hypermaternity,[3] a total assimilation of the feminine gender with the power of the procreative body, the body of a singular life that gives birth to singular lives, flesh that splits apart in the work of procreation and that vibrates—a living and pulsating body, the opposite of the weeping hard rock into which Niobe will be eventually transformed as a result of divine punishment. However, this cruel punishment is brought on Niobe not because, fulfilling her procreative power, she gave birth to seven daughters and seven sons, but because she is exceedingly proud of it, because she boasts about her feat as a fertile mother, worthy of the public honors that the Theban women undeservedly attribute to divine Latona, the mother of only two children, Apollo and Diana. In *Metamorphoses,* Ovid reports that Niobe, the happiest mother, took much satisfaction in her offspring, *progenies* (6.155). Her reversal of fortune comes about when Niobe, still beautiful in her outburst of anger, lifting her head with haughty eyes (*superbos oculos*), addresses the Theban women as they offer incense to Latona and her children: "What madness is this? Preferring gods who are known only through hearsay to gods who are seen?" (6.170–71). Thus, emphasis is laid on the visible and fully perceptible

---

2. In different versions of the myth, the number of Niobe's children varies: twelve for Homer and twenty for Hesiod; in all versions, there is an emphasis on the theme of an exceptional fertility that is equally distributed between male and female children. See Pietrobuono (2019, 46).

3. See Honig (2013, 263n62).

reality of Niobe's procreative body and of her children, in opposition to the reality of Latona and her divine children who are, instead, invisible celestial creatures. However, hybris pushes Niobe to assert that, by way of kinship, she is also divine, besides being rich, regal, and as magnificent as a goddess—as everybody can see. Yet it is not her laying claim to a divine status, in spite of her mortality,[4] that marks the climax of Niobe's offense against the goddess; it is, instead, her proclaiming herself superior in that she gave birth to seven sons and seven daughters while Latona only to two. Niobe insolently revels in her fertility, in her *progenies,* in the copious *genos,* perfectly distributed between males and females, that has emerged from her womb. How, then, can the Theban women prefer Latona—the mother of only two children, "a seventh of what my womb has delivered"? Niobe asks. "I am happy, who could deny it?," the haughty mother continues, "and I will always be." *Sum felix; felixque manebo* (6.193). This statement will be tragically contradicted. Causing the revenge of Latona, Niobe is about to be hit by the most atrocious and irreparable unhappiness—being transformed into a hard rock that incessantly drips tears of sorrow over Apollo's and Diana's murder of her fourteen children.

It is worth noticing that *felix,* in the text of Ovid, does not simply indicate joy or a sense of satisfaction. Latin *felix* is cognate with *fecundity, fertility, feminine,* and *fetus.*[5] This is a family of cognates that structurally inheres in the domain of maternity, intended first and foremost as gestation, delivery, and procreation, the labor and potency of a singular body that gives birth to singular lives in its own flesh. We are thus facing the domain of "birth" in its corporeal, materially generative, and carnal elements. The root of *felix* is, in fact, connected with the Greek verb *phuô* ("beget," "give birth to") and the noun *phusis,* meaning "nature," a word that is, in turn, cognate with the Latin verb *nascor* ("to be born"). The happiness of Niobe, whom Ovid calls *felicissima matrum* (6.155), resides in the exclusively feminine capacity to give birth; indeed, it coincides with the act of giving birth itself, with procreation as a power that belongs to the maternal body and, in Niobe's exemplary case, materializes as the perfect number, a number evenly distributed between the two genders of the children.

Niobe thus challenges Latona's maternal power, and Latona responds by sending Apollo and Diana to murder her rival's fourteen children, one by one. We find ourselves at the center of a theater of hybris, of human arrogance against gods, that provokes divine punishment and, in this specific instance,

---

4. Daughter of Tantalus, Niobe has a divine lineage: cf. Sophocles, *Antigone* 834.
5. See Hamilton's chapter.

a slaughter of innocents. In this theater, there is no pity, only infinite horror. One cannot fail to notice the crystalline logic of the story, predicated on maternity as procreative power. Just like an appendix of the maternal body, flesh of its flesh, children kill children. The mortal mother who has challenged the divine one over the number of their children is punished by her rival and reduced to a mother who no longer has children, to a sterile woman—and, soon, to a weeping rock, the mineralization of the sorrow over the loss of children, the metamorphosis of a mortal birth-giving body into an eternal rock.

In the development of *Metamorphoses*, the myth of Niobe is narratively linked with that of Arachne (6.1–145). Coming from the same area, the two women had met when Niobe, still unmarried, lived in Maeonia, Ovid says. Another example of a mortal woman punished for her hybris against a goddess, Arachne is a miraculously talented weaver who defies Minerva in the art of weaving. The goddess's revenge is inexorably brought on her reckless rival, whose body shrinks under the spell of infernal herbs and turns into the circular shape of a spider, which, with the exception of its thread-like legs, is all belly (*venter*, 6.144). Arachne, the Greek word for "spider," is thus doomed to weave her tapestry as she did before, not, however, as a human being, but as an insect. The story, which extols the spider's extraordinary weaving skills, tracks the transition from a scene wherein skilled female hands intertwine threads to weave a marvelous tapestry to one where the matter of the tapestry itself is, instead, a product of the belly. The spider literally gives birth to its tapestry, which is a product of its body. Besides being connected by the hybris of their female protagonists, the stories of Arachne and Niobe also share the emphasis on a body that materially gives birth to its own product by itself. While Arachne's specialty is a skill, a *technê*, that is, weaving as a characteristically feminine activity, Niobe's is to make children (*tiktein*), a quintessentially feminine experience, which myth delights in pushing to the extreme of hypermaternity. The fact that, becoming hybris, this hypermaternity is punished and changed into its opposite, the absence of children, does not diminish but heightens the story's relish in excess.

There is, clearly, a misogynistic element in the story. As a result of the procreative function reserved to their gender, two women clash against each other with the slaughter of innocents as the outcome. Myth patriarchally frames the theme of motherhood from a twofold angle: first, identifying women with the procreative role, it confines them within it; second, it denounces the uncalled-for pride and rivalry of mothers as birth-givers. To be sure, myth goes much beyond this predictable misogynistic frame, expressing—through excess and not without some anxiety—the uncanny that is distinctive of procreative power. One should not underestimate the fact that this is an exclusively feminine prerogative, something inherent to the very fact of life—of *bios* as a condition shared by all living beings—that is denied to men. The strife between Niobe and Latona concerns precisely that capacity of giving birth to living beings that no man has access to. What Niobe boasts about is the number of living beings (fourteen!) whom she has brought into the world: they are singular lives generated by her singular life, (visible) bodies generated by her (visible) body, flesh of her flesh. It is not by chance that, in the Ovidian version of the myth, men play no role in this story of hypermaternity: overcome by the pain for the loss of his offspring, Amphion, Niobe's husband, commits suicide; Jupiter, the gods' king and father of Diana and Apollo, remains offstage and does not interfere. Parents of the murdered and of the murderers, Amphion and Jupiter, as males, are alien to the theme of generation narrated by the myth. If one considers that in other myths Jupiter imitates the experience of the birth-giving feminine body, delivering Minerva from his head and Dionysus from the embryo that he has implanted in his thigh, it is remarkable that in the Ovidian version of Niobe's myth the king of the gods is entirely absent. Even though it is a myth about generation, about a numerous offspring that grants continuity to family lineage or new members to the *populus,* as Ovid suggests, this is not at all a myth about family, human, divine, or semi-divine. The whole story concerns maternity and describes its uncanny character, which resides not in the fact that Niobe's hybris predictably leads to predictable disaster but in the very power of generating lives. *Deinon to tiktein estin*—"Terrible it is to make children"—Clytemnestra says in Sophocles's *Electra* (770). Whoever is familiar with Greek literature cannot fail to notice the importance of the term *deinon,* a word whose meaning is notoriously impossible to render in modern languages—the English "uncanny" captures it inadequately. In maternity—in the exclusive procreative power of the female body—there is something that the Greeks perceive as terrifying, uncanny, excessive, close to animality, and even to the wild animality that Euripides casts as the profound and obscure side of the female in *Bacchae,* where we read about women who breastfeed billy goats and wolf cubs (698–702). Here too, in this kinship between woman and animal that permeates not only Greek myth, we see the emergence of misogynistic traits that feminist criticism has unmasked. That the theme of maternity attracts feminist criticism is not surprising since it is an exclusively feminine experience that is conjured. Nor is it surprising that, interrogating the maternal imaginary in this tradition, feminist criticism has mostly dedicated itself to debunking the patriarchal protocols that underlie the representation of the oblative mother, devoted to taking care of children and family, confined within the domestic sphere. It therefore goes without saying that, in a feminist perspective, to thematize maternity from an angle that refrains from debunking its oblative valence may seem a very risky enterprise. And to speak of hypermaternity in terms of generative power might be even riskier. It is as though this generative power—this experience of the living being that gives birth to other living beings, of the human animal that reproduces itself—were to be blamed for conjuring a biological vision of the maternal that it would be better to keep hidden. Interestingly enough, feminist thought has rarely investigated the obscure side of the maternal, that is, that power of procreation that inscribes itself within the physical experience of the body, within the flesh that splits apart while giving birth to singular lives—almost an articulation of the living being (you, I, anyone who is born) in the process, material and apparently impersonal, animal, and wild, of general life. The understandable fear of reducing Woman to a procreative function, and turning all women into mothers, impedes feminist speculation on this theme; it makes it reticent. Feminist criticism is also understandably suspicious of the patriarchal Symbolic order's tendency to debase women to animals, to irrational creatures that the female gender would "naturally" be closer to. Indeed, the question is complex and full of stereotypical, phallologocentric, sexist traps. Yet it may perhaps be worth it to debunk these stereotypical frames and look through the dark side of the maternal, to heed the uncanniness of the singular flesh that by splitting apart has given birth to us, experiencing the rhythms of general life, of *bios* as the condition and organic matter of the living. In the imaginary of ancient Greece, this theme occasionally emerges with disruptive force, evoking either the hybris of a potentially unlimited and omnipotent maternity—as the myth of Niobe suggests—or motherly figures who transform the uncanny character of their experience as birth-giving flesh into the horroristic gesture of the dismemberment of the son's body,[6] as we read in Euripides's *Bacchae*. With the figure of Niobe, in particular, this theme is decisively pushed to the extreme of the hypermaternal, an unsettling mirror of the power of a female body, which not only gives birth to the offspring, thus granting the continuity of family and kingdom, if not of the human race, but also, more importantly, touches upon the very process of general life, a *bios* not conceived, à la Nietzsche, as a voracious and destructive impulse, but rather as a self-growing force, the proliferation of the living, a regenerative effervescence.

After all, the lithification of Niobe's body—a mineralization of the birth-giving flesh—is not coincidental. The female participation in the process of *bios*—this uncanny complicity of the maternal body with general life, blossoming, in the case of Niobe, into seven daughters and seven sons—under-

---

6. See Cavarero (2009, 15–16).

goes a metamorphosis into hard stone, a rock that drips tears, a humid and immobile boulder. Petrified Niobe becomes, so to speak, the *anti-bios* par excellence. While *bios* is an incessant organic process, a perennial regeneration, a ferment, Niobe becomes inert inorganic matter, cold and immobile rock. More than frozen mother/earth, figure of a threatening ancestrality, she becomes a mineralized body, a monument.[7] As Aeschylus shows, Niobe's petrification exemplarily symbolizes the immobility and absolute silence to which the children's death reduces her;[8] however, it is also the flesh generative of an extraordinary hypermaternity that is here transformed into stone—unless the tears perpetually shed by the rock are themselves the sign of an eternal pain that keeps Niobe alive and preserves her humanity.[9]

It is not surprising that Niobe's lithic metamorphosis—her monumentalization, as it were—has inspired many artists, starting with sculptors. After all, Niobe's transformation incorporates the form of the medium of sculpture.[10] Since antiquity, however, painting, too has been fascinated with the Niobe theme. Richard Buxton observes that in red-figure vase painting, as one can tell from some fourth-century funerary urns,

> Niobes's was a transformation which artists took to occur—like Socrates' imagined, gradual death as described in Plato's *Phaidon* (117e–118a)—from feet upwards. Sometimes her petrification rises only as high as the shins, sometimes above the waist.... The effect of this directionality is to allow the human figure to retain, to the very last, its capacity to express emotion with the face and hands, even though the lower part of its anatomy has solidified forever into immobility.[11]

What impresses ancient artists is a process of petrification of the body that becomes more and more uncanny just as the face and arms of the person who undergoes it are still able to express its horror. When petrification reaches the head, there will be nothing but tears, water dripping from immobile and mineralized eyes. Horror, as indicated by the word's etymology, congeals and paralyzes—indeed, in this myth that emphasizes excess, it solidifies the living body, transforming generative flesh into hard rock.

Yet this process is not always imagined by artists as a progression from feet to head. In fact, Ovid himself describes it in the opposite direction. Thus

---

7. See Telò's chapter.
8. See Taplin (1972, 60–62).
9. See Forbes Irving (1990, 146) and J. Butler (2009, 78).
10. See Baert's chapter in this volume.
11. Buxton 2009, 98.

does Phillis Wheatley—African native and slave, as she calls herself[12]—in her poem *Niobe in Distress* inspired by Ovid: "A pioneer of American and African American literature," in 1773 Wheatley "became the first person of African descent in the Americas to publish a book."[13] Captured in Africa and sold as a slave in Boston, when she was about seven, Wheatley authored an extraordinary poetic output that, besides gaining much success among her contemporaries, has spurred, in recent years, a growing interest in feminist criticism, also because of her re-reading of Ovid, which inaugurates a tradition of Black women writers engaging the classics.[14] Educated in the family of her "masters," Wheatley displays extraordinary talent, soon mastering the English language, reading the classics and learning Latin. In her collection *Poems on Various Subjects,* the epyllion whose complete title is "Niobe in Distress for Her Children slain by Apollo, from Ovid's Metamorphoses, Book VI, and from a view of the Painting of Mr. Richard Wilson" (68–75) brilliantly attests to this knowledge and to her ability to modulate lines on an enchanting lyrical rhythm. Marked by the dark color of a stormy sky, the painting of Richard Wilson portrays a desperate Niobe who lifts her arms toward the daughters threatened by the arrows of Apollo and Diana. As often happens in the iconographic tradition, the painting's protagonists are the Niobids. The slaughter is about to be carried out, and Niobe is not yet transformed into stone.

Even though it echoes the text of Ovid, the first version of *Niobe in Distress* is remarkably different from the translations of *Metamorphoses* available at Wheatley's time.[15] This version does not dwell on the petrification; it ends, instead, with Niobe embracing her youngest daughter, who survived the slaughter but eventually, as fate wishes, dies in her mother's arms. Yet Niobe's metamorphosis into rock appears in a later version—in a stanza added by another hand in which we read (215–25):

    The passing air
Made no impression on her stiff'ning hair.
The blood forsook her face: amidst the flood
Pour'd from her cheeks, quite fix'd her eye-balls stood.
Her tongue, her palate both obdurate grew,
Her curdled veins no longer motion knew;
The use of neck, and arms, and feet was gone,
And ev'n her bowels hard'ned into stone:

---

12. Wheatley 2020.
13. Carretta 2011, ix. See drea brown's chapter.
14. See Spinger (2014).
15. See Thorton (2008, 245).

A marble statue now the queen appears,
But from the marble steal the silent tears.

One immediately notes that in this stanza, which is almost literally calqued on Ovid's tale (6.303–12), special emphasis is laid on the anatomic detailing in the description of the petrification of the organs: there is a progression from "up" to "down," from eyes to tongue and palate and then, through blood, to entrails and the whole body. In other words, what is striking—and different from ancient iconography—is not only the change of direction, from head to feet, but especially the detailed description, in every vital organ, of the flesh that becomes stone. In a sense, we witness a progressive mineralization of the *bios,* which, in Niobe's body, has bloomed into the exceptional, hypermaternal form of a birth-giving power. Sure, the kernel of Wheatley's poetry is centered, in the wake of the literary tradition, on the immense, irreparable tragedy of a mother deprived of her children, destined to mourn them forever in an endless silence. Sure, as suggested by other readings, the most profound meaning of this tragedy is Wheatley's denunciation of slavery, which in Southern plantations steals children away from their mothers and in Northern cities—like Boston where she lives—assigns a high market value to infertile or not-very-fertile slave women.[16] In this last stanza, we are particularly struck by the verbal rendering, enhanced by the line's alluring musicality, of the horrendous and sudden process of petrification of a body that, in myth, celebrates its procreative power with an act of hybris. The similarity to the Ovidian text in the anatomical detailing also resumes the mythical pattern of the petrified birth-giving body that seems to travel across ages and contexts through the radical evocation of the maternal uncanny. In other words, if there is something particularly uncanny in the story of Niobe, or in the remakes of all times that turn this story into a classic, it coalesces around the event of the petrification of the birth-giving body. It is as though the female body's uncanny complicity with *bios* were revealed precisely in the punitive annihilation brought about by the mineralization of the flesh. Or it is as though the truth of the very tight—too tight, irremediable, material—bond of the human animal not only with other animals, but also with organic life in general flickered most effectively in the very act of its negation. In the rock it is the ferment of life itself, the activity of self-proliferation, of growth, of generation that stops. Differently from other mythological metamorphoses that concern human beings turned into animals or trees, the rock's lifeless matter into which Niobe was transformed marks a

---

16. See Thorton (2008, 249).

radical, definitive disjunction from the world of life more than an absence of life as such.[17]

At the Uffizi Gallery in Florence, one can admire a marble statue of Niobe who embraces her daughter, the Roman copy of a Greek original by Scopas. Niobe holds on to the daughter, causing her to cling tightly to her body, so that the girl's head plunges into the maternal womb (see fig. 8.2 later in this volume). Recreated in various iconographic and statuary versions throughout the centuries, the Uffizi statue is also plausibly a source of inspiration for sculptress Antonietta Raphaël, who, in 1939, modeled some bronzes in which the embrace was intensified to such a point that the bodies of mother and daughter were fastened to each other, as though Niobe made an extreme attempt to reabsorb her daughter into her womb (see fig. 1.1).[18] (Another of Raphael's bronze statues of Niobe is reproduced as the cover of this book).

The well-known motif of the return into the maternal womb or of the maternal body's reappropriation of the children she gave birth to is subjected here to a striking torsion. What is at stake here is not only the return into the maternal womb as a remedy against death as such, that is, against the mortality that pertains to the living as individual, singular body, born and fated to die. On the one hand, in the very act of reabsorbing the daughter into her belly, of enfolding her into her fertile—*felix*, life-giving—body, Niobe does not "rescue" the girl from her irreparable mortality but from an impending death. She undoes, so to speak, the work of the impending violent death. On the other hand, one cannot ignore that the body that welcomes again the daughter into the organic and fecund shelter of its carnality is about to be petrified—and, in fact, as a statue, it is already inert matter, stone. Whereas the statues of petrified Niobe perfectly materialize, as it were, the myth, bringing to fruition the monumentality that myth itself assigns to her, the statue of Niobe that reincorporates the daughter into her womb emphasizes instead— by impossible yet stubborn negation—the uncanny expressed in the maternal body's complicity with the process of *bios*. Mother and daughter are fused into a mineral body, inorganic, without life. The incorporation of the daughter becomes petrification—not a return to the maternal sea of the organic life, to birth-giving flesh before the birth of the singular body through detachment, splitting, but a return to an exit, by means of mineral solidification, from the flux of life.

The rock on Mount Sipylus, imposing and jagged, has an uncertain shape. If one is able to recognize a glimpse of Niobe's profile, it is only because of

---

17. See Forbes Irving (1990).
18. See Bertolini (2019, 92–94).

FIGURE 1.1. Antonietta Raphaël, *Niobe,* bronze, 1939—inv. n. 23 Catalogo Generale della scultura, Centro Studi Mafai Raphaël.

its suggestiveness, that is, as Pausanias would say, "because people who enjoy mythical stories are naturally disposed to add even more wonders of their own"[19]—although the water that drips from its ravines is perhaps a manifestation of that vital humidity that Thales identified with *physis* and, with philosophical wonder, called the Whole.

---

19. See Buxton (2009, 136).

CHAPTER 2

Nihil Est in Imagine Vivum

REBECCA COMAY

I wonder what was in those arrows that shot down Niobe's children with such deadly sniper precision—high-speed ballistics, vectors of the plague, the sun's scorching rays: war, virus, climate, Apollo does it all—a perfect storm of disasters with more bad weather on its way. A violent whirlwind will abruptly transport the stony mother away from Thebes, her adopted city, back to Asia Minor, returning her to a homeland that is no longer the way she left it and to a turbulent eternity of mourning—at once insistent, legendary, and yet pushed strangely out of view.

1. STONE REMOVAL

Frozen in grief and yet overspilling her own boundaries, shrinking into solitude yet expanding into the landscape, fixed in place but defying gravity, freezing-seething Niobe turns into her own effigy, monument, and environment—a corpse, a tombstone, a tumulus, a mountain: mourner, mourned, sepulcher, and burial grounds all in one. But although she will inspire endless paintings and sculptures, and although her story will be chiseled into stone as an admonitory *monumentum*—in the temple of Zeus in Olympia, on the batiments of the Palatine, on the first terrace of *Purgatorio*—Niobe herself is not an artwork. She does not enter the sculpture garden of the *Metamorpho-*

ses either as a natural wonder or as a human artifact. Neither a monumental sculpture nor a picturesque landmark integrated into the city or the familiar landscape, Niobe's damaged body will be removed from the polis—swept back to the mountains of Phrygia, to the borderlands of Greek civilization—neither inside nor outside, not quite Greece, not exactly foreign, ejected to the margins of visibility and to the limits of representation and form.

Her petrified remainder will be known mainly by rumor and hearsay. Travelers to the region will sometimes to this day confuse Niobe with the Hittite Kybele, the oriental, orgiastic Ur-mother, whose story predates hers by several millennia and whose colossal Bronze Age statue is carved in the rocky flank of the same mountain. Pausanias (3.22.4) describes this other colossus, towering over ten meters tall on a nearby cliff face, as the "most ancient of all the images of the mother of the gods"; rumor had it that this giant statue must have been the handiwork of a demigod—even back home, Niobe has competition. These two mega-mothers in fact look nothing alike and have nothing in common apart from their prodigious fecundity, but this kind of confusion happens with this kind of mother. Too-muchness, and what mother is not this, tends to be much of a muchness.

There will be a moral to the story, at least there will be endless attempts to moralize, to transcribe Niobe's terrible story into emblem, *exemplum,* allegory, to extract moral and religious takeaway, but the lesson will remain obscure. Even Hecuba, raging in grief and outdoing Niobe's body count with her (literally) dozens of slaughtered children, makes more *sense* than the bereaved Niobe. Even Hecuba's transformation into a barking dog has more human significance. Her monstrous *sôma* becomes signifying *sêma*. The dog-tomb becomes a dog-sign, Kynossema, a place-name, a legible signpost, a point of orientation, at least for the victors. For the Greek sailors plying their way through the eastern Aegean, Hecuba's watery grave will provide a useful navigational marker. Her cenotaph will be filled with meaning. Niobe's metamorphosis, by contrast, is unmitigated anamorphosis. Pausanias, a native of the area and the only ancient writer who claims to have seen first-hand the legendary mountain, now a tourist attraction in Western Turkey, remarks that if you get too near the thing you see only a shapeless sheer of rock, but from a certain remove you can discern the profile of a weeping woman (1.21.3). Niobe's humanity can be registered only from a safe distance, becoming unrecognizable and inhuman when approached from too close. An illegible blotch in the near landscape, a death's head visible only in recession, like the anamorphic skull in Holbein's *Ambassadors,* Niobe is the image of the withdrawal of the image. This is a notable end for one who had walked in beauty and who had staked her prestige on the privilege of visibility. This had been the crux of Niobe's challenge to the gods: "What madness, to prefer gods whom you have only heard of (*auditos*) to those whom you have seen (*visis*)?" (Ovid, *Metamorphoses* 6.170). One might be tempted to say that Niobe is the image of the sublime.

2. THE COUNTDOWN

Ovid, who has left us the most detailed account of the story, including the part about the whirlwind, is as captivated by the gruesome details of the children's slaughter as by the painstaking step-by-step of Niobe's transformation. He tracks the grisly trajectory of each arrow with a gruesome, almost Homeric attention to detail—the sound of this arrow whizzing through the air, this shaft piercing the neck, this extruded clump of lung, this fountain of blood, this arrow in the gut, this tender bit of flesh behind the knee. Just before the end of his shift, Apollo hesitates, wishing he could arrest or reverse time's arrow, but the shaft has already sprung from the bow, its trajectory is unstoppable, its aim infallible. The arrow retains its exactitude even in inexactitude. It hits the mark even though it barely grazes the surface. "The young man fell smitten by the slightest wound only" (6.265–26). The most minimal (*minimo*) wound has deadly efficacy. There is no margin of error, not because the target is so elusive but because error simply does not exist in the universe of fate.

And yet there is fatigue in the telling. The story starts flagging midway through the killing spree, notably when Leto's executive order passes from Apollo to Artemis and the focus shifts from dying sons to dying daughters. As the scene changes from outdoors to indoors, from the equestrian training field to the palace interior, the lights go dim, the details become hazy, the victims nameless, their manner of death unmemorable, the storyline reduced to statistics and to the drama of the last number. It takes Ovid sixteen lines to run through the deaths of the seven daughters—the slaughter of the seven boys had taken fifty—but that we can think of nothing better to do than count lines already suggests a failure of empathy and imagination. How do you take the measure of death in large numbers; at what point do numbers start counting?

Niobe, who never stops computing right down to zero hour, manages to turn spreadsheet parenting into high drama. Her furious arithmetic forms the backbone of the narrative and generates its most startling moments. She performs her most shocking calculation at the halfway mark, weeping and raging over her sons' corpses, but still managing to taunt Leto with her superior numbers. She performs her most metaphysically precarious calculation when the scorecard has finally tipped to Leto's advantage and her own stock is on the verge of depletion. "Leave me just one, the smallest (*minimamque*), of all my many, just the smallest (*minimam*), just the one" (6.299–300). Difference is no longer measurable along a continuum of exchangeable integers, but lies in the infinite gap between something and nothing. Note the returning motif of minimalism. In the vicinity of zero, the most minimal thing—the slightest wound, the smallest child—has maximal metaphysical consequence. No injury is minor enough, no victim tiny enough—no minimum is "meremost" enough—to elude capture.

In Hades, however, on the other side of nothingness, Niobe will resume her stubborn enumeration. In Seneca's *Oedipus*, summoned from the dead by Tiresias, she will appear in the company of the Theban ancestors, voiceless but unrepentant, insolently gesticulating as she continues to tally up the shades of her children (*numerat umbras*, 615). In a related scene in Statius's *Thebaid*, this fury of enumeration will erupt into a *jouissance* of "insane," unbridled lamentation: *percenset . . . insanae plus iam permittere linguae* (4.575–78).

3. NOTHING IS ALIVE IN THE IMAGE

There is nothing alive in the image, says Ovid, shifting to the present tense as the story congeals and fast-paced narration yields to the sludge of slow-motion description. *Nihil est in imagine vivum* (*Metamorphoses* 6.305). The hair stops blowing in the wind, the tongue sticks to the palate, the womb thickens, the orifices close. Niobe disintegrates and agglutinates into a blazon of lifeless body parts, her body decomposing and stiffening into an undifferentiated stony mass—inorganic, disorganized, somewhere between forced sterilization and a body without organs. This stone does not speak, it does not leap into motion, does not quicken to the lyre, does not build on command, does not soften to the touch, does not warm to desire, does not clang with the dawn, does not spring into battle. There is no epitaph on this tombstone, no inscription beckoning the passerby with a message from the beyond. Or rather, we are being summoned, there is a message, but the script is unfamiliar and the writing eroded. There is figuration, a face in the landscape, but we glimpse it obliquely, in profile not *en face*, without opportunity for reciprocity or recognition. The statue eyes us, it solicits our attention, but it will not return our gaze.

Nihil est in imagine vivum. There is no life in this image, nothing alive in this phantom, no life in this statue, nothing living you can imagine, no life in the imagination, nothing lively or enlivening in the *imago* of the grieving Niobe. The word *imago* points in both directions: both an objective shape and a mental representation (this is why it will become so generative for psychoanalysis)—a painting, a statue, an effigy, a vision, a ghost, a simile, a metaphor, a figure, an idea. Nothing about the image of Niobe is *alive*—neither the congelation she has become nor any mental image we can form of her. Every picture of this stony mother is flat and lifeless. The imagination itself grows flaccid and brittle in the presence of this colossal grieving. There is something oppressive and hard-hearted, at once smothering and cynical, in the cliché of the all-suffering mother. Is stone-cold grief not the epitome of a dead metaphor?

And yet Niobe is not exactly dead and she is not exactly an image. The statue is not quite a statue; it is neither stationary or stable; it swoops off with the wind; it seeps and oozes; it spreads and chokes like ivy. Neither animate nor inanimate, neither living nor dead, Niobe lives on in a state of perpetual inanimation—an incessant becoming-stone, a stone that is not quite stony enough, a corpse that does not stay dead enough, continually excreting its own bodily fluids, simultaneously flooding and dehydrating, emptying and overflowing like a leaky vessel. Her *imago* toggles between drought and incontinence, between flood and desert. *By children's birth and death I am become / so dry that I am now made mine own tomb* (Donne 1967).

If it did not feel so portentously Heideggerian, we might try repunctuating. **Nihil** *est in imagine vivum.* Nothing, the Nothing, is alive in the image. In the depths of the image, nothingness itself is stirring. Nothing nominalizes itself, assumes grammatical density and dignity—it takes on a life of its own—in the secret inwardness of the image. *Nihil* **est** *in imagine vivum.* In the hollow interior of the image, nothing *is* alive, it *exists*, it *insists*, it presents itself as the nothingness of *being. Nihil est* **in** *imagine vivum. In* the image, *within* that fractured interiority, nothingness takes up its unsettled abode. Negativity opens up an internal fissure between inside and outside, a zone of intimate exteriority that breaks apart the self-enclosure of the image. *Nihil est in* **imagine** *vivum*. At the core of the *imago,* in the internal crack between objective phantom and subjective phantasm, negation intrudes: nothing, that is everything, punctures the immanence and plenitude of the *imaginary. Nihil est in imagine* **vivum***.* Nothingness is *alive,* it *survives,* it *lives on,* but barely, as a living-dead revenant, an uncanny visitor within the perforated emptiness of the image.

4. IT KEEPS ON GOING

Is Niobe a tragic character? Can she be put on stage? It is often said that tragedy is the containing, formalization, objectification, and outsourcing of mourning: women, foreigners, captive slaves are brought on stage so that the city can behold its own grief through the prism of the other's, usually a mother's, suffering. Niobe is an exemplary figure of tragic mourning—its hyperbole, vanishing point, and limit. Plato will banish her from the stage altogether. For the most famously vehement and virulent of tragic mourners, notably Antigone and Electra, Niobe will be the impossible object of desire and emulation.

She will be the model for Antigone's death-driven longing for inorganic existence, the paradigm for Electra's insatiable mourning—at once aspirational *exemplum* and horrifying example. Her stony persistence at once promises the rigor of devotion and threatens the rigor mortis of a living death. Antigone and Electra, both childless virgins, explicitly identify with this mother of mothers, audaciously modeling their bereavement on hers as they nurse and succor their own grief. Sophocles's Antigone traffics in superlatives: Niobe suffered the *saddest* death (*lugrotatan*, 823), Antigone is *most like* her (*homoiotaton*, 833), Antigone suffers the *most evils* (*kakista*, 895).[1] The grandiosity of the comparison provokes resistance in the Chorus of old men clustering around Antigone's open grave, who remind her that she is only human (as if Niobe was not), and upon her departure proceed to deflate Niobe's own exceptionality by recalling other no less illustrious examples of mortal suffering—Danaë, the son of Dryas (Lycurgus), the sons of Phineus. This expansion of suffering also "provincializes" Thebes—it breaks through the suffocating, Elsinore-like enclosure of the walled-in city, catapulting the family tragedy onto an expanded international stage: Phrygia, northern Thrace, the Bosphorus, the Black Sea . . .

No one bothers to remind either of these two virgins that Niobe had lots of children. But that would be hardly relevant to Antigone, for whom children are a fungible commodity anyway. As she will scandalously tell the Chorus, children are not the ultimate lost object, there are more where they come from, but nothing trumps the death of a brother. But in any case Antigone is bearing the multitude of the unborn. Outdoing Niobe's merely existing children, she gets to mourn all the children she will never have. Unlamented (*aklautos*) (847 and 876), unwept (*adakrutos*) (881), unmarried (*agamos*) (867), unbedded (*alektros*), without bridal song (*anumenaios*) (876 and 917), unloved (*aphilos*) (876). . . . A-a-a-a-a. The torrent of negatives keeps beating the air throughout Antigone's *kommos* like broken syllables of a lament cut off mid-throat. Not once throughout her long lamentation does Antigone (whose very name spells negativity) give voice to the full-throttled sonority of the mourner's *ai-ai-ai-ai*. Her lament is further stifled by the reticence of the Chorus, which does not provide the desired antiphonal response to her lyrical outpouring. The Chorus seals her solitude by stubbornly withholding the formal trappings of a collective ritual. But there is no limit on negative magni-

---

1. On this passage, see Rimell's and Telò's chapters.

tudes. In their abridgment the syllables of grief become bountiful, inexhaustible, self-regenerative. Speculating on the infinity of lost futures, Antigone transforms barrenness into the consummate fecundity. Reproductive futurism reasserts itself in the melancholic utopia of the not-to-be-born.

There is something self-confirming and even tautological in Antigone's performative mimesis: the very comparison to Niobe has a "Niobean" boldness. The identification also exacerbates the generational slippage and tightens the Oedipal noose. In grieving Polyneices as her own child, Antigone joins her father in matrimony and adds more tangles to the family tree. But her reference to the "Phrygian stranger" is also a dark reminder of a traumatic prehistory reaching beyond the Labdacid family tragedy—literally "pre-Oedipal" in its ancestrality—a backstory of fratricide, migrations, usurpations, dynastic interruptions, and thwarted transmissions stretching back to and beyond the violent origins of Thebes.

Can Niobe herself appear on stage? We have scraps of two tragedies by that name, combining to offer glimpses of the shoot-out and the sorrow. Sophocles (it seems) showed the terrifying action, Aeschylus the piteous aftermath. Curiously, Euripides, for Aristotle (*Poetics* 1543a29) the "most tragic," *tragikôtatos* of the tragic poets, most lavish with wailers, seems not to have written a *Niobe* play of his own. Perhaps he found the metatheatrical opportunities limited. But Euripides appears as a character in Aristophanes's *Frogs* to give a merciless parody of Aeschylus's version. Recall the scene: Dionysus goes to Hades to resurrect the recently deceased Euripides and is forced to adjudicate a posthumous contest between Euripides and Aeschylus for the crown of tragedy. The Underworld is replicating the festival agon above ground and the stakes are high: the verdict will determine the entwined fates of a declining polis and a moribund tragic culture—the salvation of Athens and the continuation of its choral festivals.

Euripides comes on stage to give a brutal plot summary of his rival's play. It sounds peculiar: minimalist, postdramatic, verging on Beckett: plotless, wordless, devoid of event, character, and action—"Aeschylean silence" at its most hyperbolic. Niobe sits speechless on the tomb of her children while everyone hovers and the audience yawns. While the actor sits frozen in silence, the spectator sits frozen in boredom, waiting and waiting for something to happen, for Niobe to say something, for the thing to be over, while the play "keeps on going."[2] Perhaps we have been trapped in an interminable prologue and are still waiting for the play to start. Or perhaps the play is already finished, and we are stuck in the endless aftermath of what never began. Stone waiting

---

2. See Telò's chapter.

for stone, a statue staring at a statue, the spectator is forcibly drawn into the (in)action. Having arrived too late or too early at the theatre, we find ourselves trapped in a drama that excludes us, simultaneously inside and outside the spectacle, interpellated into a scene to which we are denied access.

Niobe is not exactly a tragic "mother in mourning"; her grief is both more excessive and yet oddly deficient. Herodotus (6.21) recounts how when Phrynicus produced his tragedy on the capture of Miletus the whole theater reportedly burst into tears. The playwright was fined a thousand drachmas for "having reminded the Athenians of their own misfortunes," and all future productions of the play were banned from the city. Tragedy would need to find ways to contain the dangerous pathos of lament and to channel and formalize that sorrow. Niobe poses a different theatrical challenge. It is not that her grief is too distressing or debilitating for the beholder or that her story comes too close for comfort. Her grief is at once colder and more invasive. Niobe is mute on stage and the silence is intolerable to the spectator. Even more disturbing may have been the vocal explosion that will eventually shatter this silence—inhuman, monstrous, in an unknown language. "After all this nonsense, when the play [is] already halfway over," Niobe opens her mouth and emits "a dozen words, as big as an ox, with a crest and brow, some kind of terrible monster, unintelligible to the spectators" (*Frogs* 926).

Aristophanes is being funny, of course, and perhaps it takes comedy to capture the force of this strange identification—more engulfment than empathy and more tedium than terror, and with no opening for catharsis—only the stifling chill of a contactless contagion where grief and boredom converge. At the limits of tragedy, at the limits of theater, at the limits of human sociability, we confront the traumatic imbrication of two irreconcilable desires—the sufferer's demand for acknowledgment, the witness's demand for a story or spectacle on which to fasten—each veering its perilous obstacle course between the rock and the hard place of narcissism and voyeurism. The collision of these impossible desires puts a strain on every social relationship founded on the premise or promise of reciprocity and recognition. There is a cold ethical demand here, let us call it the demand for community, for lack of a better word, but it probably exceeds what theater can offer.

5. WHITE ON WHITE

Whereas Aeschylus turns theater into sculpture, the visual depictions of Niobe are for the most part highly dramatic, noisy with story, a swirl of bodies, drapery billowing, arms flailing. Even sculpture, where one might expect to see

Niobe's petrification literalized, is more theater than statuary, and like the paintings tends to be about the dying children rather than the grief-stricken mother. The best-known example, the series of Hellenistic sculptures now in the "Niobe room" in the Uffizi,[3] presents a dramatic mise-en-scène of fleeing and falling bodies, each frozen at the instant of death. Niobe stands in the center like a colossus, arm aloft, clutching her youngest in the rocky folds of her garment. None of the children are quite dead and the supply of children is not quite depleted. Niobe is still a mother. There is still another moment, still another child, still time to arrest the course of fate. Zeno's arrow has been suspended. Maternity is reclaimed in the frozen expectancy of the pregnant moment. But this is an inverted pregnancy, more of an unending stillbirth, where the suspense only reifies the inevitability of the impending disaster. This is not the kairotic expectancy of the *diskoboulos*, captured forever on the verge of throwing the disk, on the brink of a future still brimming with possibility. For Niobe every future has collapsed into the stasis of the *fait accompli*—"the paradox of an instant that endures without a future" (Levinas 1998, 9).

The surviving South Italian funerary vases showing the grieving mother at different moments of her metamorphosis are among the rare instances where Niobe's petrification is visually represented (this is perhaps because they are referencing theatrical productions rather than the myth itself): stony silence finds its objective correlative in the stillness of the well-wrought urn. Sitting on her children's tomb, slumped like Dürer's *Melencolia* by her stone, or standing like a statue within their *naiskos* (funerary temple), Niobe appears at different moments of petrification. We see her body whitening in stages as the coldness spreads from feet to legs to torso, freezing upward, like the dying Socrates, as she turns into artifact, architecture, and landscape, shrinking and expanding into stage prop, stage set, and scenic backdrop. On one fourth-century terracotta hydria (see fig. 2.1), the whiteness has reached waist-level, giving Niobe the appearance of a gigantic pillar—literally a fifth column—growing tumescently within the pillared interior of the *naiskos* with her head on the verge of bursting through the roof (just in case there was any lingering doubt that we're talking about the phallic mother). On other vases, Niobe's body expands to become a barrow, a tumulus, a mountain, absorbed into the landscape like Winnie disappearing into the sandheap in *Happy Days*. But Niobe also grows metaphysically smaller. Her leaking body becomes a thing among things, a household object, a jar (more shades of Beckett), a container for dispensing fluids, like the ones used at weddings and funerals to prepare the bodies of brides and corpses.

---

3. See Baert's and Benjamin's chapter.

FIGURE 2.1. Red-figure *hydria*, from Campania, Italy, circa 350–325 BCE, attributed to the Libation Painter. NM71.1 Nicholson Collection, Chau Chak Wing Museum, the University of Sydney.

On the front (see fig. 2.2a) of a fourth-century red-painted *loutrophoros* (a water-carrying funerary vessel), Niobe shares the space of her children's *naiskos* with two large funerary jars that flank her on either side. Both jars are painted white, matching the stony whiteness creeping up the hem of her dress as well as the stoniness of the surrounding *naiskos*. The jar on Niobe's left (our right) distinctly resembles the actual jar on which it is painted. Woman, vessel, building: containers stacked inside containers. Turn the jar around (see fig.

FIGURE 2.2a. Apulian red-figure *loutrophoros*, about 330 BCE, attributed to the Painter of Louvre. Recto. The J. Paul Getty Museum Collection.

FIGURE 2.2b. Apulian red-figure *loutrophoros*, about 330 BCE, attributed to the Painter of Louvre. Verso. The J. Paul Getty Museum Collection.

2.2b) and the mise en abyme implodes. Niobe has been replaced by a gigantic white *lekythos* (an oil-bearing ritual vessel) that occupies the entire space of the *naiskos*. The magnification draws attention to the jar's whiteness; at this scale, it looks unpainted or half-painted, as if its surface has been primed, the ground prepared, but the figure has not yet been drawn. Or maybe Niobe's petrification is completed and the figure has disappeared into the ground. Bleached and spectral, Niobe would then be indistinguishable from the jar on which she is painted and from the emptiness within it—a blank figure traced upon a blank surface, white on white.

6. EMPTY JARS

There is a two-page spread in Whitney's *Choice of Emblemes* (1586), a compilation of extracts from various European emblem books packaging for Christian readers the epigrammatic wisdom of the ancients. One page shows Niobe amidst the carnage—*superbia*: pride chastened. As if to remind the reader of her soggy destiny, the facing page shows the leaking barrel of the husband-slaying Danaids—*frustra*: pointlessness, uselessness, frustration. For their refusal of matrimony and childbirth the Danaids were condemned to an eternal afterlife fetching water in leaking pots—what better way to capture the boredom and futility of domestic toil. The layout may have been a printer's accident, but the juxtaposition of hyperbolic maternity and militant virginity is striking. The figure of the incontinent vessel is of course brimming with misogyny on many levels and there is much to say about the convergence of these different kinds of reproductive labor: housework, childbearing, weeping (the exemplary form of what we nowadays call emotional labor); the image of the punctured jar, in this context, is also awash with sexual violence. But the juxtaposition is also meta-ecphrastically suggestive. The emblem, a mute picture requiring the visual supplements of verbal *inscriptio* ("caption") and *subscriptio* ("epigram"), is itself a kind of self-emptying vessel, a signifier evacuated of immediate or inherent significance, stripped of its "symbolic" (in Benjamin's sense) or "imaginary" (in Lacan's) plenitude or semantic density, and replenished with new meaning. The visible gap between word and image makes this vacancy explicit. This labor of designification and resignification would preoccupy postclassical culture as the ancient myths were divested of their pagan content and reinvested with Christian, and later, secular-humanist meaning. This allegorical labor would be potentially unending. The passage from myth to modernity is in this sense an *essentially* (or structurally) unfinished project, which is another way to say that modernity itself is an interminable work of mourning.

Niobe will be particularly susceptible to this endless allegorical toil if only because the ultimate moral of the story remains opaque. What could Niobe have *done* to provoke such cruel and unusual punishment? Was it her arrogance, her thirst for status, her rivalry with the gods, the profligacy of her womb, the loquacity of her tongue, her prodigious reproductive and verbal *copia*? Fecundity is the last item on Niobe's brag sheet—after her pedigree, her family connections, her marriage, her wealth, her beauty—but it will be the target of Leto's rage. "On top of all this (*huc*), I have seven daughters and just as many sons" (Ovid, *Metamorphoses* 6.182–83). Niobe is also an affront to patriarchal order. That the violence against her is instigated by a woman (moreover, by a rape victim and a migrant) should not obscure this. A defiantly unassimilated immigrant, an oriental queen parading around in flashy Phrygian garments, Niobe sings panegyrics to herself, she demands recognition, she arrogates the king's authority, she asserts her tyrannical power over the Theban people. Her cautionary tale will be woven into the visual propaganda of post–civil war Rome.

Absorbed uneasily into Christian iconography, Niobe enters the sculpture gallery of the first terrace of *Purgatorio,* carved into the paving stones in the company of Lucifer, Marsyas, Arachne, and other exemplars of *superbia*—the first and most refractory of all the deadly sins. The prideful sinners doing time in purgatory are condemned to shuffle in circles around the terrace like visitors trapped in a museum, or rather like deformed caryatids holding up the museum, bent under the weight of heavy boulders reminding them constantly of their lowly status—barely recognizable as human, formless, worm-like, "defective insects," painful to behold. With their gaze continually pressed downward, these moving statues are forced to keep studying their engraved counterparts on the ground beneath their feet—sculptures walking on sculptures, stone on stone. The penitents had already passed by the splendid sculptures carved high on the marble cliffs at the entrance to purgatory—Mary, Trajan, the humble Psalmist—aspirational images offered at the outset of the journey to provide aesthetic and eschatological incentive for staying the course. The pilgrim witnessing the stony encounter is himself a stony tablet with his own weight to bear; Dante's forehead is engraved seven times with the letter "P" (for *peccatum*); these letters will be erased one by one, and his load will lighten, as he ascends the mountain—the inscription *is* the stone.

I said "uneasily" because there is something about Niobe that resists moral rehabilitation. Her chastisement seems not always to chastise. There is a stubbornness in grief that is always on the point of tipping into rebellion. This is not the endurance of the *mater dolorosa*—one reason why Hegel will unfavorably contrast Niobe's melancholia with the fortitude of Mary's mourning:[4] Niobe has no speculative capacity for infinitude; her sorrow is mired in the bad infinite of empty repetition; in other words, like the Greeks generally, she has not broken through the crust of untransfigured nature.

The conundrum, which pertains to the ambiguity of melancholia generally, is in this case that there is no stable demarcation between crime and punishment, between offence and expiation, between submission and refusal. Is petrification punishment or consolation? Injury or analgesic? Humiliation or defiance? Defeat or triumph? Is Niobe's stoniness a forcible abdication of pride or its intensification—an aggrandization, a self-monumentalizing, a self-immortalization, even a self-divinization? Niobe will become the allegory of pride vanquished, but she will also be an example of ostentatious and "odious forms of mourning" (*detestabilia genera lugendi*), as Cicero puts it (*Tusculan*

---

4. See Kottman's chapter.

Disputations 3.26). But if Niobe herself does not learn her own lesson, if grief fails to chastise, then what exactly is the lesson?

7. BOUNDARY STONE

What if allegory itself is the punishment—if Niobe were an allegory of the violence of allegory as such? In Niobe's traumatized flesh we watch suffering hardening into allegory—the painful metamorphosis of pain into image, example, instruction. Stuffed with significance, Niobe is the example of exemplarity itself. Walter Benjamin sees in Niobe's petrification the exemplification of what he calls mythic violence—a violence crystallized in the paralyzing question: *What is the meaning of this suffering? What did Niobe do to deserve this?* The very question confounds and compounds the suffering: we seek a justification for violence—a crime, a sin, a transgression. Punishment triggers the compulsion to inculpate the victim in their own suffering, to make them complicit in this suffering, to package punishment as expiation. As if it is not enough to have your children murdered you have to take the blame for it. Benjamin's point is that Niobe did not transgress any preexisting law: there *was* no law prior to the transgression and no transgression prior to the punishment. It is punishment that produces the mirage of a law antecedent to its own transgression. Punishment produces guilt and guilt prolongs the punishment. Punishment is its own tautological self-reproduction.

Benjamin sees in this porosity between law and punishment—between (what he calls) "law-founding" and "law-preserving" violence—the "rottenness" of the law itself.[5] The Hamlet allusion is surely deliberate, and underscores that myth is not an anthropological or epochal category; I will come back to this. This rottenness (a strange way to describe petrification) is structural. It is not simply that every instantiation of the law requires interpretation, opening the door to reinvention; that there are corrupt police; or even that the very authority of the law enables and requires deviations, exceptions, extralegal measures (Benjamin is writing in the early days of the Weimar Republic). It is about the repetition inherent in the law as such—put otherwise (Derrida-wise), the violence of the *archê* as the simultaneity of origin, power, and conservation; put still otherwise (again Derrida), the iterative force of every performative. The law reinaugurates itself in preserving itself; every execution of the law repeats the law's own foundational act of self-assertion; which is another way of describing the constitutive (not merely instrumental) *force*

---

5. See esp. Radcliffe's, Umachandran's, and Lezra's chapters.

of law-enforcement. The law needs to archive itself, to erect a memorial to its own power, and the guilty, anxious subject is its most enduring monument. Niobe stands as an "eternal, mute bearer of guilt," a stony tablet on which the law perpetually rewrites itself—a "boundary stone" marking the frontier between the powerful and those lacking power (I am lightly rephrasing) and establishing the rule of law as the perpetual policing and redrawing of this border. The border is not ultimately about the division of territory and does not require a physical barrier. It is a means of interpellation by which everything in its vicinity gets sucked into its orbit—criminalized in advance as an illegal (a terrorist, a rapist, an infectious agent, etc.), subjected to surveillance, incarceration, extrajudicial violence. At the origin of the law lies the traumatized legal subject. That Benjamin chooses a mother's guilt to illustrate this point—that the violence is inflicted on a woman's body and that it is gender boundaries that are being policed in this case—goes painfully unmentioned.

This rottenness explains the temporal and hermeneutical violence of law—its power to rewrite the past and capture the future within the widening gyre of the *fait,* or fate, *accompli.* Guilt is retroactively assigned from the contingency of a future that is itself accordingly reified as always already over and done with. The past becomes an unpredictable minefield of transgressions while the future is immobilized under the shadow of these transgressions. Past and future switch places; the past gapes open while the future closes. Uncertainty about what you might have done is accompanied by a certainty about the doom (call it fate) that awaits you. This is why you are anxious about the past and guilty about the future: the outcome is already decided even as the reasons demand unceasing vigilance. Dread is the dialectical convergence of these two temporal inversions: time presses opaquely with the uncertain certainty of a foreboding. Mythic space is equally confounding: the world becomes an ominous landscape of darkly intelligible ciphers and figurations. The mountain becomes a weeping woman: vaguely human, vaguely recognizable—portentous, entreating, commanding. Nature, or what we reify as such, becomes heavy with significance, demanding interpretation while remaining ultimately opaque. You are certain that there is meaning out there, but what that meaning is remains uncertain.

8. PETRIFIED UNREST

Benjamin contrasts the stasis of mythic violence, illustrated by Niobe's petrifaction, with the lightning flash of "divine" violence, illustrated by the biblical story of Korah, whose rebellion against the priestly authority of Moses is countered with brutal retaliation. Despite appearances, the contrast is not grounded on the opposition between paganism and monotheism or between Greek and Hebrew. Benjamin declares divine violence to be the "antithesis of myth in all respects" and draws up a hard division of the territories: "If [mythic] violence is lawmaking, divine violence is law-destroying; if the former sets boundaries, the latter boundlessly destroys them; if mythic violence brings at once guilt and retribution, divine power only expiates; if the former threatens, the latter strikes; if the former is bloody, the latter is lethal without spilling blood" ([1921] 1986, 297). The crisply disjunctive syntax has the declarative sharpness of a fiat. Benjamin's admirers have worked hard to get "divine violence" to work (politically, philosophically, aesthetically)—to extract anarchic-messianic-revolutionary energy from its abruption. Benjamin draws connections to the eruptiveness of the proletarian general strike. There are suggestive affinities with his later (Brecht-inspired) essay on the "destructive character" ([1931] 1986). All this will require exegetical finessing.

Suffice it for now that Benjamin goes out of his way to choose peculiar examples; neither self-evidently illustrates the distinction he is drawing and the antithesis itself may prove undialectical. There is no clear border marking the difference between the two scenarios: both Niobe and Korah defy the ruling order, both provoke the extraordinary cruelty of the gods (or God) resulting in total devastation for their people (in Korah's case, the forced disappearance of somewhere between 250 and 14,700 people depending on how you are counting). In both cases, violence is administered from the top down to enforce the unassailable rule of law (in Korah's case, the Law) and to police the border (in Korah's case, a vast bureaucracy of social distinctions). That Korah's people are "disappeared"—swallowed up by the earth rather than being gunned down in broad daylight—has no obvious bearing in this regard, and it is not obvious anyway that this disappearance is actually traceless (Benjamin's litmus test for the instantaneity and intransitivity of divine violence). The liquidation leaves no shortage of admonitory mementos with guilt and anxiety for all.

This is a deep rabbit hole. My question points in the opposite direction. Rather than flushing out the mythic latencies of divine violence, I am more interested in how mythic violence might forcibly (I use the word advisably) yield its own self-overcoming. Myth is not a stable historical or anthropological category, there is no boundary stone marking its beginnings and endings— which does not mean that it is a static universal either. It takes root wherever power reproduces and embeds itself, which is to say everywhere, but always differently, specifically, concretely. Benjamin will map the glacial landscape of myth, following its alluvial deposits across the tundra of modernity, from the "petrified, primordial landscape" of the Baroque to the frozen phantasmagorias of nineteenth-century Paris, where Niobe will encounter her double at every corner—in the corseted and corpse-like bodies of women's fashion, in the uncanny, living-dead universe of mannequins, automata, marionettes, dolls, and waxworks. Taking a cue from Baudelaire, Benjamin will add to the museum a special gallery of figurines collected under the ambiguous banner of nonreproductive sexuality: the infertile woman, the aging woman, the lesbian, the prostitute—women both excluded and potentially (but not really) liberated from the circuit of reproductive labor.

I have been talking about the various congelations of the commodity fetish—ciphers of subjectivity petrified in a world of total reification. A pessimist might see in these fossils the last traces of human freedom as this reverts to the irreversible stasis of inanimate nature. Benjamin approaches these more along the lines of the Freudian fetish—snapshots of a moment when time stood still, before the catastrophe became irreversible, before the deep freeze (it is hard to use this metaphor innocently today) of global capitalism—imprints of thwarted desire cast in the hardened lava of the Revolution.

Starting with the bad new things, on the premise that any escape from the petrified forest will require going through, and not around it, Benjamin directs his own Medusa gaze to the frozen landscape of modernity—cutting, freezing, arresting, fixing, immobilizing a world that has been immobilized in Danaid-like perpetual motion. The approach causes consternation to Adorno, who keeps accusing Benjamin of having fallen prey to the petrifying spell of myth. Benjamin will not take the bait, or at least that is a risk he is willing to assume, which in this context takes some courage, although that word probably smacks too much of heroics. The delivery from myth lies not in a divine blow delivered from on high but rather from the ground up—stone scraping against stone, stasis against stasis.

I had thought I would close off this essay by leaving Niobe in the company of Melencolia, the allegorical figure in Dürer's engraving, sitting ponderously beside her stone and surrounded by her scatter of unused objects, weighed down by the gravitational tug of earth and by the guilty fallenness of nature. But it was in the end a minor image that arrested me. In his catalogue of the Baroque image-repertoire of mourning, Benjamin pauses to quote a seventeenth-century description of the calcified but weeping heart of the melancholic: a stone that does not melt, that no tears penetrate, and that retains its rigidity even as it seeps and suppurates—a stone that "only sweats outwardly [*von außen*], when the weather is damp" (1998, 154). The stone weeps from the outside, on the surface, in full view, withdrawn but attuned to its environment, isolated and yet responsive. Its tears are not the expression of an interiority, not the disclosure of an inwardness, offer no cathartic relief from suffering, and provide no irrigation or promise of rebirth or regrowth. The stone secretes from the outside because there is *nothing* inside—no mystery to penetrate, no precious fluid to extract, no guilty secret to discharge or purge. Its emptiness is solid. No longer a hollow vessel into which meanings are poured and from which morals are extracted, no longer a tablet for the inscription or infliction of punishment, the stone presents an impenetrable thickness that nonetheless continues to secrete.

We might say that Niobe is staging a kind of "proletarian general strike" of her own—underperforming, outperforming, unperforming, refusing to perform even in her own drama. In the face of this obduracy, "allegory goes away empty-handed" (1998, 233).

CHAPTER 3

Niobe's People

Ambiguous Violence and Interrupted Labor in *Iliad* 24

BEN RADCLIFFE

Bereft of her children and petrified on a wild mountain, Niobe appears to grieve in solitude. In Sophocles's *Antigone,* the eponymous heroine compares her entombment in a lonely cave to Niobe's vigil on Mount Sipylus.[1] In *Metamorphoses,* Ovid draws out the pathos of Niobe's bereavement by striking down each of her children individually, until Niobe begs in vain for the life of her youngest daughter ("oh, leave me just one, the littlest!").[2] Niobe cannot share her grief with the family and community that she has lost, and petrification only amplifies this state of isolation, detaining her within her own traumatized body, which serves as mute testimony of the gods' reprisal against her claim to rival the maternal prowess of Leto. Niobe has thus served as a metonym for a kind of violence that establishes fatal boundaries, both between human aspiration and divine supremacy and between the grieving individual and their community. These two forms of boundary-setting work in tandem, because the violence that swats down Niobe's hubristic overreach also removes her from social intercourse, transforming her body into a figure of divine law that maintains a one-sided, imperious, menacing relation to humanity at large.

The oldest extant depiction of the Niobe myth, however, constructs a more complicated picture of the consequences of her violent bereavement:

---

1. Sophocles, *Antigone* 823–31.
2. Ovid, *Metamorphoses* 6.299.

after her children are destroyed, the Iliadic Niobe grieves with, or near, or alongside at least an assortment of peculiar communities. The context of the story is the last book of the *Iliad,* in which king Priam meets with Achilles to ransom the corpse of his son, Hector, whom Achilles slew in book 22. The two mortal enemies reach a fragile understanding in their shared experience of loss. After consenting to the ransom, Achilles encourages Priam to share a meal with him, despite his terrible grief, and to illustrate the value of commensality, he tells the story of how Niobe incurred the wrath of Apollo and Artemis (24.602–17) by comparing herself to their mother Leto; how she lost all twelve of her children in the gods' violent reprisal; how she remembered to eat food after mourning for nine days; and how she was finally petrified by grief.

Several details underscore the strange persistence of communal proximities in the aftermath of Niobe's bereavement. The first is that Zeus turns Niobe's "people" (*laoi*), her human community, into stones (*lithoi*); thus immobilized, the community is unable to perform its vital obligation to conduct a funeral for Niobe's children. But this lapse also represents a kind of ambiguous solidarity, as the community joins her in a shared cessation of the socially sanctioned practices of grief and commemoration. The gods themselves, however, ultimately bury Niobe's children, serving as a second, surrogate community in place of the human *laoi* that Zeus petrified. When Niobe herself is subsequently petrified, her body is said to reside among mountains that she coinhabits with a third community, the "swiftly dancing" nymphs, whose nimbleness contrasts obscurely with Niobe's lithic immobility. In Achilles's account, Niobe is subtracted from the web of relations and obligations that constitute normative human sociality, but she is not for this reason wholly abandoned. Rather, she is placed in constellations with a succession of human and divine beings that exist in various degrees of proximity to her, figuring modes of sociality that can persist after the pathways of ordinary collective life have been violently foreclosed.

Such figurations are especially freighted with meaning in this final book of the *Iliad,* in which the martial conflict is temporarily suspended by the two opposing leaders, Achilles and Priam, to allow time for Hector's funeral. Although the *Iliad* repeatedly assures its audiences that Troy is doomed and that Achilles's death is imminent, this pause in the final book holds open the (impossible) possibility that the warring parties could prolong their interruption of martial labor and suspend the cycle of violent reprisal between them. My object is to draw out these utopian valences in the figure of Niobe and her various "people," the para-communities that dance, mourn, and stand in shifting configurations around her.

The Iliadic depiction of Niobe is difficult to interpret because the most suggestive details are not explained or mobilized by Achilles for any explicit purpose. Like Niobe and the communities near her, the textual elements of Achilles's narrative are held in a paratactic—even lithic—proximity, interpretive crystals whose very disconnectedness makes them available for rearrangement and reinterpretation. The interpretive task is greatly abetted by Walter Benjamin's treatment of the Niobe myth in his 1921 essay "Towards the Critique of Violence," which incorporates Niobe into an analysis of the problems that arise when violence serves as a means of founding and enforcing the social order. Read alongside *Iliad* 24, Benjamin's interpretation illuminates the ambivalent character of the gods' violent reprisal against Niobe, which enforces the boundary between gods and humans even as it composes Niobe into configurations with divine and semidivine beings. In employing the resources of Benjamin's reading, I am interested not so much in reconstructing his reception of the *Iliad*,[3] but in the parallel receptions of the Niobe myth in both texts, and especially in how each text uses the myth to reflect on the ambivalent efficacy of violence, which can variously buttress, supersede, or suspend the prevailing order of things.

Achilles tells the story of Niobe more than halfway into Priam's mission to ransom Hector's corpse. During their meeting, Achilles and Priam develop a fragile understanding, shifting between admiration, amazement, and fear of the other, communicated through expressions of supplication and sympathy as well as threats and rebukes. In a gesture of goodwill, Achilles urges Priam to take a seat and tells a parable about Zeus's dispensation of good and bad fortune. Soon after, when he has arranged for Hector's corpse to be washed and prepared for transport, Achilles sits down again and encourages Priam to eat with him (24.602–17):

For even fair-haired Niobe remembered to eat,
though her twelve children perished in their halls,
six daughters and six youthful sons.
Apollo slew the sons with his silver bow,
enraged at Niobe, and arrow-pouring Artemis slew the daughters,
because Niobe likened herself to beautiful-cheeked Leto;

---

3. In his brief discussion of Niobe, Benjamin does not specify which literary instantiation of the myth he is referring to (see Ahmadi 2015). The details that he supplies are generic enough to match any of the ancient accounts, and it seems unlikely that he was drawing specifically on the Iliadic version. But, as I hope to show, Benjamin's interpretation is informed by his sense for the ambient thought-patterns of early Greek poetry and drama and offers a powerful set of conceptual resources for interpreting the Niobe *exemplum* in *Iliad* 24.

she said that Leto begot a pair, while she herself bore many;
But though Leto's children were only a pair, they slew all of Niobe's.
For nine days they lay in gore, and there was no one
   to bury them, for the Chronian [sc. Zeus] made the people stones;
but on the tenth day the Ouranian gods buried them.
And Niobe remembered to eat, when she was exhausted with shedding
   tears.
And now, somewhere among the rocks in the lonely mountains
in Sipylus, where they say are the lairs of the nymph goddesses,
who rush nimbly about the [river] Acheloios,
there, though she is a stone, she digests her sorrows from the gods.

The details of the passage have generated critical controversy, especially the last four verses (24.614–17), which critics since Aristarchus have regarded as textually suspect on the grounds that Niobe's restored appetite contradicts her ultimate petrification.[4] If Niobe overcame her grief enough to remember to eat, why was she still transformed into a grieving stone? Further, Achilles seems to undermine his protreptic by implying that Niobe's renewed desire to eat could not save her from perpetual grief. I will work with the text as we have it, but the critical unease about the last verses of the *exemplum* identifies a real tension in the passage between Achilles's benevolent intent—to encourage Priam to enjoy a shared meal—and the ghastly fate of Niobe and her children.

This tension reflects the volatile dynamic between Priam and Achilles, who should be, by all rights, mortal enemies. Commentators have recognized that the possibility of violence between Priam and Achilles looms as a central problem in the scene: an ambiguous threshold, charged with grief and anger, runs between the two men; each might unwittingly provoke violence from the other, thereby falling back into the compulsive chain of reprisals and counter-reprisals that has sustained ten years of war on the fields around Troy.[5] Beyond its ostensible purpose of encouraging Priam to share a meal, Achilles's *exemplum* is richly allusive to this volatile atmosphere. Among the many resonances that commentators have uncovered, it is especially significant that Priam, a bereaved parent, resembles Niobe, whereas "child-slaying" Achilles resembles Apollo.[6] This analogy is rooted in events prior to the ransom scene—Priam's children have already been killed by Achilles before they meet—but it also raises the prospect of continuing danger for Priam during

---

4. See Pearce (2008) and Richardson (1993, 340).
5. See esp. Redfield (1975, 215–18), Lynn-George (1988, 247–4), and Felson (2002, 47–49).
6. See Rabel (1990, 438).

the meeting. In fact, Achilles warns Priam expressly not to provoke him with precipitous demands for the return of Hector's corpse (24.560–70). The narrator (24.583–86) assigns a similar rationale to Achilles's decision to have Hector's corpse washed and anointed out of Priam's sight.

Only fifteen verses later, the Niobe *exemplum* in effect reiterates Achilles's reasoning about anger, subtly reminding Priam that he could still unwittingly provoke Achilles, just as Niobe unwittingly provoked Apollo. Achilles's warnings also raise the possibility that he could be subject to violence from Priam, not directly, but through the intercession of Apollo. Thus the analogy between the *exemplum* and the ransom scene can be reversed: Achilles could be cast in the role of Niobe, suffering retribution from Apollo if he should harm Priam and provoke the anger of the Olympians, who endorse Priam's mission (24.135).[7] In this unprecedented interaction, the guardrails of ritual and etiquette do not provide clear-cut boundaries for social conduct, and the relation between the men must be improvised verbally but also through physical proximity and gesture. After Priam makes his initial appeal for the ransom of Hector's corpse, Achilles removes Priam's suppliant hand and pushes the old man away, gently (24.508–9). The gesture is notoriously ambiguous, combining a gentle touch with a forceful push, breaking contact and reestablishing an interpersonal boundary without sparking the runaway process of violent reprisal.

The dense network of resonances between Achilles, Priam, Niobe, and Apollo/Artemis converges around this notion of proximity and boundary. In Achilles's telling, Niobe is punished for passing over the threshold between gods and humans by likening herself (*isasketo, Iliad* 24.608) to Leto and thereby impinging on her divine status. This is a prototypical transgression in Greek myth, committed by figures like Thamyris, Marsyas, and Capaneus, each of whom is destroyed for attempting to usurp or contest the honors (*timai*) of various gods. In hindsight, Niobe should have known better than to contend with Leto and her children; their vengeance appears as a gruesome but predictable response to mortal overreach. On the other hand, if the existence of a boundary between gods and mortals is an indisputable fact in the world of myth, its contours are fluid and contestable. Homeric heroes routinely vie with the Olympians, sometimes deliberately and sometimes, as it were, by default, simply by virtue of their heroic status. Characters are frequently likened to the

---

7. This danger is underscored by the resemblance between Priam and Chryses, the priest of Apollo who ransoms his daughter from the Achaeans in book 1. Like Chryses, Priam is an old man favored by Apollo in his effort to ransom his child; their two episodes bookend the *Iliad*.

gods with offhand formulae,[8] and there are more pointed encounters, such as when Apollo confronts the heroes Diomedes, Patroclus, and Achilles in battle during their respective displays of martial prowess (*aristeiai*).[9] Apollo fends off these mortal challengers with menacing and, in the case of Patroclus, ultimately fatal rebukes. But it is significant that Apollo issues his final threats only after the challengers have repeatedly charged against him. He permits these mortal heroes to attempt to vie with him, to lay claim to equality with a god. In these cases, the boundary is enforced before it can be crossed. In the case of the Iliadic Niobe, we are not told whether she had previously "likened herself" to Leto or had been warned to desist, only that, like many of her contemporaries in the generation of heroes, she tarried on the border between humans and gods and discovered, too late, that she had crossed it.

Apollo and Artemis's act of destruction thus imposes a certain distance between humanity and the gods, but the distance is asserted—marked out retroactively as a singular error—without being precisely measured or generalized. This kind of ambiguous negotiation of proximities figures centrally in Walter Benjamin's discussion of the Niobe myth in one of his best-known early essays, "Towards the Critique of Violence" ("Zur Kritik der Gewalt").[10] "Violence" translates *Gewalt*, which like "violence" can connote an illegal, destructive exercise of force. But *Gewalt* can also designate a legitimate state power or authority, in expressions such as "the power of the people" or the "authority of the court."[11] Benjamin's essay is interested precisely in the problematic circularity between these two meanings, between the legitimate authority of the law and illegitimate acts of violence. Established legal orders cannot trace their legitimacy back in time forever: they are always established by acts of violence—revolutions, coups, conquests, insurrections—that had no legal basis when they were committed. Founding acts of violence are then validated retroactively by the authorities that they found. Conversely, the law has to be maintained by the "legitimate" exercise of force, for instance, through

---

8. E.g., *theos hôs* ("like a god"); *ison . . . theôi* ("equal to a god"); *isotheos phôs* ("a godlike man").

9. Diomedes confronts Apollo at *Iliad* 5.431–46; Patroclus at 16.698–711; Achilles at 20.438–54.

10. The essay was composed in Berlin near the end of 1920, during the revolutionary tumult of the early Weimar Republic. For a history of political violence during this period, see Schumann 2009; see also Umachandran in this volume. Benjamin began writing about political issues after finishing his doctorate in 1919, and "Critique" was initially developed as part of an unfinished book-length project on politics. On the essay's history and Benjamin's early political thought, see Moran and Salzani (2015, 2–3). The essay has attracted a great deal of critical attention in continental philosophy and political theory; see in particular Derrida (1992) and Agamben (1998). My reading is especially indebted to Hamacher (1991).

11. Hamacher 1991, 1133n2.

policing. But policing exercises a kind of violence as well—often illegal, excessive, and unaccountable—that can operate as a law unto itself and undermine the legal order that it is supposed to enforce. This is the first sense in which violence is ambiguous (*zweideutig*) for Benjamin in its relation to law: it is often unclear whether violence is simply enforcing the existing order or in fact instituting new norms. We will see below that this ambiguity (*Zweideutigkeit*) has a second interpretation (*zweite Deutung,* so to speak), in the sense that Benjamin entertains the possibility that certain kinds of violence might enter into a purely destructive relation to the law *tout court*.

Benjamin typically uses "law" (*Gesetz*) to refer to systems of juridical and governmental administration, especially in modern states, but his conception of the term can be more generic, encompassing literal and metaphorical boundary markers—norms that police social conduct by setting distances between the licit and the illicit and between private persons and properties.[12] Besides contemporary European politics, Benjamin draws his examples from premodern history and religious thought, especially the Torah and Greek myth. He associates ambiguous violence with the latter term in particular and regards the figure of "myth" pejoratively, as the field of fatal and murky encounters between humans and gods. In mythical narratives, humans violate taboos or upset celestial designs that they do not comprehend until they suffer the consequences for their transgressions. Mythical violence thus anticipates the modern legal notion that "ignorance of the law is no excuse."

The example of Niobe illustrates for Benjamin the fatal circularity between mythical violence and the norms that it at once institutes and enforces:

> Mythical violence in its archetypal form is a mere manifestation of the gods. Not a means to their ends, scarcely a manifestation of their will, but first of all a manifestation of their existence. The legend of Niobe contains an outstanding example of this. True, it might appear that the action of Apollo and Artemis is only a punishment. But their violence establishes a law far more than it punishes for the infringement of one already existing.[13]

Benjamin's essential point is that the violence that Niobe suffers is simply not a *means* of punishing the transgression of an existing boundary but a sover-

---

12. Formulated generally, law is a system of received, apparently impartial norms that regulate collective life. Such norms are deeply implicated in the structures of the modern state, but they also exist in stateless societies as a means for perpetuating the social order. Hence, even though there is a daunting gulf between the concept of law in modern states and the closest Homeric equivalent (*themis*), Benjamin's notion of "law" allows one to think incisively about both. For accounts of early Greek law, see Gagarin (1986) and Ostwald (1969).

13. Benjamin [1921] 1986, 294.

eign act that institutes a new instance of division between humans and the gods. After a brief digression on Prometheus, he continues his interpretation of Niobe:

> Violence therefore bursts upon Niobe from the uncertain, ambiguous sphere of fate. It is not actually destructive. Although it brings a cruel death to Niobe's children, it stops short of the life of their mother, whom it leaves behind, more guilty than before through the death of the children, both as an eternally mute bearer of guilt and as a boundary stone on the frontier between men and gods.[14]

The redescription of Niobe as "a boundary stone on the frontier between men and gods" draws together the lines of Benjamin's reading. Through her petrification, Niobe assumes the form of a marker erected on the border between territories, like the stone markers (*horoi*) that the Greeks used historically to divide private plots of land and that are described in several passages of the *Iliad*.[15] What Niobe marks is not a spatial boundary between territories but a metaphysical boundary between the mortal and the immortal. The form of the marker preserves the ambiguity of the violence that produced it: petrification serves at once to institute a boundary and to punish Niobe for transgressing the same boundary, a semiotic murkiness redoubled by Niobe's enigmatic existence as a grieving stone.

In this initial interpretation, Niobe is one milestone in an intractable cycle of violent acts inflicted by gods against mortals to maintain the stratified order of the cosmos. The mythical pattern resonates distinctly with the patterns of violence, reprisal, and hierarchy in the human communities of the *Iliad*, and especially in the conflict between Achilles's and Priam's peoples. Indeed, for Benjamin, every existing order rests upon a history of violent transgressions and police actions, revolutions, and reactions; on the basis of this interminable cycle, law claims for itself a kind of historical necessity, which Benjamin calls "fate." The chief task of revolutionary politics is to interrupt this cycle—in effect, to abolish the state. This issue of interruption leads Benjamin to concede that there is a small loose end in the knot between fate and force that manifests itself in the Niobe myth. Although the violence inflicted on Niobe is retroactively appropriated by the gods as a means of enforcing the law of divine supremacy (Benjamin calls this species of violence "lawmak-

---

14. Benjamin [1921] 1986, 295.
15. *Iliad* 12.421–22; 21.405; 23.332. Cf. Palmer's (1950) theory that *dikē*, "justice," is etymologically connected to the archaic Greek practice of erecting stone markers on the disputed boundaries between parcels of land.

ing"), it is initially "not a means to an ends . . . but first of all a manifestation of [the gods'] existence,"[16] presumably in the sense that Apollo and Artemis first respond to Niobe out of a sense of reflexive anger, not to enforce a preconceived policy.[17] Benjamin calls this kind of violence "immediate" (*unmittelbar*) in the sense that it is *not a means*.[18] Referring to the myth of Niobe again, he remarks that,

> if this immediate violence in mythical manifestations proves closely related, indeed identical to lawmaking violence, it reflects a problematic light on lawmaking violence, insofar as the latter was characterized above, in the account of military violence, as merely a mediate violence.[19]

Lawmaking and immediate violence are closely related in mythical narratives, but this conceptual proximity admits a minimal difference. There is always the possibility that immediate, spontaneous, undirected violence might not converge with the finality of the law. Immediate violence testifies to the existence of a space of political maneuver beyond the closed circle of violence and law, a space in which violence does not necessitate the reproduction of state power.

We do not know what forms of communal life might populate this space nor what kinds of immediate violence could conceivably arrest the cycle of law-making and law-preserving violence. For readers of the Iliadic Niobe narrative, it is remarkable that Benjamin tentatively identifies the possibility of such interruption in the proletarian general strike, the complete suspension of labor by the working class, as theorized in the syndicalist tradition and especially by Georges Sorel.[20] The "immediate" character of the violence in the Niobe episode is manifested precisely in the figures that share her state of

---

16. Benjamin [1921] 1986, 294.

17. Benjamin omits the reference in the Iliadic account to the "anger" of Apollo toward Niobe's boasts (*khôomenos Niobêi*, *Iliad* 24.606)—an emotion that is probably supposed to extend to Artemis but, for whatever reason, is made explicit only for Apollo (see Most 2003). Immediately before his discussion of the Niobe myth, however, Benjamin describes outbursts of anger as an "everyday" instance of ambiguous violence: "The nonmediate function of violence at issue here is illustrated by everyday experience. As regards man [sic], he is impelled by anger, for example, to the most visible outbursts of a violence that is not related as a means to a preconceived end. It is not a means but a manifestation" (294).

18. "Immediate," like the German *unmittelbar*, has the sense of closeness and self-containment. The translation, however, loses the etymological transparency of *unmittelbar*, which is literally the negation of *Mittel*, "means" or "instrument." The term is important in German philosophy; in Hegel, for instance, the first stage of dialectic is *unmittelbar*, not yet mediated or externalized.

19. Benjamin [1921] 1986, 295.

20. Benjamin [1921] 1986, 291–92.

suspended animation, of withdrawal from the labor of everyday life. Thus, as I suggested in the introduction, although Niobe's grief and fasting are typically represented as a solitary endeavor, the cessation of labor is undertaken collectively in the Iliadic account, first in conjunction with Niobe's petrified community (*laoi*) and ultimately with the dancing nymphs of Sipylus. These two collectivities are predicated, obscurely, on co-proximities of space, on variations of motion and stillness between Niobe and the beings around her. Rather than underpinning a renewed entanglement between the gods and normative human sociality, these figures of collective proximity represent an imaginative leap out of the cycle of violence and law in which Niobe has been implicated.

In the case of Niobe's people, Achilles only mentions that Zeus "made them stones" (*laous de lithous poiêse, Iliad* 24.611). This detail is supposed to explain why Niobe's children were left unburied for nine days, but its obscurity leaves open a number of interpretive possibilities. One ancient commentator read the verse figuratively to mean that Zeus made the community feel a stony indifference (*asympatheis*) toward Niobe's dead children, since they were outraged that her impious behavior brought down the wrath of the gods on their community.[21] But the act of petrification anticipates Niobe's imminent fate (she also becomes a *lithos*), a drastically material form of *sympatheia*. The community is held in suspended animation alongside Niobe, and both refrain from conducting the ordinary rites of mourning for the dead, an indispensable religious practice by which the Greeks negotiated their relations with the gods and the boundary between life and death. Niobe and her community engage (though not by their own choice) in a general strike that suspends this ritual order and, with it, the means of situating human mortality in the divine order of things. It is in light of this anomaly that one should understand the gods' decision to bury the Niobids "on the tenth day" (24.612) after the massacre. By this act of strikebreaking, the gods apply their hands to ritual labor that humans should (and must) perform, thereby restoring the order that the gods themselves have interrupted.

The detail about Niobe's people complicates Benjamin's interpretation of the Niobe myth, which he takes as an exemplary case of law-making violence, albeit one complicated by the partially "immediate" character of the gods' retribution. By contrast, Benjamin identifies a different, "pure" species of immediate violence in a story from the Bible—God's total, unequivocal destruction of Korah and his followers, who conspire against Moses's lead-

---

21. Scholium bT at *Iliad* 24.611.

ership in the Book of Numbers.[22] Whereas Niobe's mythic fate lingers on as a mark of humanity's guilt-ridden, compartmentalized relationship with the divine, the destruction of the Korahites is so absolute that it leaves no trace, no modifying mark on humanity's normative relationship with God. In Benjamin's ever-expanding analytic, the kind of "*pure* immediate violence"[23] in the Korah narrative is "divine violence," in contrast to the "mythic violence" inflicted on Niobe.

Benjamin's typology of the forms of violence is (one suspects) deliberately unwieldy: only this shifting assortment of terms can do justice to the volatile ambiguity of the violence that Benjamin is theorizing. Indeed, as Derrida notes,[24] the ambiguity manages to exceed Benjamin's control at various points, especially in his condensed interpretation of Niobe. Although Benjamin sees Niobe as "confronted" by the figure of Korah, one might detect a certain proximity in this confrontation: by petrifying Niobe's people, Zeus is acting in the mode of the Old Testament God who smites the Korahites— Zeus's act does not restore the law of human subordination but suspends the whole order of ritual reciprocity between humans and gods by preventing the funeral for Niobe's children.[25] In place of the status quo, Zeus temporarily institutes a mode of lithic co-proximity that joins Niobe and her *laoi* in a paracommunity, a community whose internal structure has been stripped down to the minimal, radical relation of being-beside (*para-*). As Johannes Haubold has observed, early Greek poetry is impressed by the near-homonymy between *laos* ("people") and *laas* ("stone"; cf. the sound-alike synonym *lithos*), which figures in various myths of autochthony.[26] In early Greek social thought, *laos* is community in its most radical, undifferentiated sense, as the collection of "all the people" regarded in its sheer existence, at a minimal distance (*-o-* vs. *-a-*) from the fundament of inorganic (non)being. Zeus's violence in *Iliad* 24 pushes Niobe's community over this threshold into its radical basis as a collectivity of discrete bodies without temporal orientation or internal differen-

---

22. Korah organizes a revolt against Moses, his own cousin, in Numbers 16, but God causes the earth to swallow Korah and his followers. "The legend of Niobe may be confronted, as an example of this violence, with God's judgment on the company of Korah. It strikes privileged Levites, strikes them without warning" (Benjamin [1921] 1986, 297). See Deuber-Mankowsky 2019 for a reading of Benjamin's use of the figures of Niobe and Korah in "Towards the Critique of Violence."

23. Benjamin [1921] 1986, 297.

24. Derrida 1992, 30.

25. There are references throughout early Greek poetry to this kind of annihilating divine violence, e.g., in *Iliad* 16.387–88 (Zeus sends a flood to destroy a city ruled by corrupt elites) and Hesiod, *Works and Days* 240 (Zeus destroys entire cities for the crimes of a single wicked denizen—cf. Niobe, as the scholium at *Iliad* 24.611 notes).

26. Haubold 2000, 42–43.

tiation. Such a para-community cannot be instrumentalized by the gods to serve as markers of divine law or to mourn the violence that underwrites that order; withdrawn into the inertness of sheer collectivity, they pass forever out of the cycle of law and violence and thus disappear from the narrative without further description.

The intervention of the Olympians on the tenth day restores the normative relation between gods and humans and thus sets the stage for Niobe's transformation into a stone marker that delimits the boundary between these ontological domains. But there are still immediate, or noninstrumental, valences in the image of Niobe's abode among the mountains. Achilles calls these mountains *oiopolos,* which translators tend to render as "lonely," but the root sense of this compound adjective can be construed as "sheep (*oios*) tending (*pelomai*),"[27] denoting a region frequented by flocks of sheep and by shepherds. With this gloss, Niobe is thus not exactly abandoned in the wilderness; she shares a semi-agricultural periphery with an assemblage of humans and domesticated animals. Achilles underscores this state of co-proximity by placing Niobe "among the rocks, among the mountains," as if Niobe, herself a stone-being, were emplaced in an eternal para-community with other lithic beings of various dimensions.

Indeed, Niobe is not even abandoned by the gods—her neighbors, "even now," are the nymphs "who dance swiftly along the Acheloios" (*Iliad* 24.616). Dancers can appear as utopian figures in Homeric epic: the inhabitants of Scheria, an island paradise, are expert dancers who perform a virtuosic routine for Odysseus during his stay;[28] joyous young men and women are depicted dancing on the figured surface of Achilles's Shield in *Iliad* 18, a scene juxtaposed with depictions of brutal warfare.[29] Conversely, warriors in the *Iliad* call each other "dancers" to impugn their martial prowess (3.392–94; 15.508). The nymphs' energetic motion (*errhôsanto,* 24.616) around the river might seem like a disheartening foil for Niobe's immobility, but the contrast supports a composition of speed and stillness, river and stone, in the manner of a landscape description. A relevant aesthetic paradigm might also include early Greek choral dancing, which could include a soloist performing in concert with a chorus of synchronized dancers: Niobe becomes the soloist, moving

---

27. *Lexicon des frühgriechischen Epos* s.v. οἰοπόλος (I) and (II). The first element *oios* may mean "alone" or "sheep," and both interpretations were used in antiquity.

28. *Odyssey* 8.370–80; cf. 8.246–68. The blessed, peaceable Phaeacians are obsessed with dance: see Olsen (2017).

29. *Iliad* 18.590–606; see Steiner (2021, 55–57).

at her own (impossibly slow) speed, surrounded by a troop of more nimble dancers.[30]

Removed from war and from the violent interchanges that bind together actually existing societies, Niobe is set into a constellation of beings—dancing gods, shepherds, sheep, and fellow stones—that cut across the boundaries between living and inorganic, human and nonhuman, divine and mortal. Her fate thus represents something more elusive than, as Benjamin sees it, the metamorphosis of an individual body into the mark of a violent order alienated from and menacing to Niobe's former society. The possibilities contained in her para-community are obscure, but as a picture of peace, coexistence, and ontological variegation, Niobe's environment has an anticipatory, even weakly utopian quality at the end of the *Iliad* and its narrative of intractable violence. In this concluding movement, the *Iliad* promises further conflict, but it entertains, in the image of Achilles's and Priam's fragile co-proximity, the foreclosed possibility of the indefinite interruption of martial violence. Niobe and her communities redouble this possibility. Even if such valences seem to escape Achilles's conscious intentions, a temporal modulation at the end of his parable seems to bring the figure of Niobe into disarmingly close proximity with the space that he shares with Priam: "and now, somewhere," Niobe is "digesting her sorrows from the gods" (*Iliad* 24.614–17). Telescoping the interval between the distant past and the epic present, Achilles makes himself and Priam into Niobe's contemporaries. For a brief moment, it seems that the two men's digestion—of sorrows and their present meal—might synchronize with the uncanny, impossible timescales of Niobe's petrification. Can a stone finish digesting?

---

30. Steiner (2021, 38) compares the juxtaposition between Niobe and the fast-moving nymphs to that between the limping god Hephaestus and his company of robotic maidens (at *Iliad* 18.410–23). Cf. the similar description of the fast-dancing mountain nymphs in the *Homeric Hymn to Aphrodite* (261).

PART 2

Around Ovid

CHAPTER 4

Philosophers' Stone
Enduring Niobe

VICTORIA RIMELL

"Suffering motherhood," writes Jacqueline Rose in her recent book *Mothers: An Essay on Love and Cruelty,* "is a staple of maternal imagos [*sic*]—Niobe lamenting the murder of her fourteen children, killed by jealous gods; and the Pietà, the Virgin Mary grieving the dead Christ, are two of the most well-known examples."[1] Almost casually, but with intention, Rose brings together Mary's and Niobe's suffering: yet, as Andrew Benjamin explores in his response to Hegel in *Towards a Relational Ontology,* they have long been paradigmatically opposed *exempla,* the Virgin Mary standing in Hegel for "that specific logic of love," in which "love is positioned by the necessity of its accession to universality in which reconciliation, completion, and self-sacrifice occur": a conception of love, in other words, "defined as the unity of self and other and therefore of *being-at-one-with* as determined by Sameness," and by definition removed from desire.[2] Niobe, on the other hand, "is that other who, in standing in stone on the outside, complicates assimilation insofar as she is positioned outside any structure of recognition."[3] As her story is told in its longest surviving narrative form, in book 6 of Ovid's *Metamorphoses,* Niobe seems to epitomize the limit of the human where metamorphosis is located, a "zone between two deaths," as Lacan calls it, its inhabitants both dying and

---

1. Rose 2018, 12.
2. Benjamin 2015, 128, 131.
3. Benjamin 2015, 116.

remaining.[4] Transformed into a rock that continues to weep, "the presence of what one might call petrified pain,"[5] to quote Lacan's remarks on Daphne as a tree in book 1 of *Metamorphoses*, she is unreachable. While self-sacrificing Mary has become love personified, Niobe—without her beloved children, her relationality excised—must remain without love. This is what Robert Graves encapsulated when he wrote in his mythography, "all men mourned for Amphion, declaring the extinction of his race, but none mourned Niobe."[6] For Benjamin, Niobe represents another possibility for motherhood that is suggestive of what Rose is reaching for in her book—that is to say, another possibility of thinking an ethics of relation in the context of refusing, or tolerating the refusal of, *being-at-one-with* her. Or in other words, a relation in which the one is not in some way always melted into or appropriated by the other so that difference is collapsed into sameness.

Loving Niobe "would entail a different conception of life."[7] As Benjamin notes, that this might be imaginable finds a spark of potential in the "disarming clarity"[8] of Sappho's fragment 142 Voigt ("Leto and Niobe were beloved friends"), which remembers her in a close friendship, that is to say in a relation in which difference is maintained, the imperfect "were" (*êsan*) perhaps heavy with irony, the unspeakable afterward of their aggressive confrontation and Niobe's punishment for hubris.[9] But this was a friendship before motherhood. Niobe the mother transgresses, even before her offensive boast—she is proud, angry, irreverent, self-important. And the history of the idea of her centers on a double movement of both sadistically punishing that transgression—as Lacan recognizes, the world of Ovid's *Metamorphoses* is Sadean in its cruelty—and of recoiling from, denying or avoiding it. Either way, Benjamin is right: Niobe is, or has been, impossible to love. In his review article of Benjamin's book, Dennis Schmidt asks for clarity on this provocative statement: "In what sense," he asks, "is Niobe 'impossible to love' and why does this point to the question that remains as more basic still, namely, how to give justice to Niobe?"[10] As Schmidt notes, Benjamin mentions in passing Pieter Clouwet's engraving of Niobe that appeared in a 1703 translation of Ovid, in which she is caught in a moment before grief sets in, raging over the dead bodies of her children, and seems to take this as an impulse to think Niobe back into life

---

4. Lacan 1992, ch. 21 ("Antigone between two deaths").
5. Lacan 1992, 60.
6. Graves 1955, 34.
7. Benjamin 2015, 117.
8. Benjamin 2015, 162.
9. On this fragment, see the introduction.
10. Schmidt 2017, 248.

and into relation. Schmidt registers a slight uncertainty here, something not quite elucidated. In response to Schmidt, and in dialogue with Benjamin, I want in this chapter to take up the challenge that both critics seem to elide even as they acknowledge it, the challenge to be alongside Niobe not, or not only, in her hubris, in her rage, and in the initial impact of her children's murder, but in her final state of perpetual suffering, turned into stone that continues to weep. My reading will move between Homer, Sophocles, Aeschylus, Aristophanes, Ovid, and contemporary artworks, and between philosophy, psychoanalysis, and trauma theory.

My point of departure, which gives rise to the challenge I have just reproposed, is Lacan's brief commentary on Niobe in *The Ethics of Psychoanalysis*. He is referring here to the passage in Sophocles' *Antigone* (823–33) in which Antigone compares herself to Niobe as she faces the prospect of being entombed alive:

> Antigone herself even refers to the image of Niobe, who is imprisoned in the narrow cavity of a rock and will be exposed forever to the assault (*injures*) of rain and weather. It is around this image of the limit (*l'image limite*) that the whole play turns.[11]

> In effect, Antigone herself has been declaring from the beginning: "I am dead and I desire death." When Antigone depicts herself as Niobe becoming petrified (*comme Niobé se pétrifiant*), what is she identifying herself with, if it isn't that inanimate condition in which Freud taught us to recognize the form in which the death instinct is manifested? An illustration of the death instinct is what we find here.[12]

The positioning of Niobe beyond the limit of the human at which Antigone totters, as representing what Lacan calls the "second death" that nullifies the cycle of death and life and allows for the continuous "play of pain,"[13] is a fantasy that doubles down on a failure to consider the place of relationality in life. We might start by observing that what Lacan does, in the *Ethics of Psychoanalysis,* is to refuse to relate to Niobe by staying instead with the "fascinating" stance of her Sadean torturers, whose power, as he puts it earlier in the essay, is "no more than the power to support a form of suffering."[14] As Judith Butler

---

11. Lacan 1992, 268.
12. Lacan 1992, 281.
13. Lacan 1992, 261.
14. Lacan 1992, 261.

puts it, this "second death" is seen to entail the "cessation of all transformations, natural or historical."[15]

We might object that, if we engage closely with Sophocles and Ovid, and if we are interested not just in Niobe as aesthetic object that permits a certain sadistic fantasy but in Niobe as a person, Lacan maintains a kind of oedipal blindness to Niobe. But he also reminds us that it is not only by virtue of being silent, frozen, and unreachable in her grief that Niobe disrupts the possibility of love as a being-at-one-with-the-other. What Benjamin does not quite say, and what Lacan approaches obliquely through the allure of sadism, is that she also disrupts it by staging its shadow, the *terror* of identification or of being-at-one-with that itself generates the fantasy of a pure Niobe beyond metamorphosis and beyond the reach of the human. In this way, the intolerable paradox of her living death is channeled through the positionality of the torturer and defanged of its potential to inflict secondary trauma. If we relate to Niobe, she will—like Medusa—turn us into stone; this is also what happens to Theban Narcissus, figuratively, when he "knows himself" in his reflection, and beats his breast with "marble fists" (Ovid, *Metamorphoses* 3.481–82), before disintegrating. Niobe is "impossible to love" not just because of her refusal of motherhood as self-sacrifice, but also because relating to another in endless pain is terrifying, and, within the Hegelian logic of love, annihilating.[16]

The philosophical and literary tradition can only look askance at Niobe, as a figure of comparison, as statue and archetype, as if with Perseus's shield. It has only been possible to explain why confronting her is impossible, not what exactly would be at risk or under threat if that were attempted. What happens, then, when we try to look straight at Niobe, or simply sit in her presence? Close-up, Niobe's humanity tends to disappear. As second-century geographer Pausanias writes (1.21.3): "I myself saw this Niobe, having climbed the mountain at Sipylus. Close up she is a rocky crag, offering no appearance of any woman at all, much less a weeping one. But if you go farther off you seem to see a woman weeping with lowered head."

The "general issue" here, to paraphrase Stephen Frosh on psychoanalysis's investment in virtues of endurance, is that of "relational ethics": what might it mean "to find ourselves enduring an ethical encounter with another"[17] when the other stands as the limit case of that endurance? I think also here of the humanistic, Rogerian tradition in psychotherapy, which runs the risk of idealizing the therapist's compassionate "stillness" in an encounter grounded in the

---

15. J. Butler 2000, 48; see also Lacan (1992, 248).
16. On Hegel and love, see Kottman's chapter.
17. Frosh 2015, 158.

"real relationship," at a safe remove from Freudian and Lacanian hauntings.[18] How to endure Niobe, when her impermeable, oozing rock converts the stillness of our receptivity into something intolerably harder?

From fifth-century drama onward, Frosh's question, which, by the way, does not refer to Niobe, is already a live one, and centers on Niobe. In the famous intellectual contest between the two great tragedians, Euripides and Aeschylus, in Aristophanes's *Frogs,* Euripides promises to expose Aeschylus as a charlatan who "deceived" his audience, which "was already trained to be idiots" (910). He would always start, Euripides sneers, by having some solitary character sit there on stage, wrapped up so as to not show their face, an Achilles or Niobe, not even making the slightest sound.[19] And while the character sat there in silence, his Chorus would rattle off rounds of lyric one after another without a break. In this scene, the figure of Niobe becomes a passive-aggressive avatar of the perverse tragedian. Her silence and stillness make cruel mockery of the audience: she does something *to* her spectators, who are forced to just sit there, uncomfortably, *waiting for* Niobe to say something (919–20): perhaps they are on the edge of their seats, excited by the suspense, then shuffling, bored, frustrated, then as still as statues, a captive audience, or in some other sequence. Aristophanes's sketch uses humor to expose—and displace—the notion that Niobe's trauma is contagious.[20] The mechanism of the mirror, which threatens to turn the audience into stone, is double-edged, daring or even forcing the living to move, while also tempting their continued, enforced immobility: for the living, there is an anticipation or expectation that Niobe will speak, as well as a longing for her to not ignore our presence. Aristophanic Euripides's joke, taken seriously, seems to launch Frosh's core question: "How do we mine an ethical relationship out of the sheer rock of being with another?"[21] It is striking, yet also unsurprising, that in an essay on the ethics of psychoanalysis engaged specifically with the metaphor of stone, and with the symbolism of Lacan's infamous "waiting room," which in a blackly comic, almost Aristophanic way reduced the therapeutic session to "the wait," Frosh does not mention or allude to Niobe. His limit case, instead, which again avoids the shadow of endurance with which Niobe rebukes, or is imagined to rebuke, her audience, is Marina Abramović's

---

18. See, e.g., Rogers (1961) and Geller and Greenberg (2012).
19. See Dover (1993, ad loc). He is referring to the lost plays by Aeschylus, his *Niobe,* and probably the *Myrmidons,* which we think begins with Achilles nursing his anger against Agamemnon.
20. Cf. Telò in this volume: "Niobe mimetically *subjects* the audience *to* unyielding indifference" (my emphasis).
21. Frosh 2015, 159.

2010 performance *The Artist Is Present*. Here, the self-professed "grandmother of performance art" sat motionless and silent on a stage for the duration of the exhibition while visitors took turns to sit with her as she looked straight into their eyes. The marmoreal folds of Abramović's white dress pay homage to classical sculpture, and specifically, we might say, to Niobe, who was represented in a number of ancient statues, the realism of which are seen in Greek epigram to play on the contradictory nature of Niobe as artistic artefact—both inanimate and vividly in pain, both inorganic, soulless matter and a mother in mourning.[22] In the performance, Frosh implies, Abramović is a figure for the psychoanalyst, albeit not the classical Freudian one, unseen by his patient on the couch.[23] It is difficult and unnerving to be with her: she is staring and inscrutable (though not "oppressively"), offering only her presence, or a screen for transference, with no demand for confession or even for the silence-as-a-form-of-speech that unfurls in the context of the analytic session. For some it was too much to bear, for others touching, freeing, or moving, in part because, in Frosh's words, "the ethic here is one of justice" (everyone, without discrimination, receives the same gaze) and "also . . . one of love" (everyone is worthy of this gaze, "ripe for singling out"). Yet Abramović's performance, and her life path, are almost the polar opposite of Niobe's: Abramović has declared publicly that she had three abortions, as "having children would have been a disaster for my work";[24] whereas statuesque Abramović's gaze at the audience is direct, Aeschylus's Niobe does not raise her head; in Sophocles's *Antigone* and in Ovid's *Metamorphoses*, she is not a still mountain but a pulsating rock continually melting and hardening at the same time, less a psychoanalyst than a traumatized patient in the waiting room, who never even gets to see Lacan.

When Niobe does not speak, the mother who abandons us becomes the aggressor, she who must be destroyed, or destroyed again, demolished by acid, Aristophanic critique that confirms our aliveness. The alternative, if it is possible at all, is, in a sense, to become Antigone. As the Hellenistic epigram by Theodoridas collected in book 16 of the *Palatine Anthology* imagines, strangers approaching what is implicitly a representation of Niobe on a tomb (of which several survive from antiquity) will weep as they "look on the infinite mourning of Niobe." In other words, they will weep in specular response to her weeping, a significantly different experience from that of Abramović's

---

22. See *Palatine Anthology* 16.129, 130, 132, 133, 134, discussed by Feldherr (2004–5, 139–41). On visual representations of Niobe see Taplin (2007, 74–79) and Sevieri (2010); on statues of Niobe in Rome, see Feldherr (2004–5), together with Zanker (1983; 1988, 85–88), and La Rocca (1985).

23. Frosh 2015, 159–63.

24. *The Guardian*, July 26, 2016.

interlocutors, who often shed tears but in response to a neutral, calm face, inspiring a Tumblr that went viral called *Marina Abramović made me cry*:[25]

> Stand near, stranger, and weep as you look on the infinite mourning of Niobe, the daughter of Tantalus, who held not her tongue under lock and key; whose brood of twelve children is laid low now on earth, these by the arrows of Phoebus, and those by the arrows of Artemis. Now, her form compounded of stone and flesh, she is become a rock, and high-built Sipylus groans. A guileful plague to mortals is the tongue whose unbridled madness gives birth often to calamity.[26]

Like Antigone, who in Sophocles's tragedy calls Niobe ("daughter of Tantalus") a *xena*, "stranger," and feels *the same as her* (833), the stranger approaching this tomb (summoned in the vocative, *xene*) will mirror what she sees: there is a compulsion to do so emanating from the epigram that mimics an epitaphic inscription carved into stone, as the two imperatives ("Stand," "Weep") convey. This is what happens when you "stand near" Niobe and feel her grief (823–33):

> I have heard that the Phrygian stranger, Tantalus's daughter, died the saddest death, near lofty Sipylus; her did the growth of the rock, like clinging ivy, subdue, and the rains, as men tell, do not leave her melting form, nor does the snow, but beneath her weeping lids she soaks the mountain ridges. Very like her am I, as the god sends me to sleep/takes me to bed.

When the Chorus attempts to turn Antigone's disturbing identification into a bland consolation (after all it is a "great thing for the departed to have the credit of a fate like that of those equal to gods, both in life and later in death," 836–38), Antigone, truly channeling Niobe now, snaps back, insulted. The Chorus's would-be consolation does not see her, sidesteps her agony, and converts Niobe's suspended trauma into a transcendent immortality, a move replicated by Lacan.

We see a very different response in Banksy's Niobe, spray-painted in 2015 on a lonely metal door left standing in a bombed house on the Gaza Strip (see fig. 4.1).[27] The image, and the performance that surrounds it, channels Sophoclean Antigone's sarcastic, visceral attunement to Niobe, which also

---

25. https://marinaabramovicmademecry.tumblr.com. Photographs of weeping visitors are published in Marco Anelli (2010) *Portraits in the Presence of Marina Abramovic*, Bologna.

26. This and all other translations in this essay are based on the most recent Loeb translations.

27. On this image, see also Telò (2023, ch. 7).

FIGURE 4.1. Banksy, Niobe mural, 2015. Photographed by Mohammed Saber / EPA / Shutterstock.

sets up the expectation that this will be received as incomprehensible. Like Euripides's caricature of Aeschylus's Niobe in Aristophanes, she has her head in her hands, her face in shadow, and crouches on what appears to be a dripping rock.

In this published photograph, a Palestinian woman stands still looking at Niobe as if in a mirror. We see the face of neither. The encounter pulls us in and excludes us, like the door that leads to no-home. The woman's blue headscarf cannot possibly align her with the Virgin Mary, although Mary is revered in Islam; or rather, the image seems to offer up a fissuring of that old antithesis. Perhaps Mary and Niobe, like Niobe and Leto, might be friends. In the two-minute video accompanying the work on his website, which begins with the artist emerging from illegal tunnels in Gaza, Banksy seems to awaken the voice of enraged, sarcastic Niobe in Ovid's *Metamorphoses,* who dares to speak to power by mocking those who worship gods in some desperate act of self-abasement in order to avoid the violence of tyrannical divine whim: "*Welcome to Gaza,*" say the subtitles "*well away from the tourist track. The locals like it so much they never leave (because they're not allowed to). Nestled in an exclusive setting, watched over by friendly neighbours, development opportunities are everywhere.*" Niobe is mirroring herself everywhere in Gaza, he seems to say, and I dare you to look, or to look away. In both movements, we discern what is at stake in Benjamin's question, "What is it to be just to Niobe?" *We might not survive it.* That is, to be more specific, we *might not survive the vicarious traumatization.* The aestheticization of Niobe-as-icon offers a way out, a looking away, that has already taken us to a place where only a travesty of "justice," not justice itself, is possible. Banksy also alludes, perhaps more consciously, to the Niobe statue on Harry Houdini's grave, where she seems to be figure for the disabling, in death, of Houdini's capacity to escape from confinement.[28] If only we are alive, we can shift our gaze, refuse to imagine ourselves in Gaza, save ourselves by leaving the political theater.

One kind of confinement, in other words, is the sense in which we cannot *not* engage with Niobe as icon: the logic of love, which we might also term the patriarchal Ego, must overcome her particularity and render it irrecoverable, even as her aloneness is endorsed. As Jacqueline Rose puts it, in a way that is both diagnostic and satirical, "Niobe is a repository for the burden of human misery on behalf of everyone."[29] As an "embodiment of tragic aesthetics," as Mario Telò puts it in his chapter, she suffers, repugnantly, so we do not have to. It is indicative, then, that in returning again to the intimacy of Niobe in friendship in Sappho fragment 142, Benjamin turns away from Niobe the traumatized subject. Commenting on Sappho, he writes: "Not simply is she able to be loved, but, allowing for a setting in which she could be loved—a space of allowing, a space allowing love—entails an enlivening of the world."[30] Yet the issue is not whether it has ever been possible to imagine being in relation to Niobe, but whether and how it might be possible to relate to her, to love her, *now, in her unmitigated grief.*

We can observe, in the philosophical tradition, various manifestations of the need to refuse to look directly at Niobe in her pain, and therefore to affirm her universality or reproducibility. Lacan, for instance (in the passage cited above), forgets that "Niobe becoming rock" always weeps. Ancient poetry, in its particularity and radical otherness, tells it differently: in Sophocles she is "subdued" by rock that itself grows, like ivy, around her form, which both melts and does not melt the snow that, as if showing us the way, "nowhere leaves her." The ivy, itself a symbol of "rampant virility," responds to her, exerts its power over her, where *damazô* and *damnêmi* are, as Mark Griffith notes, "often used of men 'taming'/'mastering' women in and out of wedlock." God, or The Father, or Fate, "sends her" (Antigone) to sleep, but also, continuing the "marital language," or, to put it more precisely, the language of rape, he "takes her to bed" (*kat-eunazei*).[31] In Ovid, *Metamorphoses* 6, this compressed double

---

28. https://en.wikipedia.org/wiki/File:Houdini_Gravesite.jpg.
29. Rose 2018, 12.
30. Benjamin 2015, 138.
31. Griffith 1999, ad loc.

process of stony confinement/continual liquefaction is drawn out, becoming almost sequential, or circular, in the awareness that the hexameters are moving—metrical feet still dancing out their rhythm, synaloepha melting *saxum*, "rock," into the verb "to be" (*saxum' st*) in line 309—as Niobe's human feet are locked in place (301-12):

>   orba resedit
> exanimes inter natos natasque virumque
> deriguitque malis; nullos movet aura capillos,
> in vultu color est sine sanguine, lumina maestis
> stant immota genis; nihil est in imagine vivum.   305
> ipsa quoque interius cum duro lingua palato
> congelat, et venae desistunt posse moveri;
> nec flecti cervix nec bracchia reddere motus
> nec pes ire potest; intra quoque viscera saxum est.
> flet tamen et validi circumdata turbine venti   310
> in patriam rapta est: ibi fixa cacumine montis
> liquitur, et lacrimas etiam nunc marmora manant.

Now does the childless mother sit down amid the lifeless bodies of her sons, her daughters, and her husband, in stony grief. Her hair stirs not in the breeze; her face is pale and bloodless, and her eyes are fixed and staring in her sad face. There is nothing alive in the picture. Her very tongue in silent, frozen to the roof of her mouth, and her veins can move no longer; her neck cannot bend nor her arms move nor her feet go. Within, her vitals are also stone. But still she weeps; and, caught up in a strong, whirling wind, she is rapt away to her own native land. There, set on a mountain peak, she melts; and even now the marble drips tears.

A chain of stopped movement, in which form strains against content (*nullos movet capillos . . . lumina . . . inmota . . . desistunt moveri . . . nec ire*) meets a "but" (*tamen*), because Niobe weeps, and is made liquid. The marble "even now . . . drips tears," evoking and resculpting the marble statue of Niobe that Pliny tells us stood in Rome, in the temple of Apollo Sosianus in the Campus Martius; the Niobids were also depicted, famously, on the doors of the temple of Apollo on the Palatine, and adorned the handles of tripods dedicated by Augustus.[32] The nod in Ovid's line toward Augustan appropria-

---

32. See Feldherr (2004-5) and Telò in this volume. On the statues and representations on the temple doors, see Pliny, *Natural History* 36.28, with Zanker (1983; 1988, 87); La Rocca (1988); and Galinksy (1996, 213-24).

tions of Niobe, alongside representations of the Gauls' defeat on the other side of the temple doors, performs in one move the petrification and cultural requisition of Niobe as the shameful shadow of sun-god Apollo. Cast in Augustan marble rather than rock, she is not even permitted her final resting place back in Phrygia, but remains symbolically in permanent exile in Rome. The line-ending *marmora manant* ("the marbles drip") sounds and looks so close to *marmora manent,* "the marbles remain"—so close, in other words, to what might have been a declaration of Augustan monumentality, beyond the pleasure principle.[33] But (*tamen*), that is of course not what Ovid writes. Like Myrrha, one of her many sisters, Niobe is suspended between life and death (*Metamorphoses* 10.487),[34] and the duplication of syllables in the line ending *marmora manant* makes us hear her moan, *ma . . . ma,* a barbarian mother in labor: *marmora* almost become *murmura,* to be echoed later in the book by Philomela's murmuring severed tongue (*immurmurat,* 6.558), and by Niobe's other twin, Myrrha, heard muttering as she prepares to hang herself, before she is led to a worse fate (*murmura verborum . . . / pervenisse ferunt,* 10.382–83).[35] The tortured subject can utter only inhuman, infantile groans. But another way of responding to Ovid's line might be to say that the cost of relating to Niobe is to become an infant calling for its mother (*ma . . . ma*). Whereas for Sophocles's Antigone, Niobe-becoming-rock is not alone, in the sense that she is imagined in real and symbolic relation to the rock that pins her down, and to the snow that never abandons her, in Ovid her tears seem to be accompanied by sounds that both echo her children's cries and repeat her mirroring role as their mother ushering them into language, sounds that are now in our mouths as we read the poem.[36] It is never quite the case, in Sophocles and Ovid at least, that, as Benjamin puts it, "Niobe is produced as the without-relation."[37]

One of the ways in which Ovid's epic performs an "enlivening of the world," or even, in sympathy with Benjamin, a refusal to efface the primacy of relationality, is in its weaving together of dramas of tragic mirroring and disintegration that themselves imperfectly mirror each other. This allows us, in engaging with the poem, to be in contact with something other than a tragic Lacanian opposition between integrity and annihilation—a template for rela-

---

33. On *marmora manant,* see Hamilton's chapter.
34. On the parallel between Niobe and Myrrha at *Metamorphoses* 6.310 and 10.500, see Rosati (2004, 296).
35. See S. Butler (2015, 62–63) and Enterline (2000, 1–5 passim) on Philomela.
36. Cf. Telò in this volume, who compares Aeschylus's audience in Aristophanes's *Frogs* to Niobe's children, and Baraitser 2009, in a chapter which begins with weeping Niobe: "We cry, like we love, not just because we think, but because we speak."
37. Benjamin 2015, 130.

tion in which we can experience holding both similarity and difference, as the stories move. In other words, the notion that, contrary to Lacan's fantasy, there can be *no* cessation of the life of transformation, even when metamorphosis is terminal, is a fundamental one in Ovidian poetics. Throughout his works, Ovid fetishizes Niobean multiplicity as the promiscuity of the poet-lover, and his texts *both* sew together similar stories into a *carmen perpetuum* (in the fecund cosmos of the *Metamorphoses*) *and* pursue an autoimmune or pharmacological logic in which every masochistic death has the potential to generate new life, within and beyond his epic.[38] In a pattern that has already been associated with desire itself in his erotic works, Ovid returns to the *Metamorphoses* as an unfinished body in the elegiac exile poetry, where he identifies with and exceeds Niobe.[39] In both poetic corpora, Niobe paradigmatically is and is not Narcissus, or his avatar Oedipus, is and is not Pentheus, is and is not Actaeon. For example, when Ovid writes [Niobe] *liquitur* (Niobe "melts," or "breaks down in tears," 6.312), the enjambement enacting what we might imagine is the relief of tension held in the transition from Thebes (the site of trauma and civil war) to her native land, she mirrors Narcissus as he "melts, wasted by love" for a reflection he knows is not another. The longings of desire and of loss seem to merge in their entwined stories. But Niobe does not melt away like Narcissus, whose incapacity to relate is already set in relief by a third party, Echo. Snow clings faithfully to Niobe's rocky face, and in place of annihilation, there is solid pain. As Michaela Janan puts it, referring to Tiresias's famous prophecy, "Narcissus cannot know and still be an integrated subject" (at *Metamorphoses* 3.348, asked whether Narcissus will live to see old age, Tiresias replies, *si se non noverit*, "If he does not know himself").[40] Critics espy the curse of Narcissus in the poet's prophecy for Niobe at *Metamorphoses* 6.155–56 *et felicissima matrum / dicta foret Niobe, si non sibi visa fuisset* ("And Niobe would have been called the most blessed of mothers, had she not seemed so to herself").[41] Her pride, in other words, will get her killed by the jealous gods, yet there is no question of Niobe not knowing herself, or knowing herself and disintegrating (as in Banksy's installation, she stands clear and solid amidst the rubble). Her problem is the opposite one: she knows all too well that worshipping the gods is to prostrate oneself, with an absence of courage, before cruel tyrants (*Metamorphoses* 6.170–71); like Echo, she views with

---

38. On Ovidian multiplicity as the life of desire, see Rimell (2006).
39. Ovid adds a prologue to his half-burnt *Metamorphoses* in *Tristia* 1.7.
40. Janan 2009, 41.
41. McAuley 2016, 157. Compare also tragic Narcissus at *Metamorphoses* 3.466 (*inopem me copia fecit*, "my abundance has made me poor") with Niobe before her children are killed at *Metamorphoses* 6.194 (*tutam me copia fecit*, "my abundance had made me safe").

sarcastic "scepticism the institutions and rules that constitute the Symbolic."[42] She lacks nothing in her dependency on her children, who do not define her. She experiences her abundance in life not as the threat of fragmentation but as a contentment and self-actualization won through proximity with death. Motherhood, as Rose reminds us, is a "strange compromise," which is "caught between narcissism and altruism, devotion and cynicism."[43] Unlike Narcissus, Niobe is not alone.

Likewise, and more significantly, perhaps, Niobe is and is not Medusa, Philomela, Myrrha, Arachne, female counterparts rarely if ever mentioned in the tapestry of Western philosophical thinking on her. When she has been repeatedly raped and had her tongue cut out by Tereus, Philomela resolves to "fill the woods with my story and move the very rocks to pity (*conscia saxa movebo*)" (*Metamorphoses* 6.547), an uncanny reversal of Niobe's fate—to undergo unspeakable trauma before becoming the rock that weeps. In his *Letters from the Black Sea* (1.2.29–36), Ovid sets Niobe and Medusa side by side, the former turned into stone, the latter with the power to turn those who look at her into stone. In exile, he is even worse off than Niobe, who he says "lost the ability to feel pain when she was turned into stone (30)"—a hyperbolic gesture, similar to Lacan's, that must transform Niobe's suspension between life and death into a more straightforward petrification in order to preserve a fantasy of going beyond. Such is the extent to which the poet's soft suffering resists hardness, even Medusa would not be able to turn him into stone—a bid for invincibility whose logic depends on turning away from Niobe. Yet what is not quite spoken in this sarcastic envy of Niobe is that she achieves what Ovid in exile is striving for—return to the *patria* (cf. *Metamorphoses* 6.311 *in patriam rapta est*). The exile "exceeds" Niobe also in the sense that, unlike her, he must be "forever deprived" of his native land, unless the "wrath of the injured god can be softened" (*Letters from the Black Sea* 1.5.83–84). Yet what this specular opposition affords is the possibility of Niobe "melting," or us melting in response to her, in another way: might she, in parallel with the exile's fantasy of redemption and return, be forgiven for her hubris? Might her metamorphosis into a rock in Phrygia already constitute an escape or release from the sadism of the gods?

Yet there is nothing permanent about Ovid's transcendence of Niobe's limit in *Letters from the Black Sea* 1.2. In the *Tristia,* Ovid compares himself with Niobe weeping over her dead children, through whom he justifies his need to groan with grief rather than stay silent (5.1.57–58): "although Latona's

---

42. Janan 2009, 49.
43. Rose 2018, 137.

children made Niobe childless, yet they did not order her to have dry cheeks (*non tamen et siccas iussit habere genas*)," a line that reverberates with the life of his wounded lover in the *Remedia amoris*, who is compared to a mother weeping over the body of her son: "who, if not a crazy person, would forbid a mother to cry at the funeral of her child" (*quis matrem, nisi mentis inops, in funere nati / flere vetet?* 127–28). Silent Niobe speaks, or wails, but what follows also reminds us that, in Ovid, petrified pain, like suppressed desire in the *Remedia*, will grow and threaten to explode (*Tristia* 5.1.63–64):

> strangulat inclusus dolor atque exaestuat intus
>   cogitur et vires multiplicare suas

> Suppressed sorrow chokes and seethes within,
>   forced to multiply its own strength.

Whereas tragedy and epigram focus on how pain plays on the struggling surface of Niobe's body, Ovid moves, as in *Metamorphoses* 6.303–9, from her wet cheeks to her inner world, or *viscera*. Notice the heat in *exaestuat* ("seethes"), an intensive verb meaning "to boil up or overheat": frozen Niobe is a volcanic life force. But, as Ovid seems to recall, the promise of new, violent life bubbles up in Niobe at the very inauguration of the literary representation of metamorphosis that her story signposts: when Achilles in *Iliad* 24 reassures Priam that Hector's body is lying on the bier ready for the funeral ritual, he urges the father to eat, as "even lovely-haired Niobe" remembered to eat on the tenth day after her children's murder, when they were finally buried. "Now, turned to stone, she stands among the crags in the lonely hills of Sipylus . . . there she broods on the desolation the gods dealt her" (602–17). In the final line (617), the verb translated as "broods" (*pessei*) means "to soften, ripen, or change by means of heat" (*LSJ* s.v.):[44] having eaten some food, petrified Niobe now "digests" or "cooks" her pain, and/or her anger, a figure offered to Priam as an acknowledgement of his rage, but also as a promise of rekindled warmth.

As Andrew Feldherr reminds us, it is important to recognize just how ambiguous Niobe's petrification is as a conclusion to her story. Is this her final punishment, the gods' ultimate sadistic act, or might we read it as the mythological literalization of what we would now recognize as a trauma response, her body's automatic, protective defense against intolerable pain? Cicero understands petrification as a metaphor when he writes in *Tusculan Disputations* 3.63, "Niobe is imagined in stone to represent, I suppose, her silence

---

44. See Macleod on *Iliad* 24, ad loc.

in grief."[45] Yet Feldherr only asks, "Does the punishment happen spontaneously, or is it even granted to her by the gods as a token of compassion?"[46] He cannot quite approach Niobe as a traumatized subject who may be actively responding to what is inflicted upon her, despite Myrrha modeling a similar agency in *Metamorphoses* 10: having been prevented by her nurse from taking Antigone's way out and hanging herself, after sleeping with her own father, Myrrha prays to the gods to be suspended between life and death, and as she is transforming into a tree, plunges her own face into the bark (10.483–97); she "lost the old feelings with her body" (*amisit veteres cum corpore sensus*, 499)—a line Ovid reworks to refer to Niobe in *Letters from the Black Sea* 1.2.30 (*posuit sensum saxea facta mali*, "when she was turned into stone, she cast off the ability to sense pain")—yet, again like Niobe, she still weeps (cf. *flet tamen*, 6.310, 10.500).

There is now a substantial body of work, informed by neuroscience, on the freeze response to trauma, and we can understand the body's numbness, in the scene or aftermath of trauma, as a biological defense whose function is to allow victims to survive. In his book *In an Unspoken Voice*, trauma psychotherapist Peter Levine, who has developed various forms of somatic therapy for treating people with chronic PTSD, draws in a Jungian mode on Greek mythology, and specifically the myth of Medusa, Niobe's symbolic sister, in arguing for the biological universality of human responses to terror and horror. Yet in a move that is by now familiar, Levine summons Medusa as fright paralysis or trauma itself, to be approached obliquely during therapy (and thereby decapitated, with the hero's tools) in order to avoid retraumatization, forgetting that Medusa is herself a rape victim whose metamorphosis permanently captures her panicked dread.[47] The raped girl, in the ancient projection, becomes "a cruel and punishing Gorgon."[48] In practice, however, much of Levine's and others' trauma work is focused on dismantling the cultural myths that equate immobility or nonreaction in traumatic assault with the complicity or guilt of the victim.[49] It is precisely this tension between myth and reality that is put into play in the moment of Niobe's petrification in Ovid, *Metamorphoses* 6.303: *deriguit malis*. Did Niobe stiffen "from the evils she committed"

---

45. On this passage, see Matlock in this volume.
46. Feldherr 2004–5, 136–37.
47. On the story of Medusa's rape by Neptune in Minerva's temple, and her subsequent punishment at the hands of the goddess, who transformed her from the "most outstanding beauty" (*clarissima forma*) into a snake-haired monster, see Ovid, *Metamorphoses* 4.790–803.
48. Levine 2010, 37.
49. See, e.g., Herman (1992), Lopez Levers (2012), Van der Kolk (2014), and Scaer (2014).

or "from the evils she suffered"?[50] In Ovid's *Tristia* and *Letters from the Black Sea,* in which the poet's intimations of "guilt" are also evidence of the lascivious license that defines and thereby exculpates him as an erotic elegist, Niobe comes to encode this ethical choice or oscillation between blame and empathy, punishment, and forgiveness. When we can see Niobe's trauma, or even open up the question of whether or not she is to blame, it becomes possible to sit with her, and to endure it.

---

50. Cf. Feldherr (2004–5, 137), who sees an alternative between commemorating Niobe's transgression and commemorating "her grief and her humanity."

CHAPTER 5

Niobe's Tragic Cryo-Ecology

MARIO TELÒ

In this chapter, I consider Niobe as a grieving survivor—in Aeschylus, Aristophanes, and Ovid—in relation to frozen spaces broadly conceived: the Aeschylean stage, the Eurasian steppe, and the glacial landscapes posited by speculative ecology. Connecting Jacques Lacan's and Jacques Rancière's commentaries on Niobe in *The Ethics of Psychoanalysis* (1992) and *The Flesh of Words* (2004), I aim to reconceptualize her role as an icon of tragedy, which Plato codifies in his condemnation of the genre.[1] I will look beyond her grief to her coldness, a psychological and ecological trait that can be viewed as a disruption of the aesthetic-political regime of representation. Frozen in grief in Aeschylus's eponymous play, as mediated by Aristophanes's *Frogs,* and in the Ovidian corpus, Niobe is, I argue, a figure of what Gilles Deleuze calls "the mother of the steppe." Rereading Niobe in terms of coldness will lead us to connect her embodiment of tragic aesthetics with what has been called negative ecology, or "ecology without nature."[2] Niobe's glacial motherhood associates the pleasures of tragedy with Deleuze's fetishistic masochism and with a kind of death drive tending toward the inhumanity of Nature and the ontological/temporal register of life before life. To read Niobe as a mother of the

---

A different, longer version of this chapter appeared in *Greek Tragedy in a Global Crisis: Reading through Pandemic Times* (Telò 2023, ch. 7).

1. *Republic* 380a6.
2. Morton 2007.

steppe, personifying, respectively, tragedy as an aesthetic agent and Augustus as the enforcer of a frozen peace, I will initially shift between Aristophanes's Aeschylean Niobe and her explicit and implicit Ovidian appearances in *Metamorphoses* and *Tristia*. I will then connect the Niobe-like Galician (that is, eastern-central European) landscape of *Tristia* with Quentin Meillassoux's notion of glacial ancestrality, whose psychoanalytic implications I will tease out by analyzing Lacan's discussion of Niobe and of the Freudian death drive. I will end by employing aesthetic-political considerations to tie together all these psycho-ecological threads, taking my lead from Rancière's reference to Niobe in his discussion of Deleuzian antimimesis.

Analyzed together, the portraits of Niobe in Aristophanes's *Frogs* and Ovid's *Metamorphoses* make us see her notorious silence as enacting the serial temporality of her punishment. In *Frogs*, the play that constructed the proto-Nietzschean binary of Aeschylus and Euripides, Niobe is tendentiously cast by the latter as a symbol of the deceptiveness and smugness of Aeschylus and his tragic mode. In Aeschylus's eponymous play, Niobe, stripped of her many children one after another by Apollo and Artemis in retaliation for her blasphemous boasting, initially appeared as seated, immobile, silent, hiding her face. As we can infer from one of many depictions in vase paintings, where the folds of her robes, more sculptural than painterly, commingle with the stone she sits on, Niobe may have seemed like a rock even before becoming one.[3] According to Aristophanes's Euripides, the aesthetic effect of this iconic posture was that the spectator "sat waiting and waiting" (*pros-dokôn kathêito*, 919) for Niobe to "utter something" (*ti pthenxetai*, 920), while the play "went on and on" (*diêiei*, 920). In Ovid's *Metamorphoses*, at the moment of Niobe's transformation, her petrification is marked by indications of a body and a tongue immobilized as cold rock (6.301–9):

>   orba resedit
> exanimes inter natos natasque virumque
> deriguitque malis. Nullos movet aura capillos,
> in vultu color est sine sanguine, lumina maestis
> stant immota genis; nihil est in imagine vivum.   305
> ipsa quoque interius cum duro lingua palato
> congelat, et venae desistunt posse moveri;
> nec flecti cervix nec bracchia reddere motus
> nec pes ire potest; intra quoque viscera saxum est.

---

3. See figure 15 in the collection of Taplin (2007). On Aeschylus's *Niobe* (fragments 154–62 Radt) and its visual representations, see Taplin (1972, 60–62; 2007, 74–79), Seaford (2005), Pennesi (2008), and Sevieri (2010). On Sophocles's *Niobe*, see Ozbek (2015).

The mother sat down childless among her lifeless sons and daughters, and her husband, and **became rigid (*deriguit*)** because of her pains. Air does not move her hair; on her face the complexion is bloodless; her eyes stand immobile on her sad cheeks. Nothing is alive in the picture. Her tongue, too, inside **becomes frozen (*congelat*)** together with her hard palate, and her veins can no longer be moved; her neck cannot be bent, nor can her arms respond with movements, nor can her foot go. Inside, too, her vitals are stone.

In these lines, two metrical and syntactical breaks, after *deriguitque malis* and the dactylic sequence of *congelat,* translate Niobe's frozenness into an affective intensity, into the feel of formal and bodily interruption. Before the polysyndetic syntax of lines 307–9, a conglomeration of foreclosed corporeal movements, the verb *con-gelat*—a combination of the prefix *con-* ("with") and *gelu* ("frost")—marks a congealing of poetic form. It is as though this word, which encapsulates the outcome of Niobe's travails, preemptively gathers together the individual effects of immobility that she undergoes and turns them into a conglomerate of frozenness. These effects reenact the multiple, tormenting losses, each chilling blow immobilizing Niobe, killing her without killing her, reducing her to a stony/frosty presence. Returning to the Aristophanic scene, we could say that the excruciating wait imposed by Niobe on spectators is a slow accumulation of moments reflecting the seriality of her losses, of parts petrified one after another.

In a moment of Ovid's *Tristia,* the frozen landscape of Tomis, the poet's place of exile, chillingly echoes with a self-citation from the Niobe episode. In *Tristia* 3.10, where Tomis is described as "disturbing and war-torn,"[4] the same rare verb *congelo* that we saw in the Niobe passage renders the freezing of the Danube (*Hister congelat,* 29–30) amid stiffening winds (29).[5] When a few lines earlier Ovid introduces the rigors of his prison on the Black Sea with a *praeteritio*—"Why should I speak of how rivers grow, bound by cold, and brittle waters are dug out of the lake?"[6]—he seems to dramatize the silencing power of the cold air blowing over the textual surface, felt through the *f* and *fr* sounds (*frigores rivi . . . fragiles effodiantur*). As Victoria Rimell has

---

4. As Rimell (2015, 285) puts it.
5. These are the only two passages in the Ovidian corpus where *con-gelo* occurs. On the *Tristia* as a rereading and revision of the *Metamorphoses,* see Hinds (1985) and Martelli (2013, ch. 5); on this elegiac collection as a "hauntological" play with origins and lost futures, see Martelli (2021, 73–75).
6. *Quid loquar, ut vincti concrescant frigore rivi, / deque lacu fragiles effodiantur aquae?* (3.10.25–26).

observed, "In the *Tristia* . . . we . . . find many references to blocked or pierced throats and stifled voices, images which evoke not just the political censorship of subversive books, but more broadly what the trauma of exile does to the poetic voice."[7] Silencing himself, rhetorically reimposing Augustus's violence, projecting the cruelty of his (semi)divine punisher—a castrating, unnamed yet ever-present emperor—onto the "cutting" atmospherics reflected in the very name Tomis, Ovid becomes Niobe, who is explicitly evoked twice in his exile elegies as a model of infinite lamentation.[8] But there is also a sense in which the frozen landscape is Niobe herself, deprived of the phallic potency of her reproductive power. Covering the ground with a permafrost, the perpetual winter of the Black Sea region blocks time (15–18). Ovid depicts hair rattling with hanging ice, *glacie . . . pendente* (21), a phrase in which the sound *gl-* could be said to express a "vocal contortion,"[9] the sense of a broken vocality mimetically transmitted by a wasteland that passes its own loss and desolation on to the human mouth and throat. Ovid observes that the outcome of this frozen time or perennial winter is frost accreted on the face, a mouth hemmed in by a gleaming, white beard (*nitet . . . candida barba,* 22). In this description, the beard, with its gleam of vitality, is a temporal hybrid—an index of old age as shiny and uncontaminated. It is a marker of an end of time (as well as of language), which coincides with the fresh, animated ancestrality of a before-time.[10]

Ovid's self-citation enables us to perceive a cold—not simply stony—Niobe and to characterize her relationship with the tragic audience as a circulation of chilly affect and, more precisely, as an aestheticized expression of the icy motherhood theorized by Deleuze in *Masochism: Coldness and Cruelty*. Niobe's birthplace is Phrygia, an arid region with hot summers and cold winters, that, in spite of its etymological connection with "roasting" (*phrugô*), phonetically exudes the chills of Latin *frigus* (Greek *rhigos*),[11] detectable both in the Ovidian narrative of Niobe (*deriguit*) and in the no man's land of Tomis (***frig**ores rivi . . . **frag**iles*). Cold Phrygia also overlaps with ***phrix**as* (822), used by the Aristophanic Chorus to depict Aeschylus's "bristling" style.[12] This toponomas-

---

7. Rimell 2015, 285.

8. See *Letters from the Black Sea* 1.2.29–30 and *Tristia* 5.1.57–58.

9. On this meaning of *gl-* see the introduction of Bennington and Wills to Derrida's *Clang* (Derrida 2021).

10. Stevens (2009, 164) argues that Ovid's journey to Tomis has a regressive dimension—it brings him back to *in-fancy* (etymologically, "not speaking"), "the prelinguistic state traditionally attributed to human prehistory."

11. I owe this observation to David Youd.

12. Lines 822–25: see esp. 822 *phrixas d'auto-komou lophias lasi-auchena chaitan* ("bristling the shaggy-necked shock of his hirsute ridge," translated by Henderson), which itself bristles with aspirated consonants.

tic coldness is enacted in Niobe's iciness on the Aeschylean stage, as recreated by Aristophanes. Having seen her many children killed one by one despite her desperate prayers to the gods, Niobe mimetically subjects the audience to unyielding indifference—not speaking, rejecting contact, becoming an incomprehensible Other, the "disaster" that refuses to be grasped, an aloof object. The audience is placed in the position of the mortal woman supplicating indifferent gods, but, as a multitude fixated on her mouth, it also resembles Niobe's children, once dependent on her care, her words, their serial deaths reflected in the seriality of dead moments that constitute the current waiting. We can say that, in her silence, Niobe at the beginning of Aeschylus's play exemplifies the severe, icy mother figure, corresponding, in Deleuzian terms, to a female partner dominant over a male sexual partner who acts as a child masochistically caught in fetishistic disavowal, in the illusion of the maternal phallus, in fantasies of non-Oedipal or pre-Oedipal sexuality or of asexuality.[13] Deleuze extrapolates this maternal model—what he calls the "mother of the steppe, who nurtures and brings death"—from the novels and short stories of Leopold von Sacher-Masoch. In Deleuze's own description of "the woman torturer"— the quasi-maternal agent who provokes the masochistic "supersensuality" of "waiting and suspense," "an indefinite awaiting of pleasure"[14]—phonetic chills shiver through an accumulation of *f*'s and *r*'s.[15] Like Niobe, the mother of the steppe theorized by Deleuze is both "oral" (that is, loquacious) and taciturn, falling into sudden, tomb-like silence.[16] Furthermore, the Masochian steppe that grounds the Deleuzian oral mother is in Galicia, now part of Ukraine, not very distant from Tomis. The cold air of Tomis/Galicia affects the Deleuzian page; the accreted *f* words circulate impressions of the grassy fur and whipping wind tendered by the steppe.

In Ovid's aesthetic-political world, Niobe may be read as figuring Augustus, the ever-present if often unnamed addressee, not just as a castrating father, Laius or the Lacanian law,[17] but as "the oral mother," that is, a "Venus in Fur," who is "icy-sentimental-cruel."[18] As Andrew Feldherr has observed, "Niobe is the daughter of Dione, the Homeric mother of Venus, making her Aeneas's

---

13. Deleuze 1991 (see esp. chs. 2, 4, and 6).
14. Deleuze 1991, 70, 71.
15. See, e.g., *femme, figées, photo, fouet, fourrures, fonction, faire, triompher, froid*.
16. Deleuze 1991, 55.
17. Rimell (2020, 558) suggests that "Ovidian exile is staged as an oedipal drama of separation from the *patria* and from parricidal poetry which results in the fictional loss of his mother-tongue."
18. Deleuze 1991, 51. *Venus in Fur* is the title of the novella by Sacher-Masoch on which Deleuze's *Coldness and Cruelty* offers itself as a commentary of sorts.

aunt."[19] In addition, Niobe's desire to supplant Latona, to become a goddess herself "connects her to the problems of self-definition faced by Rome's *princeps* at this stage in his career."[20] Referring to the ideological importance of what we might call reproductive futurism in Augustus's political propaganda, Feldherr points out that in his *Res Gestae*, Augustus's description of his own personal loss, *filios meos, quos iuvenes mi eripuit Fortuna*, is given in language similar to what Niobe will use to predict the impossibility of hers: *maior sum, quam cui possit Fortuna nocere, multaque ut eripiat, multo mihi plura relinquet* ("I am too great for Fortune to harm; though she should snatch away many things, she will leave me many more").[21] In her rereading of Ovid's *Amores*, Ellen Oliensis has seen elements of Deleuzian masochism in the orientation of the Nasonian lover toward his beloved, Corinna—the *domina* to whom, we could say, the elegiac lover is cathectically attached in lieu of this *princeps*.[22] As Oliensis puts it, "Naso . . . demand[s] that he be countermanded, forcefully expressing his will to be made subject to the will of the other"[23] and, more precisely, to become a baby in his lover's womb. A descendant, but also, in a sense, a double of Venus, Augustus acts as a Venus in Fur, identifying with the grandiose monumentality of Rome's imperial architecture in all its seductive stoniness, its reproductive coldness. While rendering the emperor's apparently masculine power as a fetish, this cold monumentality, a maternal phallus, drives the citizens, the *pater patriae*'s children, to submit, to "remai[n] suspended or neutralized in the idea"—the all-consuming belief in an anatomical impossibility—"the better to shield . . . against the painful awareness of reality."[24] The wasteland of Tomis's steppe is, paradoxically, similar to monumental Rome.[25] The beard, whose frozenness yields a castrating speechlessness, is as "shiny" (*nitet . . . candida*) as majestic white marble. Furthermore, while promising to reset the clock, to recreate a new, pure linearity and to reconstruct psychological or moral integrity or solidity, the palingenesis of Augustan propaganda, which is physically advertised in

---

19. Feldherr 2010, 300.
20. Feldherr 2010, 301.
21. Feldherr (2010, 301) referring to *Metamorphoses* 6.195–96. On reproductive futurism, see Edelman (2004).
22. On this dynamic in elegy, see, in general, Labate (1984).
23. Oliensis 2019, 118.
24. Oliensis 2019, 145.
25. Discussing the reference to Medea's dismemberment of her brother in *Tristia* 3.9 (the poem before the description of Tomis), Oliensis (1997, 189) observes that "Ovid is at pains to depict his place of exile as the negation and antithesis of his former home," but the evocation of the mutilation of Cicero's corpse through Medea's fratricide "reveal[s] Tomis to be the very image of Rome."

the enticing severity of its marmoreal constructions and in its fertile artistic reproduction, imbues the experience of time, individual and collective, with a sense of stuckness—like the landscape of Tomis. The phrase *candida . . . gelu,* applied to the frozen beard of Tomis's inhabitants (3.10.22), also refers to the earth, a mother frozen like a statue: *terraque marmoreo est candida facta gelu* ("the earth was made white by marmoreal frost," 3.10.10). In the insistent images of "waves immobilized by frost" (31–32), of "frozen waters" (38, 48), and of "a sea blocked" (37), as well as of ships congealed in marble (*stabunt in marmore puppes,* 47) and fish imprisoned in ice (49), we see the raging *tristitia* of the exile Ovid. He appeals to but, to an extent, also attacks the Emperor, allegorically depicting the temporal and psychological consequences of the so-called Pax Augusta:[26] a generalized sense of suspension, of arrested development, of attraction and assimilation to a Niobe-like Mother Nature that acts as a Venus in Fur or "marble body" or "Venus of ice."[27] The ships in the sentence *stabunt in marmore puppes*—almost a formal preview of *stabat mater*—resemble majestic objects, marmoreal receptacles, similar to Roman monuments celebrating imperial stasis. In an elegiac collection that claims to have come to life without a mother (*de me sine matre creata / carmina,* 3.14.13–14), the charged language of these female containers immobilized in marble-like ice points to a glacial motherhood that we can see, for example, in the monumental, gelidly receptive Ara Pacis.[28] The repetitive rhythm of Ovid's description in this poem exudes a fetishistic *jouissance* fueled by "the cruelty of the ideal"; the language bespeaks a temporality moving toward the "freezing point."[29] The cutting, evental force of the Augustan father seems to give way to the fetishistic duration, to the "timeless eternity"[30] induced by the cathexis to the maternal phallus, the "ideal" that we can read into the line *terraque marmoreo est candida facta gelu,* where *marmoreo . . . gelu* functions syntactically as a cold supplement to the body of the maternal earth, as a fetishistic appendage somewhere between materiality and immateriality.

---

26. On the raging *tristitia* of Ovid in *Tristia*, see Oliensis (2004, 316), who suggests that poetry of the exile constantly implicates Augustus even with Ovid at the center because, as she puts it, "within Ovid's poetry . . . the naming of the one conjures up the rivalrous shadow of the other." On the idea of the Pax Augusta, see Cornwell (2017).

27. Deleuze 1991, 53. Williams (1994, 14) sees the "eternally hard and frozen" landscape of Tomis as a version of the Iron Age, of "post-Saturnian" times. My reading deconstructs this representational model.

28. The Ara Pacis is a marmoreal receptacle conceived as a celebration of fertility and reproduction: on the monument's connection with the mother Ceres, see, e.g., Spaeth (1994).

29. Deleuze 1991, 52.

30. McNulty 2015, 114.

Niobe can also be considered an icon of nature as an inhuman force, as theorized in dark ecology. Using Deleuze's words, we could say that as a mother of the steppe Niobe embodies "the catastrophe of the glacial epoch" and reveals "the secret of Nature"—that is, that "Nature . . . herself is cold, maternal, and severe."[31] In *On the Principle of Cold*, discussing the "coldness" (*psuchrotês*) that people around him look for in the summer when they move to "the lower parts" (*tôn katô*) of their homes, Plutarch envisions this movement underground as a loving embrace of the earth—or, we might say, of nature as a cold crypt.[32] In his 2009 book *Cold World*, Dominic Fox theorizes the "dejection" stemming from the perception that nature "has a way of existing . . . completely indifferent to our aesthetic and moral values."[33] In this perspective, nature is the object of an "unrequited longing,"[34] as Timothy Morton calls it in his theorization of dark ecology as a form of melancholic ethics. "By setting up nature as an object 'over there'—a pristine wilderness beyond all trace of human contact," ecology "re-establishes the very separation it seeks to abolish,"[35] while dark ecology urges us to accept and, to an extent, embrace this separation. This view of "nature as an ideal world apart," as "an external, foreign, unknown . . . unknowable space" or a wild oppositional space has feminist and queer potential, as Stacy Alaimo has shown, inasmuch as it troubles the hierarchy of the subject-object/culture-nature binary.[36] Imagining nature as a radical alterity may induce us to think of time beyond the present and look at the present "as suspended between prehistorical catastrophe and anticipated extinction."[37] Providing an ecocritical (or eco-eschatological) interpretation of Derrida's *à venir*, Ted Toadvine has suggested that "our awareness of an ancient geological past that precedes us opens our imaginations to an indefinitely distant future after us."[38] This future corresponds to an exteriority not different from a stone, which, in an eco-deconstructive perspective, is always from another time, "like a meteor, a fossil, or a glacial erratic."[39] The nature theorized by Morton corresponds to a notion of the earth as a realm that "must be ambiguously read as beyond the *ends* of the human, as it is irre-

---

31. Deleuze 1991, 53, 54.
32. See Plutarch, *On the Principle of Cold* 954b *en ankalais gês agapêtôs* ("in the arms of the earth, lovingly").
33. Fox 2009, 37.
34. Morton 2007, 196. On this point, if from a different perspective, see Kottman's chapter.
35. Morton 2007, 125.
36. Alaimo 2000, 88; and Alaimo 2008, 252.
37. Toadvine 2018, 53.
38. Toadvine 2018, 54.
39. Toadvine 2018, 75. See also Nancy (1993, 92).

ducible to any anthropological subject, egological consciousness, or *Dasein*."[40] We could say that nature's or the earth's refusal of a "bridge, an isthmus"—a trigger of "the desire for world or the want of a world," in Derrida's words—turns it/her into an inhuman Deleuzian mother of the steppe, separated from the human child by "an infinite difference."[41]

The ancient geological past referred to by Toadvine can be linked with Quentin Meillassoux's notion of ancestrality. Meillassoux offers ancestrality as a response, in the mode of speculative realism, to the erasure of the nonhuman world that arises from the Kantian and post-Kantian theorization of the inaccessibility of the object in itself to the human subject. For Meillassoux, ancestrality is associated with an epoch of the world that precedes consciousness broadly conceived—an age of inanimate life before the emergence of organic life.[42] This ancestrality is impressed upon the *arche-fossil*—in Meillassoux's words, "a material indicating traces of 'ancestral' phenomena anterior even to the emergence of organic life."[43] The idea of ancestrality restores the full alienness of the stone by locating it in a world without subjects, that is to say, an external frame of being chronologically and ontologically anterior to and severed from consciousness. In a complementary, though reversed, perspective, the fossil is for Lynn Huffer "a strange time-twisting mirro[r] of 'the ends of man,'" that is, "a proleptic trac[e] of our own extinction"—the projection of a world without us, or even without organic life.[44] Similar to ancestrality, the "cold earth" posited by Herschel Farbman "is [a] kind of substrate of life"—an image of the world without us that will survive us after our extinction. As he puts it, "We may die of the heat we create in our environment, but the earth to which we return in dying will always be cold."[45]

The preorganic life of ancestrality is an *archê*, an imagined point of origin that constitutes the goal of the Freudian death drive, an inanimate destination symbolized, for Lacan, by the petrified Niobe. In *The Ethics of Psychoanalysis,* during his famous discussion of Antigone, Lacan explicitly connects

---

40. Lynes 2018, 117. See also Neyrat (2018, 9), who following Merleau Ponty's point that "Nature is the primordial—that is, the nonconstructed, the noninstituted" (2003, 13), conceives of "the earth-withdrawn, non-objective and irreducible to a body . . . the nocturnal side of nature."

41. Derrida 2011, 31.

42. Meillassoux (2006; 2014). Povinelli (2016, 8–9) uses the term *geopower* in relation to the "time before the life and death of individuals and species," "a time of the *geos*."

43. Meillassoux 2014, 13.

44. Huffer (2017, 81, 82), commenting on "Monsters and Fossils" in Foucault's *Order of Things*.

45. Farbman 2012. See also Toscano (2018) on Engels's identification of the demise of humanity with a nature no longer warmed by the sun.

Sophocles's (and Ovid's?) Niobe with Freud's theorization of the death drive, the regressive rushing perversely energizing each human organism from the beginning of consciousness:[46]

> In effect, Antigone herself has been declaring from the beginning: "I am dead, and I desire death." When Antigone depicts herself as a Niobe becoming petrified, what is she identifying with, if it isn't that inanimate condition in which Freud taught us to recognize the form in which the death instinct is manifested?[47]

In the lyric song from Sophocles's *Antigone* referenced here, Niobe is not simply petrified while continuing to shed tears. She also seems to be turned into something literally frozen, as suggested by the formal parallelism between *petraia blasta* ("stony growth") and *chiôn* ("snow"), two complementary yet distinct materialities that effect her nonhuman transition.[48] Looking at Aristophanes's Aeschylean Niobe as a mother of the steppe can help us consider how the grieving mother adds a Deleuzian as well as a genuinely Lacanian spin to Lacan's Freudian interpretation of her death-driven symbolism. It can also enable us to view Niobe—in her intricate Aeschylean, Aristophanic, and Ovidian entanglements—as a site of intersection between psychoanalysis, speculative realism, and aesthetics. In their long wait, Aristophanes's Aeschylean spectators experience the death drive in a Lacanian register: as *jouissance,* the pleasure in pain of an endless, futile circling around. The seemingly endless deferral is generated by Niobe's quasi-death, which is fashioned as nonlife projected toward life or, more precisely, toward the Symbolic—that is, toward the emergence of language (in her case, a reemergence), a moment in which she "says something." The audience—in effect, her children—are in a similar state: forbidden to move by the "law" of theatrical seeing, frozen in their seats (*ekathêto*) but also animated by a kind of fervor, ardent for movement and relationality, the markers of life that are captured by the *towardness* of the prefix *pros-* in the participle *pros-dokôn,* "waiting" (in the present tense and, therefore, incomplete).[49] We could also say that through this waiting, that

---

46. Freud 1920.
47. Lacan 1992, 346.
48. See lines 827 (*petraia blasta damasen*) and 830 (*chiôn t' oudamai leipei*), which present the same syntactical structure. On this passage, see Rokem in this volume. According to Harris (2013, 255), Lacan's Niobe is Ovid's Niobe, whom Lacan would connect with another Ovidian character, Narcissus.
49. This kind of cold fervor is a feeling comparable to Derridean archive fever, in its various manifestations, which in *Archive Feelings* (2020) I posit as distinctive of tragedy's death-driven aesthetics.

is, through the temporality of fetishistic idealization triggered by the maternal phallus, the spectators of Niobe trespass into a glacial present—the ontological condition that is a counterpart of the oral mother—something like the ancestrality posited by Meillassoux. Tracy McNulty identifies Meillassoux's "glacial world" with the Freudian "preorganic," the state of originary nonlife toward which the death drive pushes the organism (human or nonhuman) as soon as life begins. For McNulty, "fetishism *is* a speculative realism"—it creates a kind of speculative ontology through a psychological condition that brings glacial ancestrality into postancestral life, spectrally importing the preorganic state pursued by the Freudian death drive.[50] In postancestral life, this haunting ancestrality approximates nature in its radical alterity, nature as the pre- or extrahuman externality of a nonhuman world whose ontological distance correlates, psychologically, with the unfillable gap opened by the maternal phallus, the anatomical fantasy generative of the fetish. The material hardness (stony, marmoreal) of the fetishistic object models the fetishist's masochistic hardening into illusion and into ancestrality itself—a further hardening of nature, of the impenetrable (in)difference that exceeds the human subject. Niobe's cold motherhood—enacted on the Aeschylean/Aristophanic stage and in the Masochian landscape of Tomis—brings together, in hardness, nature, the fetishist, and the fetishistic object. Still ostensibly alive, perpetually shedding tears—whose liquid, vital movement is immobilized by their very repetition—Niobe in her postmetamorphic embodiment as a rock in a frozen landscape encapsulates ancestrality's paradox of a nonliving life, a life before life.

Along with the registers of psychology and speculative realism, Niobic glaciality has aesthetic-political resonances, including a necropolitical dimension. On the Aeschylean stage, Niobe is subjected to a treatment on the threshold between taxidermy and necropolitics. Taxidermy is a practice that works through death while apparently keeping the nonhuman other alive; what Achille Mbembe has called "necropolitics," on the other hand, is the exercise of state power to maim, to inflict a mutilated life, killing the other by denying them death, subjecting them to what Rob Nixon has called "glacial" violence.[51]

Yet in the glacial Niobe of the beginning of Aeschylus's play we can also see, à la Rancière, a different aesthetic-political dynamic, by which the artificial life of the eventful Aristotelian plot comes up against the more lifelike condition of boredom—a kind of nonlife. For Rancière, it is when literature pursues the nonsense of life, "the empiricism of life as it unfolds," becoming

---

50. See McNulty (2015, 117): "The 'glacial epoch' . . . that masochistic suspension seeks to isolate appears as a depiction or construction of the phallic mother."

51. Mbembe (2019) and Nixon (2011).

"mute," that it fosters political change, altering what he calls the distribution of the sensible, the perceptive parameters that regulate hierarchy.[52] In *The Flesh of Words*, regarding Deleuze's aesthetics—the (lawless) law of "[the] molecular world, un-determined, un-divindualized, before representation"[53]—Rancière refers to Hölderlin's rendition of the passage from Sophocles's *Antigone* where Niobe is mentioned ("I know that she has become like a desert"):[54]

> The translator's treason effected by Hölderlin is exemplary of the passage from one signifying system to another. In fact the Niobe of Sophocles and mythology survived the metamorphosis permitted to the laws of the world of representation. According to a simple mimetic principle, the grief-stricken mother became a rock wet with tears of despair. On the other hand, the Niobe of Hölderlin, the Niobe of the era of literature, leaves the signifying system of *mimêsis*. She becomes a desert, a rocky expanse where figure and meaning are abolished, where *pathos* is equal to the apathy of inert matter.

Even though Hölderlin participates in the diachronic play of representation, committing "treason" against the Sophoclean text by changing Niobe from a rock into a desert, this imagistic metamorphosis, a representational alteration, radicalizes the antimimetic, that is, nonsignifying force of Niobe, her identification with a core of resistant materiality that defies representation's effort to capture her through meanings. Rancière invites us, in a sense, to regard Niobe as a figure of representational opacity—as nature, which cannot be subjected to the constraints of representation, in all its variations; which cannot be reduced to any figurative schema; which denaturalizes, deforms *mimêsis*. He sees Niobe as the mythological figure who brings together the Deleuzian emphasis on the "logic of sensation" as part of the deterritorialization of the subject—the subject's becoming imperceptible, or turning into an intensity— and his own concern with the aesthetic-political disruption or even extinction of representation, a consensual police, through radical moments of perceptive dissensus.[55]

Such dissensus can be perceived in one of the surviving lines of Aeschylus's *Niobe*, which drags down the poetic scales of *Frogs*—the instrument ostensi-

---

52. Rancière 2010, 164; Rancière's discussion of Aristotle's theorization of plot appears in the ironically titled *La parole muette*, or *Mute Speech* (2011).
53. Rancière 2004b, 150.
54. Rancière 2004b, 150.
55. Rancière (2004b, 149) refers to Deleuze and Guattari (1987, 6), who speak of "reduc[ing] oneself to an abstract line, a stroke, . . . find[ing] one's zone of indiscernibility." When Rancière (2004a, 6) remarks that "the task of art is to undo the world of figuration or of doxa, to *depopulate* that *world*" (my italics), he evokes a kind of ecological catastrophe.

bly measuring his and Euripides's value. The "weight" of verbal texture, of crafted *poiêsis* is felt in the seamless succession of assonant nouns and adjectives describing *thanatos* ("death"): *monos theôn gar Thanatos ou dôrôn erai* ("Alone among the gods, Death does not love gifts"). Like Niobe's death-like silence, the impassive, rigid, heavy, cold blocks delay the emergence of verbal action till the end (*erai,* "it/he loves").[56] The formal structure of this line makes us see Niobe as an artwork's "grimace of the 'desire to speak,'" in the phrase of Boris Groys, who claims that "it is . . . [the] desire to speak on the part of the picture . . . that is systematically suppressed in the modern age."[57] The verbal spark kindled by the bisyllabic *erai*—akin to Niobe's flickering into language, into speaking life before her final petrification—interrupts the formal solipsism of nominalization, but only partially, since desire as such is an expression of *lifedeath,* encompassing mobility and immobility, hotness and coldness; it is a "crystal image," troping Niobe's frozen suspension between silence and speech.[58] Even as the excruciating duration staged by Aeschylus numbs the eye and the other sense organs like the Euxine or Galician winter, it connects us with an alluring glacial ancestrality, nature's inhumanity, beyond the human yet embedded in the human experience as, in Freudian and Lacanian terms, death is within life, perpetually haunting it.

Whether we locate her on the tragic or comic stage, in the world of Ovidian elegy or epic, on the Masochian or Tomian steppe, the glacial Niobe codes an aesthetic freezing without any cathartic thawing. Before speaking, as in her petrified afterlife, she, like nature, hoards life, grieving the ungrievable lives of her children. As Niobe strives to remove herself from time, she immobilizes representational and thanato-political imperatives while mobilizing an icy virtuality before and after consciousness.

---

56. Aeschylus, fragment 161.1 Radt.
57. Groys 2012, 225.
58. On *lifedeath,* see Derrida (2020). Commenting on Lacan's pairing of Antigone and Niobe in relation to the death drive in *The Ethics of Psychoanalysis* (see above), A. Benjamin (2016, 144) observes that "dying and living on, living and dying define [Antigone's] stand."

CHAPTER 6

Tears from Stone

JOHN T. HAMILTON

Contestation presumes parity. In a self-evident but crucial way, every incitement to compete asserts some basis of equivalence with one's chosen opponent. Even though a contest is designed to determine superiority, instigating a confrontation is premised on the provoker's belief that he or she is evenly balanced with the party provoked. Accordingly, the series of matches between mortals and immortals in books 5 and 6 of Ovid's *Metamorphoses* entails troubling ramifications; for it implies that humans, including mortal-born heroes, can stand on equal footing with the gods. The singing tournament between the Pierides and the Muses (5.250–678), the weaving contest between Arachne and Minerva (6.1–145), and the vicious battle between Niobe and Latona (6.146–312) depend on a purported commensurability with the divine. All three mortal contenders exhibit prideful arrogance and, as a consequence, endure a miraculous transformation: the Pierides are changed into magpies, Arachne into a spider, and Niobe into a stone figure. In each case, the metamorphosis would appear to be what one would expect: a punishment that aims to reinforce what is proper and just. Yet the import and complexities of this sequence of contests, nearly midway through the poem, should not be passed over too rashly. Hardly an isolated set of cautionary tales against hybris, these mythic accounts seem in fact to relate to the overall plot of a work that concludes with the divinization of Julius Caesar (15.745–870). That is to say, human rivalry against the immortals, with its implication of equality, appears to play a key role in understanding the significance of the question that motivates the entire poem—namely, how the mortal Caesar became a god.

Of particular relevance is the tale of Niobe, who challenges Latona because she fails to see any essential difference between the goddess and herself. As usual, a relation of sameness, however delusional, encourages the queen to challenge the divinity head-on and attempt to prove her superiority. Certainly, the contest does not go well for her. Yet what is striking is her ultimate fate: she is not simply transformed into a marble statue but specifically into one that weeps (6.312): "and tears even now trickle from the marble" (*et lacrimas etiamnum marmora manant*). At least in terms of the *mythos,* the statue is not a sculpture but rather what Niobe has become. The matter complicates the *logos* that generates the mythic expression. On the one hand, the figure is not an artistic representation of her, like the numerous Niobe statues viewable across Augustan Rome, but rather the bereaved woman herself, transformed into stone. On the other hand, however, both as a living, breathing queen and as a petrified image set on a mountain peak, she is nothing but an artistic representation, incorporated into Ovid's epic. The ambiguity of being at once both a work of art and not coalesces in the image of a statue that "weeps nonetheless" (*flet tamen,* 6.310): a piece of inanimate marble, yet somehow still sentient, still mourning, still in tears.[1] Thus, in addition to being a story of mortals competing with gods and its implicit claim to equivalence, the myth seems to address the very status of artistic representation, including poetry, and its relation to life. In both regards, the Niobe episode should be read as programmatic, as articulating the broader concerns of the *Metamorphoses* as a whole.

Although in the opening lines, the poet claims to offer a "continuous song" (*perpetuum carmen*) "from the origin of the world" (*ab origine mundi*) "to the present times" (*ad mea tempora*), the epic does not always respect chronological order and generally foregoes historical orientation. Rather, the narrative flows from one episode to the next often on the basis of connecting themes, transitional motifs, or an overarching frame story. Accordingly, the sequence that culminates with the Niobe episode in book 6 commences at the head of book 5. That is, before the queen of Thebes challenges a goddess and undergoes petrification, the mortal Phineus arrogantly and unjustly rivals the demigod Perseus, who punishes his assailant by brandishing the Gorgon's head and turning him into stone.

---

1. The relationship between the mythic account of Niobe and her sculptural representation in Rome provides the basis for the reading of Feldherr (2004–5).

Just before the fatal transformation (5.227), Perseus assured Phineus that he would become "a monument that will last through the ages" (*mansura . . . monimenta per aevum*). The future participle *mansura*, from the verb *manere* ("to remain, to stay"), not only resonates immediately with the noun it modifies—*monimenta*, from the verb *monere* ("to remind, to warn")—but also anticipates the verb *manare* ("to trickle"), which will conclude the description of Niobe as a statue, where "tears even now trickle (*manant*) from the marble." The petrified image of Phineus thus foreshadows and informs the figure of Niobe in stone—a morphological continuity discernible through slight modulation: *monere—manere—manare*, "warning," "lasting," "trickling."

The poet's initial promise, announced in the work's first line, to tell of "forms changed" (*mutatas . . . formas*), applies both to the events described and the mode of description (1.1–4):

In nova fert animus mutatas dicere formas
corpora; di, coeptis (nam vos mutastis et illa)
adspirate meis primaque ab origine mundi
ad mea perpetuum deducite tempora carmen!

Into the new—my mind moves to tell of forms changed into new
bodies; O gods, on my undertakings (for you have changed even them)
breathe and from the first origin of the world
draw out a continuous song to my present times!

Ovid's playful manipulation of the epic tradition begins with the very first word. One would expect an accusative object in the initial position: a substantive that would represent the theme of the poem at hand, e.g., the "wrath" (*mênin*) of the *Iliad*, the "man" (*andra*) of the *Odyssey*, or the dual "arms and the man" (*arma virumque*) of the *Aeneid*, the epic that Ovid is primarily emulating and challenging. Instead, the *Metamorphoses* opens with a prepositional phrase denoting movement: *in* plus an accusative object (*nova*): "into the new." Motion and change come forward as the poem's theme, not declaratively, but rather performatively through a grammatical act that is carried over to the second line, where an accusative object is given in initial position: *corpora* ("bodies"). The appearance of these *corpora*, moreover, has the effect of a revision.[2] The first reading of *in nova* as "into the new" (taking *nova* as a substantive form of the adjective: "into the new things") is recast and redirected

---

2. A rich variety of revising effects in Ovid's oeuvre are fully analyzed by Martelli (2013).

in the second line: (*in nova*) *corpora,* "into new bodies." The poem is changing shape before our eyes.[3]

Likewise, the other accusative phrase, *mutatas . . . formas* ("changed . . . forms"), which does serve as the poem's titular theme, however postponed, is not only a translation of the conventional Greek title, *Metamorphoses,* but also a nearly exact replication: both the Greek term and its Latin translation contain five syllables; both feature an initial *m* and a final *s,* as well an internal *t, a, f,* and *r.* The reader is thus witness to transformation transformed. These grammatical and morphological shifts on the level of description further underscore the myriad physical alterations that will be described in the present work—poetic and narrated mutations, finally, that are related and performed by the poet and the gods alike: "for you [gods] have changed even them [my initial undertakings]."

The narrative sequence that moves from Phineus to Niobe is similarly driven as a verbal performance: from a monumental warning (*monere*) and persistent remaining (*manere*) to the tragic trickling of tears (*manare*). As such, both the stories and their presentation illustrate Ovid's poetic project, which consistently negotiates between formal permanence and change. Like Phineus, Niobe may become *monimenta* that "will last" (*mansura*) "through the ages" (*per aevum*), yet one that "nevertheless" (*tamen*) continues to express herself in tears, in time.

The cautionary tale of Phineus, which ends with Perseus wielding the Gorgon's head to change his assailant into monumental stone, seamlessly leads or shifts into the subsequent episode. As the son of the mortal Danaë and Jupiter, Perseus has always relied on guidance from his divine sister, Minerva, who now enters the scene. The goddess travels to Mount Helicon to visit the Muses and see for herself the fresh spring, which broke out when Pegasus struck the ground with his hoof. Again, thematic and verbal connections motivate the change of scene: Pegasus is the winged horse born from the neck of Medusa when Perseus beheaded her, while the animal's Greek name, *Pêgasos,* clearly relates to the "spring" (*pêgê*) that bursts forth on Mount Helicon. As Urania, the chief Muse, shows Minerva the rushing stream, nine magpies are heard, lamenting their fate with human voices (5.296–99). Minerva learns that the birds were once the daughters of Pierus, also nine in number, who, swollen with pride, dared to challenge the Muses to a "singing battle" (5.305).

The daughters of Pierus, the Pierides, thus intensify the theme of rivalry broached in the Phineus episode. Now, instead of a mere mortal instigating a mortal demigod (Perseus), we have human girls provoking the immortal

---

3. See Heath (2011–12), who characterizes this effect as a "poetics of simultaneity."

Muses. The arrogance colors the song selected. The eldest of the Pierides performs the myth of Typhoeus, the monster who terrified the Olympians and drove them into Egypt where they hid "in lying shapes" (*mentitis . . . figuris*, 5.326): Jupiter as a ram, Apollo as a crow, Bacchus as a goat, Diana as a cat, and so on (5.327–31). That is to say, they present the Pantheon in an Egyptian manner, portraying the gods in the shape of animals. In response, Calliope, the Muse of epic poetry, overturns this theriomorphism with a song that depicts the Olympians in human bodies. The strategy succeeds: the Pierides lose the contest and are turned into magpies, a transformation that is again characterized as "lasting," now with the verb *remanere*—"and even now in feathers their old eloquence remained (*remansit*)" (5.677). The consequences of the Muse's song are ambivalent. When the gods are said to have human shape, mortals have more reason to emulate them as models; yet, sameness also implies parity and therefore might encourage mortals to compete with deities. Anthropomorphism invites humans to aspire to be gods, yet in such aspiration, they fail to understand the nature of divinity.

Hence, at the beginning of book 6, the story about the Pierides reminds Minerva of Arachne, a girl who once challenged her to a weaving contest. Whereas the Pierides belonged to a royal family but had inferior skills in art, Arachne is of low birth yet possesses artistic talents that are undeniable. The neighboring nymphs marvel at her tapestries. At first, Minerva, disguised as a frail old woman, tries to persuade Arachne to be pious: "Yield place to the goddess and with your voice beg pardon, reckless girl: she will grant pardon to her who asks" (6.32–33); but Arachne has too high an opinion of herself. Even after Minerva discards her camouflage, the girl persists in provoking the goddess to contend at the loom.

Minerva sets to weaving her famous victory over Neptune on the Acropolis for control of Athens. The lesson is obvious: having once conquered another god, she would certainly vanquish a mortal. To underscore her point further, she produces four scenes in the corners of the fabric depicting mortals who rivaled the gods and suffered punitive transformations (6.87–100). Despite the clear lesson, Arachne is not deterred but rather portrays Jupiter as the white bull that once seduced the maiden Europa. Here, the theriomorphism implies that the gods are deceptive. Unlike the song of the Pierides, however, Arachne's tapestry is superb—"you would think it was a real bull, real waves" (6.104). The deictic gesture, which pulls the reader into the scene as a witness, corresponds to Arachne's art, which overcomes the separation of art and reality. Just as the extratextual audience is dragged into the text, so have the Jovian bull and the tumultuous waves been woven into the textile. They are "real" (*vera*), or so "you would think" (*putares*). The possible metamorphosis of life into art accords with the ambitions of the Pierides and Arachne, namely, that "real" human beings might become gods, who subsist in poetry, statuary, and painting. The narrative path that leads toward the Niobe episode is well paved.

After Arachne has finished at the loom—with further images of Jupiter and Neptune acting deceptively in animal disguise—her weaving is deemed flawless: "neither Pallas nor Livor could revile that work" (6.129–30). In anger, Minerva strikes Arachne with her wooden shuttle, and in despair the maiden hangs herself. The extreme act rouses pity in the goddess, who transforms her into a spider. Again, the metamorphosis permits survival: "live on, indeed, yet nonetheless hang, wicked girl" (*vive quidem, pende tamen, inproba,* 6.136). The contrastive adverb (*tamen*) will perform the same function at the conclusion of Niobe's story: as in the case of Arachne, transformation promises Niobe monumental longevity, a kind of deathlessness through death, "yet nonetheless" she remains alive, "weeping" (*flet tamen,* 6.310).

Though Arachne's contest of skill ended with a dead heat, power alone reasserts the hegemony of the divine—a might-is-right outcome that strikes human society as unjust. The story spreads eastward to Lydia and Phrygia, where Niobe learns the terrifying fate of Arachne, whom she once knew personally. This cautionary tale, however, has no effect. Instead, when Niobe marries Amphion, the king of Thebes, royal power and her prodigious fecundity—having borne fourteen healthy children—swell her pride to untold limits, which leads to an ominous prediction (6.155–56): "And Niobe would have been called the happiest of mothers, if she had not seemed so to herself" (*et felicissima matrum / dicta foret Niobe, si non sibi visa fuisset*). What might have been *said* of her (*dicta*) is undermined by how she seemed (*visa*) to herself.

Regardless, bearing in mind the episodes that preceded this moment, Niobe is well positioned to contest divine supremacy: in their battle against the Pierides, the Muses reasserted the gods' physical resemblance to humans; and in her duel against Minerva, Arachne proved that human skill could match that of a deity. Both cases might spur a mortal queen, especially one who saw herself as most fortunate, to rival a goddess or attract divine envy. Indeed, before Niobe commits blasphemy, it is the goddess Latona who intrudes on the scene as if to instigate the arrogant lady, just as Minerva made the first move in deciding to visit Arachne. Unlike Minerva, however, Latona makes her presence known through her prophetess, Manto, the daughter of Tiresias, who in the name of the goddess commands the Theban women to worship at Latona's temple: "Latona commands through my mouth" (6.162). Tellingly, the will of the goddess is knowable only through a human vehicle.

It is during the cultic procession that Niobe arrives, emphatically in motion until she comes to a halt (6.165–69):

> ecce venit comitum Niobe celeberrima turba 165
> vestibus intexto Phrygiis spectabilis auro
> et, quantum ira sinit, formosa; movensque decoro
> cum capite inmissos umerum per utrumque capillos
> constitit, utque oculos circumtulit alta superbos.
>
> Behold, Niobe comes thronged by a crowd of companions,
> a notable figure in Phrygian robes with woven gold
> and, as much as anger permits, beautiful; and moving with her seemly
> head her hair, which hangs down on each shoulder,
> she stands firm, and loftily casts about her haughty eyes.

Amid the faceless participants, Niobe is singled out by her wealth, beauty, and foreignness, wearing her native Phrygian robes in Thebes, "with woven gold" (*intexto ... auro*, 166). The woven gold lightly evokes Manto's injunction to the people to "wreathe their hair with laurel" (*lauro*, 6.161)—a feature that contrasts with Niobe's "loosened hair" (*inmissos ... capillos*, 168), which she tosses about (*movens*, 168). This movement is precisely what will be abolished in the final metamorphosis, when the first sign of her petrification occurs in nearly the same terms: *nullos movet aura capillos*, "the breeze stirs no hair" (6.303). Once again, the poem's transformative energy affects the language as well, here with yet another echo of the "gold" (*auro*) in the "breeze" (*aura*) that fails to stir the hair that once moved so freely.

For now, however, it is Niobe who puts a stop to her movement. She stands firm (*constitit*, 169), observing the procession, holding herself tall (*alta*, 169). The verticality of her attitude is underscored by her eyes, which are described as "proud" or "haughty" (*superbos*, 169) and convey her sense that everyone else is beneath her. In anger, she cries out (6.170–71): "What is this madness, to prefer celestial beings who are heard about (*auditos*) over those who are seen (*visis*)?" The complaint acts as a gambit, engaging Latona as an opponent, which reveals that Niobe numbers herself among the celestial deities. The exclamation further expresses Niobe's conviction that she has an edge, now by enlisting the legalistic power of evidence over mere hearsay. She is a goddess who is visible, standing presently before everyone's eyes, while Latona is absent, invisible, a figure merely "heard about" and therefore open to doubt. At least on the level of the *mythos*, Niobe is not incorrect. Although the gods may produce visible effects in the world, their physical presence is solely accessible in art, poetry, and sculpture; and as everyone knows from Hesiod, the Muses who inspire artistic representation are not without the capacity to lie (*Theogony* 27–28): "We know how to speak many false things that resemble the truth / And we know, when we wish, how to proclaim true things." Still, the validity of Niobe's statement, which exalts herself in terms of visibility (*visis*) over the goddess about whom one only hears (*auditos*), recalls the fateful portent pronounced at the start of the episode, that Niobe would have been reported (*dicta*) as the most fortunate of mothers, had she not seemed (*visa*) to herself as such. The queen may presently be a marvel to behold (*miranda*) yet will soon be explicitly identified as someone wholly "lamentable" (*miseranda*, 6.276).

It is not yet necessary to insist that, on the level of the *logos*, Niobe too is but a figment of poetic discourse and therefore equally liable to the charge of hearsay. For now, it would be better to remain within the mythic milieu. Niobe "stands firm" (*constitit*, 169), and so does the verse, for *constitit* forms a dactyl and thereby creates a noticeably halting pause after the first foot. The pause is apt: motion implies movement in time, and it is time that qualifies the human condition. In presuming divinity for herself, Niobe aims to exempt herself from the temporal limitations that define every mortal being. This fatal misconception drives her arrogant blasphemy (6.171–72): "Why is Latona being worshipped at her altars, while my divinity is as yet without incense?" (*cur colitur Latona per aras, / numen adhuc sine ture meum est?*). The rhetorical force of this exasperated question—the asyndeton, the paratactic placement, the chiastic ordering of the opponents (*Latona per aras / numen . . . meum*)—accentuates Niobe's opinion that she stands eye-to-eye with the goddess. In this regard, she intensifies the pretense of those who preceded her in the narrative sequence. Distinct from the Pierides and distinct from Arachne, Niobe is not simply another mortal who challenges a deity but rather one who presumes divine power, *numen*, for herself.

To demonstrate her superiority to all other mortals and her equal footing with the immortal Latona, Niobe provides an impressive list of possessions, beginning with her lineage (6.172–79). Her mother was one of the Pleiades, who were the daughters of the Titan Atlas, while her father, Tantalus, was the son of Jupiter, who incidentally also sired her husband, Amphion. These conventional appeals to ancestral legitimacy, however, are compromised by what Niobe fails to mention. The name of Tantalus, though once a favorite of the Olympians, would have made her audience shudder, since he abused this relationship by sharing ambrosia with his mortal companions, before butchering his own son Pelops and serving him up as a meal to test the gods' omniscience—a *contemptor deum*, just like her arrogant daughter. From a different angle, given Jupiter's notorious promiscuity, having him as both grandfather and father-in-law might come across more as a joke than a claim to divinely ordained potency. As for Atlas, Niobe is eager to point out that he supports the entire heavens on his shoulders yet refrains from noting that this burden is a punishment, just as she omits the story of how the Titan was turned into stone by Perseus wielding the Gorgon's head—a detail that would seem to be a forewarning of her imminent fate.

Thus, Niobe persists in claiming preeminence in dubious ways: "the Phrygian people fear me" (*me gentes metuunt Phrygiae,* 6.177), though she left Phrygia as a young woman and now resides in Thebes; "the realm of Cadmus is under my dominion" (*me regia Cadmi / sub domina est,* 6.177–78), though she is formally but the consort of the king; and hence, the misleading exaggeration: "the city walls, constructed by my (*mei*) spouse's lyre, together with the people are ruled by both me (*a me*) and my husband" (6.178–79). In addition to the rather weak rhetorical legerdemain, the sequence is noteworthy for the emphatic repetition of the first-person pronoun (*me . . . me . . . mei . . . me*), which recalls the anaphora commonly found in hymns to a deity. In fancying herself to be on a par with a goddess, Niobe does not hesitate to recite a hymn to herself.[4] Yet her self-adulation cannot conceal a self-contradiction: she says she has "beauty worthy of a goddess" (*digna dea facies,* 6.182), which only reminds us that she is not, in fact, an immortal.

All the same, Niobe seems perfectly convinced that she ranks with the divine Latona, and is thus prepared to fight. She calls attention to her great quantity of offspring, seven sons and seven daughters, a number that far exceeds Latona's two children, Apollo and Diana (6.182–83). On this basis, while standing physically present before the Theban populace, Niobe ridicules Latona, whom no one can see, and insultingly alludes to the goddess's shameful history, that, according to myth, no place in heaven, earth, or sea was willing to give Latona a place for her to rest and give birth, until Delos, an island that floated aimlessly on the seas, felt pity for the vagrant deity (6.189–91). As with the prior claims, Niobe deceitfully passes over a crucial part of the narrative: she does not mention that Latona was exiled and pursued by Juno, whose jealous wrath over Jupiter's erotic affairs is famously severe. In any event, Niobe's reliance on a merely numerical argument—that fourteen children are greater than two—is patently weak. As any military strategist knows, the belief that quantity alone would be a sufficient criterion for judging relative power is delusional. Equally misguided are the conclusions Niobe draws (6.193–96):

> sum felix; quis enim neget hoc? felixque manebo;
> hoc quoque quis dubitet? tutam me copia fecit.

---

4. See Anderson (1972, 176–77).

maior sum quam cui possit Fortuna nocere,
multaque ut eripiat, multo mihi plura relinquet.

I am fortunate; who indeed would deny it? And fortunate I shall remain; this too who would doubt? Abundance has made me safe. I am greater than anyone, whom Fortuna would be able to harm, and let her snatch away many, she will leave me many more.

Again, Niobe stands firmly in place, stubbornly immobile in her arrogance. Like a goddess, she believes she is free from time itself, immune to the vagaries of Fortune, of what might still happen. She speaks as though her present circumstances will remain the same eternally: *sum felix . . . felixque manebo,* "I am fortunate . . . and fortunate I shall remain." The chiasmus, together with the shift from the present to the future tense, underscores Niobe's recklessness, which feebly employs a temporal condition to deny the effects of time. This foolish disposition explains her many prior omissions: evoking Tantalus and Atlas without reference to their fates; recounting Latona's expulsion without reference to its cause. In each case, she abstracts one moment from the ongoing flow of time. In her view, happy now means happy forever.

The adjective *felix* is pertinent, and not only because it reiterates the initial portent that would have cast her as "most fortunate" (*felicissima*). The primary sense of *felix* is "fruitful" or "productive"—cognate with words that involve childbirth like *fecundus, fetus, faenus* ("monetary interest on capital"), and *femina*. This semantic field characterizes the state of being fortunate as being subject to temporal limitations, for what is born is also slated to die. Again, Niobe precariously sets too much stock on the present forms. She may, at present, be "beautiful" (*formosa*); yet, at least in the eyes of Roman culture, beauty is particularly vulnerable to the ravages of time. Consequently, the poet alludes to mutability with a telling qualification: Niobe was "beautiful, as much as anger permits" (*quantum ira sinit, formosa,* 167). Despite what Niobe thinks, quantity will not be a very strong suit. Apollo will soon avenge his mother by entering the "flat field" (*planus . . . lateque patens . . . campus,* 6.218) and slaughtering every one of the queen's offspring. The flatness emphasizes the battleground as a level playing field, on which the match between immortals and mortals will be definitively decided—a horizontal arena that defuses Niobe's prior appeals along the vertical axis. Consequently, she can do nothing but stand still as the number of her children is reduced to none; and as her finely formed beauty will be mutated into stone, yet another form suffering change.

Whereas the Pierides and Arachne staged their rivalry on the basis of art—singing and weaving, respectively—Niobe makes her bid solely on the claim that she, too, like Latona, possesses divine power (*numen*). And this assertion is true insofar as divine status depends on mortal worship. To be a god means to be revered as one. This proviso is precisely what worries Latona, as she complains to her own children, Apollo and Diana: "whether I may be a goddess is in doubt and through all the ages I shall be shunned from worship at the altars, unless you, my children, hasten to help" (6.208–9). The statement is odd and sheds light on Latona's resemblance to her challenger. Like Niobe, the goddess is "proud of having given birth" (*vobis animosa creatis*, 6.206), yet pride and motherhood are not the only features the goddess shares with her opponent, for Latona is also given to rhetorical embellishment: Niobe has not explicitly cast doubt on Latona's divinity, but rather simply claimed that she, Niobe, is a superior divinity based on her fecundity, on the quantity of her offspring.

Parenthood has conventionally been seen as a viable path for a mortal to attain immortality insofar as one's children can survive one's death. Accordingly, at the very end of the *Metamorphoses,* the noblest achievement ascribed to Julius Caesar—an apotheosized man—is being the father of his glorious son, Augustus (15.750–51). Similarly, this is the principle that drives Niobe's audacity. Even after her seven sons have been struck down by Apollo's bow, while admitting her misery in contrast to the goddess's felicity, she persists in asserting her quantitative supremacy (6.284–85): "More survive miserable me / than happy you; after so many deaths, I am still victorious" (*miserae mihi plura supersunt, / quam tibi felici: post tot quoque funera vinco*).

Nonetheless, despite her perseverance, Niobe has begun to change radically—a change likewise expressed as a matter of quantitative degree: "Ah! How much this Niobe from that Niobe differed" (*heu! quantam haec Niobe Niobe distabat ab illa*, 6.273). The central repetition is iconic and powerfully demonstrates change in what formally endures by juxtaposing the same name, *Niobe,* first in the nominative and second in the ablative case. The shift in grammar undercuts the identity of form. Moreover, the exclamation (*heu!*) inserts the narrator and therefore the reader directly into the scene.[5] In contrast to the opening distinction between what is said and what is seen—*dicta* and *visa*—the poet now steps forward both to see and tell. The extratextual intrusion will give way to intertextual resonances, when Niobe utters her miserable taunt: "Feed on our grief, cruel Latona" (*pascere, crudelis, nostro, Latona, dolore*, 6.280). In addition to interweaving successive references to

---

5. See Bömer (1976, 82).

herself and her rival, the line engages in the broader epic tradition, alluding to the earliest extant appearance of the story in the *Iliad*. Here, in order to persuade the bereaved Priam to eat, Achilles evokes the figure of Niobe, who did not refrain from food, despite her devastating loss (*Iliad* 24.602–17).[6] According to the logic of competitive parity, Niobe, who once ate despite her grief, now goads her enemy to ingest that very grief.

Behind Niobe's provocation is her sustained assertion that she is a goddess in her own right. And, although in terms of the *mythos*, this claim is clearly invalidated, it appears to acquire some verification on the level of the poetic discourse. To be sure, as her daughters begin to perish, Niobe comes closer to utter defeat. Even by her own quantitative reasoning, she loses the battle as soon as she is left with only one remaining child (6.296–98):

> latet haec, illam trepidare videres.
> sexque datis leto diversaque vulnera passis
> ultima restabat.

> This one hides (*latet*), you might see her trembling. And with six given over
> to death (*leto*), having suffered various wounds, the last one remained.

Of course, this last remaining child will soon be killed, but before that definitive moment, Niobe's children, at least, are verbally identified with the murderous goddess: first, by means of the verb *latet* ("hides"), which immediately evokes Latona, as well as her earlier expulsion, pursued by Juno's wrath; and next, by the word *leto* ("to death"), which perfectly spells the goddess's Greek name.[7] Surprisingly, in the end, the victims come to resemble the goddess on the level of the signifier. The verbal phenomenon (a *dictum*) is thus further corroborated as a visual event (a *visum*): "you might see her tremble." The insertion of the reader into the episode corresponds to the narrator's textual presence, noted above, and moreover reaches back to Arachne's tapestry, in which "you would think it was a real bull, real waves" (6.104). Throughout, the effect is the same, confirming the equivalencies that motivate the entire series of contests: an abolition of distinctions, between the said and the seen, art and life, immortals and mortals.

Niobe's fate puts every one of these distinctions into question; for her final transformation into a marble monument that weeps indicates that the statue is not a representation but rather the woman herself. Her stony presence antici-

---

6. See Radcliffe's chapter in this volume.
7. On this reading, see Feldherr (2004–5, 135–36).

pates and corroborates Pygmalion's famous assertion in book 10 that "art *hides* itself by its own art" (*ars adeo* latet *arte sua*, 10.252). Again, the statement posits a distinction through sameness: here, between art and art. The nominative (*ars*) is equal to and different from the ablative (*arte*), just as, in 6.273, "this Niobe" (*haec Niobe*, in the nominative) differs from "that Niobe" (*illa Niobe*, in the ablative). In Niobe's case, the difference between art and life is erased just as her claims eliminate the border that separates living mortality from deathless divinity.

Although punishment may aim to reassert the hierarchy that subordinates mortals to immortals, it also lays the basis for a general leveling. The vagueness of Niobe's transformation stresses this ambiguity: while the petrification may be understood as a straightforward punishment for blasphemy, it may just as well be seen as more in line with Arachne's metamorphosis, which was portrayed as an act of compassion on the part of Minerva. Or perhaps it is but a realization of Niobe's core character, her rigidity, her stubbornness.[8] A fragment attributed to Hesiod, as well as a passage in Pindar, proposes the etymological link between "stones" (*laes*) and "people" (*laoi*).[9] More immediately, though, the myth of Deucalion and Pyrrha in book 1 of the *Metamorphoses* (313–415) has already accustomed the reader to associating human life with hard stone. Following the global flood, the heroes replenished the human population by casting stones—the "bones of the great mother" (*ossa . . . magnae . . . parentis*, 1.383)—behind their backs, producing a new, more durable human race, whose existence replaces the former species that Prometheus created from fragile clay (1.82–83).[10] As stone, Niobe may have never been more human.

Most provocatively, her transformation is not ascribed to any explicit agent (6.303–12):

deriguitque malis; nullos movet aura capillos,
in vultu color est sine sanguine, lumina maestis
stant inmota genis, nihil est in imagine vivum.   305
ipsa quoque interius cum duro lingua palato
congelat, et venae desistunt posse moveri;
nec flecti cervix nec bracchia reddere motus

---

8. Otis (1966, 151) remarks that "the metamorphosis is not punishment at all, not even an act of divine pity, but the very image of Niobe's final condition." For a concise overview of the many possible interpretations, see Frécaut (1980, 136–37).

9. "[Deucalion and Pyrrha] founded a race of stone, and they are thus named *laoi*" (Pindar, *Olympian* 9.45–46). Cf. Hesiod, fragment 234 West.

10. For this reading and its relation to the Niobe episode, see Boyd (2020).

nec pes ire potest; intra quoque viscera saxum est,
flet tamen et validi circumdata turbine venti   310
in patriam rapta est: ibi fixa cacumine montis
liquitur, et lacrimas etiamnum marmora manant.

She grew rigid from evils: the breeze moves not a hair, in her face is color without blood, her eyes stand motionless in her sorrowful sockets, there is nothing alive in the image. That tongue within is also frozen to the rigid palate, and her veins cease from being able to pulse; neither can her neck bend nor her arms move nor her feet walk; inside too her entrails are stone. And yet she weeps and she is snatched up by a surrounding whirl of wind to her homeland: there, fixed on a mountain summit she cries, and tears even now trickle from the marble.

She "grew rigid with evils" (*deriguit malis*), though it is unclear whether her own sins or Latona's vengeance are the cause. Did the goddess transform her punitively or was it a purely spontaneous event? In either case, all movement is negated. The image is utterly lifeless, both on the surface and within—a list of body parts is congealed, ending with the "entrails" (*viscera*), which likely refers to her womb. She will no longer be *felix*, no longer fecund. "And yet nonetheless she weeps" (*flet tamen*). Though incapable of moving, a strong wind delivers her home to Phrygia, where she rests to this day, "and tears even now trickle (*manant*) from the marble."[11]

As already indicated, what the concluding verb, *manare*, semantically proposes is that Niobe, though inanimate, lives on (*manere*). She might not have remained fortunate, despite her previous claim (*felixque manebo*), but remains nonetheless. She is a story without end.

The mortal Niobe thus attains the immortal status of art; she has become her own memorial or *monumentum*—not simply an undying testament to her mourning but a work that accords with Ovid's artistic ideal as expressed in the poem's epilogue. After recounting the apotheosis of Julius Caesar and after alluding to the lasting glory of Caesar's heir, Augustus, the poet steps into the poem to declare (15.871–79):

iamque opus exegi, quod nec Iovis ira nec ignis
nec poterit ferrum nec edax abolere vetustas.
cum volet, illa dies, quae nil nisi corporis huius
ius habet, incerti spatium mihi finiat aevi:

---

11. On this passage, see also Rimell's and Telò's chapters.

> parte tamen meliore mei super alta perennis 875
> astra ferar, nomenque erit indelebile nostrum,
> quaque patet domitis Romana potentia terris,
> ore legar populi, perque omnia saecula fama,
> siquid habent veri vatum praesagia, vivam.

> And now I have completed a work, which neither Jove's anger nor fire
> nor the sword nor voracious old age will be able to abolish.
> Whenever it will, that day, which has no power except over this body,
> let it limit the extent of my uncertain life.
> Still, with my better part, above the high stars
> I shall be borne everlasting, and my name will be indelible,
> wherever Roman power lies over conquered lands,
> I shall be read by the mouths of the people, through all the ages in fame,
> if the prophecies of the poets have any truth, I shall live.

Like his contemporary, Horace, Ovid has erected a monument—*exegi monumentum* (Horace, *Odes* 3.30.1)—a memorial or tombstone in poetry that will survive the ages. Though corporeal death is inevitable, the poet will remain alive in his work, just as Niobe remains alive in sculpture, still mourning, still weeping. The power of song will last *per omnia saecula*, "through all the ages"—the selfsame phrase that Latona employed, fearful that she will be "shunned through all the ages" (6.208). Though timeless, the goddess is as concerned with time as her human competitor and her human poet. There is both divine authority (*numen*) and motion (*motum*) latent in the *mo-numentum*, both Niobe's and her poet's. Which recalls that the monument is ultimately also a text: not a corpus of meanings forever set in stone but rather a poem that will continue to lament and continue to change "into new . . . bodies," re-readable and therefore revisable, by the author, Ovid, as well as by us.[12] Thus, as one of the poet-prophets named in the final line (*vatum*), Ovid resembles the proud queen in challenging the gods. If the deities are knowable only through poetry, sculpture, and painting, then they are the glorious offspring of the artists alone. Yet uncannily, in resembling a punished woman who is rendered into marble and expelled to the East, Ovid also seems to predict his own shameful expulsion, after the *Metamorphoses* has been fixed as a poem, figuratively written in stone, yet always subject to revision. Like the immobile Niobe who weeps alone on a remote mountaintop, unsure whether anyone notices her, Ovid will enter a state in which he will continue to sing,

---

12. Cf. Martelli (2013, 15).

while being unsure whether anyone is listening any longer. For now, the apotheosis of Caesar, with which this *carmen perpetuum* ends, validates this risky, audacious gambit—that mortals are on a par with the immortals, not despite but precisely because of time, the time in which every form may change but also the time for the song to be perpetuated, moving toward what is yet to come, at least in terms of a fallible yet durable art that hides itself.

CHAPTER 7

Shadow and Stone
Niobe between Platonism and Stoicism

ANDRES MATLOCK

Niobe is a fragment. Where comparable figures, like Antigone, are shaped by the generational relationships of mythic cycles and the interpretative histories of the stage, Niobe appears prismatic, always slightly different from our last glimpse of her. Even in Ovid's canonical retelling, the poet's singular focus on her revolt and its suppression by Leto's children is obstinate in its circumspection. We learn little about the motivations behind Niobe's vitriol against Leto, and her claim to a mythical genealogy as the daughter of Tantalus is undermined by the divine violence that seems to be the point of the story.[1] As often in Ovid's poem, metonymy takes precedent.[2] Niobe's actions stubbornly repeat Arachne's arrogance toward the gods, and her metamorphosis remains, somehow, incomplete: "Inside her body, she is stone. Yet she weeps still and, seized by a powerfully whirling wind, she is swept away to her own homeland. There, perched on the peak of a mountain, she dissolves (*liquitur*), and even now tears flow from the marble."[3] Narrative cannot explain this recalcitrant Niobe, somehow both solid and fluid, heavy as a stone and light enough to be carried on the wind. Instead, as I propose in this chapter, we might approach these prismatic fragments of Niobe with a view not to restore their totality,

---

1. See *Metamorphoses* 6.170–202, for Niobe's futile genealogy.
2. On the slipperiness between transformation and transference in Ovid's poem, see Mikkonen (1996, 322–24) and *Metamorphoses* 6.146–51 for connections with Arachne.
3. *Metamorphoses* 6.306–9.

but rather to trace their outline as a problem for philosophy. As an object of philosophical attention, Niobe represents a material polarity that conjoins and separates Platonism and Stoicism, a durable marker in the ontological expression of these modes of thought.[4]

Before turning to examine Niobe's impact in Platonic and Stoic texts, I foreground the polarizing quality of three aspects of her myth that are otherwise only loosely connected in the narrative tradition. It is in a "Stoic" or a "Platonic" response to these polarities that we can locate Niobe as a problem of thought:

1. Niobe's motherhood. In the last book of Homer's *Iliad*, Niobe appears in Achilles's speech to Priam, where her example is used to convince the bereaved old man to break bread with his son's killer. Achilles selects this mythic fragment not just for its clear relevance to the killing of a parent's children, but for the perhaps unexpected reason that, "Lovely-haired Niobe was mindful of food, even as her twelve children perished in her halls."[5] This theme returns at the end of the speech when Achilles recalls that, "even as a stone, [Niobe] broods over (or "digests," "matures," *pessei*) her grief sent by the gods."[6] Achilles's wordplay leaves the inanimate figure of Niobe digesting forever, hungry for more. At the same time, her failure to ensure the "maturation" of the children from her own womb is also contained in the verb, *pessô*. As a stone, Niobe abstains from food but is sustained by the "grief sent by the gods." As a mother, to be "mindful of food" even in grief emphasizes the banality of trauma and the ultimate futility of maternal nourishment.

2. Niobe's friendship. In a fragment of a fragment, Sappho reveals a glimmer of backstory: "Leto and Niobe were very dear companions (*philai etairai*)."[7] The passage from this shared friendship, comradery, or sexual union—however we should interpret this early use of the term for "courtesan"—to enmity and pedicide is merely suggested. The attachments of their former relationship were, somehow, supplanted by the new attach-

---

4. I refer less to the historical philosophical schools and more to manners or patterns of thought that reappear ahistorically. On the modern construction of this opposition, see Nietzsche's programmatic claim to "invert" or "reverse" Platonism and its fallout: e.g., Heidegger (1991, 154), Deleuze (1990, 253–7), Robinson (2009, 128–29), Lane (2011), Badiou (2008, 1–32). Niobe's example, in fact, helps to articulate a salient turning point in the (dis)continuity between these modes of thought.

5. *Iliad* 24.602–4.

6. *Iliad* 24.617; for the connection between mourning and food as an aspect of Iliadic warrior culture, cf. 19.225–33.

7. Fragment 142 Voigt. On this fragment, see the introduction and Rimell's chapter.

ments of motherhood, implying an irreconcilability between intra- and extrafamilial affection. To be a friend, Niobe cannot be a mother, and to be a mother means entering an actively antisocial relationality, destructive both within and outside of her family. The loss of Leto as a friend foreshadows the loss of her children as a mother.

3. Niobe's sense. In the Ovidian canon, Niobe's expression of sorrow is metamorphosed into a trickle of moisture. These tears from a stone are the last vestige of Niobe's ability to signify—to impress herself on the world, even if, in her transfiguration, this sign manifests only as self-erosion (*liquitur*). Yet another characterization of Niobe's grief attested in the fragments of Aeschylus's lost play as well as in Cicero's *Tusculan Disputations* removes even this last ability to make her mark: silence.[8] In a list of mythological mourners, Cicero's speaker comments briefly, "Niobe is rendered in stone, I believe, to represent her eternal silence in grief."[9] Similarly, in the opening of Aeschylus's play,[10] Niobe seems to have been seated and shrouded in front of the audience, maintaining resolute silence, unwilling or unable to speak even as the Chorus prompts her, and the audience chafes uncomfortably at this breach of theatrical convention.[11] And yet, of course, her silence speaks volumes. Niobe's "eternal silence in grief" surpasses the communicative potential of her former garrulousness—the cause of all her trouble, after all.[12]

In each of these instances, Niobe lays the groundwork for confronting the limits of humanity's materiality itself. Her stoniness reifies the tenuous boundaries that define embodied experiences of maternity (nourishment/hunger), friendship (love/hate), and sense (speech/silence).

As a problem of the limit, therefore, Niobe finds a different home in Platonism and Stoicism, but one whose doors, we might say, open onto a shared conceptual field. In the philosophical literature of antiquity and its modern

---

8. This silence is also present at an earlier point in the Ovidian transformation, when her tongue "freezes" (*congelat*) inside her mouth, 6.306–7; see Telò in this volume.

9. *Tusculan Disputations* 3.63.

10. See fragment 154a.5–8 Radt: "And you [yourselves] can see the final outcome of this marriage: this is the [third (?)] day that she has been sitting at this tomb, a living mother brooding over her dead children, with the unhappy beauty of her form [melt]ing away" (translations from Aeschylus throughout from Sommerstein 2009). Note that unlike the *Iliadic* image of "brooding" as digestion, here we have a more straightforward maternal representation of a hen sitting over her eggs (*epôizei*).

11. For a suggestion about the audience's reaction, see Aristophanes, *Frogs* 907–37.

12. Aeschylus's Chorus warns (fragment 153a.17–18 Radt), "seeing that one is mortal, one should cherish the [prosperity that comes from the gods (?)] and not be rash in speech."

responses that I consider from Emmanuel Levinas and Gilles Deleuze, Niobe articulates a human relation to the inanimate, the incorporeal, the real. For a Platonist, the contradictions contained within Niobe's petrified image disclose the erosion of the real. A Stoic instead excavates Niobe's mineralogy, heeding her summons to disanimation. For Platonic thought, the intransigence of Niobe's stoniness is a mark of the false substantiality of the image, and a call for philosophy to demarcate the real from its shadow. At the same time, and through this same erosion, Niobe reconfigures Stoic ontology as an ethics of inanimacy. These two poles are held in tension by the oscillations of her myth. The problem of Niobe requires the philosophical observer to confront the predication of maternal nourishment, friendly attachments, and sensible expression on their dissolution.

Niobe provides Platonic philosophy with an allegory of the image, a mythos of mythos itself—not just a work of art, but the possibility of artwork. In an essay that offers a Platonic explanation for the aesthetic impulse,[13] Emmanuel Levinas establishes Niobe in this role through a discussion of the temporality of the image. Framing his position against the Bergsonism of mid-twentieth-century French philosophy, he argues that it is has become accepted as a "truism" that "the continuity of time" is the "very essence of duration."[14] According to this chronological axiom, any discontinuity of duration can only be an "illusion of a time grasped in its spatial trace, an origin of false problems for minds incapable of conceiving duration." Opposing this reduction of time to duration, and its unitary assumptions about being and becoming, Levinas contends,

> We on the contrary have been sensitive to the paradox that an instant can stop. The fact that humanity could have provided itself with art reveals in time the uncertainty of time's continuation and something like a death doubling the impulse of life. The petrification of the instant in the heart of duration—Niobe's punishment—the insecurity of a being which has a presentiment of fate, is the great obsession of the artist's world. . . . The eternal duration of the interval in which a statue is immobilized differs radically from the eternity of a concept; it is the meanwhile, never finished, still enduring—something inhuman and monstrous.

---

13. See Levinas (1989, 134–37) for the explicit Platonic grounding of the essay. On Levinas and Platonism more generally, see Narbonne and Hankey (2006, 42–100).

14. Levinas 1989, 140; this passage continues below. On Bergsonian duration and Levinas's response, see, e.g., Narbonne and Hankey (2006, 106–19) and Lin (2013, esp. 17–78).

Niobe's punishment—"the petrification of the instant in the heart of duration"—reveals the "presentiment of fate" that is the purview of the artist as image-maker. As a prefiguration of the artistic impulse, Niobe's transformation unveils a discontinuity between being and becoming, with the artist and her image on the side of becoming, or "the meanwhile, never finished, still enduring—something inhuman and monstrous." The artistic image produces a shadowy, perverse form of "eternal duration" that belongs not to truth and reality but "to the interval in which a statue is immobilized," artificially isolating one moment in the ontic flux for preservation. This punctuated frozenness opposes the creative eternity of concepts to which the philosopher aspires. As a mythotype of artistic creation, Niobe's metamorphosis reveals the "death doubling the impulse of life" that haunts all subsequent plastic or otherwise mediated images. By contrast—and this is where Levinas's Platonism really strikes home—alone of all human endeavors, philosophy, especially dialectical philosophy, strives to separate this shadow from its reality, embracing the "eternity of a concept" in its luminous truth.

Reading Plato's *Republic* with Levinas's interpretation in mind helps to clarify his scattered references to Niobe as they relate to the nexus of aesthetics, ethics, and the law. In his introduction to the education of the Guardians in books 2 and 3, Socrates censors the Niobe myth particularly because it contravenes his definition of divinity. Socrates argues that, for the Guardians to have a theological grounding for their concepts of justice and the good, the gods must be represented to them according to divine nature as it really is, and "A god is, of course, good in reality and must be spoken of as such."[15] According to this fundamental division, nothing that is good can cause harm, and if it cannot cause harm, then it cannot do evil. Consequently, since a god is good, "No one else is to be held responsible for the good things, but for the bad things we must look for any other cause but the god."[16] When it comes to representing divinity in art, therefore, Socrates urges:

> We must [n]ever allow the young to hear that, in Aeschylus's words: "For mortals god implants guilt / Whenever he wishes to ruin a house utterly."[17] But if anyone writes anything in verse in which these lines occur, for example the sufferings of Niobe, or those of the house of Pelops, or the Trojan Wars, or anything else of this sort, then either we must not let them say that these are the work of god, or if they are, then they must search out the reason

---

15. Plato *Republic* 379a–b; translations from Plato throughout are from Emlyn-Jones and Preddy (2013).
16. *Republic* 379c.
17. Quotation: Aeschylus, *Niobe* fragment 160 Radt.

that we are pretty much looking for now and say that god carried out good, just deeds, and that the people responsible have profited by being punished.[18]

Picking up this idea later on, Socrates uses Niobe—again in her Aeschylean appearance—to reemphasize the need for philosophical oversight by situating the detrimental effects of such false narratives on the audience: "everyone will excuse himself for being evil if he is convinced that they do and have done such things, even: 'Those akin to the gods / those close to Zeus, / whose altar of the ancestral god / is high above around Ida's rocky crag / For them the blood of the gods has not yet lost its power.'"[19] If poets depict heroes or gods as "close to Zeus," as Apollo and Artemis expressing their power through vengeance and violence, what is to stop average citizens from crafting exculpating narratives about their own wrongdoing? Niobe's fate thus stands alongside other prominent mythical examples, such as Orestes, as a warning about the power of narrative art to distort and influence an audience's perception of divinity, the good, and their own responsibility. The only sensible response to this danger, for Socrates, comes from a philosophically informed system of artistic restrictions.

Beyond providing an exemplary basis for Kallipolis's philosophical censorship, Plato relegates Niobe to punishment before the law since her image stands before being, resisting dialectical reason and eluding conceptualization under the eternal truth of philosophy.[20] This critical response is elucidated by seeing Socrates's resistance in Levinasian terms, in which the erosion of Niobe's mythic features calls us to observe the shadows of the real. The stubbornness of her Aeschylean theatrical representation, in which her transfigured stoniness stands as a durable reminder of the gods' capacity for evil and the powerlessness of mortals over fate, cannot be excised, and so must be outlawed. The other contradictory features of her myth—the predication of maternal nourishment on a mother's hunger, of friendship on violent enmity, and of communication on silence—demonstrate the "inhuman and monstrous" quality of the image and image-production. Artwork that embraces these contradictions, as Plato affirms Aeschylus's tragedy does,[21] keeps truth at a distance, projecting for audiences instead the warped reflection of "death

---

18. *Republic* 380a–b.
19. *Republic* 391e; quotation: Aeschylus, *Niobe* fragment 162 Radt.
20. On Platonic censorship of literature as a part of his philosophical program, see esp. Naddaff (2002) and Collobert (2011).
21. We should be skeptical of Plato's interpretation as a source for understanding Aeschylus's play; see Sommerstein (2009, 160–61); cf. Murray (2011, 187). But clearly, he reads the tragedy as emphasizing the culpability of the gods.

doubling the impulse of life." The Socratic censorship of these image-producing tendencies—not their total prohibition, but the creation of an elaborate system of rules and conditions under which they *can* contribute to the Guardians' education—is an attempt to use philosophy to close that gap, to bring the viewer closer to a glimpse of the thing-in-itself via its shadow.

Given the role that Niobe plays in enforcing an ontological division between reality and its image, the force of her myth ripples outward into phenomenological aspects of Platonic thought. For instance, in the same books of the *Republic* that deal with the education of the Guardians, mothers reoccur as a focal point in the development of a child's ethical and aesthetic sense. In his guise as the lawgiver, Socrates lays a special injunction on bedtime stories: "There again let not mothers, persuaded by these poets, terrify their children by telling these stories wrongly that there are some gods who go the rounds at night in the guise of all different kinds of stranger, so they do not blaspheme the gods and at the same time make their children afraid."[22] On the one hand, this injunction seems like a naïve plea to the power of nurture over nature. But, on the other hand, and viewed through the Niobic prism, the Socratic call to wrangle those mothers, who have been "persuaded by these poets," to the side of his philosophical project lays bare the crucial division between nourishment and hunger that Niobe's motherhood stubbornly refuses. If philosophy cannot discern the truth of maternal sustenance, how can it inform a broader educational structure in which children will grow into just citizens?

In another ripple, we can see the Platonic consequences of Niobe's eternal silence for another of Cicero's exemplary figures in his book on grief: Artemisia of Halicarnassus. Echoing Niobe's silent sorrow for her children, Artemisia's grief at the death of her husband, Mausolus, is intransigent. But, in Artemisia's case, this immovability is explicitly figured as a work of artifice in the famous Mausoleum, which Cicero calls that "noble *sepulchrum*." Their correspondence is deepened by Cicero's description of Artemisia's mourning: "for as long as she lived, she lived in grief and finished her days in the same state until she was consumed (*contabuit*)."[23] Like Niobe's stony silence, Artemisia's *sepulchrum* reifies a moment that is not allowed to pass. Although her body is finally consumed and rots away (*contabuit*), nevertheless she remains frozen "in the same state" until the very end of her life.[24] In Niobe

---

22. 381e, trans. modified; cf. 377c. On the relationship between this symbolic nourishment and more literal sustenance, see esp. the regulation of breastfeeding at 460d. For Platonic mothers more generally, see, e.g., Walcot (1987), Alford (2000), and Murray (2011, 189–93).

23. *Tusculan Disputations* 3.76.

24. For the philosophical background of this passage see, Graver (2002, 117–20); for a biographical reading, see Englert (2017).

and Artemisia's response to grief we register the countless ways that humans mediate their lives in order to cope with the real, the emergent, the truth of existence. As the Aeschylean Chorus says of Niobe in a section not quoted by Plato, "A [mortal] afflicted is nothing but a shadow."[25] The affliction, in the Platonic view, is this very tendency toward artifice and mediation. Only philosophy offers a remedy for humanity's retreat from the real into the shadow.

For Platonic thought, therefore, the erosion of Niobe's features—the polarities that she stubbornly represents—demonstrates what Levinas calls, using a coinage from Jean Wahl, the "trans-descendence of the real."[26] The intractable undecidability of her stoniness reminds us of humanity's inability to perceive, at least without the accoutrements of philosophy, what is true, eternal, and divinely existent. But further compounding this reminder of human fallibility, our aesthetic infatuation with her jagged fragmentation demonstrates, for the Platonic line of thought, that she herself offers no solution to the problematic materiality of our existence. Instead, she must be legislated, punished, and corrected by the philosophical injunctions under which Plato maintains her.[27]

From a Stoic perspective, the erosion of Niobe's features sweeps these Platonic injunctions into an immanent becoming. Niobe does not hold a different structural position in Stoic ontology: as a figure of the limit, she marks the hither side of being. Instead, the movement of thought has changed. For Platonic thinking, Niobe is an aporia that cannot be passed, and so must be processed legislatively. Stoic ethics, by contrast, can be entirely oriented around approaching this limit bodily, physically, in reality through word (or an absence of words), action (or inaction), and affect (or disaffection). The very polarization of the figure of Niobe holds open the possibility of realizing this limit, as an instantiation of the Stoic sage's commitment to affirmative existence, effortlessly assenting to the *logos* of the universe.

Niobe appears prominently in Diogenes Laertius's account of the death of Zeno, the founder of the Stoa. As often in Diogenes's biographies, the death of the philosopher offers a mise en abyme of his core teaching or commitment.[28] It is striking then, to find Niobe, already a mythotypic figure, as the stubborn ground on which Zeno, literally, falls:

---

25. Fragment 154a.9 Radt.
26. Levinas 1989, 137; cf. Wahl (2016).
27. On Niobe and the law, see the chapters of Lezra, Radcliffe, and Umachandran on Benjamin.
28. On this feature of ancient biography and Diogenes's work, see, e.g., Chitwood (2004), Critchley (2009), and Grau (2010).

He died in the following way. Leaving his school one day, he tripped and fell, breaking a digit ("toe" or "finger," *daktulon*). Striking the ground with his fist, he quoted a line from the *Niobe*: "I'm already on my way, why are you calling for me?" (*erchomai: ti m' aueis?*) And, throttling himself (or "exhaling his breath," *apopnixas heauton*), he died right then and there.[29]

Niobe's summons to inanimation—the call of stone—rings loudly in the Stoic's ear. Zeno's clumsy tumble results only in a broken *daktulos*. Yet his reaction escalates rapidly from an expression of frustration to apparent suicide. The cause of death is communicated by the impenetrable phrase, *apopnixas heauton*, which implies either that he forcibly suffocated himself or, perhaps, exhaled all the air from his body and simply never drew in anew. Diogenes's explanation for Zeno's behavior comes from the brief quotation—only four words in Greek—that he tells us derives from a *Niobe* by the fourth-century BCE "New Music" radical, Timotheus.[30] The philosopher assumes the role of actor in his last breath, performing an exit-line that has been waiting for its enunciation at just this moment.

The quotidian quality of this death-note suppresses its recursive significance for Stoic thought.[31] There is nothing particularly poetic about the line— "I'm already on my way, why are you calling for me?"—or distinctive in its word choice or syntax, but its delivery transforms Zeno's otherwise unremarkable slip and fall into a moment in which the aporia of materiality is embodied and surpassed. Although we do not know the content of Timotheus's poem, Diogenes's reference to Niobe as its titular character raises the question: who is playing Niobe in this scenario? Is she, as would be fitting, the ground on which Zeno bangs his fist, the stony surface under which the philosopher will pass after death? Or, as might be equally plausible, is she the philosopher himself, captured in mid-transformation, addressing herself as she watches his

---

29. *Lives of Eminent Philosophers* 7.1.28. For a biographical interpretation, see Erskine (2000, 60).

30. We have only one other attestation for this Timothean work in a reference from one of Machon's *chreiae*. Machon's lines also involve mythological figures—Charon and Fate (*Moira*)—summoning the speaker toward death; see LeVen (2013). On Timotheus and New Music, see, e.g., d'Angour (2006), Csapo and Wilson (2009), and LeVen (2011).

31. Berrettoni (1989) relates this account to Stoic ideas about fate and interprets Zeno's broken *daktulos* as a divine sign of his loss of logical abilities. Cf. Grau (2010, 350): "Indeed, Stoics, and particularly Zeno, used complex symbolic gestures to represent some elements of his doctrine. . . . In these gestures, the finger was essential: the finger is both simultaneously the tool and the symbol of knowledge; so, breaking the finger is equivalent to being no longer capable of knowing or researching. . . . Following Stoic logic, which he had just invented, Zeno deduced that the breaking of his finger was a sign, sent by the Earth, that he should finish his philosophical career, and thus his own life."

body disanimate and calcify? Yet this latter perspective, in fact, subsumes the former. As Niobe, Zeno is both the speaking, embodied figure and the impersonally silent ground that is summoning her. Similarly, Zeno's enunciation of this line puts Niobe into contact with Stoic theories about representation and knowledge, as is indicated by the symbolic injury to his *daktulos*. Deprived of this digit, which is employed in Zeno's performative demonstrations of rational assent,[32] the clenched fist of certainty becomes instead a futile gesture of submission to the call of the stone. Even the uncertainty surrounding the cause of death contains this significance: whether Zeno violently ends his life by "throttling himself," or just runs out of breath—in his performance of Niobic submission, what is the difference?

It is in this turn from grasp to submission that Niobe appears in her stage dress as a sage. We can unpack her sage-like qualities by turning to Gilles Deleuze's extensive engagement in *Logic of Sense,* which is dedicated to the possibility of realizing, albeit in a modern idiom, the Stoic ideal.[33] Although Deleuze never refers directly to this anecdote or to Niobe,[34] she grounds his interpretation of Stoic ethics in two key ways: first, he identifies in the theory of the "quasi-cause" through which the sage acts, a distinctive "bipolarity" of "impassibility and productivity, indifference and efficacy."[35] This bipolarity characterizes the "immaculate conception" of the sage—in Daoist terms, his *wu wei*.[36] The sage's bipolarity finds its mythotype in the polarizing qualities of Niobe's myth, yet it reframes them as something simultaneous, copresent in the moment of her transformation: her maternal nourishment produces the impassible hunger of her mineralized existence, and her stony indifference effectuates an eternal mark of her friendly attachments. As she is transformed, she comes to identify with the incorporeal effects of her corporeality, just like the sage who even when just walking identifies with "the walk," which acquires a body through him.[37] As such, and this is the second aspect of Niobe's sagacity, her transformation marks not the reification of an

---

32. For Zeno's demonstration of *katalepsis* using the image of a fist, see Cicero, *Lucullus* 145.

33. On Deleuze and Stoicism, see, e.g., Sellars (1999), Beaulieu (2005), Sellars (2006), and Bennett (2015).

34. The absence of any specific discussion is less notable considering the intensely "compressed" nature of Deleuze's treatment of ancient philosophy; see, e.g., Bennett (2015, 26–28) for an expansion on Deleuze's use of Stoic causality.

35. Deleuze 1990, 144; this passage continues below.

36. Deleuze makes an explicit connection with "Zen"; on the relationship between Daoism and Stoicism more generally, see, e.g., Yu (2008).

37. See Deleuze (1990, 146–47). Deleuze adapts this image of the sage walking from Chrysippus's discussion of the eternal present; see Stobaeus 1.106.5–23 = Long and Sedley 1987, 1.304 (51B) with Goldschmidt (1979, 43).

aporia—an end that knows no end—but is rather evental. It possesses a present instantiation—the body of the woman formerly known as Niobe—yet is realized in the future and the past of the "impersonal and pre-individual, neutral, neither general nor particular, *eventum tantum*"[38] that her disanimation represents. Like Maurice Blanchot's description of death as an event, Niobe's stony suspension is personal and definitively situated in her body, its history and suffering, and yet, at the same time, is *in*corporeal and grounded only in the timeless thingness of itself.[39] In her evental bipolarity, Niobe stands *sub specie aeternitatis* as a figure of the sage who, to use a phrase from *Cinema 1*, in her "absolute defenselessness," transgresses every logo-rhythm of wisdom.[40] In her stoniness, she has ceased to require her own maternity, companionship, or *logos*; instead, she no longer needs to begin, to move, to speak in order to be a mother, friend, and sage. She exists entirely affirmatively in inanimation—finally, a body without organs.

We find the ripples of this sagely Niobe in a consolatory letter by the Stoic Seneca. This letter, one of the *Moral Epistles* addressed to Lucilius, adopts a conventionally Roman, performatively masculine attitude toward grief. Yet with the appearance of Niobe we can reframe its central question: what would it mean to be friends with/as a stone?

> I am grieved to hear that your friend Flaccus is dead, but I would not have you sorrow more than is fitting. That you should not mourn at all I shall hardly dare to insist; and yet I know that it is the better way. But what man will ever be so blessed with that ideal steadfastness of soul, unless he has already risen far above the reach of Fortune? Even such a man will be stung by an event like this, but it will be only a sting (*vellicabit*). . . . Let not the eyes be dry when we have lost a friend, nor let them overflow. We may weep, but we must not wail. Do you think that the law which I lay down for you is harsh, when the greatest of Greek poets has extended the privilege of weeping to one day only, in the lines where he tells us that even Niobe took thought of food? It is because we seek the proofs of our bereavement (*argumenta desiderii*) in our tears, and do not give way to sorrow, but merely parade it (*non sequimur sed ostendimus*). . . . Shame on our ill-timed foolishness (*infelicem stultitiam*)! There is an element of self-seeking (*ambitio*) even in our sorrow.[41]

---

38. Deleuze 1990, 151.
39. See Blanchot (1982, 87–159).
40. Deleuze 1986, 185. For an emphasis on the "mineralogy" of Deleuzian ethics, see Kaufman (2013); cf. Ramírez (2021).
41. Seneca, *Letters* 63; translation by Gummere, modified.

Seneca's advice on moderation in mourning is suitable for a Roman *vir*. This cultural expectation receives the trappings of philosophy with a reference to the ideal of emotional extirpation, a topos in Roman adaptations of Stoicism that emphasizes the removal of all forms of belief—as Stoic psychology characterizes grief and the other "passions."[42] Yet Seneca also keeps his addressee fully aware of the embodiment of grief by describing its effect even on the man who "has already risen far above the reach of Fortune" with the metaphor of a bee sting (*vellicabit*).[43]

Seneca's consolation, therefore, filtered through his reference to Homer's Niobe, might offer us instead a thinking through of the embodied incorporeality that is our experience of grief at the death of a friend. In this understanding, Niobe's hunger does not demonstrate maternal callousness any more than Lucilius's tears contain infallible proof (*argumenta*) of bereavement or "longing" (*desiderium*) for his friend. Rather it is *in* the affirmative embodiment of hunger that we experience grief not for ourselves but in and of itself, just as, by extension, Niobe's submission to her stony form contains within it the traces—the crystalline veins—of the friendship that Sappho tells us Niobe and Leto enjoyed. This figure of submission—the turning of "impassibility and productivity, indifference and efficacy"—is written into the logic of sense with which Seneca closes the passage. Our "foolishness" (*stultitia*) or inability to make sense of/at the moment of the friend's death is "ill-timed" (*infelicis*) because it carries an evental charge: our friend's death is a present that reaches out to encompass past and future. Instead of "giving way to it" (*non sequimur*)—enacting it, participating in it, as Niobe did via her transformation—we encircle it self-servingly (*ambitio*) and grasp at it as a false sign (*ostendimus*). As Derrida says (and Montaigne before him, and Cicero before him), "O my friends, there are no friends!"[44]

In her connection to representation and signification, this sagely Niobe retains an attachment to the problem of the image to which she is intimately tied in Platonism. This attachment is also apparent in Deleuze's description of the sage as an actor of the real. Like Zeno, who delivers his perfectly timed line from Timotheus's *Niobe* at the moment of his death, "the actor redoubles this cosmic, or physical actualization, in his own way, which is singularly superficial—but because of it more distinct, trenchant and pure. Thus, the actor delimits the original, disengages from it an abstract line, and keeps from

---

42. See Cicero, *Tusculan Disputations* 3.13 with Nussbaum (1987), Graver (2002, 83–85), and Thorsrud (2008).

43. Cf. Varro, *On Agriculture* 3.16.

44. For the quotation, see Derrida (1997, 2); for the idea of "loving as if sometime we might hate" in Cicero, see *On Friendship* 59.

the event only its contour and its splendor, becoming thereby the actor of one's own events."[45] In keeping with the Nietzschean project that Deleuze sets for himself in *Logic of Sense* to "reverse Plato," the actor as philosopher—as more than philosopher, as one who can act *through* philosophy—marks the very turning post that Niobe occupies between Platonism and Stoicism.[46] As shadow or stone—seductively (de)materialized or the very stuff of being—Niobe weighs down the shared fabric of ancient philosophy at just this point where ontology becomes ethics, ethics becomes aesthetics, and the real becomes the enlivened matter of human experience and reflection.

It is in this guise as the object of the philosopher's aestheticizing gaze, the undigestible hunger of thought itself, that Hugo von Hofmannsthal's Lord Chandos sees Niobe. Amid a cognitive, artistic, and emotional breakdown, Chandos is suddenly confronted with a vision of the milk cellar on his dairy farm where he had recently ordered a rat infestation to be treated with poison. He describes his fevered fantasy:

> A mother was there, whose dying young thrashed about her. But she was not looking at those in their death agonies, or at the unyielding stone walls, but off into space, or through space into the infinite, and gnashing her teeth as she looked! If there was a slave standing near Niobe in helpless fright as she turned to stone, he must have gone through what I went through when the soul of this beast I saw within me bared its teeth to its dreadful fate.[47]

This is the fantasy that philosophy restages with Niobe: to watch, like a slave struck "with helpless fright," as she petrifies, her eyes looking not back at us, the audience, or even toward her dying children, but "off into space, or through space into the infinite." The philosopher fears and longs to bear within his own soul the "dreadful fate" of this mother that we share with, but apart from her.

---

45. Deleuze 1990, 150.
46. See above note 4.
47. Von Hofmannsthal 2005, 172. On this text, see, e.g., Brett (1978) and Deleuze and Guattari (1987, 240).

PART 3

Art and Aesthetics

CHAPTER 8

The Weeping Rock
Paragone, Pathosformel, and Petrification

BARBARA BAERT

The point of departure for this chapter is the centerpiece of Ovid's *Metamorphoses* (6.146–312): Niobe's transformation into a weeping rock. Niobe's transformation incorporates the form and matter of the medium of sculpture. According to the humanist *paragone* debate, painting and sculpture compete to be the medium with the highest qualities of virtuosity. In the first part of the chapter, I explore the iconographic deployment of Niobe in the *paragone* rivalry, taking up examples from the field of tension between the second and third dimensions, between grisaille and stone, between figurative and nonfigurative.

Aby Warburg refers to the Niobe motif's *Nachleben* in his *Tafel 5: Beraubte Mutter. (Niobe, Flucht und Schrecken)*. This displays the images of both the bereaved mother (Niobe) and the murderous mother (Medea). The montage also introduces the theme of the descent to the Underworld. It becomes clear how the cluster of motifs around the figure of Niobe—hybris, *lamentatio,* and the chthonic substrate—functions as a direct entry to a bipolar hermeneutics of the visual medium: the "historical psychology of human expression" that navigates between Apollo and Dionysus. By extension we can consider how the Niobe motif is an externalization of the furthest boundaries of what human artistic expression can achieve: the unending tribute to love, but also the ceaseless struggle against death.

The "weeping rock" that according to legend still stands on Mount Sipylus in Turkey draws upon deeper anthropological patterns. Petrification indicates inertia, frigidity, and a Medusan psychosis of fear. In nature, stones and rocks have a slumbering insistence that can be captivating. Stones are after all visible but impenetrable; they index an irrevocable absence in their presence and have their abode in an otherworldly region of utter blindness and silence. From a psychoanalytic perspective, Niobe's petrification symbolizes the straitening of her life and the loss of anima within a culture divorced from authentic feeling, nature, and instinct. Here Niobe meets Echo. Looking at this from the perspective of the artistic medium, the final image, Niobe's petrification returns as the first image: the brute matter in which art lies locked, the Urform in which artistic eruption is already heralded. This elision reveals Niobe's transformation as the most radical conceivable form of "iconogenesis": the visual arts sprout from a paradoxical inertia and continue to be watered by Niobe's bitter tears.

1. *DUMQUE ROGAT, PRO QUA ROGAT, OCCIDIT*

In Ovid's account, the divinely exacted penalty for Niobe's pride is the gruesome murder of her children. But this is followed by a second punishment: petrification by sadness. The actual metamorphosis takes place during her petition: *dumque rogat, pro qua rogat, occidit* (*Metamorphoses* 6.301). She "dies" within her despair. This is the point of no return in a radical and irrevocable sclerosis: petrification. The transmogrification exchanges the horror of loss for another horror: being forever turned to stone before the eyes of others, without the release of being able to disappear into Hades, delivered to the moment just before all consciousness vanishes and so still cruelly aware of the fourteen perished children. This is why this particular stone weeps, making marble a metamorphosis within the metamorphosis, an image of an image. The choice of stone—*lacrimas etiam nunc marmora manant* (312)—is by no means a random one. *Marmor* comes from the Greek *marmairein*, which means "to shimmer, to shine like the surface of the water." In the *Iliad*, Homer speaks of the shimmering sea (*hala marmareên*, 14.273); the ancient and medieval commentaries on Ovid interpreted Niobe's turning to marble in a variety of ways.[1] The Greek writer and traveler Pausanias provides an extensive description: in his accounts of his journeys through Greece he claims to have seen the rock for himself.[2]

---

1. Lesky 1936, 643–706; and Wiemann 1986, 6–9.
2. Pausanias, *Periegesis* 1.21.3.

The comic poet Philemon regards the petrification as a symbolic image of Niobe's suffering: psychic and bodily rigidity.[3] The Greek mythographer Palaephatos (fourth century BCE),[4] who was later followed by the Byzantine scholar Johannes Tzetzes,[5] contended that the motif derived from an actual funeral monument in Sipylus and that the sculptor had diverted water from a nearby spring to run from the eyes of the statue. The twelfth-century Byzantine writer Eustathius says that the myth was based upon an existing natural phenomenon at that location.[6] Giovanni Boccaccio, in *Genealogy of the Pagan Gods* (1360), mentions that petrification is a result of shock and sadness.[7] And the image in Sipylus weeps simply because ground water seeps through the cold stone.

The Renaissance also saw the emergence of a monumental iconographic tradition regarding Niobe.[8] The episode generally appears in private spaces as part of series on Diana and Apollo. Tintoretto painted Niobe among sixteen ceiling octagons, commissioned in 1541 for the bedchamber in the Palazzo San Paterniano of the Venetian count Vettor Pisani, under the title: *Niobe mutata in sasso ed i figli saettati da Apollo* (see fig. 8.1).[9] The composition is said to go back to a now lost work by Giorgione for the Casa Sorenza in Venice, described by the painter Carlo Ridolfi.[10] Here again the description reads *Niobe cangiata in sasso e di lei figliuoli saettati da Diana e da Apolline*. Tintoretto's *raccourci* references the ultimate gesture of despair, the moment that Niobe, in Ovid, imploringly raises her arms: *ad caelum liventia brachia tollens* (*Metamorphoses* 6.279). The foreshortened perspective provides a symbolic form that heightens the drama. The viewer is drawn into this anagogy of suffering, which at the same time is so close: only one desperate arm's length away.

Niobe also appeared in public spaces, in the famous frieze by Polidoro da Caravaggio (1499/1500–1543) on the façade of the Palazzo Milesi in Rome.[11] Here too the massacre itself was depicted together with Niobe's consequent despair. This *chiaroscuro* frieze was much copied and has also been preserved

---

3. Fragment 102 Kassel–Austin.
4. *On Unbelievable Tales* 8.
5. Tzetzes, *Chiliades* 4.463.
6. Eustathius, *Commentary in Dionysus's Periegesis* 87.
7. *Genealogy of the Pagan Gods* 12.2.
8. On the ancient iconography, see the extensive and very recent discussion in Zeidler (2018).
9. Now in the Galleria Estense, Modena; see Wiemann (1986, 31).
10. Polati 2010.
11. On Polidoro's and Maturino's Roman façades, see Gnann (1997, 90–117) and de Castris (2001, 108–72).

FIGURE 8.1. Tintoretto, *Niobe Turned Into Stone and the Children Shot by Apollo* (1541–42), Modena, Galleria Estense.

in Enrico Maccari's etches from 1876.[12] It was the last frieze that Polidoro painted before the Sack of Rome in 1527. Giorgio Vasari celebrated the mastery of grisaille and the virtuosity of the *paragone* effect of bronze figures: "un' infinità di figure di bronzo che non di pittura, ma paiono di mettallo."[13] This brings us to the theme of the *paragone*.

2. THE SELF-AWARE IMAGE[14]

Ovid generally describes his metamorphoses with great plasticity. In the tragedy of Niobe too, the metamorphosis is a descriptive finale: the wind no lon-

---

12. Wiemann 1986, 71; and Maccari 1876.
13. Vasari 1853, 62.
14. After Stoichita (2015).

ger stirs her hair, the blood drains from her visage, her tongue freezes, and it is not a mild breeze but the furious storm that carries Niobe back to her Asian homeland where she remains as weeping marble.

In his *Metamorphosis in Greek Myths*, P. M. C. Forbes Irving discusses the two archetypal characteristics of petrification in classical mythology: complete lifelessness (in contrast to transformation into a tree or a bird, for example); and the immutable location of stone as a landmark, as a *monumentum* and thus also as a *monumentum* frozen in time.

The "stone figure" mostly indicates a radical disjunction between humanity and divinity, mirroring an equally shocking pattern of behavior. We cannot discuss all of the many examples in the literature, but Medusa is particularly well known.[15] Irving primarily finds the punishment of being turned to stone in a context of blasphemous talk and sexual aberration.[16] It is a particularly pitiless transformation. After all, having to endure in a "stony death" is a life without desire: not living but hanging between the animate and the inanimate.[17] The stone figure is a "compromise between natural material and human form, between men and the other world."[18] Stones cannot speak; they are immobile and fixed in their emotional sclerosis. The stone figure is in a condition of absolute silence, everlasting blindness, and permanent coldness.[19] To be turned into rigid stone symbolizes not only erection but also castration.[20]

Niobe's petrification is of a piece with these archetypes. Her punishment dismantles her prideful talk—now she is forever silent—and her pride in her fertility is exchanged for infertile rock. But Niobe also deviates from tradition. First of all, there is no connection to the punishment of male lust.[21] Secondly, she corresponds to a condition of being that she had already reached psychically and physically.[22] In her hardening by grief, Niobe receives her permanent mantle. Niobe herself becomes the many-headed tombstone that she weeps over, comparable to the smiling stone on which Demeter sat lamenting Persephone in self-imposed mourning.[23] Thirdly, her stone is not completely petrified: she weeps, retaining a trace of her former human state. In this sense

---

15. See, for example, the iconic Kristeva (1998).
16. Forbes Irving 1990, 139.
17. Forbes Irving 1990, 143.
18. Forbes Irving 1990, 141.
19. Forbes Irving 1990, 146.
20. Fenichel 1937, 6–34.
21. Crompton (2003, 51) mentions that in Sophocles and Plutarch one of Niobe's sons appeals to his homosexual friend.
22. See Barolsky (2005).
23. Forbes Irving (1990, 142 and 146) on how petrification in Sophocles is the equivalent of a tomb.

she is suspended between inanimate nature, which has no feelings of sadness, and animate creatures, such as birds, that do.[24]

In his "Ovid, Bernini, and the Art of Petrification," Paul Barolsky plumbs the relationship between the *Metamorphoses* and artists' self-reflection.[25] Gian Lorenzo Bernini's (1598–1680) *Apollo and Daphne* (1622–25) is a well-known *Metabild* for the metamorphoses that are possible in the hardness of marble. The nymph's transformation is so sensual, so lifelike, so caught in the process itself, that it seems as though Bernini must have kneaded the marble with his fingers.[26] The apex of this masterful *paragone* is the wind: this invisible, wonderful stimulator of movement—breath and psyche together—gives the image life.[27] And the viewer's shock at such virtuosity transfers petrification to the viewer themself, who is struck still by amazement at an artist who can create life from inert matter.

Niobe is in every respect the opposite transformation. Ovid tells us that Niobe's hair could no longer dance in the wind, and the same wind becomes a brutal *raptor* that abducts her stony form. But Niobe is also a remarkable "retrograde petrification." The counterpart of Niobe's petrification can here be identified: Pygmalion's girl, described by Ovid in *Metamorphoses* 10.247–97, that comes to life from sculpture.[28] Where Ovid describes how Pygmalion felt the beating of the girl's veins, how her flesh became warm and suffused with blood, and how she blushed up to her face upon seeing her creator, he describes how Niobe's blood drew from her face, her tongue stiffened, and all her senses vanished into a weeping rock.

In Agnolo Bronzino's version now in the Uffizi Gallery in Florence, we see that the theme was being used in the *ekphrasis* and *paragone* discourse.[29] Bronzino deviates from iconographic tradition by placing the eye contact (*lumen*) with Pygmalion outside of the confines of the painting to where Bronzino was standing, and thus the first person the girl saw was her true creator, the painter (and not the sculptor), just as the text in Ovid's story says: the light and her creator.[30] The position of Galatea's arm is also ambivalent;

---

24. Forbes Irving 1990, 149.
25. See Barolsky (2005).
26. Barolsky 2005, 154.
27. See Pardo (1991) and Baert (2013).
28. Unlike marble, ivory is composed of inorganic and organic matter; in other words, ivory contains all the elements of life. As a material it is also very close to human skin. A selection of basic literature: Mülder-Bach (1998), Weiser (1998), Zeuch (2000), Binczek (2007), Stoichita (2008), Vogel (2008), and Bettini (2008).
29. https://www.wikiart.org/en/agnolo-bronzino/galatea-and-pygmalion. See my analysis of the Pygmalion myth in Baert 2018.
30. Falciani and Natali 2010.

she appears to be pointing at herself: the "self" of the creation and the artwork come to life has been realized. This "self" is not Pygmalion's ego, who kneels in his own isolated amazement. No, the "self" is the self of Bronzino, who is saying: "Look, you're alive now!" All these subtle adaptations of the Ovidian myth contribute to the mise en abyme of the medium, of the self-referential image.

I acknowledge—at least at this stage of the argument—that Niobe does not participate in this iconographic self-reflection. Her petrification, the metamorphosis itself, is not the subject of visual reflection. In painting I had expected to find blood draining, bare flesh turning cold, under a bleak grisaille brush, or references in sculpture to the material of the stone itself. Her main role seems primarily to be that of the stricken mother, the center point of unbearable horror and murder depicted in a frieze. Niobe does not support the *paragone* aesthetic and the self-aware image. In a humanistic context that praised artists for their *pneuma,* the life that they can put into an image, she is the reverse path.[31] Pygmalion's Galatea is embraced in the ideals of what art is able to achieve; she exemplifies what is at stake. Niobe's petrification, in contrast, lies at the amorphous origin of images, not at their perfected extreme. This is why only her sorrow, her horror, can be the subject of "narrative." What she contributes to art is diachronous pathos, the massacre in private space, the doleful *exemplum* for mothers in a patriarchy,[32] but not the synchronous apathy at the mountain top, where she will overrule that sorrowful role in thunderous silence. I will return to this issue in the fourth part of this essay.

3. BERAUBTE MUTTER

In Aby Warburg's *Denkraum,* the *Nachleben* of the *Antike* plays a crucial role.[33] This means that the concept can be found in his oeuvre, in both a theoretical and an iconographical way. In this section, I will connect the Niobe motif to Warburg's concept of *Pathosformel* or internal transfer (transport) of antiquating formal energies—*Pathosformeln*—that navigate between bacchanalian exuberance and classical soberness, between the realm of Dionysus and that of Apollo. According to Warburg, this polarity is part of a universal dynamic in the anthropology of imagery, a dynamic that keeps refreshing itself over the

---

31. Barkan 1993. On ancient imagology, see Goldhill (2001) and Steiner (2001, 3–26).
32. Gilby 1996, 152: "The classical Niobe is a figure of power who emanates the solid sub-terra strength of Greek female culture despite the obvious minatory goals of the myth's creators."
33. Warburg 1999, 585–86.

eras. Indeed, Aby Warburg is describing a history of polarities that results in an anthropology of the history of western civilization in which philology, ethnology, history, and biology converge into the *Zwischenraum* where the turbulences of the magical and symbolic thinking of cultural memory are at work. Only within this interspace will it be possible to find any basis for understanding and curing the schizophrenia of human culture. Imagery is precisely where the *polarité pérenne* of history—this *psychomachia* of the Warburgian method[34]—and energy are unearthed and left behind.[35]

Warburg's fascinations, obsessions, techniques, and desires to chart his *Pathosformeln* culminated in the Mnemosyne project. He launched the project in 1924 together with Gertrud Bing (1892–1964) along with the so-called *Bilderatlas*.[36] Mnemosyne is the goddess who gave all things a name, and she is also the mother of the Muses. The choice of this goddess is not without meaning, since it connects the notion of inspiration (Muses) with the semantic difficulties of naming the meaning of an image and expressing it in language. Aby Warburg places Niobe in Plate 5 of the *Bilderatlas*. On the left side of the panel are three sculptures from the iconic group in the Uffizi, known as the "Niobids" (see fig. 8.2). The statues were found in 1583 near St. John Lateran on the Esquiline Hill of Rome and were moved to the garden of the Villa Medici.[37] Modern research has dated the group as a Roman work (first century BCE to first century CE), possibly after a Greek model. The group had once formed part of an open group of sixteen sculptures described by Pliny the Elder as "Niobe, her fourteen daughters and the paedagogos."[38] Pliny places the group at the temple of Apollo Sosianus in Rome. The find had an impact on the aesthetic discourse of the time comparable to that of the discovery of the Laocoön group, dug up on January 14, 1506, in a vineyard near the Roman Colosseum.[39] Remarkably, Warburg does not show the best-known sculpture from the group, namely, Niobe herself pleading that her last daughter be spared. Johann Joachim Winckelmann devoted lyrical passages to this specific sculpture, which he took to be exemplary of the "high" or "sublime" style that

---

34. Didi-Huberman 2013, 8.
35. Baert 2016b, 25.
36. Warburg 1992.
37. Wiemann 1986, 146; North 2012, 114–15; see also Welcker (1836). In his "The Age of Fable," Thomas Bulfinch (1796–1867) records one form of *paragone* relating to petrification: "In the Uffizi gallery in Florence, there is a plaster cast of an ancient marble statue of Niobe. The sculpture depicts a beautiful and incredulous Theban queen embracing her horrified child. A Greek axiom is connected with this sculpture, 'To stone the gods have changed her, but in vain; the sculptor's art has made her breathe again'" (2007, 106).
38. Pliny the Elder, *Natural History* 29.36.
39. See Richter (1992) and Loh (2011).

he dated to the late fifth or early fourth century as *Ausdruck der Figuren aus der Heldenzeit*.[40] The caption to plate 5 reads:[41]

> Antike Vorprägungen. Magna mater, Kybele. Beraubte Mutter. (Niobe, Flucht und Schrecken). Vernichtende Mutter. Rasende (beleidigte) Frau. (Mänade, Orpheus, Pentheus). Klage um den Toten (Sohn!). Übergang: Unterweltsvorstellung (Raub d. Proserpina). Griff nach d. Kopf (Mänade, Kassandra, Priesterin! [Tafel 6]).

On the left we see the group around the Earth Mother: mothers intentionally (Medea) or unintentionally (Niobe) involved in the murder of their children, children of mothers symbolically sacrificed (the castration of Attis, son of Cybele). The central bloc consists of figures from the myth of Dionysus, the god of orgy and sacrifice, with Orpheus and Euridice as prototype. On the right are examples from Hades, with the rape of Persephone as prototype. The earth mothers—Cybele, Niobe, Medea, Demeter—are therefore read together with sacrifice, the ritual cycle of life and death.

In the montage of plate 5, the ancient *Versuch der Einverseelung vorgeprägter Ausdruckswerte bei der Darstellung* is thematized in the *Pathosformel* as the fury, as *Leidenschaft* in the Niobe, as the bacchanalian delirium dance motif of the Maenads, as the cycle of death and fertility. Even as death by the gaze itself. And so the *Pathosformeln* of these earth mothers become figures of Dionysus. "E così i suoi avversari, sbranati dalle donne in preda all' enthousiasmos, diventano figure di Dioniso."[42]

For Aby Warburg, the conflict between the dramatic, chaotic image and the mild, loving image is a personal truth.[43] To him, images are a threat as well as an embrace: they tack between Dionysus and Apollo. In every image, there is also death. "In other words, Warburg's aptitude for the *astra* (concepts) always brought him in proximity to the *monstra* (chaos)."[44]

We can now understand the Niobe group in Plate 5 as a paradigm of humanity's deepest panic sublayer, and so as Niobe's chthonic position in iconography. Paul Verhaeghe argues that the chthonic image should not be interpreted metaphorically but rather "phorically," that is to say, as "bearing," as

---

40. North 2012, 112.
41. Centanni et al. 2000.
42. Bordignon 2012.
43. See Baert (2014).
44. See Didi-Huberman (2012). See Deleuze and Guattari (1991, 20): "It is as if one were casting a net, but the fisherman always risks being swept away and finding himself in the open sea."

FIGURE 8.2. *Niobe and Her Youngest Daughter,* first half of the second century CE, Galleria degli Uffizi, Florence.

"carrying," as a first and necessary step in a confrontation with what is deemed "unimaginable" within the real.

> A processing of the unimaginable makes it bearable, prepares signification, so that it becomes bearable. . . . It tries to shape the unutterable. . . . Chthonic art differs from and contrasts with oedipal art, which in one way or another always involves a sexual genital processing of this originally undifferentiated and terrifying force. The oedipal development is the final phase of this process, as it channels and socialises *eros* and *thanatos*. . . . Sigmund Freud calls this mourning process *Trauerarbeit,* and equates it to analytical *Arbeit,* the work performed in psychoanalysis. In both cases, the identity of the person may be deconstructed by destroying the identification layers that form the ego.[45]

Where Bernini's Daphne and Bronzino's Galatea were intended to display the utmost *paragone*—the beauty of the marble and coloring, Apollo smiling at such virtuosity, the light of the *astra* reflected on the medium—Niobe is the implosion of its opposite, of stony death, of Dionysus's grimace, of the engulfing darkness of the *monstrum*.[46] Niobe stands on the edge of the abyss, Hades visible on the further side, but she is still living among us. The image still barely belongs to the human, embodying the excess of what the gaze can just bear without destroying. *Du lebst und tust mir nichts.* In this sense she is like a stone *monumentum* between Euridice and Orpheus, like a landmark, that we should never forget: *In every image, there is also death.*

Giorgio Agamben argues that Warburg's *Pathosformeln* are autonomous hybrids of archetypes. They possess an equivalent "first-timeness" (the *primavoltità*).[47] Every photograph taken as part of the Mnemosyne project constitutes an *archè* and, consequently, is archaic. Or as Wolfgang Kemp formulates it: "Each recollection must be stored in the collective memory, where it is rooted in the primal experiences of sorrow, ecstasy, and passion that have left their indestructible 'engrammes'[48] on the psyche of humankind. When a memory arises from these depths, it must work in a 'polarizing' way, as

---

45. Verhaeghe 2013, 80. The Polish clinical psychiatrist Ewald Rumpf (1985) developed the "Niobe Complex." Niobe's tragedy illustrates the mother who is unable to view her children as separate from herself; therefore losing her children means losing her life.

46. See also Didi-Huberman (2001).

47. Agamben 2009, 28–30.

48. The term *Engramm* is borrowed from the German zoologist Richard Wolfgang Semon, who used it to describe the biologically inherent memory trail of a species. See Semon (1908, 190).

'explosive,' as a formula of liberation and activation."[49] This means that the *Bilderatlas* is not only an atlas of the *Pathosformel*, but also an instrument of the *em-pathos*, as Georges Didi-Huberman argues in his study *Hepatische Empathie. Die Affinität des Inkommensurablen nach Aby Warburg*.[50] In 1892, after correcting the second proof of his doctorate on Sandro Botticelli, Warburg decided to add a short prelude.[51] In this text, still at the beginning of his exceptional biography and career, Warburg connected the renewal of his method to three concepts: *Nachleben*, *Pathosformel*, and *Einfühlung*.[52] The last concept he defines as follows: "dass dieser Nachweis für die psychologische Aesthetik deshalb bemerkenswerth ist, weil man hier in den Kreisen der schaffenden Künstler den Sinn für den ästhetischen Akt der ›Einfühlung‹ in seinem Werden als stilbildende Macht beobachten kann."[53] Georges Didi-Huberman considers Warburg's methodical parameters of *Einfühlung* as the ultimate key in reading and understanding the Mnemosyne atlas. The cognitive affect of empathy—seemingly "ambivalent" or "paradoxically" situated between "emotional feeling" and "cerebral thinking"—is reflected in the heart of Warburgian dialectics:

> Ist das nicht im Grunde ein elementares Paradigma aller Erkenntnis, die versucht, ausgehend vom Sinnlichen zu Intelligiblem zu gelangen? Und besteht darin, nebenbei bemerkt, nicht die hauptsächliche Arbeit eines jeden Archäologen oder Kunsthistorikers?[54]

4. BACK TO THE WEEPING ROCK

As I wrote earlier, Niobe lies at the amorphous origin of images, not at their ultimate extension into mimetic perfection. This is an image of the image in the sense of alpha and omega, of a *longue durée* that attempts to embrace *Bildwissenschaft*, of which Aby Warburg once said: "ganzen Skala kinetischer Lebensäußerung phobisch-erschütterten Menschentums." Niobe's metamorphosis to stone is the beginning: the Ur-image; the *primavoltità*.

The mystery of a stone that arrived in its location without human intervention, craggy, not shaped by human hands, appeals to the creative power of

---

49. Kemp 1991, 88.
50. Didi-Huberman 2010.
51. Warburg 1892.
52. Didi-Huberman 2010, 3.
53. Warburg 2010.
54. Didi-Huberman 2010, 6.

nature.[55] "La pierre comme élément de la construction, est liée à la sédentarisation des peuples et à une sorte de cristallisation cyclique. Elle joue un rôle important dans les relations entre le ciel et la terre."[56] The stone is fashioned by a nature that breaks, fractures, tears, scours, carves, and washes. Weathering creates an image that does not derive from human ideas but will inspire them.

A divine origin is often ascribed to stones. They fall from heaven or are cast earthward by gods. The *Geworfenheit* of a stone is the manifestation of the divine. Although it had no figurative features, the "stone cast from heaven" was thought to preserve the image of the god. These were often black, meteoric rocks. When Pausanias visited the cult location of Pharai in Achaia, he was amazed at the veneration of thirty square stones. The author refers to them as *argoi lithoi* or *baitulia* ("meteorites").[57] In early antiquity there was a belief that the gods themselves had cast down these stones. They are the first "embodiments" of the gods, reaching humanity as a raw and unworked mass, rudimentary signs of their existence. Yet in all their aniconicity these stones were still regarded as "portraits." The meteorite was inherently animated by the goddess, encased in stone despite its lack of face or limbs. Pausanias has already been quoted above describing Niobe's rock: close by it is indiscernible, but from further away her profile becomes recognizable. "When you are near it is a beetling crag, with not the slightest resemblance to a woman, mourning or otherwise; but if you go further away you will think you see a woman in tears, with head bowed down."

Niobe too goes back to the Ur-image where form and matter have not yet separated but lie enclosed in one another.[58] Niobe is a descendant of such images fallen from heaven. The greatest taboo—the unthinkable taking place under the eyes of one mother at the prompting of another mother—demands the greatest totem: the ultimate gravity of aniconic rock. The rock is the only monument powerful enough to block the catastrophe, the trauma, wrapped in deep layers of silence. The dolmen of a throat sewn shut.[59] The furthest possible point of banishment in time: perhaps when humans first walked erect.

Niobe is the mouth of the dormant crater from which all other images will erupt. Now we can understand why Mikhail Bakhtin found "the sexless and 'perfect' Niobe and her daughter" in the Uffizi such a paradox. He did not

---

55. See Baert (2004).
56. Chevalier and Gheerbrant 2002, 751.
57. Pausanias 7.22–24. See Freedberg (1989, 67).
58. See Baert 2017.
59. Here again I see a relation between the fantasm of Niobe on the mountain and the "shock" of the Laocoön. "What is a scream other than the disarticulation of speech? The utterance that fails to communicate. The thought that cannot yet crystallize. Sensation rising to the surface" (Loh 2011, 399).

understand Winckelmann's tribute. "In classical antiquity the human body is entirely enclosed and complete. It is a lonely singular body distanced from all others. Therefore all the indications of growth, of incompleteness and procreation are removed and the eternal imperfection of the body is hidden, conception, pregnancy and birth hardly occur."[60] In the marble amorphous *lithos*, however, Niobe is deconstructed to her archaic, furious—almost Homeric— essence, and after Warburg's Mnemosyne she can return home a second and final time. *The identity of the person may be deconstructed by destroying the identification layers that form the ego.* The inconceivable—a woman, deprived of her motherhood and her identity—can only return to the universal matrix of the earth itself: afigurative. In this chthonic place of rest, she no longer needs her identity, mimesis, *paragone*, even *Pathosformel*.

I would go a step further. Is Niobe not the stumbling block, the *skandalon* according to the hermeneutics of *la violence (désir) mimétique* developed by the anthropologist and philosopher René Girard in mythology? "Chez tous les écrivains majeurs, je pense, la rhétorique des oxymores constitue une allusion significative aux vicissitudes de l'interaction mimétique et rejoue obscurément l'essentiel drame humain de la pierre d'achoppement mimétique, le skandalon que nulle interprétation linguistique ne pourra jamais appréhender."[61] Girard makes an idiosyncratic reflection on the ideal of the stumbling block. The Greek word *skandalizein* is derived from "limp," "stumble." *Skandalon* derives from "stumbling block." If you follow someone with a limp, Girard writes, you will see that it seems as if that person repeatedly appears to want to (or is going to) coincide with his shadow without ever succeeding. Girard's image strikingly evokes how limping—the "scandal"—comes closest to the grotesque drama of humankind, namely, to be unable (or not allowed) to coincide with the "self." The "scandal" shows in all its deficiency, in all its imperfection and *tristesse*, the loss of the absolute reflection and the impossibility of eliminating the dichotomy.

The meaning of "stumbling block" is hence highly ambivalent: it is the defect but also the opening to insight; the obstacle but also the possibility. As if, in the stumbling, everything is briefly lit up, as if there is hope. "The paradox implies that Niobe's petrification has simultaneous potency and impotence. Her story is an enigma of pretension, perpetual grief, masochistic desire, self-awareness, providential fury, and glory."[62] Glory: in Niobe's Ur-image the womb again swells with fruit, like the still undressed black stone of Kybele. Demeter becomes her friend and her daughter Persephone the consolation

---

60. See North (2012, 71); see Bakhtin (1995).
61. Girard 2011, 46–47.
62. Gesell 2013, 12.

for the loss of the seven other daughters. Niobe—the image of the image—has become a second *omphalos*.[63] Not a monument at the perfected end, but a landmark for an eternal beginning. This enormous stumbling block—*l'essentiel drame humain de la pierre d'achoppement mimétique*—is needed to parry the *skandalon*. The tragedy is unbearable and terrifying from close up (no foreshortening here), but from a safe distance becomes watchable and healing. And Niobe herself looks out over the open landscape; she is restored in her Homeric *teichoscopia*.

Niobe opens to our eyes a scopic regime in which a deep consciousness of the elements, of wind and rain, are part of our *Gefühlsraum*[64] and of our (artistic) experience.[65] Niobe's tears cut wrinkles through her petrified body: erosion as mourning. But the fluid is also a cautious sign of fertility regained.[66] Niobe's image is therefore also a comfort. Her tears irrigate the land. And is marble not the murmur of the sea? In this sense Niobe has found the power for a different sort of hermeneutics of the image: "stoniness." The anthropologist Tim Ingold in his *Being Alive* describes this as "materials against materiality."[67] Like a friendly iconoclast, Ingold argues for the study of our material culture as an integrated process of the natural elements and surfaces of materials, of interactive views of buildings, sculptures, even dolmens, menhirs, and rocks like Niobe. "Stoniness, if you will, is not constant but endlessly variable in relation to light or shade, wetness or dryness, and the position, posture or movement of the observer."[68] "Stoniness, then, is not in the stone's 'nature,' in its materiality. Nor is it merely in the mind of the observer or practitioner. Rather, it emerges through the stone's involvement in its total surroundings—including you, the observer—and from the manifold ways in which it is engaged in the currents of the life world. The properties of materials, in short, are not attributes but histories."[69]

Niobe has become, at last, her history. Indeed, the *istoria* discussed by Leon Battista Alberti will move spectators when the men painted in the picture outwardly demonstrate their own feelings as clearly as possible. Nature provides—and there is nothing to be found more rapacious of her than she—that we mourn with the mourners, laugh with those who laugh, and grieve

---

63. Gilby 1996, 153: "The Niobe complex as this situation may be called is primarily an exploration of funerals and fertility, gender and family relationships, with a tinge of race and class issues involved."
64. See Schmitz (1981, 264–76).
65. DeBlieu 1998; Ingold 2005, 97–104, and 2007, 19–38; and Hsu and Low 2008, 17–35.
66. Sidgwick 2014, 157.
67. Ingold 2011, 19–32.
68. Ingold 2011, 30. See also Tilley (2004).
69. Ingold 2011, 32.

with the grief-stricken. Yet these feelings are known from movements of the body.[70] But also when images, like Niobe, are petrified in aniconic stoniness, when they are materials against materiality, they can survive as *istoria*. That is what Ingold understood in Niobe's plea in the plea: *dumque rogat, pro qua rogat.*

This is the difference between Niobe and Echo.[71] From her own tragedy, Echo offers no comfort, no glory. Echo has no perspective on the hills and the mountains. Echo merges entirely into nature. There is no fluid. There is no final irreducible silhouette on a mountainside, no stumbling block. No *teichoscopia*. See, her clothes are not yet consumed, but her bones are already as soft as wax. And her face has completely vanished beneath the moss. Echo fully and heroically undergoes *l'essentiel drame humain de la pierre d'achoppement mimétique* in the opposite of mimesis. She partially made possible Niobe's "perpetual grief, masochistic desire, self-awareness, providential fury, and glory."

The question must be confronted of why Echo was obliged to surrender herself to this form of petrification, even more pitiless than that of Niobe herself. The question arises what *skandalon*, what taboo Echo had to counter, that was so gigantic and so crushing that she could only avoid it by vanishing? The disaster known as Narcissus? The catastrophe of the origins of the image in a mirror?

---

70. Loh 2011, 393.
71. See Baert (2016a).

CHAPTER 9

Schelling's Niobe

MILDRED GALLAND-SZYMKOWIAK

In Schelling's writings on the philosophy of art between 1802 and 1807, Niobe appears not only as a figure from Greek mythology but also as a singular work of art. The latter was the group of *Niobe and Her Youngest Daughter,* and more broadly the Niobids, now in the Uffizi Museum in Florence (see fig. 8.2). By 1800, the *Niobe* belonged to a select constellation of *essential individualities,* a small number of Hellenizing statues that were repeatedly taken up in aesthetics as paradigmatic of specific aspects of beauty and its theorization (the Laocoon group in the Pio-Clementino Museum, the Niobe and the Niobids in the Uffizi, the Apollo in the Belvedere, the Medici Venus, the Juno Ludovisi, etc.). Each of these names referred not only to an individual creation, but also to an artistic-theoretical complex and thus to an interweaving of thing and theories. Winckelmann's *History of the Art of Antiquity* (1764) played a major role in the development of such constructions; in addition to his remarks on the *Apollo* and the *Laocoon,* he gave a description of and commentary on the *Niobe,* to which I will return.

The aim of this chapter is to unravel the different layers of symbolization at work in Schelling's Niobe. As a result of this hermeneutic inquiry, the figure of Niobe will be that in which nature and art, the plastic arts and poetry, activity and passivity, the sensible and absolute reason are interarticulated in an original way.

Abbreviations: SW = Schelling 1856–61; AA = Schelling 1976–; PhK = Schelling, *Philosophie der Kunst* (SW V; AA II, 6,1); *Phil. Art* = Schelling 1989.

1. *PHILOSOPHY OF ART* (1802–5): NIOBE AS A SYMBOL OF NATURE, SCULPTURE, AND ART

Absolute Identity as an Infinite Productivity

In his "philosophy of identity," Schelling sought between 1801 and 1807 to understand the totality of beings in a systematic way based on the principle of the absolute identity of subject and object. In this identity subject and object, infinite and finite, ideal and real are not brought together: they are in the identity as the two aspects of its self-affirmation. The absolute is self-affirming insofar as its idea is immediately also its being. Schelling posits as a consequence that "the absolute is by nature an eternal act of producing. This producing is its essence."[1] The fact that the essence of the absolute is conceived as absolute productivity, and moreover the Schellingian thesis that the absolute does not go out of itself,[2] require us to think of its products not as dead effects of the productivity, but as the becoming-visible of the dynamics of their production. This perspective makes it possible to think a continuity between, on the one hand, Schelling's *Naturphilosophie*, insofar as the thought of *natura naturans* is primordial in it, and on the other, his philosophy of art, structured by the double movement of *Einbildung* of the absolute: autonomization of the image/product, as well as presence of the absolute in its image.

However, in *art*, the absolute affirmation of the One is no longer merely unconscious, but appears through the conscious (and unconscious) activity of genius. Artistic creation, *poiesis* in its most general sense, makes the dynamics of the absolute visible in objects: "Art is the direct reflection of the absolute act of production or of the absolute self-affirmation."[3] It is then as an archetypal representation of generation, of an infinite productivity inseparably natural *and* human, that the figure of Niobe will become an image of the absolute in art: as an image of maternity, even of hypermaternity.[4]

Niobe, Symbol of Nature

For Schelling, "the Niobe of the plastic arts who solidifies (*erstarrt*) with her children" is the "image" of nature.[5] The signification of this solidification or

---

1. Schelling, *PhK*, SW V, 482; AA II, 6,1, p. 206; *Phil. Art*, 99–100.
2. Schelling, *Darstellung meines Systems der Philosophie*, SW IV, 120.
3. *PhK*, SW V, 631; AA II, 6,1, 322; *Phil. Art*, 202.
4. See Cavarero's chapter in this volume.
5. *PhK*, SW V, 631; AA II, 6,1, 321; *Phil. Art*, 202.

"freezing" resonates at three distinct levels of understanding: (a) the *myth,* in which the freezing is the disappearance of life, in the death of the children and the petrifaction of Niobe; (b) the presentation in *plastic form,* the instantaneous and mute summary of the mythic narrative, of the passage from life to death; (c) the statue in its *materiality,* the cold, hard, yet animated marble. And yet, something unites these three levels in our experience of the artwork: the fact that each one shows us both life and death, the productive principle *with* its products—products that are simultaneously linked to the principle (the mother) and separated from it (death).

However, nature does not show us absolute productivity as such: this one "veils itself in an other, a being."[6] Nature includes the two opposite aspects of *natura naturans* as infinite productivity and of its immobilization in products, *natura naturata.* If one agrees to see in Niobe, "hyper-mother," the productive principle, then the group of Niobids gives intuitive access to the duality of nature, which is theorized in the *Naturphilosophie.* Niobe "frozen with her children" is shown in her fecundity *and* in the immobilization of this fecundity, thus symbolizing the natural productivity stopped in its products. The strength of this symbol lies in the fact that it shows the moment of *passage* from one to the other of these opposite determinations. What is meant here by "symbol"? The Niobids do not *refer to* nature; rather, the *articulation of productivity and stopping* that essentially characterizes nature is at the same time a defining feature of the mythical scene. This articulation is, moreover, presented just as much by specifically artistic means in the sculptures: the moving draperies, the gestures and positions, the expressions of the faces, all converge to produce a vivid sense of the passage from expanding life to mortal contraction. This condensed signification present at different levels of reality—in the forms of the statuary group given to our sensibility and feeling, in the narrative imagination and memory constructing the mythical scene, in the philosophical rationality understanding the identity of opposite dimensions—is precisely what Schelling calls a symbol, *Sinn-Bild,*[7] the sense-image where sense completely saturates the sensible.

Niobe, Symbol of the Plastic Arts

The group of Niobids symbolizes nature as duality of *natura naturans* and *naturata naturata*: the vital principle, the productive activity, united to its

---

6. *PhK,* SW V, 631; AA II, 6,1, 321; *Phil. Art,* 202.

7. See *PhK,* SW V, 411–12; AA II, 6,1, 149; *Phil. Art,* 49. On symbol in Schelling's philosophy, see Whistler (2013).

products by maternity and separated from them by death—but also already by birth. The slaughter committed by the children of Latona only accomplishes the inevitable destiny of any natural *product,* detached as such from the universal life, and doomed indissociably to generation *and* corruption—maternity being then the announcement of death.

At a second level, the statue of Niobe, symbol of living Niobe becoming stone, also symbolizes the crystallization of the universal *poiesis* in material things. In the plastic arts (music, painting, architecture, sculpture), as in nature, the infinite productivity is presented in a material that, at the same time as it manifests it, remains opposed to it. These arts give images of the absolute productivity in "corporeal objects,"[8] whereas the arts of the word (epic poetry, lyric, dramatic) put it in image in an ideal materiality, the language, more "transparent"[9] to the self-affirmation of the absolute.

The petrifaction characteristic of the art of the sculpture but also of the destiny of Niobe symbolizes more largely the coagulation of the divine Word in the plastic or formative arts:

> the formative arts are only the dead Word, and yet nonetheless Word, the act of speaking; the more completely this speaking dies—up to the sound petrified on the lips of Niobe—the more sublime is formative art in its own fashion. In contrast, on the lower level, in music, that living element that has passed over into death—the Word *spoken* into the finite—is still perceptible only as sonority.[10]

Niobe thus embodies not only the principle of the formative arts in general, but also the *telos* of their dynamic system, the perfect realization that directs their philosophical setting in order. In other words: the more a plastic art makes visible the infinite affirmation *as frozen,* the more it approaches the *Niobe,* and the more it will be perfect as plastic.

This freezing (*Erstarrung*) however is not a death. Niobe in the myth is not dead, but petrified, and the statue in the Uffizi shows her in the very moment of becoming stone. Ovid, on whom Schelling certainly relies, emphasizes that petrified, "yet she weeps (*flet tamen*)."[11] This makes Niobe a dead woman who remains alive: a living woman who has died to the world because of the loss of her children, or, as well, a dead woman who carries with her the ever-living pain, the endless weeping.

---

8. See *PhK*, §72, SW V, 481; AA II, 6,1, 206; *Phil. Art,* 99.
9. *PhK,* SW V, 484; AA II, 6,1, 208; *Phil. Art,* 101.
10. *PhK,* SW V, 484; AA II, 6,1, 208; *Phil. Art,* 101 (translation modified).
11. Ovid, *Metamorphoses* 6.301–3, 310.

In that it is the image of the plastic arts, which are "the dead Word, and yet nonetheless Word":[12] not as the material extinction of the infinite productivity, but as the very *tension* of its *materializing* (in melody, drawing and combination of colors, setting in form of the stone). The principle of the systematic succession of formative arts consists then in the more and more perfect conciliation of the infinite affirmation and its freezing in individual condensations.

At a first level, *music* presents, in the succession of sounds, the condensation of the absolute productivity like an event, therefore in a transient way; the resonance fades, without being frozen. Music is "the art form that divests itself to the highest degree of corporeality by portraying pure movement as such, separated from the object."[13] In *painting*, the condensation goes up to the contour and the figure,[14] as individual beings take shape, with their space. However, their form appears only through the play of the light and the shade in the color: the painting can only "describe space without filling it."[15] But *sculpture* creates its own space, because its symbolizing material is stone or wood in the shape of a human body—the living organism, seat of the reason, capable of thinking the absolute, and as such doubling the biological life in a rational one. To this extent, the human body bears its own symbolism, which Schelling explains in detail.[16] Now in the sculpture, the idealized human form gains an additional symbolic dimension by becoming the form of a god.[17]

For Schelling, sculpture is the symbolic art par excellence, insofar as there is a perfect resonance, an in-forming repetition (*Ein-bildung*) between its different aspects: the human organism as the seat of the life of the spirit, the idea of a god or goddess as a particularization of the "divine" life, and finally, the concrete statue in its forms, its proportions, and its expressiveness, as holding the equilibrium or the *indifference* between particular form and living ideality. This indifference defines its beauty.

Niobe, Symbol of the Sculpture

Niobe as myth and as sculpture symbolizes the *telos* of the plastic arts. It means, on the one hand, that its *passage* from infinite life (hypermaternity)

---

12. *PhK*, SW V, 484; AA II, 6,1, 208; *Phil. Art*, 101 (translation modified).
13. *PhK*, SW V, 502; AA II, 6,1, 221; *Phil. Art*, 116.
14. See *PhK*, SW V, 518; AA II, 6,1, 234; *Phil. Art*, 127.
15. *PhK*, SW V, 507; AA II, 6,1, 225; *Phil. Art*, 119.
16. See *PhK*, SW V, 604–9; AA II, 6,1, 300–304; *Phil. Art*, 184–87.
17. *PhK*, SW V, 621–22; AA II, 6,1, 314; *Phil. Art*, 195.

to petrifaction shows the general direction of the rational classification of the arts (from pure mobility to determinate individuality). On the other hand, it means that the *being*-petrified of Niobe realizes the essence of sculpture—namely, to make the living appear *as* dead, the infinite productivity *as* objectivity, without eliminating either of them. Sculpture "portrays the highest contact between life and death,"[18] "life and death encounter one another there, so to speak, at the highest point of their confluence";[19] because, according to the lessons given in Jena,

> the finite and the infinite, the form, which is death in itself, and the essence, which is the infinite life principle, come together in sculpture in the highest indifference.[20]

The myth of Niobe, the "absolute mother" petrifacted, presents us with this point of contact: not death replacing life and suppressing it, but life as death, frozen life. And the statue of Niobe in the Uffizi symbolizes this myth by realizing the petrifaction in an existing thing. This statue thus becomes the archetypal image of sculpture.[21] The *Niobe* is a sculpture that gives the intuition of the essence of all sculpture.

Niobe's Calm: From Winckelmann to Schelling

The face of the Uffizi *Niobe* presents us with a very particular calm: it is a kind of deactivation of the expressiveness itself, a strange calm, almost inexpressive. Schelling's understanding of this "calm" is part of his reelaboration of Winckelmann's views on ancient Greek sculpture. There is nothing new in noticing that Schelling extensively and explicitly relies on the writings of Winckelmann, whom he describes as "the father of all science of art, whose views are still the ultimate and will always remain so."[22] Now, as far as the expression of emotions and passions in sculpture is concerned, Winckelmann had insisted on the *psychological-artistic* necessity of limiting the deformation of facial (or more broadly expressive) features, thus to show a state of calm, without too strong intensity of either passion or action, in order to preserve

---

18. *PhK*, SW V, 618; AA II, 6,1, 312; *Phil. Art*, 193.
19. *PhK*, SW V, 618; AA II, 6,1, 312; *Phil. Art*, 193.
20. *Schelling's Vorlesungen über die Ästhetick. Jena, im Winter 1802. Nachschrift Schlosser*, AA II, 6,2, 461.
21. *PhK*, SW V, 625; AA II, 6,1, 317; *Phil. Art*, 197.
22. *PhK*, SW V, 557; AA II, 6,1, 264; *Phil. Art*, 153.

beauty.[23] Schelling takes up the idea that a beautiful expressiveness should remain controlled and not distort the features.[24] But his concern is *artistic-metaphysical*: to understand how this calmness can take on, in the work of art, not the sense of an absence of life but that of a mode of the absolute identity of passivity and activity, of being and acting.

In this context, three statues already privileged by Winckelmann play, with no surprise, a paradigmatic role in Schelling's reflections: the *Apollo* of Belvedere, the group of *Laocoon,* and the Florentine *Niobe*. Winckelmann, considering the *Apollo* as the supreme model,[25] had noticed that the contempt visible in the lip, the anger in the nostrils, remain subordinated to the unshakeable peace that can be read on the forehead. The *Apollo* becomes for Schelling the image of an absolute activity, which does not need to oppose the passions, because it masters them. The *Laocoon*, which Winckelmann had analyzed as the image of "the greatest suffering and pain,"[26] is for Schelling the figure where, even in the greatest passivity of pain, "we see the soul triumph and arise as a divine light of incorruptible serenity above the figure":[27] here activity pierces passivity, the ideal through the real. Calm is shown as won *through* pain and in spite of it.

The *Niobe* also shows a form of serenity that does not descend from the ideal but rises from the real. However, this "calm" does not emerge through the passions. Let us take a closer look at how Schelling rewrites Winckelmann's text. The latter, having characterized Niobe as "an image of the fear of death,"[28] writes:

> The daughters of Niobe, against whom Diana directed her deadly arrows, are represented in this indescribable fear, when feeling is numbed and stifled (*mit übertäubter und erstarrter Empfindung*) and the presence of death takes from the mind all capacity to think. The fable provides an image of this lifeless fear by the metamorphosis of Niobe into stone.... Such a state, in which feeling and thought cease, and which is akin to indifference (*Gleichgültigkeit*), changes no aspect of shape and appearance, and the great artist could fashion here, as he did, the very highest beauty—for Niobe and her daughters are and remain the most exalted ideas of it.[29]

---

23. Winckelmann 2006, 204.
24. Cf. *PhK*, SW V, 559; AA II, 6,1, 26; *Phil. Art,* 154.
25. Winckelmann 2006, 333.
26. Winckelmann 2006, 206.
27. *PhK*, SW V, 557; AA II, 6,1, 264; *Phil. Art,* 153.
28. Winckelmann 2006, 206.
29. Winckelmann 2006, 206.

Schelling rewrites the text as follows:

> A similar image is that of Niobe with her daughters. The latter, at whom Diana aims her deadly arrows, are depicted in indescribable fear with numbed feeling (*mit übertäubter Empfindung*), where numbness/freezing/petrifaction (*Erstarrung*) itself brings back the calm (*Ruhe*) and that high indifference (*Gleichgültigkeit*) that agrees best with beauty and does not change any features of the figure or form.[30]

Winckelmann's analysis is referring to a psychological state, in order to make plausible Niobe's strange expression of inexpressive calm. An inner state of intense anguish produces an interruption of feeling and thinking, thus a facial expression that no longer expresses anything. The mythical transformation of Niobe into stone makes real the psychological metaphor that designates this anesthetization as "becoming petrified." By what seems to be an expression of indifference, but which is rather that of the paroxysm of terror, the beauty of the Florentine Niobe appears "like an idea conceived without the help of the senses."[31] What Winckelmann theorizes here is thus a *coincidence* between the anesthetic effect of the violent anguish and Niobe's beauty seeming uncreated, eternal, beyond the passions; he does not seek to elaborate an internal, immanent relation between the two.

Schelling's rewriting of this passage drops the concern for verisimilitude and the psycho-poetic justification of petrifaction. Instead, he introduces the idea of the aftereffect of petrifaction, producing calm, thus beauty: *Erstarrung* (meaning "numbness" *and* "solidification") "itself brings back the calm." The polysemy of the term *Erstarrung* leads us to understand this idea on two levels. (a) In the myth, Niobe's becoming stone allows her to go out of pain. Ovid presented in this sense the petrifaction as desirable to escape from inordinate suffering.[32] (b) In the statue, the *Erstarrung* is that produced by the art of the sculptor. It is then the becoming-art of the myth that brings back the calm. The statuary art in the singular features of the face and gestures of the *Niobe* shows by its own means a passivity that is no longer defined as the opposite of activity. The strange inexpressiveness of the Florentine *Niobe* is not to be understood as *resembling* a psychological indifference but as *manifesting* the metaphysical indifferentiation between the passive and the active.

---

30. *PhK*, SW V, 558; AA II, 6,1, 265; *Phil. Art*, 153 (translation modified).
31. Winckelmann 2006, 233.
32. See Ovid, *Letters from the Black Sea* 1.2.34.

Art Commenting on Itself: Niobe, Symbol of Artistic Symbolism

How does this reversal of affect into beauty take place? Schelling specifies it just after identifying the *Niobe* with "the archetype (*Urbild*) of sculpture," in a decisive passage:

> All life is based on the joining of something infinite in itself with something finite, and life as such appears only in the opposition (*Entgegensetzung*) of these two. Wherever their highest or absolute unity is, we also find, viewed relatively, death, and yet for just that reason also the highest degree of life. Since it is indeed the work of sculpture to present that highest unity, then the absolute life of which it shows the images already appears in and for itself—also compared with the appearance itself—as death. In the *Niobe*, however, art itself has uttered this mystery by presenting the highest beauty in death. Furthermore, it allows *that* calm (*Ruhe*)—the one inhering only within the divine nature itself and completely unattainable to *mortals*—to be gained in death itself, as if to suggest that the transition to the highest life of beauty, at least as far as that which is mortal is concerned, must appear as death. Art is thus doubly symbolic here: it becomes additionally the interpreter (*Auslegerin*) of itself such that that which all art seeks stands before our very eyes here, expressed in the *Niobe*.[33]

For Schelling, mortals feel life only in the opposition between an infinite (an activity) and a finite (a passivity). For a finite being, caught in the empirical network of relations and oppositions which define reality for him or her, the suspension of these oppositions would mean a passage to nothing, or a death. But from the philosophical point of view, this suspension has the signification of the original identity of opposites, the One and All, the very source of all life. By presenting to us in its features the calm *in* the anguish, the *Niobe* gives us access to this absolute identity. This is the first degree of artistic symbolism. But in what sense is there a "double" symbolism?

The suspension of the oppositions, the realization of their unity in a finite sculpture, can be carried out in two ways.[34] On the one hand, as a perfect fusion of matter and idea, as in the case of the Vatican *Apollo*. It is the "divine nature" (see the passage above), the coincidence of the human form and the divine, perfectly reversible one into the other in their pure identity. On the other hand, this unity can be reached through the sacrifice of finitude: in the

---

33. *PhK*, SW V, 625; AA II, 6,1, 317; *Phil. Art*, 197–98 (translation modified).
34. As noticed in Cirulli (2015, 129) and Unger (2018, 168).

Niobe, natural life (infinite fecundity) is shown as nonliving in relation to a higher life—a life that is however at the same time *given to the spectator* in the beauty of the statue. This statue not only offers us, like the *Apollo,* a view of absolute identity; it also gives us the view of this view from the phenomenal world, that of mortal existence. The *Niobe* symbolizes not only the metaphysical content that is common to the artistic setting in form and to philosophical thought; she simultaneously shows the mode of access properly artistic to this content. Art makes us see the absolute indifference in a sensible thing, but through the death of the sensible as sensible: "the highest beauty, in death," in a negation of the finite, mortal existence, a negation that the figures of the gods, immediately infinite, cannot present. As such, the *Niobe* suggests that art realizes the exhibition of the absolute in the sensible only by negating at the same time the sensible as such.

The thesis of the double symbolism of art in the *Niobe* is also the confirmation of the Schellingian conception of aesthetics as a *philosophy* of art, whose object cannot be the sensible as such, but only the absolutized sensible.

2. CONCERNING THE RELATION OF THE PLASTIC ARTS TO NATURE (1807): NIOBE, SYMBOL OF THE BOUND

In 1807 Schelling, deviating from Winckelmann, reinterprets Niobe's calm as a manifestation of grace, a grace that is not mawkish but powerful. I would like to show here that in this new context, the statue of *Niobe and Her Youngest Daughter* gives intuitive access to the essence of the now redefined absolute.

Art Makes Visible the Productive and Organizing Force of Nature

In Schelling's discourse *Concerning the Relation of the Plastic Arts to Nature,* nature has, above all, the sense of "the world's holy, eternally creating primal force,"[35] which produces all that is. This force is not irrational; it harbors a creative and unconscious knowledge, a "living concept"[36] that drives an "in-formation," a shaping of the primal force in a form by closing in on itself. The first stage of this natural in-formation is the petrifaction (*Versteinerung*);[37] it is followed in the scale of beings by the more and more determinate individuation of the original productivity in plants, animals, and human beings.

---

35. Schelling, *Über das Verhältnis der bildenden Künste zur Natur* (1807), SW VII, 291–329 [= *Akademierede*], 293; Schelling 1968 [= *Relation*], 325 (translation modified).
36. *Akademierede*, SW VII, 301; *Relation,* 331 (translation modified).
37. *Akademierede*, SW VII, 304; *Relation,* 335.

In the artist's activity, this living but blind concept becomes consciously productive. The function of art in general is to seize this "spirit" present in nature and to make it visible.[38] This means that, in the work of art, the form appears admittedly as a negation of the original force, but also as its concentration, its re-formation in an individual whole.[39] The determination of the form is thus not so much a limitation as an affirmation of the absolute.

Niobe's Sublime Beauty—"High Style"

Nature progresses from closed inorganic forms to the absolute organicity of the human body. In the same way, we can distinguish three modes of presentation of the absolute in sculpture,[40] which are also three historical stylistic stages: (a) the severe style, marked by the hardness of the sensible forms: the spirit asserts itself in its separation, and the form reflects this separation; (b) the beautiful style, high style, "the sublime beauty in which fullness of form does away with form itself";[41] (c) the graceful style, in which the contours are entirely softened, with an almost sensual charm (the *Venus* of Praxiteles). Grace appears as a spirituality of the natural as such, the whole figure is imbued with it.[42]

However, there is also, as Winckelmann observed, a *nonsensible grace* belonging to the high style, and pertaining to the sublime and not to the sensual. It is that of the Florentine *Niobe*,[43] whose beauty is powerful, thus neither pleasant nor seductive. Everything happens here as if the spirit of nature had broken its natural ties,[44] suddenly going out to a beauty that is one with goodness, with the "soul."

Beauty in Death: Niobe's Grace

Schelling first rephrases the analysis he had given in his lectures. In the *Niobe*, anguish turns into superior calm; the finite negated in its finitude[45] becomes visible revelation of absolute indifference in the sensible, thus beauty. *Grace*,

---

38. *Akademierede,* SW VII, 301; *Relation,* 330.
39. *Akademierede,* SW VII, 304; *Relation,* 334.
40. See *Akademierede,* SW VII, 310–14; *Relation,* 337–42.
41. *Akademierede,* SW VII, 305–6; *Relation,* 336–37.
42. *Akademierede,* SW VII, 311; *Relation,* 342.
43. *PhK,* SW V, 613; AA II, 6,1, 307; *Phil. Art,* 189–90.
44. Cf. *Akademierede,* SW VII, 311; *Relation,* 342.
45. See *Akademierede,* SW VII, 302; *Relation,* 332–33.

however, is now designated as that which transforms "pain, benumbedness (*Erstarrung*) and even death itself into beauty."[46] The sensible forms, outlines, and proportions, as well as the movements and expression of the face of the Florentine *Niobe*, "soften" the expression of horror

> by the fact that pain, passing beyond all expression, annuls itself again, and beauty, which seemed impossible to save alive, is preserved from violation by the nascent petrifaction (*durch die eintretende Erstarrung*).[47]

The term "grace" names then, and this is new, the articulation between petrifaction and beauty, as a result of artistic creation. The grace is what has been created by the sculptor, the aesthetic property not deducible a priori[48] and which is offered to the intuition of the spectator; it is the sensible mediation through determined plastic contours between the climax anguish and its reversal in ideality.

The Soul in Niobe: Maternal Love

In a second step, Schelling, in order to explain the particular grace and calm of Niobe, invokes the concept of the *soul*. This allows a new interpretation of Niobe's calmness.

While in Schelling's *Aphorisms on the Philosophy of Nature* (1806) the "soul" of each thing was defined as that which relates it to the One and All, or that which "dissolves it into eternal existence,"[49] in the 1807 Discourse Schelling focuses instead on the self-affirmation of the absolute as/in the *human* soul. All creatures are moved by the "spirit of nature," but in the human being the soul is the principle of knowledge and *poiesis*. The soul is not a faculty, but the active, productive presence of absolute unity;[50] it is therefore also that which raises the human being above egoism, above concerns for the self.[51]

Schelling describes the presence of the "soul" in the grace of the Uffizi Niobe as follows:

---

46. *Akademierede*, SW VII, 314; *Relation*, 345.
47. *Akademierede*, SW VII, 314; *Relation*, 346.
48. "In this domain, what was not apprehended in the idea appears incarnate before the eyes" (*Akademierede*, SW VII, 292; *Relation*, 324).
49. *Aphorismen über die Naturphilosophie*, no. LXXXI, SW VII, 215; AA I, 15, 231.
50. See *Akademierede*, SW VII, 311–12; *Relation*, 343.
51. *Akademierede*, SW VII, 312; *Relation*, 343.

In the mother's countenance we see not only grief for those of her children who already lie like broken blossoms, nor only terror for the salvation of those that remain and of the youngest daughter, who is seeking refuge at her bosom, and not indignation against cruel deities, least of all cold defiance, as has been alleged; we see all this, but not by itself, for through grief, fear, and indignation there radiates, like a divine light, everlasting love—the only abiding thing—and in this love the mother proves to be a mother who was not, but is (*die es [= Mutter] nicht war, die es ist*), who remains bound to the beloved by an eternal bond.[52]

Schelling's perspective has shifted. The annihilation of the feelings that seems to take place in the grieving Niobe is no longer their suppression; it no longer corresponds to a going out of the domain of the affective. It is rather understood as their reabsorption into their common basis, in the matter from which they all draw their existence and their meaning and direction, and in which their particularities are erased—namely, maternal love.

Yet Schelling has a concept to designate this totalization of particularities that, without canceling themselves, are indifferentiated in a common being: the concept of *chaos*.[53] In the lectures on the philosophy of art, the philosopher named "chaos" the fusion of all the colors in the pictorial representation of the flesh.[54] He also characterizes language as a chaos, meaning not a disorder or an indistinct mixture, but "the material (*Stoff*) of all tones and sonorities reduced to indifference";[55] or, to quote a phrase of Jean-François Marquet, "the *neutral* medium where the various forms exchange, abolish and consume each other."[56]

In the complex neutrality of Niobe's face, the spectator experiences the feelings as chaos, that is to say, through the fundamental activity of which they are only particularizations: the maternal love, which shows itself as anguish for the life of her children as well as mourning and defiant refusal of their loss. It is no longer the intensity of the affects that allows their reversion into indifference, but rather their multiplicity, which the sculptor's work causes to appear through their common substance, love—grasped not as tenderness or sorrow, but as ecstatic concern for the other (or the soul), "eternal love" and "eternal bond." At the death of her children Niobe does not in any way cease

---

52. *Akademierede*, SW VII, 314; *Relation*, 346 (translation modified, but emphasis original).
53. See Galland-Szymkowiak (2019).
54. *PhK*, SW V, 540; AA II, 6,1, 251; *Phil. Art*, 141–42.
55. *PhK*, SW V, 635; AA II, 6,1, 325; *Phil. Art*, 204.
56. Marquet 1973, 261; emphasis original.

to be a mother: she becomes an eternal mother, an eternal ecstatic position of self in other individuals.

Niobe, Symbol of the Absolute as Bond

Now love, or the Bond, is precisely the definition of the absolute that Schelling's metaphysics arrived at in 1805/6. What changed between 1802/3 and 1807 was the shift in Schellingian metaphysics from a conception of the absolute as absolute identity and as self-affirmation to the redefinition of this absolute identity as the Bond.

The absolute identity, the Bond between the finite and the infinite, is unconditioned, absolute, only if it is nothing *other* than the binding of what it binds, i.e., if it does not face the elements that it binds but is itself identical to their binding. Schelling expresses this idea in the circular characterization of the Bond as "the Bond of oneself and the bound."[57] This is to emphasize that the absolute is not simply the unity of opposites (the finite and the infinite), but the identity of the infinite that is finitized and of the finite that is infinitized. To redefine absolute identity as the Bond is therefore to focus on the *internal* link between the infinite and the finite, and to develop a conception of the finite as originally essential to the self-affirmation of absolute identity. It is at this price, Schelling insists, that we will be able to understand absolute identity in its *actuality*: "*this Bond* is the only effective and completely real absolute identity."[58]

To understand absolute identity as the Bond means to emphasize the coincidence of the absolute with its *self-revelation*, i.e., the fact that in its unity it always poses itself simultaneously as multiple, knowing itself as the One precisely through this multiplicity. This double movement is also elucidated by Schelling as *infinite self-love*.[59] This love is not a sterile self-contemplation, but the generation of an infinite number of individual beings that not only repeat the unity of the absolute but are *indispensable to its reality* (*Existenz* is thus another name for the Bond itself).

In my view, the expressions "eternal love" and "eternal bond" in the description of Niobe in 1807 must be understood in direct connection with this conception of the absolute as the Bond developed in 1806. Schelling rein-

---

57. Here I draw on Galland-Szymkowiak (2011, 269–73).

58. Schelling, *Darlegung des wahren Verhältnisses der Naturphilosophie zu der verbesserten Fichteschen Lehre*, 1806, SW VII, 60; AA I, 16,1, 107 (emphasis original).

59. Schelling, *Über das Verhältnis des Realen und Idealen in der Natur* (1806), SW II, 362; AA I, 16,1, 183.

terprets the strange calm of Niobe as a figuration of (sublime) maternal love and suggests that it gives us an intuitive insight into the essence of the absolute as the Bond. Niobe is, on the one hand, the proud woman who loves herself in her children—as the absolute binds to itself through its own products. The children, however, are also autonomous creatures, which is (painfully) evidenced in their death; the absoluteness of natural products is likewise achieved in the negation of their finite lives: the bound outside the Bond is nothing. And finally Niobe loses the movement of life at the death of her children: in the same way, if the bound disappeared, the Bond, as the Bond of oneself and of the bound, would be deprived of all actual life.

Thus the meaning given by Schelling to Niobe *is not tragic*. Niobe's calmness, her strange inexpressiveness, is now interpreted not as anesthesia, or as a deactivation of the feelings, but rather as their immanent transfiguration through the maternal love that makes their unity, thus symbolizing the essence of the Bond. Beyond its significance for the philosophy of art, the Uffizi Niobe bending over her daughter presents us with the eternal movement of being, or ex-sistence.

•

Niobe is a powerful and central symbol in Schelling's philosophy. Interpreting Niobe opens up several fundamental theses of his philosophy of art: the continuity between *Naturphilosophie* and the philosophy of art, the reworking of the Winckelmannian theory, the primacy of sculpture in the plastic arts, the symbolic intuition of the dynamics of the absolute in individual artworks. What interests Schelling in Niobe is not the punishment of arrogance, it is not infinite sadness, nor even a tragic fate. What is ultimately central in his eyes is the properly artistic sublimation, in the *Niobe and Her Youngest Daughter* of the Uffizi, of mortal motherhood into a symbol of the absolute Bond.

CHAPTER 10

The More Loving One
On Postmelancholic Life

PAUL A. KOTTMAN

1.

Pandas crave bamboo, pigs wallow in the mud, children seek ice cream as they seek parental love. All creatures are moved by objects of satisfaction. The connection between need and satisfaction is unavoidable. This is—Kant would say—a synthetic a priori truth: it is discovered through experience alone and yet it also appears to be the transcendental principle for any empirical psychology whatsoever. Freud simply called this "the pleasure principle."

But as Gregg Horowitz (2001) points out, in the *Critique of Judgment* Kant asks a haunting question: How can anything other than the satisfaction of interest (need, desire, appetite, craving) give rise to pleasure or satisfaction? When Kant thinks about the pleasure principle (without ever having read Freud, of course) he concludes that the link between need and pleasure is interrupted only by "taste in the Beautiful" which "alone is a disinterested and *free* satisfaction; for no interest, either of Sense or of Reason, here forces our assent."[1] If *anything* can give rise to pleasure or satisfaction—other than the

---

This chapter stems from my contribution to an October 2022 Festschrift event for my friend, Gregg Horowitz. Section 1 of this paper reworks, paraphrases, and makes occasional verbatim use of, pages 30–37 of Horowitz (2001). Rather than disrupt the reader's attention by frequent quotation marks, I begin with this blanket acknowledgment of my use of Gregg's words in Section 1 below.

1. Kant 1987, § 5, 52.

satisfaction of interest (need, desire, appetite, craving)—then, offers Kant, it is taste in the Beautiful.

While the importance that Kant attaches to taste in the beautiful has had a long and well-known afterlife in aesthetic theory, the significance of Kant's haunting question for ethics or psychology remains less discussed.[2] More generally, insights from aesthetic theory remain isolated from ethical and psychological reflection; one aim of this chapter is to press against that. So, in addition to Kant, I will also turn to Hegel's notion of "love without desire," as well as his treatment of certain aesthetic-mythic figures—Abraham and Niobe (as Hegel contrasts Niobe to Mary), especially—to see whether these can be made available as theoretical-reflective material for ethics and psychology. I will not ask whether Hegel's interpretation of Niobe or Abraham is "correct." Instead, I want to reflect on these mythic figures less as static objects of interpretation than as self-conceptions in formation—which may offer a chance to talk about what melancholy affords, and whether it might at least point in the direction of postmelancholic life.

For creatures who are driven by an imperative for satisfaction—by a need that never doubts itself—being alive means being driven by something unquestionable. Again: pandas crave bamboo, children seek ice cream and love from parents. Whom I love looks touchable to me, and when I hunger food looks tasty. Kant, however, views natural necessity from the perspective of the autonomous ("civilized," "disciplined," "moral") subject. Natural necessity starts to feel like a compulsion only when it is antagonistic to some other (disciplining) force that might resist it. After all, natural pleasure hates reflection. Children do not want to think about whether they *should* want ice cream or their parents' love. But, eventually, morality—culture—requires that children learn to fear and even loathe their own nature. Through such fear and loathing, on this view, children become "subjects" and attain "autonomy" by foregoing the pleasures that it is in our nature to pursue.[3] Before augmenting this story, we can draw two conclusions from this cursory sketch.

---

2. Although philosophical treatments of Kant with Freud are not absent, recent discussions tend to focus on the connection between Kant's transcendental philosophy and Freud's metapsychology. Béatrice Longuenesse has redrawn our attention to the historical fact that, as she puts it in the summary of her 2022 Isaiah Berlin Lectures at Oxford University, "Freud is the direct heir of a nineteenth century school of naturalistic philosophy of mind which called itself 'physiological Kantianism.'" See also Longuenesse (2017, 204–25) and Deigh (1996, 113–32). Horowitz (2001) places Kant's aesthetic theory in direct conversation with Freudian psychology.

3. Pursuant to conversations with Mario Telò about Judith Butler's *The Psychic Life of Power*, I attach the following footnotes. Butler puts the point made here as follows: "A vexation of desire, one that proves crucial to subjection, implies that for the subject to persist, the subject must thwart its own desire. . . . A subject turned against itself (its desire) appears . . . to be a condition of the persistence of the subject" (J. Butler 1997, 9).

First, to feel alive, as undepressed creatures do, is—from the point of view of the autonomous subject—to follow a demand for satisfaction that (in Kant's words) "does not leave us the freedom to make an object of pleasure for ourselves out of something or other."[4] To be free and to feel alive (as an undepressed creature) are antinomies. To be naively (say, childishly) undepressed is—from the point of view of an autonomous subject, and thus *for* any autonomous subject—to be unfree, but also to be in the grip of a logical imperative for satisfaction that we feel when we feel alive, that we need *in order to feel alive*. To follow the pleasure principle is to be in the grip of natural needs, not freedom—so, the undepressed creature's feelings of aliveness come, so to speak, at the cost of autonomy.[5]

Second, because what comes into conflict in the autonomous subject are (1) feeling alive and (2) freedom, depression belongs to the transcendental genesis of the autonomous (culturally disciplined) subject. From this Kantian perspective, the autonomous-free subject just *is* an interruption in the animal connectedness of need and pleasure, where the moral law belligerently establishes its autonomy from nature.[6] Whom I love looks touchable to me and when I hunger food looks tasty. It is, again, *this* link between interest and pleasure that is severed in the autonomous-depressed subject, for whom estrangement from nature is formative. The depressed subject is not without needs or appetites (not without loves or hungers). But, because those needs are cut off from satisfaction, and perhaps even from the possibility of mourning the loss of that satisfaction, they offer no guidance in the world toward which they are inevitably turned.[7]

---

4. Kant 1987, §5, 52.

5. To put the point differently, borrowing again from Butler, "the effect of autonomy"— since it is "conditioned by [a] founding subordination or dependency [that is] is rigorously repressed," because "no subject, in the course of its formation, can afford fully to 'see'" its dependency and neediness for parental love—emerges only "in tandem with the unconscious" (J. Butler 1997, 7–8).

6. This identification of autonomous subjectivity with melancholy has become familiar to us via psychoanalysis. Indeed, a point Butler has famously (at least, for academic types) made about the "melancholic formation of gender" can be expanded to support this general conclusion: although side effects may vary, to be an autonomous subject or a cultivated person just *is* to be depressed. Freud's "account of melancholy is an account of how psychic and social domains are produced in relation to one another" (J. Butler 1997, 167).

7. This is also a point developed by Butler, who underlines Freud's distinction between the repression and the foreclosure of desire in subject-formation. Whereas Freud seems to suggest that a repressed desire might have once lived apart from its prohibition, a "foreclosed desire is rigorously barred, constituting the subject through a certain kind of preemptive loss." And, relevant to the discussion that will follow here, J. Butler (1997, 223) continues: "The foreclosure of certain forms of love suggests that the melancholia that grounds the subject . . . signals an incomplete and irresolvable grief."

Depressed people regard the world disinterestedly, as without interest or possible use. Depression is the inversion of the pleasure principle. Depression, as Horowitz puts it, is like being buried alive because one's purposes fail to conjure an interesting world. In Kantian terms, depression is discovered through experience alone yet it nonetheless appears to be the transcendental principle for any *non*empirical psychology whatsoever.

2.

However, the autonomous subject is not only the interruption of the animal connectedness of *need* and pleasure. The autonomous subject is also the interruption of *morality* (culture) and pleasure.[8] In other words, we should notice at this junction that the autonomous "disciplined" subject does not even *feel* free, does not *enjoy* autonomy—since, in her, not only need and pleasure, but also autonomy and her pleasure (the feeling of aliveness) have come apart.[9] After Freud, of course, it no longer comes as a surprise that culture demands the severance of need and pleasure; the insight itself may be losing whatever therapeutic effect it might have once had. Perhaps this is also because we can find ways, as Freud noted, to creatively wring sadomasochist enjoyment out of the severance of need and pleasure. Although, importantly, it is not clear that sadomasochistic enjoyment can be wrung from the severance of morality and pleasure. Indeed, depression teaches that even sadomasochism's "pleasures" can cease to be enjoyable. In which case, the possibilities for postmelancholic life cannot simply run through a restoration of the link between need and pleasure (which is not to say this link does not also need repair). For, we would still need to suture freedom and feeling, restore a *feeling* not only of natural appetite but also of freedom.

I will return to Kant's treatment of this issue. But let me now turn to what I think of as Hegel's variation on Kantian disinterested pleasure. By this, I mean

---

8. Eros may be at odds with culture, but if so then this is only because culture first interrupts the bond between eros and satisfaction. This interruption is what Freud called *Das Unbehagen in der Kultur*.

9. Recall, the importance of the moral law, for Kant, lies in its being impossible to discover its force in any natural appetite or desire. For Kant, "the moral law ... does provide a fact absolutely inexplicable from any data of the world of sense or from the whole compass of the theoretical use of reason, and this fact points to a pure intelligible world—indeed, it defines it positively and enables us to know something of it, namely a law" (Kant 1956, 44). When we act from recognition of what the moral law requires and for no other reason, we act freely. So, for Kant, the freedom of the moral law is predicated on its not being explicable, and on not being practically *experienced* to be explicable, as the satisfaction of appetite or desire.

what Hegel in his *Lectures on Fine Art* calls "love without desire" (*begierdelose Liebe*). For Hegel, "love without desire" characterizes parental love or what he sometimes calls religious love.[10] The kind of attention required by "love without desire" is also, for Hegel, the form of attention appropriate to beholding the art of painting.[11] As Hegel notes, no doubt with Kant's notion of disinterested pleasure in mind, when we look at a painting (as fine art) we do so non-appetitively, and yet devotedly. So, the very form of such beholding raises the question with respect to its ethical content: What calls for devotional beholding, for love without desire? Just as Kant's notion of disinterested pleasure has implications for ethics as well as for aesthetic theory, so too, I think, Hegel's notion of "passionless love" from his treatment of the art of painting bears transposition into ethics and psychology. So, let us see what happens if we reimagine the transcendental genesis of autonomous subjectivity and depression with Hegel, rather than only with Kant and Freud.

Like "disinterested pleasure," "love without desire" is enigmatic—although differently so. A lack of desire or appetite would seem not only to interrupt love, the experience of loving someone, but also to be—more strongly—an impediment to feeling love or, for that matter, an impediment to living. To be without desire, or libido, is a hallmark of depression, a condition that can be life-threatening. So, what could love without desire be?

To understand this, we need to consider how desire goes lacking in the first place. In other words, we should continue to bear in mind the formative severance of desire and satisfaction. Following Kant, we just saw how the imperative nature of morality blocks demanding-childish neediness; and we saw how the subject is the site at which morality belligerently establishes its autonomy from nature. What Judith Butler called "the psychic life of power" may also be a good name for this general account of (self-)subjection. Nevertheless, we should also now ask: Is such self-subjection "in" the autonomous subject really what interrupts the pleasure principle? And let us ask further—and with a bit more demand for detail—how else is the pleasure principle disrupted, and with what implications?

3.

Consider that social norms get established *as* obstacles most sharply, most unforgettably, when they stand between the promise of satisfaction that we

---

10. "Love without desire" (Hegel 1975a, 816).
11. See Kottman (2020, 41–66).

perceive in what, or whom, we love *and* those very same love objects in whose company we seek satisfaction. I want to suggest that autonomy from neediness is belligerently established not *in* the autonomous subject (as the site of conflict between morality and nature), nor by self-subjection to the moral law above us, but (1) between us and nature, *and* (2) in words and actions and fugitive experiences between subjects, intrasubjectively.

This view is crucial to the thrust of the young Hegel's response to Kantian morality. In his early writings, Hegel saw the crucible of autonomy and nature in what he simply called "love" and "life." In a posthumously published text, nowadays entitled "The Spirit of Christianity and Its Fate," Hegel considers the problem at hand: namely, the traumatic severing of natural neediness and satisfaction, or the disruption of the pleasure principle and its fallout in our ethical and psychological lives. By reading Hegel, I want now to augment the Kantian and "psychic life of power" account given thus far by considering two formative crucibles for ethics and psychology. First, there is the disruption of the pleasure principle, the interruption of the unavoidable connection between need and satisfaction in a creaturely lifeworld. Second, there is the withdrawal of love, or the interruption of need and satisfaction precisely where love between people could have been, may yet have been. Because both traumas unleash contagions that, like a plague, overflow individuals and enter the mainstream of ethical life, I will follow Hegel in calling them floods.[12] With this, then, let me now turn to Hegel's discussion of the mythic figures, especially, of Abraham and Niobe.

A Flood

Hegel begins with an interpretation of the biblical "flood in the time of Noah." Although nature furnishes the conditions of possibility for our survival, as well as of our pleasure and satisfaction—although we *need* nature, and although our own nature is needy—the flood in Noah's time showed that Nature, in her relation to us, "made none of the distinctions which love might have made but poured savage devastation over everything." This flood, in other words, not only marks an elemental disturbance of the pleasure principle's primacy; it is also the traumatic discovery that the natural world does not love us, does not need us as we need her. Our natural neediness makes us infinitely vulnerable

---

12. I hasten to emphasize: this is not to say that there are only, or can only be, two floods.

to natural elements that are capable of "general manslaughter."[13] Our relation to nature is an unrequited bond—and hence, can feel like a terrible betrayal.[14]

> The impression made on men's hearts by the flood in the time of Noah must have been a deep distraction and it must have caused the most prodigious disbelief in nature. Formerly friendly or tranquil, nature now abandoned the equipoise of her elements, now requited the faith the human race had in her with the most destructive, invincible, irresistible hostility.[15]

Hegel imagines three possible responses to this primordial trauma, each figured mythically. Each response amounts to the inauguration of radically different futures for what the young Hegel calls "the development of the human race"—for living human life.[16] It is the contrast between the first, on the one hand, and the second two responses, on the other hand, that is most decisive, and most worth recalling in this context.

Hegel sees the first response in the Greek myth of Deucalion and Pyrrha. After the flood, this "beautiful pair" invited human beings "once again to friendship with the world, to nature, made them forget their need and their hostility in joy and pleasure, made a peace of *love*."[17] Although Hegel regards this as "the more beautiful" and "reconciled" way of life, he does not offer much elaboration in this context as to how exactly this reconciliation was made.[18]

The second and third responses are figured by the biblical figures of Nimrod and Noah, respectively. Both Nimrod and Noah respond to the trauma of nature's hostility by trying to master nature. "Against the hostile power [of nature] Noah saved himself by subjecting both it and himself to something more powerful," writes Hegel, "Nimrod, by taming it himself." Nimrod, Hegel suggests, seeks mastery in practical activity (the construction of a material world capable of withstanding or resisting nature's hostility). By contrast, "it was in a thought-product that Noah built the distracted world together again . . . realities were reduced to thoughts, i.e., to something mastered."[19] "Both"

---

13. Hegel 1975b, 182.
14. See also Telò's chapter on this "unrequited bond."
15. Hegel 1975b, 182.
16. Hegel 1975b, 182.
17. Hegel 1975b, 184–85.
18. The myth itself involves the throwing of stones taken for the bones of mother earth.
19. Hegel 1975b, 183.

Nimrod and Noah, says Hegel, "made a peace of necessity with the foe and thus perpetuated the hostility."[20]

The decisive point, then—for which Hegel offers no explanation because he takes it to be generative of, though not responsive to, *why?* questions—is this: in response to the traumatic discovery of our unrequitable need for a potentially hostile nature, everything turns on the difference between a "peace of love" and what Hegel calls a "battle against need" (the "perpetuation of hostility through a necessary peace").[21] The latter path is searingly depicted by the young Hegel in his interpretation of Abraham:[22]

> Abraham . . . tore himself free altogether from his family in order to be a wholly self-subsistent, independent man, to be an overlord himself. . . . The same spirit which had carried Abraham away from his kin . . . led him through his encounters with foreign peoples during the rest of his life; this was the spirit of self-maintenance in strict opposition to everything. . . . He was a stranger on earth, a stranger to the soil and to men alike.[23]

What strikes Hegel is that Abraham's longed-for "autonomy" is forged through what Stanley Cavell will later call "the withholding or the theft of love."[24] In Hegel's memorable phrasing: "Abraham wanted *not* to love, wanted to be free by not loving . . . wanted to be free from . . . relationships."[25] This wish to be free by *not* loving—this willed withholding of love—characterizes, for Hegel, Abraham's response to the trauma of nature's hostility. The pursuit of mastery over nature, the "battle against need" in response to the initial trauma of the flood *just is* the withholding of love from others, which means this response composes (I think) a still-to-be-grasped prehistorical response to the flood, taken repercussively (by Hegel) as a transcendental wanting not to love—a

---

20. Hegel 1975b, 185.

21. By "everything," I mean—also—how this discovery is of something prehistorical, yet taken (by Noah and Nimrod, on Hegel's reading) as transcendental. More on this below.

22. Insofar as Hegel is critical of Abraham *and* identifies him as "progenitor of the Jews," an antisemitic attitude and prejudice is legible in Hegel's text. To block its furthering, I am trying to treat (against the letter of Hegel's text) "Hegel's Abraham" only as prefiguring a general, fateful, sharable human response to the trauma of nature's hostility—without identifying that response with the historical determination of the Jewish people or any other self-identifiable people or tribe. Moreover, as I will make clear in a moment, I locate the crux of the critique in the withholding of love, and not in self-subjection to monotheistic authority.

23. Hegel 1975b, 185–86.

24. For instance, Hegel notes the contrast between Abraham and "Cadmus, Danaus, etc., [who] had forsaken their fatherland too, but they forsook it in battle; they went in quest of a soil where they would be free and they sought it that they might love." See Cavell (2022, 32).

25. Hegel 1975b, 185.

wish, that is, to separate love from wanting, to sacrifice the former for the sake of the latter.[26] Again, note: Hegel sees both Abraham's "battle against need" and Deucalion and Pyrrha's "peace of love" as alternative responses to the traumatic perception of nature's hostility; responses which cannot, so to speak, simply be explained *by* something in human history insofar as such responses must also help us to explain something of why they themselves are so generative of "*why?* and *why not?*" questions *for* subsequent human histories, for later ethical and psychological formations. In the Kantian terms invoked earlier—these two alternative responses are discovered through experience alone, yet they nonetheless (for Hegel) appear as the transcendental principles (while, I am suggesting, nevertheless being prehistorical events) for any *non*empirical psychology whatsoever.

To help underscore the significance of this point for the present discussion, allow me to briefly contrast my understanding of the stakes here with the interpretation of the young Hegel offered by my colleague Jay Bernstein.[27] By following what I noted earlier as the "psychic life of power" viewpoint, Bernstein, I think, gets Hegel's point exactly backward. Bernstein claims that (for Hegel) it is Abraham's "self-subjugation to transcendent authority" [God, the moral law] which establishes

> an ethical geometry of horizontal and vertical, in which the horizontal and so immanent relations of love and life are displaced by a vertical relation to a projected externality. . . . Because there is no actual external authority but only the self-subjecting stance of taking oneself to be so subject, then the meaning of the vertical relation is realized through what the attempt to secure it does *to* the horizontal relations of love and life.[28]

Bernstein's reading seems to me to reinstall the awesome and destructive power of the ("projected") moral law in the very place where Hegel wants, on the contrary, to reveal its relative impotence—its status as symptom rather

---

26. Adding an important detail, Hegel is careful to insist that Abraham had not been harmed by his father or his family—rather, Abraham withdrew from them "without the grief which after a wrong or outrage signals love's enduring need, when love, injured indeed but not lost, goes in quest of a new fatherland in order to flourish and enjoy life there." That is, for Hegel, Abraham's withdrawal of love is not a symptom of deprived neediness—like adolescent rage, or righteous anger—but a primary and decisive "severance which snaps the bonds of communal life and love."
27. J. Bernstein 2003.
28. J. Bernstein 2003, 399.

than illness, so to speak.[29] Hegel is not here attributing to "self-subjugation-to-morality" the power to harm or ruin bonds of love. Hegel's point, I think, is opposite to this: for Hegel, the severance of the bonds of love summons a need for self-subjugation to morality, giving rise to the need for a relation to the world mediated through almighty God in the first place. The meaning of a "vertical" attachment to the moral law is not realized through destroyed horizontal bonds; rather, such "vertical" self-subjugation is one psychic and ethical fallout of withdrawn love.

So, I think we can more productively read Hegel as seeing the withdrawal of love as itself decisive for human fates, and hence as prompting us to further reflect on why (and how and when and where) love's withdrawal has been so destructive. One sign of its destructiveness can be seen in how the withdrawal of love, while prehistorical, appears (even to Hegel) to be repercussively transcendental. I want to start again, then, by seeing Abraham's relation to God as a way of living out Abraham's altered relation to nature, to *his own* nature, in the pursuit of mastery and autonomy. Which is to raise a question that Hegel exposes, but perhaps does not adequately pursue as prehistory. What in Abraham's (or, our) past induced this altered relation to nature?

4.

Abraham, Hegel observes, was depressed. As we have seen, depression belongs to the transcendental genesis of autonomy and self-mastery, and so it should not surprise us that Abraham's pursuit of autonomy brought on depression. But Hegel furnishes a crucial twist to our previous discussion. While the pursuit of autonomy and mastery are within Abraham's power, "love alone was beyond his power." *That* depressed him.[30] Abraham's wish to separate love from wanting, by sacrificing the former in the name of the latter, remained

---

29. One risk in Bernstein's reading, I think, can be seen in the way that he, elsewhere, extends this view (namely, that "self-subjection to transcendent authority" does harm "*to* horizontal relations of love and life") into the basis for a purported rational reconstruction of the binding of Isaac, in the stipulation that Abraham's faith was "world hatred, in human terms . . . the murder of Isaac." Seeing the withdrawal of love as the impetus to, and not the harm wrought by, self-subjection to God—as I am urging here—might allow room to understand "faith" as something other than world-hating murderousness. For instance, self-subjugation and faith might also come to be seen as symptoms of suffering in need of redescription and better understanding. See J. Bernstein (2017, 267 passim). See also J. Bernstein (2003, 404–6).

30. "Even the one love he had, his love for his son . . . could depress him, trouble his all-exclusive heart and disquiet it to such an extent that even this love he once wished to destroy; and his heart was quieted only through the certainty of the feeling that this love was not so strong as to render him unable to slay his beloved son with his own hand" (Hegel 1975, 187).

unsatisfied; frustrated and blocked by his love for his son. Abraham found himself unable to *un*love Isaac passionately; unable to love him passionlessly. So long as Isaac lived, so too, would desire continue to infect Abraham's love. Abraham's intent to sacrifice Isaac, then, marks what the mature Hegel calls an attempt to "love without desire." Note that, in direct contrast to (the mature Hegel's) Niobe and Mary, (the young Hegel's) Abraham attempts to separate love from desire by sacrificing the bonds of love to his own desire for autonomy. As if only resurgent and triumphant desire, to be consummated in the binding of Isaac, could anesthetize his depression.

Hegel is not here offering a phenomenology of Abraham's binding of Isaac. He is alerting us, with flashing red lights, to the depths to which depression can lead. That is, he is pointing to the lengths to which we might go in withholding the love we are powerless not to feel, in the attempt to separate love from desire. In Abraham's response to the flood, suggests Hegel, we see a possible human response to the traumatic perception that—no matter our neediness, no matter our dependence on nature's gifts—nature does not love us, does not make "the distinctions which love might have made but poured savage devastation over everything."

In watching Abraham and Isaac, in other words, we observe: if the distinctions love *does* make (those particular loves we cannot help but feel) do not appear nature-made to satisfy our needs, then the distinctions love draws can nevertheless point us to where we might pour our *own* savage devastation.

5.

So, the withdrawal of love unleashes another flood. Just as the flood in the time of Noah taught us that nature does not love us back, does not need us as we need her—so, too, those we love, and whose love we seek, often appear unable to love us back as we wish. I have in mind situations in which love for another is felt to be not so much unrequited as unrequitable. Various "flood" situations are picturable here, beyond Noah, Abraham, and Isaac. There are also the kinds of situations that Freud mentions in "Mourning and Melancholia," when he notes that melancholia arises in "reaction to the loss of a loved object . . . (when) the object has not perhaps actually died, but has been lost as an object of love (e.g. in the case of someone who has been jilted)."[31] Or, we might add to this, when a parent does not (*appears* unable to) respond to the neediness of their child. Or, when our friendships remain frustrating and dis-

---

31. Freud 1917, 244.

appointing, their growth stunted by wanton pursuits of autonomy. Or, when strangers and fellow citizens withhold kindness and courtesy. Or, when one's love for a depressed friend or lover cannot be met—again, not exactly because the love is not requited (it may well be requited "in their heart," who knows?), but because it *appears* unrequitable. To love a depressed person is to have as love object one who is, from the point of view of the needy lover, sometimes just as good as dead and yet tantalizingly, beautifully *there*.

With your imagination set thus to work, consider the difference that Hegel sees between Niobe and Mary in his discussion of painting in the *Lectures on Fine Art*.[32] At issue in Hegel's distinction between Niobe and Mary are the same issues raised by Freud in "Mourning and Melancholia": our conception of, and response to, painful loss and love.

Hegel's remarks in these pages from the *Lectures* are elusive, but it seems clear that the passage from Niobe to Mary parallels what Hegel sees as the transition from what he calls the classical to the romantic, and from sculpture to painting.[33] This matters, because Hegel sees art proper as borne of a traumatized response to the perception of nature as dead—that is, forged in the experience of nature not just as what Hegel calls the "external world" of "inflexible foreignness" (as stones and water might appear to a young boy playing on the shore), but the more sober apprehension of nature as deprived of liveliness, of nature as dead.[34]

For Hegel, the classical form embodied by Niobe (in sculpture) entails an intricate dialectic. On the one hand, for Hegel, the depiction of Niobe in classical sculpture is the appropriate depiction of her; the appearance of Niobe's stony "cold" form is the proper exhibition of her "independent divinity and freedom." In the sculpture of Niobe, the presentation of artistic spirit appears *as if* it were a claim of dead nature; just as (sculpted) dead nature *appears* here as if it were animated. On the other hand, dead nature, despite the appearance of liveliness in art, is finally inanimate. Indeed, for Hegel, it falls to classical sculpture—in the wake of Egyptian mummification—to drive home the lesson that nature is not just spirit's "other" but also irredeemably deprived of spirit: truly dead. For, to see Niobe's cold, independent freedom and nobility, we must also see that the hard matter of which she was fashioned remains powerless to shape and pose itself freely.

---

32. Again, I am less interested in asking whether Hegel offers "correct interpretations" of Niobe or Mary than in understanding what Hegel's view might be, and might help us grasp.
33. For instance, Hegel says that Marian "love without desire . . . enters here in place of the quiet grandeur and independence of the figures of antiquity" (Hegel 1975a, 817) that we see in figurations of Niobe.
34. Hegel 1975a, 31.

The point to be taken here from this condensed outline is that the classical sculpture of Niobe is forged (as spiritual activity) by precisely what prompted Niobe's own grief: namely, the traumatic perception of death, of inanimate nature in human form (corpses). In the figure of Niobe, mourning thus takes the form of a completed *work*—the work of artistic culture itself being a mournful response to our apprehension of death in nature.[35] The (sculpture) form of Niobe-in-mourning is at the same time the content; it is the mourning itself. Niobe's mourning itself, in other words, is here exhibited as the work that artistic beauty was (or did). For, again, the medium of art beauty is dead nature that appears—but *only appears*—to be lively. To apprehend Niobe's sculpted liveliness as *only appearance*—merely as artistic beauty—is therefore to mourn that human form's lost capacity to satisfy living desire. As Kant would say, the sculpture can now be regarded with disinterest; or, as Hegel would put it, insofar as the sculpture cannot respond to any living desires, leaving our desires for real liveliness unrequited, art responds to spiritual interests alone.

And yet the sculpture does not depict Niobe herself as having achieved, *in the sculpture,* the mournful apprehension of beauty that the sculpture affords to its viewer. The one sculpted—Niobe herself—did not and could not see her dead children as beautiful. This is both a formal limit of the artwork *and* of the ethical content of Niobe's experience. It is a formal limit of the artwork because sculpture, as I just noted, presents beauty as a *work of art,* whereas no one knew better than Niobe that her children were not art products! And it is a limitation in Niobe's lived experience because she could not simply withdraw her interests in and desire for her children's liveliness *just* by apprehending that, no matter how they appear, they are dead. To look upon the bodies of dead loved ones mournfully, grievingly—where "grief and pain are final"—is to be unable to look with disinterested pleasure, to be unable to find artistic beauty *there*.[36] Our apprehension of Niobe's beauty is predicated upon her inability to see beauty along with us, which also means our apprehension of her beauty blocks us from weeping for her children with her—even though it is her mournfulness that makes her beautiful in our eyes.

By contrast, when Hegel looks at Christian depictions of Mary's lamentation, he is struck by how Mary's face appears when she looks at her child. Which is to say, Hegel is struck by how Christian painting depicts Mary's

---

35. In Hegel's words: "In the ideal figures of antiquity, on the other hand, we do see, apart from the above-mentioned trait of quiet mourning, the expression of the grief of noble beings, e.g. in Niobe and the Laocoon. They do not lapse into grief and despair but still keep their grandeur and large-heartedness" (1975a, 31).

36. Hegel 1975a, 31.

apprehension of her son, *and* her son as he is apprehended (by her and by us at the same time). As with Niobe—and for the very same reasons: namely, a correspondence between an ethical limitation in mourning and an aesthetic limitation of the artwork—Mary herself cannot see (and cannot be seen to see) her dead child as artistically beautiful. At any rate, to conclude that Mary looks on Christ with disinterested pleasure must be off the mark.

Nevertheless, in contrast to the sculpture of Niobe, we see (over and over, in painting after painting) Mary look upon Christ without desire. So, what do we see? Hegel's enigmatic suggestion is that we see love: passionless love, religious love, maternal love. Hegel further characterizes maternal love as something that one might think impossible—namely, egalitarian love:

> the unique love which affords bliss and an enjoyment of heaven rises above time and the particular individuality of that character, which becomes a matter of indifference ... in the sight of God all men are equal, or piety, rather, makes them all actually equal so that the only thing of importance is the expression of that concentration of love which needs neither happiness nor any particular single object.[37]

Mary, that is, displays indifference not to Christ's passion and death, but to any essential connection between his passion-death (his ethical value) and his particular appearance. The value of his life and the meaning of his death cannot be properly "seen" in the display of his body, and *this* is what Christian painting "shows." Indeed, this is *why* Christian painting shows us Mary's beholding of her son. She loves him, we see, *no matter how he looks.* Mary's love is maternal—and joins the ethical and the aesthetic in the sense we intend when we sometimes say of someone that he has a face only a mother could love.[38]

6.

Put aside the myth and iconography for a moment. There is the risk, I think, that the figures of Abraham or Niobe or Mary can lead us to think that only parent–child relations, or certain "types" of love are at issue (maternal, for instance). Instead, imagine that you love someone who—not only because

---

37. Hegel 1975a, 818.
38. Or, in Hegel's words: "because individual characterization is the non-essential element ... not absolutely fused with love's spiritual kingdom of heaven, it acquires here a greater determinacy" (1975a, 819).

of death, but perhaps because of illness, or depression, or abandonment or estrangement—is absent from you. And your heart breaks in lamentation, because of the loss—not only because desire is not now satisfiable, but also because desire and love are coming apart at the seams. In such moments, perhaps, we can feel what it would be to react, like Niobe—such that love does not survive the interruption of need and pleasure. And, taking up Hegel's aesthetic theory of Niobe, we can perhaps also imagine how *that* traumatized reaction freezes mournfulness into melancholic beauty by setting the apprehension of dead nature into the work of artistic culture. Niobe's independent and free beauty transcends the cycle of life and death, but only by "working" in and through the dead nature whose mere *appearance* of liveliness it persistently confronts. By contrast, we might feel what it would be to react to the interruption of need and pleasure with a quasi-parental regard sustained without desire, for the one who cannot return a lively response. The latter reaction, according to the myth, might be why Mary herself did not die, exactly, but rather was assumed. As if her body's passionate expressiveness were the precise cost that she paid for the love she suffered. While striking, Mary's imagined fate is not obviously a viable picture of human postmelancholic existence.[39]

In asking how anything other than the satisfaction of interest can give rise to pleasure, or how there can be love without desire, are we tracking possibilities for postmelancholic life at all?

Let me return one last time to Kant, for whom disinterestedness must be capable of becoming the site of a renewed necessity, and freedom from need thereby the occasion for the resurgence of life and natural feeling within the subject.[40] *The Beautiful*. To many, this sounds like romanticism, like cliched romantic love even. Or, at least, like the kind of romantic love sometimes seen in people in the grips of a midlife crisis affair who will swear they "feel alive again for the first time in years." But Kant is quick to caution us that the subject in the throes of beauty is in the strictest sense in the grip of nothing since beauty is not "objectively" in the world. This might mean that: "The beautiful object is the illusion the autonomous subject is compelled to generate in order to undergo pleasurably the force of its own disavowed nature."[41] Beauty is only experienced by the depressed, in just same way that art is the illusion of a culture befitting humanity (as Nietzsche put it).

---

39. Here is Hegel making this point: "Looked at physically, this is a love which is death, a death to the world, so that there hovers there as something past the actual relationship of one person to another" (1975a, 817).

40. Horowitz 2001, 35–37.

41. Horowitz 2001, 36.

Or perhaps: The pleasure felt by the disinterested is the *feeling* of being free—a feeling generated of *necessity*, because generated in the wake of the severed connection between need and happiness, interest and pleasure. Judgments of beauty entail a distinct lack of self-awareness on the part of the judge—"who will [necessarily] talk [mistakenly] about the beautiful as if beauty were [which it is not] a characteristic of the object."[42] For Kant, beauty is the illusion the subject must conjure to undergo the pleasure of feeling alive—but such beauty cannot be recognized by the judger as the illusion it is (our midlife crisis problem again).

But if we stick for a moment longer than Kant does with the way in which what comes together in judgments of beauty is *feeling* and freedom, then what the melancholic subject might also be bound by is not only the return of natural aliveness within culture, but first of all the return of feeling to freedom: the *feeling* of being free, of *freedom as a pleasure*, as something nonobjective—not locatable in the world. As I said earlier, the autonomous subject is not only the interruption of the animal connectedness between *need* and pleasure; the autonomous subject was also the interruption between *morality* and pleasure. The subject of disciplining morality does not *feel* free—and this is why, in feelings of disinterested pleasure, beauty binds us not only with the force of lost nature but, for the first time, with the force of *felt* freedom. I do not think this way of putting things—my emphasis on feeling and freedom—distorts Kant's thinking too much, since Kant himself wants to conclude that the truly free subject is neither the natural-creaturely one nor the moral-autonomous one, but the one for whom compulsive judgment is experienced as the delirious undergoing of beauty.

7.

So in asking how pleasure can be felt by the melancholic and how love can persist without passion, we are—after all—also tracking how the pleasure and freedom come together as possibilities for postmelancholic life. But is taste in the Niobe-like melancholically beautiful the only possibility for us?

For another possibility, consider W. H. Auden's poem, "The More Loving One":

Looking up at the stars, I know quite well,
That, for all they care, I can go to hell,

---

42. Horowitz 2001, 37.

> But on earth indifference is the least
> We have to dread from man or beast. 4
>
> How should we like it were stars to burn
> With a passion for us we could not return?
> If equal affection cannot be,
> Let the more loving one be me. 8
>
> Admirer as I think I am
> Of stars that do not give a damn,
> I cannot, now I see them, say
> I missed one terribly all day. 12
>
> Were all stars to disappear or die,
> I should learn to look at an empty sky
> And feel its total dark sublime,
> Though this might take me a little time.[43] 16

Niobe's melancholic beauty persists, but whatever work of mourning art may have once afforded is closed off to us: beauty shines from a past in which we cannot take up residence. For her part, Mary's egalitarian love comes at the cost of passionate investment. In Auden, however, other possibilities come into view. As in Kant, so in Auden's poem, to be able to judge a starless sky beautiful is the prerogative of the melancholic subject, a feeling wrung out of the experience of finding one's needs to be not only unmet by the universe, but unmeetable. Only because nature does not love us back, leaves our needs unrequited, can nature be judged beautiful.

But Auden's poem furnishes an additional wrinkle to this. The chance to feel nature's beauty requires—and perhaps also *is*—the survival of unrequitable love, the sting of love withheld, the perception of nature's indifference staring back at us in the form of someone whose love we could not help but crave, but which craving finds no satisfaction. The traumatic disruption of the pleasure principle and the withdrawal of love appear, in the experience of the poet, not as two separate crucibles for ethics and psychology but as two faces of the same unrequitable need.

Depression is, I think, contagious—it is always "caught" from depressed others, survivors of floods. At the same time, the withdrawal of love symptomizes how we forget that we could also be, in the face of unrequited love,

---

43. Auden 1960.

what Auden here calls "the more loving one." Can poetry remember such forgetting? In its central couplet, Auden's poem challenges us to spy in this predicament a difference between melancholia and postmelancholic satisfaction. What kind of pleasure, what feeling of freedom, and what ways of living less painfully with others might be unlocked, by finding it within oneself to say:

> If equal affection cannot be,
> Let the more loving one be me. 8

CHAPTER 11

~

Niobe's *Nomoi*

DANIEL VILLEGAS VÉLEZ

The law (*nomos*) is not inscribed in stone. But the transgression of divine law—the boundary that sets apart gods from mortals—can be petrifying. *Nomos* is not a mere statute or decree (*thesmos*); it is not an empirical law but the ultimately anterior ordering that precedes and authorizes all human laws. *Nomos* is neither the inscribed law, nor the stone on which laws are inscribed, but rather *that* the law is (or will have been) inscribed. Perhaps *nomos* names the act of inscription itself, or even the condition of its inscription, one that, as a condition, is confirmed with its transgression. In declaring herself equal—even superior—to the goddess Leto, Niobe exceeds the boundary that her punishment makes visible. Niobe becomes the border stone demarcating this very limit, the spatialization of the *nomos* that keeps gods and mortals separate yet bound. Transformed into a spatial border, into a separation, this *nomos* simultaneously joins what it divides, thus undoing the law it meant to establish. In this way, the monstrous act of punishment is the confirmation, the repetition, and hence the inscription—but also the undoing—of law itself.

This condition or organizing law—the separation and its transgressions—is a recurrent subject matter in Baroque courtly opera. Its paradigmatic form is Orpheus's descent into the underworld, transgressing the boundary to snatch Eurydice from death through his enchanting song. The Orpheus myth's recurrence in the history of opera needs no special reaffirmation, except to point out that its concern with human and divine limits—the matter of sovereignty—is central to its operatic adaptations. The myth of Niobe is equally concerned with the *nomos* of the human and the divine, and more closely engages with the question of sovereignty, turning as it does around the history of the Theban kingship—the fate of Amphion and Zethus as usurpers of the Cadmian throne. Yet—and this is a stunning, exceptional silence—there is only one extant opera on Niobe (against hundreds of Orpheuses), Agostino Steffani and Luigi Orlandi's *Niobe, Regina di Tebe* (Munich, 1688), the focus of this chapter.[1]

This is a notorious absence in the operatic repertoire. The story of Niobe is recounted with spectacular detail in Ovid's *Metamorphoses*—a common source of themes for Baroque librettists—and was revisited through sculpture, etching, and painting throughout antiquity and again from the Renaissance through the nineteenth century.[2] One might explain this omission by arguing that the story of Niobe's punishment does not involve the magical power of music that makes Orpheus such a paradigmatic operatic theme, except that, as this chapter will show, magical music also plays a central role in the story: Amphion built the walls of Thebes with the sound of his lyre, animating stones in the same way that Orpheus tamed the beasts. This is precisely how Niobe mourns Anfione at the end of Orlandi's libretto, ironically anticipating her own fate: "*Ahi che trafitto privo d'alma, / e di vita in terra stassi / chi diè vita alle pietre, anima à i sassi*" ("Alas, how pierced through, / deprived of soul and of life, on earth you lie / who gave life to the stones, soul to the rocks").[3] Erecting the walls of Thebes through music—tracing the boundaries of the citadel, determining its order, its *nomos*, through a musical performance—would seem to offer princes a paradigmatic opportunity for allegorical self-representation, arguably the central objective of Baroque opera. And yet, this eminently musico-political act is still not Niobe's but her husband's, and so it seems that, with her petrification, Niobe was condemned to an eternal silence.

---

1. Orlandi and Steffani 1688. Strohm (2007) mentions three other operatic works on the subject of Niobe from the seventeenth century: a music for tournament performed in Mantua in 1652, likely composed by Antonio Bertali; a pasticcio titled *l'Anfione dramma per musica* (Milan, 1697–98) and Jean-Claude Gillier's *Amphion, tragédie en musique* (Paris, 1696). Giovanni Pacini's 1826 *Niobe (dramma eroico-mitologico)*, premiered during his successful tenure at the Teatro San Carlos in Naples, was never published, but is the subject of Franz Liszt's 1837 *Grande Fantasie sur des motifs de Niobe*, S.419. Musical representations of Niobe in antiquity are also scarce. Most notable is a *nomos* by the controversial *kithara* player and singer Timotheus of Miletus (450–360 BCE), of which only two fragments are preserved: *Poetae Melici Graeci*, fragments 786–87.

2. For an overview of the ancient representations, see, e.g., Zeidler (2018); for the Renaissance, see Baert in this volume.

3. Orlandi and Steffani 1688, 84.

Have we ever listened to Niobe, or is her silence another aspect of her paradigmatic "non-relationality," as Andrew Benjamin observes? This is the question that animates this chapter. What can we learn from the unique case in which she was given center stage?[4] How can we listen to Niobe's petrified—and petrifying—silence? And what does *nomos* have to do with this silence? To answer these questions, this chapter considers Steffani and Orlandi's *Niobe, Regina di Tebe*. Throughout the chapter, I test the thesis that what is at stake in the musical *nomos* and its early modern operatic recomposition is the ordering spatialization of *nomos*—the process of tracing boundaries and the regulative authority that issues from them. What this examination of Niobe's musical afterlife demonstrates is how musical performance—the iteration of myth on stage—constitutes an internal ordering of musical elements and the external delimitation of social and political orders (who performs what for whom, and with what aims). But, insofar as it is an iterative performance, taking place anew every time, this organization and ordering undoes itself, like the boundaries inscribed by *nomos*.

NIOBE'S UNSUNG VOICE

Separated by four books in Ovid's *Metamorphoses*, it remains significant that Niobe and Orpheus appear together in panel 5 in Aby Warburg's *Bilderatlas*, where she is described as a "bereaved mother" while he appears—in the center of the composition—as the victim of the "frenzied (insulted) women," the Maenads who dismembered the singer.[5] As transgressors of *nomos*, the two form an odd couple, indeed. Orpheus is the son of Apollo, hence Leto's grandson and an indirect target of Niobe's boastful challenge. Niobe's unmeasured upward reach mirrors the verticality of Orpheus's descent into the underworld, her glacial punishment the converse of the bard's dismemberment. The chiasmus is pure Ovid: "Her very tongue is silent, frozen to her mouth's roof" while his "lifeless tongue mournfully murmured," (*flebile lingua murmurat exanimis*, 11.52–53), creating a mournful chorus with his *flebile* lyre and the *flebile* banks of the stream (*flumen*) just as Niobe's tears continue to flow (*flet*). Issuing forth from his disembodied head, Orpheus's tongue continued to sing—becoming the very paradigm of operatic song. Niobe, on the other hand, was never to be heard again.

---

4. Benjamin 2015, 116.

5. Ohrt and Heil 2020, 5–6. See Baert's essay for an analysis of the role of Niobe in this panel.

Are we not waiting, still, to hear Niobe? How can we listen to her if, after all, her punishment was to be eternally, monstrously visible—monumentalized—but forever silent? How can we listen to Niobe if, as Benjamin writes, she is the very figure of "that other who, in standing in stone on the outside, complicates assimilation insofar as she is positioned outside any structure of recognition"?[6] Niobe remains turned into a stone, exposed yet inaudible. Indeed, her petrification continues to be repeated in the multiplicity of statues and paintings that iterate her "enforced silence."[7]

Voice (*phônê*), Aristotle states, is a sound made by a living animal endowed with a soul (*On the Soul* 420b 7–15). Yet while the human shares *phônê* with other animals, only the *zôon politikon* ("a social animal") is endowed with rational speech, with *logos* as the capacity to indicate right and wrong (*Politics* 1253a15). Hence, as Mladen Dolar points out, the distinction between *logos* and *phônê*, between rational speech and mere sonorous articulation, is a political distinction, tracking—or rather grounding—the boundary between *bios* and *zôê*, between the qualified life of political beings in the interior of the *polis* and its external delimitations: the less-than-human, the inhuman, the monstrous, but also, at the other extreme, the divine.[8] There is a political ordering, a degradation, then, rather than an audible difference, that qualifies a sound as *logos*, *phônê*, or *psophos*, a spatialization of the order of *nomos* that distributes the space of the political as an inside and its outside, the human and its borderline others, the space that Niobe transgresses in her haughty elevation and of which she becomes a marker, its boundary stone.

To be petrified—to be punished with a frozen tongue—is to be silenced, to be denied a chance to utter one's *logos*. Antigone calls Niobe her semblant, likening her own punishment of underground imprisonment to Niobe's petrification. Yet a crucial difference between the two is that Antigone preserves the possibility of articulating the laws (*nomous*) she obeys and those she challenges, even as Creon dismisses her claims as the "songs and lamentations" (*aoidas kai goous*, Sophocles, *Antigone* 883) of someone condemned to death. Unlike the more dignified and poetic *thrênos* ("lamentation"), *goos* ("wailing") is the sound of a borderline human, a creature at the edge of life. Pindar uses the word *goos* to qualify the sounds made by the dying Gorgon, and is more generally associated with the feminine, the monstrous, and thus what is outside or beyond *logos* (*Pythian Odes* 12.21). Through her sonorous exclamations—on the threshold between *logos* and *phônê*—Antigone expresses the injustice of her punishment at the hands of the tyrant Creon, even as her

---

6. Benjamin 2015, 116.
7. Benjamin 2015, 123.
8. Dolar 2006, passim. On the aesthetics of sound, see also S. Butler (2015).

exclamations are declared to be monstrous. Conversely, Niobe is punished for her boastful claims of superiority—exceeding her human delimitation—by being rendered silent, unable to account for herself and her actions. Niobe's and Antigone's topological similarity lies in the extremes between Antigone's meaningless songs and lamentations and Niobe's frozen, silenced tongue—the extremes that frame the *logos* (and hence political inclusion) that, as a punishment, is denied to both. Aristophanes carries this very motif further in his parody of Aeschylus, whose *Niobe* would make the character "sit there muffled up," as the spectator waited "for the moment when his Niobe would make a sound" (910–20). Not only is she denied speech, mournful song or wailing, but even a murmur.

In other words, Niobe is denied both speech (*logos*) and voice (animated sound or *phônê*); a rock, she is only capable of *psophos*, mere noise. Her glacial, unbroken silence is her punishment, a petrification that means an exclusion from the political and even the living even as she remains a monster, an abominable landmark to admonish (*monstrare*) mortals of the divine order she crossed.[9] Critically listening to the series *logos*—*phônê*—*psophos* that delimits the human voice from the less-than-human *goos* of the Gorgon Euryale and Antigone and the inanimate sound produced by a stone, is what is most at stake when (with Benjamin) we consider the kind of space—and its *nomos*—that must be opened, a space in which "allowing for speech becomes an affirmation of the relationship between space and being-in-relation."[10]

THE ORDER OF *NOMOS*, THE ORDER OF SONG

A man—Aristotle writes—"that is by nature and not merely by fortune cityless is either low in the scale of humanity or above it" like the "lawless" (*athemistos*) man "reviled by Homer" (*Politics* 1253a7). Beast or sovereign, the lawless is a being at the extremes of humanity, the complementary sides of a distribution of the political identification of *logos* as *phônê semantikê* ("signifying voice") and *bios* as qualified life. At stake in this distribution is the undecidable duplicity at the heart of the term *nomos*: on the one hand, *nomos* refers to an apportionment, division, distribution, or sharing, while on the other it implies the designs of fate and the (usually but not exclusively unwritten) customs, normative practices, and established forms of behavior. Within the sense of distribution and apportionment is included the ritual distribution of

---

9. Here I add to the series *manare*—*manere*—*monere* in Hamilton's, Rimell's, and Baert's essays.

10. Benjamin 2015, 138.

land and, by implication, the sense of an undivided space, a pasture or abode (*nomós*) inhabited by nomads and animals as well as its subsequent transformation into a regulated space, where it crosses over into the second sense of the customary regulations of a people.

For Martin Ostwald, the most general sense of *nomos* is "an order of some kind," from the order of *kosmos*—the distribution between the divine and the human (and the obligations of the latter toward the former), the source of its normativity itself—to the habits of animals and the customs of different peoples. Consequently, the history of *nomos* is that of its transformation from a divine order toward a statutory *isonomia*, where the religious and pastoral origins of the customary *nomos* become equivalent to *thesmos* to acquire the meaning of an "authority to issue norms and as the political norms and regulations which a people accepts as valid and binding for itself."[11] This is the tension between Creon and Niobe's semblant Antigone, between a man-made law and her observance of how things should be done: "Hades demands these *nomous*" Antigone says, in defiance of the *nomos* of Creon's "tyrannic decision" to leave Polynices without burial (Sophocles, *Antigone* 515). The undecidability of the term is expressed in Antigone's exclamation, as she is led to her tomb, that Thebes can witness "how unwept by friends, under what laws (*nomois*) I come to the heaped-up mound of my strange tomb" (842). Hence, *nomos* is both "order" as distribution and as command, or more precisely, the normative capacity that issues from a given distribution, an order of orders: a circular economy in which the distribution receives its legitimation from the very order it announces as the norm, and of which Niobe serves as demarcation.

In a more polemical interpretation, written in Berlin during World War II and published in 1950, Carl Schmitt emphasizes the pastoral meaning of *nomos* as *nemein*, which he interprets as meaning both "to divide" and "to pasture." For Schmitt,

> *nomos* is the immediate form in which the political and social order of a people becomes spatially visible—the initial measure and division of pasture land, i.e., the land-appropriation (*Landnahme*) as well as the concrete order contained in it and following from it.[12]

In contrast to Ostwald's, Schmitt's examination of *nomos* is not a merely philological inquiry but one that aims to contest the merely legalistic sense of

---

11. Ostwald 1969, 158.
12. Schmitt 2003, 71.

positive law (*Gesetz*) as normative power, which he calls a degraded "metamorphosis of is into ought"—nothing more than the arbitrary law of the stronger.[13] For Schmitt, the original meaning of *nomos* is the very act of legitimacy, a constitutive historical event "whereby the legality of a mere law first is made meaningful."[14] Schmitt likewise argues that *nomos* is primarily a spatial, not a religious concept: its normativity does not issue from a divinely ordained disposition or a ritualized distribution and apportioning of social roles and responsibilities but from "an original, constitutive act of spatial ordering . . . established by land-appropriation, the founding of cities, or colonization."[15] If this land-appropriating act is still too close to the natural right of the mightier, Schmitt later clarifies that "a land-appropriation (*Landnahme*) is constituted only if the appropriator is able to give the land a name (*Name*)."[16] What he fails to acknowledge, of course, is that "naming" here reinscribes the violence of the land-appropriating act. This is poignantly understood by colonized subjects, whose *logos*—their articulation of right and wrong—is consistently reduced to the status of the borderline human sound, of *phônê*.

Scholars who deal with the problematic polysemy of *nomos* often take its musical sense (that is, the musical genre known as "nome") as secondary—at best a source for the kind of witty wordplay in Plato's *Laws*.[17] A notable exception is Thanos Zartaloudis, who closes his thorough examination of the concept with an analysis of *nomos mousikos* in which he emphasizes the organizing role that *mousikê* plays in ancient Greek society as a mimetic mechanism for preserving and transmitting the mores and ethos of the community.[18] As Zartaloudis suggests, the musical senses of *nomos* (as song in general and as a genre) involve the senses of ordered regulation, the preservation of social organization through performative ritual, customary, local adaptations (*êthos*), and even the harmonic order of the *kosmos* in Pythagorean traditions.[19] In other words, the musical senses of *nomos* seem to be not merely derivative of or ancillary to its broader signification but rather paradigmatic of its multifarious meanings.

In addition, I suggest that what is musical in *nomos* concerns also, if not primarily, the performative act of repetition, the rhythmical marking and remarking, the demarcation of time and space through performance, the

---

13. Schmitt 2003, 73.
14. Schmitt 2003, 73.
15. Schmitt 2003, 78.
16. See Stergiopoulou (2014, 118–19).
17. For example, at 722e and 799e.
18. Zartaloudis 2020, 363–64. See also Villegas Vélez (2022).
19. Zartaloudis 2020, 384.

intervallic distribution of sounds—their heightened spatialization and rhythmical temporalization.[20] What is "performed"—carried out, accomplished—in musical performance is precisely this ordering of space and time, the division, distribution, and transmission of the community's mores and ethos. Musical performance, in other words, accomplishes—carries out while inscribing—the community's *nomos*.

NIOBE, REGINA DI TEBE

Let us turn now to Niobe's early modern iteration. Steffani and Orlandi's *Niobe, Regina di Tebe* must be situated within the genre of Baroque courtly opera, approached here as a performative mechanism for repeating—iterating—the spatialization of *nomos* to define early modern European absolutism in imitation of the ancient past. This mechanism was developed across seventeenth-century Europe through an agonistic—read, mimetic—struggle between absolutist courts: the dukedoms in Northern Italy, the kingdoms in Naples, the papal monarchy in Rome and the oligarchic republics in Venice; Louis XIV's court at Versailles; and the various Habsburg courts in Austria and the Spanish Netherlands.

One can distinguish, albeit somewhat analytically, between two conceptions of spectacle that informed the development of late seventeenth-century courtly opera. On the one hand, the commercial approach of the Venetian public opera houses that emphasize the representation of mythical and historical subjects, often reinterpreted as class-based heteronormative romantic dramas, to provide opportunities for the virtuosic display of singers and sophisticated machinery whose repeatability served to amortize costs. In this case, representation is understood as the repeated display of spectacle for the consumption of paying audiences. On the other hand, the "courtly" opera developed in the Italian dukedoms and kingdoms, and later in Versailles, conceives of representation as the self-display of the court itself, mixing medieval courtly rituals (triumphal entrées, tournaments, ballets, and *intermedi*) with the techniques of public-house opera to shape mythological narratives that authorize and legitimize dynastic claims to absolute power across empires.[21] Through this chain of courtly imitations—Habsburg courts imitating Versaille's imitation of Italian opera, itself intended as an imitation of ancient drama—European courts constructed themselves as the inheritors of the

---

20. Villegas Vélez 2020.
21. For an account of the "two origins" of opera, see Bianconi (1987, 162).

ancient world, mobilizing ancient myth to draw its borders against the Eastern empires and legitimize their imperial claims upon the so-called New World.

Steffani and Orlandi's *Niobe* is a paradigmatic work of this mimetic historical and geopolitical configuration. An Italian composer trained in Rome and Paris and employed at the Munich court under Maximilian II Emanuel, Prince Elector of Bavaria, Steffani was at the center of the stylistic and political forces that shaped the phenomenon of courtly opera and the borders of early modern Europe. Composed for the 1688 Carnival—Steffani's last at Munich— *Niobe* marked the turning point of Max Emanuel's military and imperial aspirations. After taking over the regency of his uncle in Bavaria in 1680, a young Max Emanuel entered an alliance with Holy Roman Emperor Leopold I in 1682, through which the Elector committed fifteen thousand soldiers to defend Habsburg territories against the growing advances of the Ottoman Empire. The arrangement would soon become critical when Grand Vizir Kara Mustafa Pasha laid siege to Vienna in 1683. Max Emanuel joined Charles V, Duke of Lorraine and John III Sobieski, King of Poland and defeated the Ottoman armies, an event that marked the beginning of the end of the Turkish Western expansion. Max Emanuel then married Leopold I's daughter, Archduchess Maria Antonia, in 1685 and again joined Charles and the Holy League in the campaign to retake Buda after 145 years of Ottoman control, in a brutal campaign that culminated with the murder of the Muslim and Jewish populations of the city—an act of Imperial ethnic cleansing at the hands of the Christian soldiers. The destruction of the Jewish community is recorded in Isaac Schulhof's 1686 *Megillat Ofen* [*The Book of Buda*]. As András Riedlmayer recounts, the city was sacked, mosques and synagogues were burned with people inside them, and "those who survived the siege and its aftermath, including several hundred Jews and six thousand Muslims, were taken by the Christian troops as chattel to be sold as slaves or held for ransom."[22] Finally, in 1688, Max Emanuel led his own campaign against the weakened empire of Mehmed IV, briefly capturing Belgrade in 1688, although it was retaken by the Ottomans in 1690 when the Nine Years War between France and the Habsburg empire broke out at the other end of Europe.

Orlandi's libretto sets the scene of Niobe's punishment—her fourteen sons and daughters shot by divine arrows, her husband Anfione stabbing himself with his sword—at the climax of act 3, situating the event as part of the tragic history of the Theban dynasty. The dramatic action in *Niobe* is mostly centered around the rivalry between two claimants to the Theban throne: the melancholic king Anfione, who rules Thebes as a usurper but who withdraws

---

22. Riedlmayer 2001, 268–69.

from his ruling duties, leaving Niobe in charge, and Creonte, the legal heir to the throne as a descendant of the line of the Theban founder Cadmus. (In the traditional version, Creon takes the Theban crown only after Laius, who is restored to power after Amphion's death, dies at the hands of his own son Oedipus.)

The conflict between the two rivals involves magical feats that also test the boundaries between the human and the divine. As a defense against Creonte's first assault on the city in act 1, Anfione builds the fabled seven gates of the Theban citadel by using his magical lyre—rendered onstage through an elaborate set of theatrical *machine*—a feat that prompts Niobe to declare him a god rather than a mortal king. In act 2, Creonte disguises himself as the god Mars through the magic of his counselor, Poliferno, and kidnaps Niobe. Under Poliferno's spell, Niobe believes to be herself a goddess, a conviction that, combined with her anger after the spell is undone due to the intervention of Latona's priest and seer Tiresias, prompts her boastful challenge to the divine order and thus her tragic downfall.

Act 3 tracks closer to Ovid's narrative, as Niobe interrupts the celebrations of Latona and organizes a triumphal parade as an apotheosis for her own children. The final scene displays the wrath of the gods—Latona, Diana, and Apollo and their "deità compagne"—in all their operatic might. Descending in a chariot in the midst of thunder, lightning, and an earthquake that destroys the buildings of the city, the vengeful gods shoot arrows at the Niobids who, unlike in Ovid's telling, are given no lines as they fall. Seeing her dead husband and offspring, Niobe is petrified: "Mà negandomi i pianti immenso affanno / Cinta l'alma di nube horrida, e tetra / già mi rende di pietra" ("But my immense sorrow denies me tears / my soul is surrounded by horrid bleak clouds / now I am turned to stone"), she sings in an interrupted chromatic ascent in the closing *cavata* that seems to stop before its allotted time, the final *settenario* anticipating the rhyme *tetra/petra* ("bleak"/"stone") that breaks the flow of the two preceding *endecasillabi,* as if the singer was suddenly frozen before reaching the end of the line. Finally, triumphant Creonte banishes the magician Poliferno (thus saving himself from the same fate as Niobe) and takes the city among a majestic ballet of celebrating soldiers that ends the opera in the French courtly style.

THEBAN HAUGHTINESS, OTTOMAN PRIDE

But what does it all mean? In the dedicatory preface to *Niobe,* librettist Luigi Orlandi celebrates Max Emanuel's military accomplishments against "Asiatic pride," thus suggesting an allegorical parallel between the events of the war against the Ottoman Empire and the expulsion of the usurpers in Thebes—Niobe was, after all, the daughter of Tantalus, king of Phrygia in Anatolia. After quoting from Ovid's *Metamorphoses—et felicissima matrum / dicta foret Niobe, si non sibi visa fuisset* ("And Niobe would have been called the happiest among mothers, if she had not seemed to be so to herself," 6.155–56)—and comparing the Elector to the humble sun, whose light upon others he himself does not see, Orlandi marks the allegory in explicit terms:

> And see how the greatest Light today, as a symbol of your supreme attributes, overthrows Theban arrogance with a thundering hand, which no less represents to the terrified shadows of Asiatic pride the victorious lamps of your acclaimed powers.

As is often the case with operatic appropriations of ancient myth, however, the intended allegorical meanings are often obscure and rarely unproblematic. By convention, the main character in the opera—the royal couple of Anfione and Niobe—would be read as a representation of the dedicatee, the Elector Max Emanuel and his wife Maria Antonia, in the same way that Vincenzo Gonzaga in Mantua was represented in Monteverdi's *Orfeo*, the paradigmatic work of its genre. The particularly elaborate role of Anfione, which stands out among Steffani's best parts, seems to suggest an immediate identification with the Elector Max Emanuel, himself an accomplished dilettante musician.[23] Yet this reading is immediately compromised as soon as one considers not only the allegorical reading suggested in the dedicatory preface but also the prideful character of the mythological couple (contrasted with the Elector's humility in Orlandi's preface) and their tragic fate. Moreover, Orlandi's Anfione is not only a usurper but especially a world-weary king who, at the beginning of the opera, passes the scepter on to Niobe, even appointing her former lover Clearte as her assistant. He is, indeed, the operatic version of the *Trauerspiel*'s indecisive tyrant, as analyzed (via Schmitt) by Walter Benjamin: "The prince, with whom rests the decision concerning the state of exception, shows that, as soon as the situation arises, a decision is nearly impossible for him."[24] This suggests a moralistic or didactic intention behind *Niobe*, less a representation-as-deification of the ruler than an admonishing examination of sovereignty, issued for a prince whose imperial ambitions were already evident and which would be realized some decades later as his son, Karl Albrecht, was crowned

---

23. Timms 2003, 221.
24. Benjamin 2019, 56.

Charles VII, Holy Roman Emperor, fulfilling Max Emanuel's desire to replace the Habsburgs as rulers of the empire.[25] Just as petrified Niobe is a *monumentum* of the *nomos* that divides the human from the divine, so is this *Niobe* an admonishing message about the proper measure that absolute rulers—Max Emanuel's sole ambition—must maintain.

COMIC SOVEREIGNTY, TRAGIC FATE

No sooner does Anfione appoint Niobe and Clearte as regents of Thebes than he faces the very emergency he, as a sovereign, is meant to avoid. Spurred by the magic and vindictiveness of Poliferno (the brother of Dirce, wife of Lycus, whom Anfione assassinated to become king of Thebes), Creonte and the future king of Alba Longa, Tiberino, mount an assault to reclaim Thebes for the Cadmian dynasty. Anfione's response in the face of this attack is to request support from the "popoli" who once enjoyed his music and ultimately from Giove (Jupiter), his father—an appeal to his political, artistic, and divine legacy as Theban ruler—requesting that the god punish "with your flashes of lightning the boldness of the malicious and villains."[26] Yet, in place of armies and lightning, the ensuing scene is a mixture of mechanical *meraviglia* and comedy, as Anfione himself is marveled by the magical—yet evidently unintentional—effect of his song, as the walls of Thebes begin to rise: "Ma che miro? Che scorgo? I marmi, i sassi, / animati al mio canto / forman di Tebe i muri" ("Yet what do I behold? What do I see? / The marble, the stones / animated by my song / form the walls of Thebes").[27]

Then, reinforcing the effect of comic inverisimilitude, Nerea, Niobe's chamber nurse (a role traditionally played by a male actor), storms onto the scene in panic, singing an agitated aria whose opening *quinario* verses with *sdruccioli* endings (accented on the antepenultimate syllable) mock the Venetian convention of the "magic scene," culminating with an ironic, unwitting prolepsis of Niobe's ultimate petrification:

Assistetemi,
soccorretemi,
Numi del Cielo.
Fra quei sassi

---

25. For a similar reading, see Kuen (2019, 236).
26. Orlandi and Steffani 1688, 31.
27. Orlandi and Steffani 1688, 31.

che s'aggirano intorno ai passi,
io divengo di pietra, io son di gelo.

"Gods in heaven, stand by me, help me. Between these stones here that move under my feet, I turn to stone, become ice."

In Venetian opera, as Ellen Rosand explains, *sdruccioli* verses became closely associated with incantations and mad scenes due to their perceived jarring quality, "associated with the darker elements of life: with the uncivilized, the demonic, magic, and also, on occasion, the comically rustic."[28] All of these qualities of the borderline human punctuate—and undermine—Anfione's greatest mythical claim. In Ovid's *Metamorphoses*, Niobe boasts of this very accomplishment, claiming that the very walls built by her husband's lyre and the people—*moenia cum populis*—acknowledge the couple as their rulers (6.178–79). In Orlandi's libretto, the paradigmatic musician-king—who received his lyre from Hermes/Mercury himself—becomes a helpless, impotent ruler whose devotion to Niobe and cosmic music (his best scene is an elaborate aria to the Harmony of the Spheres, to the *nomos* of the *kosmos*) bring about the downfall of his house.

It is this episode that activates Niobe's obsessive claim to divinity, as she reacts to Anfione's feat not by acknowledging Giove's support but by declaring her husband to be "worthy of being called a god."[29] The blind prophet Tiresias promptly warns of the consequences of Niobe's call for building altars "for the new Theban god," announcing that the bold and haughty claims of these "mortal kings" who "pretend to usurp from the eternal gods / the honors due to them on earth" will bring about the vengeance of heaven upon all.[30] Satisfied with this act of political performance—a musical display of divine power—Niobe crowns Clearte as king of Thebes and declares Anfione to be a god, leaving themselves vulnerable for the redoubled attack of Creonte.

This scene thus articulates the political, spatial, and musical senses of *nomos* under examination here. Creonte and Tiberino's attempt at retaking the city of Thebes from the usurpers prompts its further fortification, the erection of a visible, defensive boundary whose immunitary logic—an isolating defense that becomes harmful for the organism that produces it—paradoxically brings about the city's demise.[31] Rather than a protection, the walls become themselves a threat. In appealing to Zeus for support, Anfione breaks

---

28. Rosand 1991, 344.
29. Orlandi and Steffani 1688, 33.
30. Orlandi and Steffani 1688, 34.
31. See Esposito (2011).

the very boundary that Tiresias remarks with his prophecy: the stony walls of Thebes mark not only the inside and the outside of the *polis*—the regulated from the unregulated, the political from the lawless—but also the boundary between mortals and gods. At the end, the walls fall as easily as they rose up by another act of divine intervention. Throughout, the materiality of the walls serves as a prolepsis of the story's outcome in another perfect chiasmus, as the animated stones of the wall are reversed in Niobe's frozen repose. Replacing them after they fall, Niobe becomes another wall, a boundary that marks and remarks the porosity of the *nomos* it sets to demarcate.

Even if shrouded in comedy, that the walls are created through a musical— read, performative and iterative—act is significant. The mythical act stages the inscriptive role that Deleuze and Guattari assign to the Refrain or *ritornello,* as a combination "of rhythmic vowels and consonants that correspond to the interior forces of creation as to the differentiated parts of an organism" that takes place in "the sublime act of the foundation of a city."[32] With the concept of the Refrain, Deleuze and Guattari uniquely identify the function of musical performance as a territorial assemblage for marking, remarking, and demarcating spatiotemporal boundaries, that is, for creating interior and exterior orders, performing and carrying out their *nomos.*

Nomos is neither inside nor outside, neither the law that exists within the walls nor merely the space they demarcate. Rather, it is the demarcation itself, the erection of the borders, the territorializing inscription that defines the space of the law and its outside. What is inscribed in Baroque courtly opera— in the ostentatious performances of absolute power that punctuate the history of European empires—is Europe's self-differentiation from its others in the East through the appropriation and reinscription of ancient mythology as Europe's proper past and identity. Like the Ovidian narrative it emulates, *Niobe, Regina di Tebe* does involve the deification of its dedicatee.[33] As we have seen, it is unlikely that Anfione was intended to allegorize Max Emanuel. Orlandi's contextualization of the plot with respect to the Great Turkish Wars rather points to Sultan Mehmed IV, whose preference for hunting over warfare was blamed as the cause of the Empire's losses in the 1680s, while his subordination to his mother Turhan marked his rule as the "Sultanate of Women." Creonte and Tiberino are possible yet still unlikely candidates, as their campaign against Thebes is ultimately orchestrated by the magician Poliferno. This leaves us with the last and most troubling suggestion, that Max Emanuel should be seen as none other than Apollo, the real "sun" that expelled the

---

32. Deleuze and Guattari 1987, 311.
33. See Hamilton's essay in this volume.

Theban usurpers. If this is so, then the gruesome slaying of the Niobids has a clear historical parallel in the sacking of Buda and the murder of its Muslim and Jewish populations, an act of divine vengeance of which a humble Christian ruler might be rightfully proud. The claims to absolute power of European rulers—Louis XIV, Leopold I, Max Emanuel—are tempered through the iteration of ritual punishment of its others—haughty Ottomans—and the erection of exemplary admonishing *monumenta* or boundary stones—Niobe's silent weeping—that demarcate the "proper" way of European absolute rule: one accomplished not through the vacuous performance of symbols and "laws" but through the very real, violent inscription of *nomos* via the joint operation of land-appropriation and genocide.

PART 4

Philosophy, Poetry, Social Justice

CHAPTER 12

Niobe between Benjamin and Arendt—and Beyond

MATHURA UMACHANDRAN

Between the writings of Hannah Arendt and Walter Benjamin, a curious lacuna around the concept of violence exists.[1] This silence has not gone unnoticed in the voluminous scholarship on the intellectual and personal lives of these two towering figures of twentieth-century European thought. Theorizing violence—its political and intellectual functions, its cultural and historical forms—is a profound and ongoing concern for both thinkers. This essay offers an attempt to address the pointed silence between these otherwise intimate interlocutors, not by producing with a flourish a hitherto lost piece of archival evidence, an overlooked note, or a newly deciphered scribble in the margins of a letter. Rather, I fashion a speculative gamble into the silence, drawing on the animating impulses behind Arendt and Benjamin's respective critiques of violence. In the second half of the essay, I linger on and with Niobe, the mythological figure that receives analytical short shrift in Benjamin's "Towards the Critique of Violence" (or, "Critique of Violence") and whose opacity has opened up leeway for speculation and interpretation for those of us contributing to the present volume. Navigating with Arendt's insistence in her essay *On Violence* that it is possible to think with the Greeks in articulating political

---

1. Various scholars have already run this experiment of thinking between Arendt and Benjamin's accounts of violence. Most instructive for the writing of the present essay was Swift (2013), who examines the concepts of "life" and the respective critiques of vitalism between the two essays.

projects in the present, I press on what a Niobean politics of resistance might yield, or how otherwise Niobe might direct our political imagination.

•

Subsequent to Walter Benjamin's death by suicide at the Franco-Spanish border in 1940, his friends and close interlocutors sought to secure his intellectual legacy and not without disagreement among themselves.[2] In 1968 Arendt published a landmark collection of Benjamin's essays translated under the title *Illuminations: Essays and Reflections* (hereafter *Illuminations*). It is worth pausing over what kind of editorial exercise Arendt is performing with *Illuminations* in her choice and arrangement of material, to better demonstrate the pointed absence of "Towards the Critique of Violence." Directed at an Anglophone audience, the *Editors' Note* explains the nonappearance of two essays in particular from the collection, described as "very regrettable exceptions": "the study of Goethe's *Elective Affinities* . . . and the article on 'Karl Kraus.'"[3] Arendt goes on to justify her decision: "since Karl Krauss is still practically unknown in English speaking countries and since the Goethe essay consists to a large extent of a polemic against Friedrich Gundolf's *Goethe*, equally unknown, these two essays would have needed so many explanatory notes that the thrust of the text itself would have been ruined." The implication here is that *Illuminations* eschews a definitive representation of the sum of Benjamin's essays, prioritizing common cultural understanding instead.

Moreover, Arendt's editorial interventions have been enormously influential in how Benjamin's thought has been received. In her expansive opening essay, Arendt gives us a complex portrait of her friend—complex in the sense of consisting neither of hagiography nor objectivity, full of affection and admiration but not without a grain of something grittier, closer to contempt. She sets up Benjamin's intellectual activity through an elaborate system of deferral:

> To describe adequately his work and him as an author within our usual framework of reference, one would have to make a great number of negative statements, such as his erudition was great but he was not a scholar, his subject matter comprised texts and their interpretation but he was no philologist.[4]

---

2. See the grumpy correspondence between Arendt and Adorno, translated into English by Gillespie and Hill (2019). Adorno had published Benjamin's collected writings as *Schriften* with Suhrkamp Verlag in 1955.
3. Arendt in Benjamin 1968, 265.
4. Arendt in Benjamin 1968, 4.

These hedged definitions determine Benjamin as neither theologian, nor translator, nor historian. Among them is literary critic ("he reviewed books and wrote a number of essays on living and dead writers but he was no literary critic"),[5] conspicuous by virtue of being precisely the portrait which *Illuminations* seeks to make. Hence, later: "The chief aim of this volume is to convey the importance of Benjamin as a literary critic."[6] Covering work published between 1931 and 1950, five out of the ten essays included in *Illuminations* showcase Benjamin's interpretative acumen on writers that he most admired and that inspired his analytical imagination such as Baudelaire, Brecht, Kafka, and Proust. But Arendt also includes essays that would go on to establish Benjamin's philosophical credentials such as "The Work of Art in the Age of Mechanical Reproduction" or "Theses on the Philosophy of History" and which, moreover, can hardly be said to serve the aim of creating an image of Benjamin as a literary critic.[7] Given this disjunction between stated aim and included material, *Illuminations* could plausibly have collected "Towards the Critique of Violence"—it did not have to be disbarred on the grounds of being a philosophical rather than a literary critical essay.[8]

It is not only the editorial omission that constitutes Arendt's silence on "Towards the Critique of Violence." Its absence sounds all the more loudly because in the year after *Illuminations* appeared, Arendt published her own focused, essay-length philosophical exploration of violence. While by no means the only place in which Arendt meditates on the place of violence in organizing human relations across time and the political mechanisms by which violence can be circumvented or sublimated, *On Violence* (1970) is a concentrated account. Moreover, it presses the question of her nonengagement with Benjamin on the concept of violence. *On Violence* expands and develops an essay written the previous year in the *New York Review of Books*, in which Arendt is speaking to an elite reading public at a moment in which the authority of political and education institutions was facing serious challenges from the anti–Vietnam War and Black Power movements.[9] Arendt expresses distaste for the methods and motives of the latter in particular, even

---

5. Arendt in Benjamin 1968, 4.
6. Arendt in Benjamin 1968, 265.
7. Obviously, Arendt's framing of Benjamin can be and has been pushed back on: a classic counter statement is Weigel (1996) on Benjamin's multidisciplinarity.
8. The chronological issue—namely, that "Towards the Critique of Violence" (1921) was published a decade prior to "Unpacking My Library" (1931)—is not sufficient to explain Arendt's selection.
9. Arendt 1969.

as she extrapolates from contemporary events a philosophical distinction between power and violence.[10]

Disambiguating power and violence conceptually enables Arendt to ground an argument for social institutions in which collaborative political activity can be cultivated. Arendt explicitly engages with the contemporary philosophical debate around violence, taking on early twentieth-century French Syndicalist thinker Georges Sorel's conceptualization of the general strike as myth. While Sorel's arguments for the violent class struggle appear to her to be "modest" since they culminate in a proposal for nonviolent strike, she is sensitive to the willful (mis)readings of the real world of his ideas. She also addresses the compelling arguments for anticolonial violence as politically valuable and morally justified that Frantz Fanon offers in *The Wretched of the Earth* (1961). She reserves special scorn for Jean-Paul Sartre's incendiary preface to Fanon's work, and accuses him of the "glorification of violence."[11] For Arendt, these three strands of political thought are not only poor observers of history but also poor readers of that place given by Marx to revolutionary transformation. Given that major interventions into and philosophical derivations of the concepts used to justify violence clearly interested Arendt, the absence of Benjamin's essay-length meditation on violence in *Illuminations* is stark.[12]

Beyond the felicitous coincidence of publication dates and a common object in the concept and critique of violence, Benjamin shares with Arendt an engagement with Georges Sorel's *Reflections on Violence* ([1908] 1999) As Alberto Toscano notes, this is the most-cited text in Benjamin's essay, as well as appearing in the bibliography for several of the philosophical fragments that accompany it.[13] To that end, it is much less rhetorically hostile than Arendt's engagement. Sorel's apologia for the revolutionary potential for

---

10. At the opening of *On Violence,* Arendt makes a differentiation between "power" and "violence" and separates these contrasting terms from "strength" and "force." Thus, she counters a (perceived) failure in contemporary political thought, namely its imprecision: "It is, I think, a rather sad reflection on the present state of political science that our language does not distinguish between such key terms as power, strength, force, might, authority, and, finally, violence—all of which refer to distinct, different, phenomena.... It is only after one ceases to reduce public affairs to the business of dominion that the original data in the realm of human affairs will appear, or, rather, reappear in their authentic diversity" (1970, 42–43).

11. Elsewhere Arendt explicitly calls the rhetorical excesses of Sartre and other revolutionary thinkers "irresponsible" (1970, 20).

12. R. J. Bernstein (2011) notes the through lines between *On Violence* and Arendt's major works, for example, showing how in *The Human Condition* (1958) Arendt determines that violence has, via its instrumental role in "fabrication," a place in political activity if not human life *tout court.*

13. Toscano 2021, 197.

violence had been seized upon by fascist gangs in the 1910s and continued to serve as a basis for attempts to justify fascism well into the National Socialist period. Benjamin found Sorel's marking the difference between types of strike, political and revolutionary, and mobilized it in "Towards the Critique of Violence" to formulate a way of breaking out of the perverse ouroboros of mythic lawmaking. In other words, Benjamin was turning to Sorel, who had already found a way to raise a question mark over the systemic and self-justifying power of the state via the collective political action of the proletarian subject. It is precisely this instrumentalization of violence that disturbs Arendt—and why Sorel above all draws her critical ire, since his case clearly demonstrates how intellectual justifications can be co-opted and codified into totalitarian political ideology. This is, in effect, a refusal to endorse the transformative potential of violence, an aspect that Benjamin situates at the heart of his critique, following a move that Fanon and Sorel had respectively made. If Arendt's silence on "Towards the Critique of Violence" indexes her distaste at her friend's use of Sorel's ideas on the revolutionary strike, their shared engagement with the French Syndicalist is one of two common moves. The other shared move is a turn to classical antiquity for thinking through the philosophical problem of violence. For Arendt and Benjamin, these turns do not represent isolated engagements with classical antiquity. Arendt in particular is engaged with ancient Greek and Roman political principles and institutions as paradigmatic throughout her oeuvre.[14]

Where Benjamin's mobilization of the Niobe myth forms a significant (if inscrutable) part of his argument about the nature of mythical violence, Arendt only briefly gestures to ancient political thought and forms as part of her disambiguation of power from violence. As noted previously, in part two of *On Violence* Arendt underscores a distinction between the useful specificity of ancient political vocabulary and the fuzziness of contemporary terminology. Enacting a little fuzziness of her own, she observes how twentieth-century thinkers such as Mao Tse Tung and Bertrand Jouvenel operate with an identical set of terms as the ancients, and only mentions vaguely that the ancients were "exempl[ary] to the . . . men of eighteenth century revolutions when they ransacked the archives of antiquity and constituted a republic."[15] She goes on to insert seamlessly the modern idea of bureaucracy (government by no one, in which accountability is invisibilized) into a taxonomy of ancient political forms, namely, monarchy, oligarchy, democracy, and aristocracy. And it is precisely the ancients' conceptual acumen with political theory and naming that

---

14. See for instance the recent special issue, "Hannah Arendt and the Ancients," *Classical Philology* 113.1 (2018).

15. Arendt 1970, 10.

Arendt wishes to present as their saving grace. So, while she acknowledges that the Greeks and Romans constructed slave economies and insists that these systems ran on hierarchical principles of "obedience," Arendt implies that these historical systems of domination can be offset by the ancients' elaboration of political theories based on equality. Thus, she writes: "When the Athenian city-state called its constitution an isonomy or the Romans spoke of the *civitas* as their form of government, they had in mind another concept of power which did not rely upon the command-obedience relationship."[16] Arendt's use of the ancients as a stimulus for applying pressure to her contemporaries' thinking around violence, as well as her use of ancient political theory for a positive paradigm, is helpful as a corrective to Benjamin's opacity.

If a better understanding of Benjamin's Niobe is the main quarry of this volume, my attempt to crosshatch his reading with Arendt's impulses is driven by a certain dismay at his articulation of Niobe, namely, as the mere paradigm of mythic violence. Picking away at this conception of Niobe in turn allows us to observe the polarity upon which this essay's categorial formulations rest, one that is particularly evident in the formulation of the concepts of "mythic" and "divine" violence, and the examples chosen to illustrate these concepts.[17] While it is not the place here to delve deeply into Benjamin's use of the story of Korah from the Book of Numbers as a contrastive example (i.e., of divine violence), his use of it to insist on the existence of mechanisms that can break the interminable feedback loop of mythic violence is idiosyncratic. The story narrates the perils of collective political action in the face of divine will, when the priest Korah mounts a challenge to Moses and is punished for doing this by a sinkhole wiping out of his family, property, and immediate community. If this story demonstrates that divine violence operates along the principle of fiat, it appears to be a flat-out contradiction to use it to support an argument *for* collective political action, namely, the strike as a way to break the self-justifying violence of the state.

Such binarism between the Greek and Hebrew paradigms is frustrating in a thinker as dialectically astute and inclined as Benjamin. He consigns Niobe to *only* being the instantiation of mythic violence and the witness to its effects. In offering only one way to understand the Niobe story, he forecloses the possibility of immanent critique of mythic violence, that is, breaking apart the arbitrary violence by which states legitimate themselves from the inside out. In short, thinking about Niobe undialectically leaves the spell of mythic

---

16. Arendt 1970, 10.

17. "In its archetypal form mythic violence is a mere manifestation of the gods. Not a means to their ends, scarcely even a manifestation of their will, but in the first instance a manifestation of their existence. The legend of Niobe contains an outstanding example of this" (Benjamin 2021, 55).

violence intact. If smashing mythic violence is Benjamin's ultimate aim in this essay, it is not a mere whimsy to explore alternative tactics for reading Niobe (as showcased in this volume). Rather it constitutes a serious attempt to reprise the potential of myth, as opposed to mythic violence. As Amir Ahmadi observes in the conclusion of his reading of Benjamin's Niobe, "Benjamin's conception of mythic life as fateful reduction to guilty silence before the gods—and in the extreme and paradigmatic case, Niobe's metamorphosis into stone—can hardly be an acceptable interpretation of this constellation."[18] Lastly, the emphasis on collective political action might be a useful point for cross-pollinating the silence between Arendt and Benjamin. We do not need to follow Arendt's definition of power (as differentiated from violence) in order to be guided by her insights about collectivity and political action.

AS STONE, AS SUBJECT: REPOLITICIZING NIOBE

To reach a more dialectical understanding of Niobe, we can start by asking: what can she offer us other than a mute witness to mythic violence? Benjamin's rendering of her as an example is an abstracting move. He empties out her inner world, up to and including her capacity for agency and desire. Niobe as mute witness to and of mythic violence is all externality, existing only as proof of a concept. It is a positioning that forecloses political possibilities—a trap. Contra this reading, we can insist that the stone can be taken seriously as a subject, that she might have an interiority. From there, our intuitions might radiate outward, framing a second set of questions about her stony subjectivity. What might Niobe feel, and what does she desire—can these change over the course of her transformation into stone? Once turned into stone, can she be implicated in affective processes other than grieving? These questions urge us to consider Niobe's materiality, particularity, and placed-ness. Moving under both sets of questions is an intimation framed by Sara Ahmed in a recent interview that the "registering [of the impact of violence] is also the creation of a possibility for being otherwise."[19] Note that there is a slim but important distinction between Ahmed's "registering" as a provisional start-

---

18. Ahmadi 2015, 66.
19. Ahmed makes this claim by highlighting the context in which Audre Lorde wrote the poem "Power" (1978): "Lorde talked about writing that poem after stopping the car because she heard about the acquittal of a white police officer for the murder of a Black child. She had to stop the car, she said, otherwise she was going to have an accident. She had to stop the car, and a poem came out. She had to stop the car to get the poem out. That's the connection, I think, between my auntie, and Lauren, and Audre—the absolute willingness to register the impact of violence, so that that registering is also the creation of a possibility for being otherwise" (Ahmed and Binyam 2022).

ing point for political reimagination and Benjamin's positioning of Niobe as *Markstein,* confirming the capabilities of the existing order and tied up with abstraction and exemplarity. I will follow Ahmed's intimation in two directions, one toward thinking about Black maternity in connection with Niobe. The other direction tends more queerly, away from reproduction as the thematic sinews of this myth and toward petrification as its own mode of politically resistive being, and being together.

Other scholars have explored the political potential of the myth of Niobe through its reception history. Nicole A. Spigner makes the case for the power of the reversioning of Niobe in her examination of Phillis Wheatley's ballad "Niobe in Distress for her children slain by Apollo, from Ovid's Metamorphoses, Book VI, and from a view of the Painting of Mr. Richard Wilson" (1773, hereafter "Niobe in Distress"). The ballad's title advertises a close engagement with Ovid's Niobe at *Metamorphoses* 6.146–312.[20] As a formerly enslaved woman, Wheatley was hailed in her lifetime for her erudition and literary talent, not least via her engagement with Greek and Latin texts. Wheatley's ballad cleaves close to the epic telling, moving the story across to rhyming English couplets with various rhetorical flourishes such as an updated invocation of the Muse in the framing stanza.[21]

Unique to Ovid's treatment of the myth is the addition of Niobe's challenge to the worship of Latona, building out from her claim to greater fertility. Wheatley reveals how Niobe need not merely narrate and co-sign the operations of power, as Benjamin would lead us to believe. At the end of the ballad, Niobe begs for the life of her last daughter ("'Ye heavn'ly pow'rs, ah spare me one,' she cry'd," 210) before her transformation into stone, or "grew stupid at the shock." The request for mercy and the transformation, however, do not formulate an object lesson about *superbia*. Instead, investing the myth with a specific subject position and rendering the story in the context of slavery reveals Niobe as a place in which the abuse of power is not accepted as such. Connecting subject matter and her experience of being an enslaved and highly educated person, Spigner comments: "Wheatley speaks to the power of black motherhood, something that is otherwise, specifically in the Atlantic Slavery context, framed and experienced as denigration. By highlighting Niobe's rebellion against a totalizing power, Wheatley reclaims black motherhood as a site of resistance, not just one of vulnerability."[22] Thus, Wheatley's intervention suggests a scenario in which Latona is imagined as white, in the sense of pow-

---

20. Spigner 2014; and Spigner 2021.
21. Wheatley 2001, 53–59.
22. Spigner 2021, 320.

erful and anxious, concerned with quashing any contestation of the normative hierarchy of divine and mortal by defending her own status.

Scholar of transatlantic slavery Saidiya Hartman indicates how Black female enslaved subjectivity and the myth of Niobe are mutually illuminating. Hartman recounts in a searing passage of her auto-ethnographic *Lose Your Mother: A Journey along the Atlantic Slave Route* the experience of "standing in the dark recesses of the holding cell for female slaves. I felt both the pull and the impossibility of regaining the country lost. . . . Like the myth of the mother, return is all that remains in the wake of slavery."[23] Reflecting on the notion of return, Hartman concludes,

> *I shall return to my native land.* Those disbelieving the promise and refusing to make the pledge have no choice but to avow the loss that inaugurates one's existence. It is to be bound to other promises. It is to lose one's mother, always.[24]

I want to suggest that Hartman arrives at naming a particular disenchantment via Niobe and the Niobids and therefore understands disappointed recuperations (of the return to idealized places or parents as they once were) as leading to previously unimagined territory that might be politically revelatory. For those who refuse to put store by the "myth of the mother," a shift in understanding of the basic conditions of being can happen, such that being is no longer organized around belonging. This reorientation thus opens up "other promises" for those who are living in the wake of having being snatched from land and originating family.

Losing one's mother, then, is not simply a single traumatic event but an unfolding process of reckoning (indicated with Hartman's "always"). Where the slaughter of the Niobids registers the murderous dispossession of people from their lives as well as violent severance from family, Niobe's experience is focalized through a bereavement that reorients her being in the world. Thus, Niobe resonates with Hartman's figuring of loss by inverting our attention toward the mother as also a subject who must avow her losses (the mother who loses, always). What all of this "promises" remains open-ended: it may well be new political commitments, different ideas of self-integrity, alternatives patterns of relating individually or collectively to the world structured by histories of violent dispossession. Nonetheless, we can now emphasize that specifying subject position renders Niobe more than mere mute witness and

---

23. Hartman 2007, 99–100.
24. Hartman 2007, 100.

instead positions her as a site for actively refracting the ongoing and generational effects of violence, in this case the violence visited on the bodies of Black mothers by the transatlantic slave trade.

ROCKS THAT DESIRE: MORE THAN HUMAN NIOBE

Maternity and its griefs, however, are not the only way to disassemble Benjamin's Niobe. As Gloria Gaynor so memorably insists in *I Will Survive* ("At first I was afraid, I was petrified"), petrification is not the end of the story. While Gaynor's iconic disco anthem is concerned with celebrating life after the failure of romantic love, the movement of the song's narrative grants me license to think more closely about the nature of Niobe's rocky life after punishment. It is also useful to invoke Gaynor's camp call to the dance floor here to key into the queer possibilities of Niobe's story, ones that do not adhere to reproductive logics.

To move into this reading, it is worth noting Benjamin's framing of Niobe's punishment as orientated by and toward the divine. Of mythic violence, he writes:

> [Violence] stops short of taking the mother's life, which it leaves behind as an eternal, mute bearer of guilt and as a stone marking the border (*Grenze*) between human beings and gods, a life now, through the children's death, more inculpated than before.[25]

Of all the borders that Niobe marks, Benjamin calls particular attention to the boundaries of the human as allegorizing the violence of the state. Rather than clearly fixing this category through violence, we can offer a clear rejoinder: how can a *stone* mark the limits of the category "human"? Not so much *who* but *what* is Niobe when, as a rock, she retains a capacity for deep feeling, as well as for demonstrating such feeling. Her humanity is not canceled out but rather seems to be augmented, more than intact, by her transformation into rock. Niobe's rockbody must surely exceed and blur the category "human" rather than define it clearly, even in the sense that her rock existence means that her weeping extends her life beyond a "normal" human time frame. In considering the strange temporality of her indefinite feeling, one that breaks the biological frame, we have now shifted perspective away from placing Niobe in exclusive relation to the gods and are instead exploring what

---

25. Benjamin 2021, 55.

the rock offers when not rendered as the exclusive proof of divine existence or state violence.

At this point, the analytical resources of queer inhumanism make a welcome intervention. In invoking these frameworks and pointing to registers of sexuality (as opposed to fecundity) in relation to Niobe, I am intentionally pushing far beyond the parameters of any ancient telling of the myth.[26] But to invoke queerness vis-à-vis Niobe is to elaborate the possibilities and rich meaning of her polyvalent weeping, her body indeterminacy, her clearly ongoing rocky subjectivity. Queerness as a concomitant to the blurring, even the collapsing, of the category "human" sharpens our understanding of the politics of refusal that Niobe's rockbody proposes. Ultimately, we are feeling around the edges of the Niobe to find the opening for something more than a myth about the violent policing of humanity via fertility. Lifedeath/stonebody—the story of Niobe offers generative ambiguities in the ontological messiness of her petrification.

To launch their exploration of queerness as always extraneous to the conceptual apparatus of the human, Dana Luciano and Mel Chen turn to a self-portrait by lesbian Chicana photographer Laura Aguilar, *Grounded* #114 (2006).[27] The image is of the artist's "queer, fat, brown" body, back to the camera, folds of skin and flesh abundant, sitting on the ground in a desert-like landscape. Behind this person is a boulder that, though bigger, shares their contours. Contra the defanged sensuality that other commentators have seen, Luciano and Chen insist on the *sexiness* of the image in how the softness of body bleeds into the durability of stone, in how the human body in the center of the image is expansively part of and engaged with the landscape. In addition, the person's resistance to being gazed upon suggests an erotics to which the viewer, able to engage with only a part of these circuits of desire with the land, is not privy. The person mimicking rock is not available to be witnessed, shielding herself from the violence of being turned into spectacle—her attention is elsewhere. Luciano and Chen write: "To follow Aguilar's turn toward the boulder, then, is not to turn away from questions of objectification or dehumanization; it is, rather, to consider how these questions already anticipate the contemporary 'nonhuman turn'—to examine . . . how those categories rub on, and against, each other, generating friction and leakage."[28] In fact, class, race, gender, sexuality, and ability are the ontological vectors along

---

26. For a queer reader, following the reflex to attend to the one extant Sappho fragment on Niobe (fragment 142 Voigt) does not readily yield what I might hope for, that is, the nub of an ancient narrative of queer desire between Niobe and Leto. See the introduction.

27. Luciano and Chen 2015.

28. Luciano and Chen 2015, 186.

which what it is to be human has been categorized. Therefore, those who are marginal or outside of the normative categories reveal the contingency of these attempts to control and taxonomize.

Returning these insights to Niobe, we can recognize what opens up when we do not circumscribe her story to one of regulating humanity. To insist that Niobe-rock has a sexuality completely apart from fertility is also to think critically about how much value of the human is derived from reproductive bodies. Could we imagine Niobe also with her back turned away from us, embroiled not in the god-given mandate of weeping but in being part of a wider landscape of wanting, desiring, feeling? Rather than a story of punishment, this could be a story in which the act of being materially evacuated from a humanoid body is the escape hatch from regulated productivity. Niobe, after her petrification, might enjoy the sensation of mosses growing on her and sending root tendrils down into her cracks. She might enjoy being hammered by hail, or the caress of a summer breeze, or the feeling of tears turning into ice forcing her apart. Perhaps after a sudden landslide she delights in the feeling of being closely packed around by soil and rubbing up against other rocks, having been exposed on a hillside for so long. Not just subject to processes of the natural world but responsive to them—if we imagine Niobe as mourning, then we also have to imagine that the rock is charged with feelings and desires that we cannot access. Or maybe Niobe is a stone butch in her queer afterlife who does not want to be touched at all?

A queer more-than-human Niobe fumbles toward theorizing a petrified subject with desires unto herself, one who holds out the possibility that alongside weeping and suffering, there are other felt sensations and dynamic sensations that she might experience. Tavia Nyong'o recounts the performance of Regina José Galindo's *Piedra* (2013), tracking his experience of viewing this provocative artwork.[29] Galindo crouches naked on the ground for nearly forty-five minutes, covered in layers of black charcoal, while three people (two invited men and one uninvited woman) urinate on her back. Wrestling with how to construe this voluntary self-abjection, Nyong'o inquires about how to view this work ethically, and ultimately arrives at the insight that what he might have been waiting for is the rock to get up and move away. The possibility that this person who has become a rock might exercise her own agency does not resolve the uneasiness that the performance has generated, but it does usefully frame the sense that the serial urinations are not the whole story. The temporariness of the performance engages the idea that Galindo's rock-body is not only for being looked at. It has agency. It could move. It might

---

29. Nyong'o 2019, 99–112.

devise an escape. In brief, Galindo's performance and Nyong'o's sense that he is waiting for the rock to move prompts me to insist that Niobe is not the objective sum of her abjections of power. For Niobe, too, I want to hold on to the idea that to be a rock is also to move and to move beyond a world that so violently demands the spectacle of her desire, a narrow performance of the human. We are not supposed to gaze at Niobe and subject her to further objectification—rather, when we speculate about her desires that we do not recognize, we are revising what is possible in the realm of our own desires beyond those that have been sanctioned.

•

Niobe is not a monolith. At the very least, the ancient testimonia and visual representations of the myth attest to this heterogeneity. In the speculative gambit of this essay, I have suggested that Niobe—construed as multiple in her meanings—might well guide us in thinking about resistance to violence as a structuring condition of the world, if only we have the imagination to think about a politics organized by those who have always fallen outside of the normative category of humanness. That way lies a collectivity in which the political capacity of feeling is valued—it is explicitly not the collectivity of reasonable actors cherished by Arendt's ancient paradigms of political organization. Above all, I have sought to offer a corrective to Benjamin's reduction of Niobe as evidence *par excellence* of mythic violence, the proof of the gods' existence and the interminable cycles by which states accredit themselves with power and authority.

CHAPTER 13

Countering Injury
On the Deaths of the Niobids

ANDREW BENJAMIN

1.

In the following epigram, John Donne situates himself in a tradition that dwells on Niobe's predicament:[1]

> By children's births and death, I am become
> So dry, that I am now my own sad tomb.

While "children's births and death" are noted, mother and children are separated. What matters is lost. Separation predominates. Questions of relationality remain unposed.[2] Despite the evocation of the "tomb" Niobe did not die. After the death of her children, and the suicide of Amphion (her husband), she still survived—surviving through petrifaction. As stone she continues to cry. The final line in Ovid's account of Niobe presents petrifaction, tears, and her continual presence, *et lacrimas etiam nunc marmora manant* ("and even now the marble flows with tears," *Metamorphoses* 6.312). If this *etiam nunc*

---

1. Donne 1967, 149.
2. Niobe is only ever a series of Niobes; hence there is only ever the figure of Niobe. While her presence in Ovid, *Metamorphoses* book 6 is granted a certain privilege in the argument presented here, it is equally true that her presence in the *Metamorphoses* is continually illuminated—as a result of both opposition and affinity—by her presence elsewhere.

("even now") marks the presence of Niobe, what of the Niobids? She continues. They died.[3] How are those deaths to be understood? The project of this chapter is twofold. In the first instance, it is to answer these questions concerning the deaths of the Niobids. The second aspect to be addressed concerns the nature of Niobe's survival. What is the status of this *nunc* ("now")? How is this instance of the temporality of survival to be understood? Niobe is condemned to endless mourning as the result of the way her children die. Cicero described her as prolonging "her silence in mourning" (*in luctu silentium*).[4] The concern here however is not with the literal means by which the Niobids died, namely, shot by bow and arrow. There is another account of their deaths that repositions the literal as an effect. The conjecture here is that they died as the result of immediacy. They died as the result of the refusal of mediation, thus of im-mediacy as the presence of that refusal.

In Ovid's *Metamorphoses,* as Latona was outlining what she takes to be the wrongs that had been done to her, Phoebus interrupts: *"desine" Phoebus ait "poenae mora longa querella est"* ("'Stop,' Phoebus says, 'a long lament is a delay of punishment,'" 6.215). That interruption is staged. A cessation or stop demanded—a positioning that is enacted through the use of the imperative form *desine*. The insistent cessation occurs such that there is a closure of any space of deliberation or negotiation. As the line makes clear, the "punishment" (*poena*) cannot be delayed. The absence of delay means that the death of the Niobids follows immediately. A sense of urgency prevails. It is the nature of this immediacy that will have to be taken up. (And in the end a countermeasure sought.) Immediacy has to be linked to the recognition that Niobe's endless mourning is not just because her children died. Rather, their deaths were the result of justice's refusal. Even if the refusal of justice is defined by the history of the myth's reception in terms of Niobe's failure to respond appropriately to Latona's status as a god, and, as is clear from the presence of Niobe in Boccaccio's *De mulieribus claris,* the continuity of her presence in both literature and art functions as a reminder to all women to avoid the arrogance that could slide into independence, it remains the case that history here is the history of differing modalities of injustice.[5] Again, part of the general

---

3. Pausanias (2.21.10), while not really believing the account himself, reports a story that two of the Niobids survived: Amyklas and Meliboa.

4. *Tusculan Disputations* 3.63.

5. Indeed, the problem of the relationship between historical detail and what can be called the philosophical occurs at this very point. The indispensable volume edited by Andrea Bruciati and Micaela Angle (2019) has provided both the most sustained presentation of images as well as texts surveying those images. While detail is essential, the question that has to be noted concerns their relation to philosophical engagement. There is no attempt here to diminish the necessity to take up detail. The questions being addressed concern the evaluation—thus

argument is that immediacy—though the full force of the term will need to be developed—closes the space that is the precondition for the possibility of justice. As a result, justice needs to be understood not as a matter of rights to be predicated of individuals; rather it depends upon the presence of the open space—the space of negotiation and deliberation—in which it can be sought. (A space in which appearance is essential even if precarious.[6]) Central to justice is not the givenness of individuals but the preconditions for the possibility of living a just life. Integral to that life is as much the prevention of injury as it is the provision of resources—identifiable possibilities of protection and appeal—were injury to occur.

Precision is necessary here. Injury is not the wound. It cannot be equated with what occurs to the body. While the body is implicated, injury and wounding need to be held apart. In order to capture its force, injury needs to be recast as *in-jury*. This recasting recalls the term's historical reference to *iniuria*. Justinian argues that in general *iniuria* is defined as that which *non iure fit* ("is done contrary to law").[7] While this opens up the question of how law is to be understood if it is not equated directly with prevailing and historically delimited statues, it is still the case that the presence of law as a possible abstract condition means that injury needs to be accounted for in terms of the presence of acts that undo right and thus close down the possibility of an opening to justice. In-jury has a constant and ineliminable affinity therefore with in-justice. The reverse side of which is, of course, the possibility of law's constancy, namely, a definition of law in which it is defined in terms of the constancy of its opening to unconditional justice.[8]

While there can be no doubt that Latona was implicated in the death of Niobe's children, that position is however not as straightforward as it might seem. There are other presentations of their relationship that mention a possible friendship. With that possibility a different setting has been created. Note

---

judgments made—in relation to that detail. This need not be the province of the philosophical. Richard Neer, for example, has argued that what the Niobe statutes evidence is "misogyny" (2010, 169). The approach here is furnished by a specific understanding of biopolitics; namely, the organization and control of life—including processes of rendering life precarious—that are part of the effective organization of power.

6. The allusion here is to Hannah Arendt's conception of the "space of appearance." For her, appearing is not just intrinsic to human being; it is linked to both speech and action and thus to the relational. The space of appearance is thus an instance of spaced relationality. Arendt describes it thus: "The space of appearance comes into being wherever men are together in the manner of speech and action, and therefore predates and precedes all formal constitution of the public realm and the various forms of government, that is, the various forms in which the public realm can be organized" (1958, 199).

7. Justinian, *Institutes* 4.1.

8. On law's constancy see Benjamin (2019; 2020).

the famous fragment 142 by Sappho.⁹ Within the fragment Niobe and Leto appear together. The fragment announces the ending of one set of possibilities and the beginning of another. The fragment reads:

Λάτω καὶ Νιόβα μάλα μὲν φίλαι ἦσαν ἔταιραι

Leto and Niobe were beloved friends.

The key point is that they "were" (ἦσαν) friends. A friendship made more complicated by the possible erotic implications of the word ἔταιραι.¹⁰ Nonetheless present here is a description that while true of the past is projected as no longer true. One plausible conjecture is that Niobe's boasting and her interactions with Leto, which the latter found demeaning, led to the end of the friendship. (Though the actual reason, were there in fact to have been just one, is left unaddressed within the context of the fragment.) If, however, another source is located, namely, the wall painting attributed to Alexandros of Athens at Herculaneum (first century BCE), a different set of possibilities emerges. In the painting the assumption is that Phoebus is present encouraging Niobe with a gentle push to reconcile with Leto.¹¹ Were this painting to set the measure, then friendship is presented as holding open the possibility of reconciliation. The "were" would have ceded its place to a "still." The possibility remained, if only in this configuration. In fact, another reality took over.

It is important to note in this regard that in his discussion of the different positionings gods and humans have in relation to friendship Aristotle writes in the *Eudemian Ethics* that human "well-being" necessitates relationality. He is precise. It occurs καθ' ἕτερον ("with relation"). The gods, on the other hand, have a sense of "well-being'" that is self-defined. It falls beyond any inscription within relationality. Hence the formulation: αὐτοῦ τὸ εὖ ἐστίν ("well-being belongs to him").¹² If the Sappho fragment is just read in light of the equation of friendship and relationality, then the "well-being" of Leto and Niobe would have had an important reciprocity. "Living well" as an end would necessitate the effective retention of that relationship. Were they to have been friends, they would have wanted "well-being" for each other, and they would have been aware that they were co-implicated in its realization. They were there, one for the other. This sense of human "well-being" in Aristotle, and its connection to friendship, means that friendship is a particularized

---

9. The text here is cited from Campbell (1990).
10. See Telò's introduction to this volume.
11. See http://arthistoryreference.com/t145/20380b.htm.
12. *Eudemian Ethics* 1245b20.

relation, as it can be seen as forming part of the general description of human being as *being-in-common*. While the presence of the gods within this setting complicates how relationality is to be understood, it remains the case that the references to "well-being" need to be conceived as much in terms of the individual as they do in regard to the presence of "well-being" resulting from and maintained by other modes of relationality.

Clearly, in the context in which Aristotle is writing, the presence of relationality should be set against both the simultaneous presence of hierarchies of power—e.g., slavery and the subordination of women—and specific modes of governmentality that can be linked to ostracism. While Aristotle's own description of ostracism in the *Politics* (1284a), in which it is presented as a way of regulating either excessive power, or rule, as the result of populism, has important local determinations, ostracism more generally can be understood as the severance of the possibility of relationality. The force of ostracism resides in the proposition that, following Heraclitus, the "city wall" (*teichos*) discloses the space of human sociality.[13] The defense of the wall therefore is the defense of the space of the human. However, the overall point remains that the interplay of "well-being" and friendship cannot be thought other than in terms of relationality. Claudia Baracchi writes of friendship that what she describes as its "distinctive feature" is "listening to the other, the resounding space that welcomes, understands, and gives back."[14] What is important about her description of friendship is the way that it is thought in terms of both spatiality and relationality. The problem however is that while friendship is indeed a form of reciprocity that necessitates the spatial and thus becomes an instance of the interplay of "well-being" and spaced relationality, the question that needs to be addressed is the extent to which this description might have greater extension. Before addressing that question, it is essential to stay with the end of their friendship.

There is a specific concern at work here. Is the cessation of their friendship that which opened the way for the deaths of the Niobids to occur? The question is too stark. Between friendship and its opposite there might have been a form of indifference. The point is, of course, that a relation of indifference between Niobe and Leto need not have resulted in the deaths of the Niobids. However, that would only have been true if what endured within

---

13. Heraclitus, fragment 44 Diels and Kranz: "The people must fight for its law as they would defend the city walls." The copresence of *nomos* and the city as definitional to human being is one of the most significant elements in Heraclitus's thinking. On the necessity to think human life and life in general in relation to the city as an important aspect of Greek thought, see Brill (2022, 34–38). See also Di Cesare (2020).

14. Baracchi 2022, 212. For an extension of her argument, see Baracchi (2020).

such a form of indifference also involved the interplay of spatiality and reciprocity as already having provided the body's location. There would be a link therefore between forms of indifference and a form of letting-be. Again, the connection between spatiality and reciprocity cannot be merely formal. It has to become that which delimits specific forms of life. The presence of the formal and the continuity of its devolving into the particularity of forms of life means that what is continuing to unfold here is the basis of a philosophical thinking of life. Not biological life, but life thought biopolitically, intrinsic to which is both relationality and spatiality. The refusal of life therefore cannot be equated with killing. Life is more than the physiological, thus more than bodily presence. Hence the defense of the Niobids would itself always have to be greater than a mere claim to the right to life, as the latter is conventionally understood, namely, as predicated on an individual's bodily continuity. Once this position is continued, then what emerges is a place—a site—one that is as much spatial as it is relational. It is the space of life and as such is integral to the definition of human being. Moreover, one configuration that it enables is friendship. However, it cannot be restricted just to friendship since friendship has its own distinct register. Friendship becomes therefore a particular instance of spaced relationality.

An initial friendship need not have saved the Niobids. However, it would have maintained the setting in which deliberation was possible. It might have occasioned forms of reflection and understanding that then could have resulted in the continuation of life rather than literal death. Again, the key point is not friendship, if friendship is understood as no more than a human relation. As noted above, what friendship necessitates is the space that maintains its own continuity. This is the space in which the implications of friendship—and this will always be of a specific and thus always nameable friendship—and therefore the responsibilities and forms of care to which it uniquely gives rise can be acted out. And yet, it is essential to differentiate between friendship, the singularity of any one friendship, and relationality taken more generally. Friendships are defined by their singularity. Being a friend, or becoming a friend, are relations of determined duration. Friendships always begin. Equally, they can end. Entry into friendships need not even be intentional, as Maurice Blanchot wrote in relation to his friendship with Dionys Mascolo, "On était amis et on ne le savait pas."[15] Starting and ending friendships need not therefore be deliberate. The distinction between friendship and the conception of relationality that defines *being-in-common* is that the latter entails always already having entered a space that has neither

---

15. Blanchot 1996, 9.

beginning nor end. That setting has an additional important quality. Namely, that while having entered can always be assumed, the capacity to live out the consequences of relationality and equally the sense of place that commonality entails bring additional demands into play. The prevailing presence of disequilibria of power means that the full realization of "well-being," now construed as a potentiality rather than an inevitability, is marked by an almost inevitable precarity. What attends is the ineliminable possibility of in-jury. This is not a claim that singularizes individuals. Rather, what is jeopardized is the interplay of spatiality and relationality that defines *being-in-common*. As a result, what becomes important is twofold. First, there has to be a defense of *being-in-common*. The second element however concerns the ground or the basis of this defense. In sum, what these elements point toward is the possibility, if not the necessity, that there be a noninjurious response to injury. (The latter—injury/in-jury—is present as an attendant threat though equally as an already given reality.)

While it might be argued that the collapse of the friendship between Niobe and Leto created the possibility for the death of the Niobids, such a claim only has force to the extent that the collapse is not understood in strictly interpersonal terms. Rather, what ended with the friendship was the presence of the setting—the place of what Baracchi identifies as "exchange" and "welcome"— in which discussion and deliberation could have taken place. The collapse of the friendship has to be understood therefore in terms of the ending of spaces of mediation and thus the increasing isolation of the parties involved. Hence the push attributed to Phoebus in the wall painting by Alexandros of Athens acquires an additional quality. It is not about individuals. Rather, it concerns spaced modes of relationality. Hence, what has to be brought back is not friendship. It is not a question therefore of hoping that Niobe and Leto renew their friendship. The project does not depend upon attributing a vain salvific force to friendship. In other words, what has to be allowed is the possibility that there could be spaces of mediation that were not dependent upon the presence of friendships. In part this is also because, as has already been noted, friendships have to be particular. What makes them matter philosophically is the presence of a space of mediation—however, the nature of that space does not depend upon those involved in it having to be friends. Rather than friendship there has to be a commitment to maintaining and safeguarding that space, namely, the suspension of immediacy in the name of the always more original presence of the spacing allowing for the discontinuous continuity of mediacy. The spacing is occasioned by the city wall. In more emphatic terms there has to be a commitment to life. While a lot more needs to be adduced at this point, the defense of life will always demand forms of immanence. Law's constancy is an immanent condition; equally, the defense of spaced relationality demands a commitment to the possible actualization of an immanent condition whose presence, at any one point in time, may only obtain as a potentiality.

2.

In order to return to the possibility of a site of mediacy and mediation as bearing, and bearing on, life in the context of an engagement with the figure of Niobe, what has to be traced are the ways in which immediacy comes to dominate in the presentation of Niobe in Ovid's *Metamorphoses*. As has already been noted for these present concerns, Niobe will continue to be linked to the way she is presented in book 6 of Ovid's poem. At the outset of the section in which she occurs, she is described as "the happiest mother" (146). And yet, once that description is given, it is then complicated. Added to it is the further qualification that this "happiness" is tenuous and will, in fact, be undone as a result of her uncompromising pride and her self-declared relation to the gods. Boasting of her fecundity, she refuses to acknowledge the effect she has on others. And yet, there is far more at stake. There is not just the refusal to acknowledge the power of the gods; there is her own self-identification as a god. The latter, she claims, should obtain given her lineage and her fecundity. She claims to be as "worthy" as a god (6.181). These two points then combine. She positions herself beyond the hold of fate. What is important to note here is that the claim that is being made is about Niobe herself. The language used is prior to the actual slaying of the Niobids. What has to emerge is that precisely because their deaths are the result of immediacy, they result from the operation of fate. This then opens up the proposition that the space of mediation and the suspension of fate have to be thought of as coterminous. There is continual move away from the centrality of the individual to the necessity to maintain relations as the locus in which human being occurs. What this means, of course, is that if Niobe is in error, it is simply because she thinks that the suspension of fate is no more than an act of individual will. In broader terms what this means is that the move from the primacy of the individual is not to the refusal of the singular, but to the incorporation of the singular within the relation. The resultant position is that singularity is not presupposed by the relation. It is produced by it.

Niobe is punished for what she has said. The question to be addressed, in this instance, is, what does it mean to punish Niobe? What type of law is involved? What in this context would count as a response to one who claimed comparability to the gods and who believed, in addition, that her actions would stem the tide of *Fortuna*? The story is well known. In the first instance the children of Latona kill Niobe's sons. In the context of Ovid's *Metamorphoses,* the descriptions are dramatic. The death of Alphenor, for example, occurs while he is lifting up the body of one of his brothers. He too is struck by an arrow. Life flows from him (6.253). Another son, Ilioneus, raises his hands and shouts to the gods. He pleads. While asking for his life to be spared he dies. A presentation of the moments in which life and death coincide can be found on the Roman sarcophagus (circa 160–170 CE) in the Glyptothek in Munich (see fig. 13.1). On seeing the horror unfolding, Amphion—Niobe's husband, the children's father—commits suicide. The sons have been killed; revenge is now exacted on her daughters. At this point one of the dramatic sets of lines in this section occurs (6.298–301):

> ultima restabat; quam toto corpore mater,
> tota veste tegens "unam minimamque relinque!
> de multis minimam posco" clamavit "et unam."
> dumque rogat, pro qua rogat, occidit.

> The last daughter remained; covering her with her whole body, with her
>   whole dress,
> the mother cried out, "the youngest one, leave me this one.
> Of so many I am asking this one, the youngest."
> While she asked, the one for whom she asked, was killed.

The last line here is central. The use of the conjunction *dum* in the line *dumque rogat, pro qua rogat, occidit* reinforces the sense of immediacy and thus the drama of the deaths. In Ovid's version after these events Niobe turns to marble and is carried by the wind to her "native land" (*in patria*).

What occurred? Latona acted. However, what then emerges is the enacted presence of the relation between the gods and the law (the law of the gods). In other words, what occurs is premised on the impossibility of mediation. The punishment of Niobe becomes the enacted presence of pure immediacy. As will be suggested in what follows, while Niobe may have thought herself to be a god, the fact that she is subjected to the dictates of immediacy, while at the same time attempting to undo the immediate by demanding mediacy, indicates that her refusal of fate, even if not articulated as such, is in fact the attempted refusal of the immediate. This position sets up a set of connections in which the temporality of mediation and deliberation is refused. Niobe is subject to immediacy. The punishment is exacted however on the

FIGURE 13.1. Roman sarcophagus, circa 160–170 CE. Apollo and Diana kill Niobe's fourteen children. Glyptothek, Munich.

Niobids. While it will be essential to stay with Ovid, it should be noted that in Aeschylus's *Niobe* she speaks after the event. In so doing, it can be argued, she is attempting to explain and discuss her predicament. What that means is that she enters into the realm of deliberation. Mediacy takes the place of immediacy. Mediacy is that which no longer nurtures either fate or the equation of law with the dictates of the gods. Mediacy demands deliberation; injury is no longer a necessity. In other words, in-jury is no longer fated.

The relationship between the immediate and the possibility of mediacy occurs in a number of different ways in this section of the text. In the first instance, it is clear from the line cited above: *dumque rogat, pro qua rogat, occidit*. The "asking" is simultaneous with the "killing." As noted, initially this is enacted by the temporality staged by the conjunction *dum*. Moreover, the repetition of *rogat* together with the use of the present tense for both verbs—*rogat, occidit*—reinforces the presence of immediacy. Here the asking is literally simultaneous with the killing. There is no intervening set of spatial relations. Immediacy closes off any possibility of such a setting. This is the equation of law and retribution that is structured by fate. The words spoken by Niobe were without any point. The saying was as much an asking as it was a nonsaying. Niobe in this setting—despite speaking—was silenced. The same state of affairs pertains to the plea uttered by Ilioneus (6.264). The term he used in this context is important. Ovid writes that he addresses the gods. He raises his hands and shouts to the gods. The fact that he uses the imperative form *parcite* ("spare me") cannot be ignored. A response is demanded. He asks for a space to be created in which he can talk, in which he can be both heard and spared. Sparing is an allowing and thus a letting-be. For Heidegger sparing is linked to "peace." In Heidegger's terms "real sparing" (*eigentliche Schonen*) is an allowing to dwell which means "to remain at peace within the free."[16] There is a productive affinity here insofar as Ilioneus is asking for the suspension of immediacy and thus of not being subjected to fate's operative presence and the violence it necessitates. The force of the imperative is that it opens the space of the mediate (mediation). At work within this setting is the implicit recognition that not to be subject to fate—thus not becoming the subject of fate—is to be spared. Sparing is the continuity of relationality. In sum, therefore, the space and the time of deliberation are invoked, albeit in the dramatic form of an imperative. That invocation is however always already too late. The arrow was already in flight. Despite speaking and asking for a space of mediation to appear, the term *parcite* is direct speech, and thus the possibility of being able to appear in that space has been undone in advance. Even though there is the presence of direct speech, there is, nonetheless, a genuine sense that nothing has been said. The failure of the imperative to function as a performative does not mean that Ilioneus has been literally silenced. Rather, the operative presence of immediacy undoes the possibility that the demand may have an end.

Speech is not just the presence of the spoken imperative. Consequently, there has to be another tack. Hence opened up here is the need to work with the supposition that speech entails as much a reciprocity between speaking/listening/observing subjects as it does there having to be a place of exchange. Mediacy demands the open as the space of relationality. And yet, it is not as though Niobe is silent. More significantly she needs be understood as having been silenced. In a number of instances, she speaks. She may have tried to explain her actions. If Athena at the end of *Eumenides,* in the undoing of the Furies and thus the demand that divine law no longer obtain, can be understood as suspending the work of fate and her expectation that the Furies are henceforth "minded to find the path of fair speech" (γλώσσης ἀγαθῆς ὁδὸν) (888–89), then there is a possibility that Niobe may, in the end, have sided with Athena and thus with the possibility that justice can never be the result of the immediacy of divine law. No matter how flawed her actions may have been, in talking, and thus by accounting for herself, not only were forms of justification sought, she may also have attempted to present another account of what she had said. What matters is not her talking as such but what the act of speaking presupposes, namely, the presence of a space of exchange.

---

16. Heidegger 1993, 351; and Heidegger 2000, 151.

3.

In the Campanian hydria in the Nicholson Museum at the University of Sydney, Niobe is located in a *naiskos,* a small temple associated with funerary activities (see fig. 2.1). The link to the funeral and to death is therefore both clear and direct. However, Niobe is not dying. In fact, if the famous description of her in the *Greek Anthology* (5.129) is allowed a central position, then her living on in stone has a far more complex presence than is usually assumed. The move from life to an afterlife becomes fundamental.

> From a living woman (*ek zôês*) the gods turned me to stone; from stone (*ek lithoio*) Praxiteles allowed me to live (*zôên*) again.

Here Niobe is speaking. This is to be contrasted of course with Poliziano's translation from the *Planudean Anthology,* in which petrification results in that which *est idem cadaver et sepulchrum sibi* ("the corpse is the same as a tomb for her").[17] Such a final positioning is even there in Ovid's own description of the statue: *nihil est in imagine vivum* ("Nothing in the statue is alive," 6.305). Niobe keeps turning between life and death. After all, on one level, petrification is not just the becoming stone—it is the enforced withdrawal from spaced relationality. Therefore, it is the abnegation of human being. It is, as it were, the ultimate injury. The afterlife that Praxiteles might have allowed her moves in a number of directions. There is the evocation of the constancy of a form of vigilance and thus the refusal to forget. Niobe lives on precisely because she can be seen as remembering; to return to Cicero's formulation, she can be seen to be "mourning silently." And yet, the important point here is slightly different. While the site of survival can be singularized, what Praxiteles allowed was a form of presence that was not just explicable in terms of the afterlife of the work of art, it was necessarily supplemented by the fact that integral to that afterlife is the recognition that the work of art needs to be understood as the continual coming-into-relation that defines the coincidence between seeing and interpretation. What this means is clear, namely, a different measure will have been set.

The Campanian hydria fixes Niobe. Fixes her as active. Tantalus kneeling is reaching toward his daughter. Her hand is in the air, a gesture that will be repeated in, for example, seventeenth- and eighteenth-century illustrations of Ovid. One of the most famous is by the German engraver Johann Wilhelm

---

17. Poliziano 2019, 74.

Bauer (1607–40). (The engravings served to illustrate editions of Ovid.)[18] While the whole engraving warrants detailed commentary in its own right, what is of significance here for the current concerns is the presence of her raised hand. The engraving also captures the movement of petrification. The folds of the material allow for the translation from clothing to stone as an effect of the engraving process. Encroaching shadows aligned with the continuity of lines mark the movement. In fact, it might be suggested that the move from light to dark in Bauer's engraving serves to dramatize the movement of the hand. Movement and stasis work together. Niobe's body is doubled in advance. Given this configuration of her body's presence, what then is to be made of her raised hands? The question pertains both to the hand in the engraving and to the hand on the hydria.

The first part of any answer is the fact that the hands are raised. They are held up. Muscles, blood, bodily tension, perhaps even the interplay between the purely physiological and the will (or intention) combine to maintain the hand in the air. The hand is as much the registration of shock as it is the hand which, in cutting the air, pleads for a cessation or an undoing. In other words, there is a doubling of gesture. The presence of this doubling means that what is at work here is the presence not just of form, but of form that is always already informed. In addition, gesture as a result cannot be reduced to, or equated with, a locus of meaning as though the body were not somehow implicated. Equally, gesture cannot be identified with the movement of the body if that movement is taken as an end in itself. The presence of the doubling of gestures means that can never be the "gesture as such." In other words, gesture can never be "the exhibition of a mediality" and therefore be no more than the "process of making a means visible as such."[19] Gesture is always the interplay of bodily movement and meaning.[20] This is the case even if the conditions or determinations of any one gesture, or set of gestures, and thus meanings are neither settled nor unified. Hence the continual possibility of gesture's doubled presence. Here the raised hand is both the shock at what is occurring and the demand for the space of mediation. In fact, in moving between image and text, since what is at work here is Niobe's figured presence, there is an affinity between Niobe's raised arm, and Ilioneus's use of the imperative form *parcite*. Both comprise forms of intervention with this doubled presence. The interventions in question are neither mere movement, nor simple demand. In both instances there is the attempt to create a space that

---

18. http://baencd.freedoors.org/Discs/Baen%2003/WebSite/ovid/niobe.html.
19. Agamben 2000, 195–98.
20. I have tried to develop this conception of gesture—a project that begins with a critique of Agamben—in my *On Gesture: Classical and Renaissance Expressions* (2024).

allows for the interplay of appearing and sparing. What results is a form of insistent demand. While acknowledging the inherent fragility of the demand for the spatiality that marks relationality and in which deliberation, judgment, and contestation take place, the presence of such a demand cannot be avoided. Moreover, the demand in question is not for a space linked to any form of utopian project. It is a space that is regulated in advance by the recognition that mediacy is the necessary correlate to the placed nature of human being.

At work here therefore is a countermeasure. If in *Metamorphoses* 6.251, *desine* closes the space of mediation and deliberation, not only does this assume and evidence the primacy of relationality, it demonstrates that immediacy has to be understood as the closure of the possibilities afforded by always having allowed for the originality of relationality. As such immediacy is inextricably bound up with injury as in-jury. The raised hand moves beyond simple protection. Indeed, it is not for protection as though what pertained related only to the presence of the individual's body. The contrary is the case. The raised hand is intended to undo the possibility of in-jury by insisting on actualizing the possibilities that are always already inherent (hence the earlier references to immanence) in the spaced relationality that is constitutive of human being and thus the modes of relationality that are the preconditions for the possibility of justice. The raised hand is therefore the countermeasure to the enforced presence of injurious immediacy.

If it is true to argue that the Niobids died as a result of the refusal of mediacy and thus their deaths were premised on the impossibility of justice, they died therefore injured, and this creates the setting in which it is possible to return to Niobe's tears, tears that are there "even now" (*etiam nunc*). The question to be addressed, as stated at the outset, concerns the status of the "now." If there is a further image that will allow this question to be addressed, then it is the famous sculpture of Niobe protecting her youngest child that forms part of the Uffizi Niobe Group (see fig. 8.2). Staged by this sculpture is an emphatic form of care. Niobe seeks to protect her child from harm. What becomes clear is not the failure to care, nor is it the failure to protect. After all, the Niobids died. Rather, the point is that care is not sufficient to stem the threat of injury. Dante in *Purgatorio,* Canto 12, views Niobe *con . . . occhi dolenti* ("with sad eyes"), the same eyes that appear in *Rime* 25 as linked to *pietà del core* ("heart's anguish"). He is troubled and disturbed by what he sees. And yet, the affective response, as with care's dramatic sculptural presentation, does not involve the turn to justice. Injury remains. Presented here—again in both image and text—is the necessity and the limit of care. What endures "now" is the reminder that the only possible response to the presence of injury/in-jury and the continual threat of immediacy is to maintain the conditions that allow for and sustain justice. In other words, what continues "now"—evidenced by the continuity of her tears—is the necessity to insist on spaced relationality as that which yields the only possible response to immediacy. Care depends upon justice.[21]

---

21. Pursuing the relationship between care and justice is the central concern of the last book by Elena Pulcini (2020). Her work is the indispensable starting point for any engagement with a philosophy of care and its eventual relation to justice.

CHAPTER 14

~

Lacrimae Rerum
Institution of Grief

JACQUES LEZRA

For Giggy Lezra, 1934–2023

I am writing these words about Niobe's grief with other loss before my eyes—as others have, no doubt.[1] My mother, lucid, strong of heart, died five weeks ago. My father, nearly a centenarian, is spinning into silence, forgetfulness, the dark. Sergio Chejfec died suddenly. César left us too. And of course public loss is everywhere on screens and phones: COVID, war, school shootings, the insults of predatory neoliberalism bring grief everywhere to us; they market it to us and bring us to mark it.

The long history of Niobe's allegories keeps me company. It presses in different directions from her story's knots. I will not write that Niobe's story is unique in this way, since I recall so many other, multiplying myths. Has any other of the West's stories, though, so tightly tied together the matters of number and grief, tied them together in such a way that the very number of retellings of the story also brings us to grief? Only perhaps—and it is a suggestive coupling—the story of Narcissus. Perhaps if literary culture had left just one story, or a single or even primary way of imagining Niobe's stories (Ovid: *unam minimamque relinque*),[2] then I could find my way more easily to the question, How do I grieve for you alone? But Niobe is *procax*; her allegorizations are wanton, undisciplined. She figures *superbia* and stony

---

1. Chejfec 1994, 142.
2. Ovid, *Metamorphoses* 6.299.

insensitivity (Alciatus: *Est vitium muliebre Superbia, et arguît oris / duritiem, ac sensus, qualis inest lapidi*).[3] She represents a mother's ceaseless love, pride in a child, unending grief. She doubles herself: *Statuae statua, et ductum de marmore marmor.* She is the limit of the sculptor's art (Juan de Arguijo, in a seventeenth-century sonnet echoing sources in the *Anthologia Graeca*, has her exclaim: "A todo me dejó restituida, / mas no al sentido, l'arte poderosa").[4] She offers politics, sociology: Jean Hardouin's 1716 *Apologie d'Homère* scandalizes Mme. Dacier by maintaining that in the *Iliad,* "Niobé c'est la Grèce. Ces douze enfans, ce sont les Grecs, hommes et femmes, que les arbalétriers et chassèurs de la campagne de Troye tuerent les neuf premières années du siege." "Rien n'est plus divertissant," Mme. Dacier ironizes in reply: "Voilà assurément une profondeur du génie bien étonnante," she adds, before "defending" Homer from Hardouin's "annoying" incoherences.[5] Nietzsche's Niobe arouses the "envy of the Gods," as the "too favoured mother."[6] For Walter Benjamin, she stands as "an eternally mute bearer of guilt and as a boundary stone on the frontier between men and gods" or, in Julia Ng's recent translation, "an eternal, mute bearer of guilt and as a stone marking the border (*Grenze*) between human beings and gods, a life now, through the children's death, more inculpated than before."[7] For Judith Butler, commenting on and extending Benjamin, "it may be that Niobe's tears provide a figure that allows us to understand the transition from mythic to divine violence."[8]

What does it mean to grieve only for one? Is my question like asking whether *just one* "Niobe" organizes the long and incoherent history of her allegories?

Or let me put it like this. Aulus Gellius (*Attic Nights* 20.7) notices the "remarkable, even ridiculous variation . . . to be noted in the Greek poets as to the number of Niobe's children. For Homer says that she had six sons and six daughters; Euripides, seven of each; Sappho, nine; Bacchylides and Pindar, ten; while certain other writers have said that there were only three sons and three daughters."

Is my grief at losing some number, any number, greater than what I feel when I must lose just one, only one, call him Isaac or call her Iphigenia or Selia or Beatriz Viterbo? How to reckon singletons together, say, six boys and

---

3. Alciato 1621, Embl. 67.
4. "A una estatua de Niobe, que labró Praxíteles, de Ausonio," in de Arguijo 2011, n.p.
5. Hardouin 1716; and Dacier 1716.
6. Nietzsche 1991, 315: "Envy of the gods. The 'envy of the gods' arises when he who is accounted lower equates himself with him who is accounted higher (as Ajax does) or who is made equal to him by the favour of fortune (as Niobe is as a mother too abundantly blessed)."
7. Benjamin [1921] 1986, 295; and Benjamin 2021, 55.
8. Butler 2012, 89.

six girls, or seven or nine or ten of each, or only one? This question has of course the most difficult logico-mathematical, religious, and ethical history. The answers that Niobe's stories provide are disconcerting in their diversity—the number of Niobe's allegories, like the number of her children, troubles our reckoning—but also in their structure. For they ask, in Niobe's name: what is *one* life?

In Ovid's telling of her story, desperate Niobe argues for one life on two contradictory lines. The gods attend to neither argument, but Niobe's grief is *instituted* to repeat, guard, and retain the incoherence she desperately expresses. (An institution as classically understood is a sort of *statue*; it is erected; it stands in stone, repetitive, to ward off finitude; because it stands against time, it makes my acts recognizable and legitimate over time; it stands you now within its closure, now outside; and it sets me outside at times, within at others.)

How to save *just one*; to fail; and then to learn how to grieve *just one*, the least one, one only, distinct from all the others: *et unam,* the last daughter. As the numbers still living drop, the weight of the minimum increases, *de multis minimam*: the last one bears the weight of all my children; she stands for them. Leave me one, leave me the unit, so that I can count how many and how many worlds I have lost—since, without one, without the one, I will not be able to count my loss. Artemis, Apollo, Latona, cold gods—you should want me to tell my grief, to count my dead, now and forever, tear by tear, one and one and one child lost. Leave me one, so that I may number and mourn the others. Through and in her I will recall them and grieve for all of them in her. The Sanhedrin Mishnah (4.5) famously and controversially says—after warning witnesses in capital cases of the gravity of bearing false witness, of the dangers of uncertainty and ambiguity—that "anyone who saves a single soul [from Israel], he is deemed by Scripture as if he had saved a whole world."[9]

---

9. Neusner's translation of Sanhedrin Mishnah 4.5J–K (1991): "Therefore man was created alone, (1) to teach you that whoever destroys a single Israelite soul is deemed by Scripture as if he had destroyed a whole world. And whoever saves a single Israelite soul is deemed by Scripture as if he had saved a whole world." The controversy Israelite/any human is not just editorial, of course, but it is that as well. Here is Smith (1970) on the ways in which Jervell (1960) seeks "to prove that 'man' means 'Israelite'":

> Jervell uses Mishnah Sanhedrin 4.5, which he reads as saying, "the Biblical text indicates that anyone who destroys one Israelite life is as guilty as if he destroyed a whole world." It also remarks that Beer-Holtzmann, in their edition of the Mishnah, said that some MSS omitted the word 'Israelite' and preferred this reading. This preference, Jervell says, was a mistake, due to the fact that they did not understand that "man" means "Israelite." Thus the reading proves the principle and the principle determines the reading (and the circle is the most elegant form of argument).

(To save a single soul, one only, *any* soul, is to save a world.) Save me just one, so that I can count the worlds that I have lost, that you have taken from me.

Just for this reason I must deprecate the last. For just because the last one *may* count for them all, may be the one and one for each one, just because counting on her and with her she may bear the weight of all my children, you may think that she can stand for them all, and that by taking all but her you will have left me the rest *in her*. So I must say instead: leave me with nothing, and I will call her one, the minimum, the least of them. Leave me the one closest to none, the least of them, the last one. I will call her just one because she does not count as one; she is just that, the *minimam*, the last. I do not love her most or least; she is just the one left. Indeed, I will take from her what made her mine alone, what made her my youngest, what made her my dearest: all that was her life I will take, so she will be just this last, *minimum* thing you leave me. Look: leave me just the last one, alone, *et unam*, and she will not add up to her siblings, indeed she will add up to nothing, not even to herself. I cannot count her as *mine*: she cannot be a thing of mine that I can hold. She is the one who cannot be made to count. (Ovid uses the expression *et unam* on one other occasion in the *Metamorphoses*, at 6.525, describing Tereus's rape of Philomela. Here the repeated *et* in *et virginem et unam*, "a virgin, all alone," works as an intensifier: a virgin, and alone; not one attribute added to another, but by their intensification both subtracted from Philomela. In Tereus's hands she is rendered *nothing*, unattributable, without a relation to father, sister, or even to the gods. In my despair, this, even this, is what I promise I will carry out upon my last child, if only the gods will spare her, just one, only one, *et unam*, alone.)

Niobe's grief holds together these two incompatible renderings of the one—the "one" that is each individual, the cardinal *one* that you will leave me so that I may count and grieve in counting them for each of the others, one and one and one like the dark beads of a rosary; but also the "one" that cannot be made to count; the last, the ordinal *one* (although there can only ever be one *last* one, just which one is last has no importance: her lastness is all); the *one* that you will leave me just because she will never even count, not even as one, for her lone last self, and more: because I will sacrifice what makes her "one" to the ordinal quality of her lastness. She will not even be one, being just the last.

Grief pushes Niobe to fold one "one" into the other. For her, it is the way of despair, the last argument, the "one" she turns to when all other arguments have failed. Fruitlessly. Folding cardinal "one" into ordinal "last one" will not persuade the gods. No "one" can be saved by *adding* the just-one child to the just-last child.

What sort of operation would it be, to try to add a cardinal "one" to an ordinal "last"? *Cardinality* is the primary feature of a number; it is what comes first in its order of attributes, the quality on which all others, the arithmetical or syntactical qualities of relation-to-other numbers, hinge. The technical question posed by the order of number's attributes hides at the center of Niobe's grief: just what is finitude? What does it mean for one body to begin, and to end? The knot of Niobe's story here leads me to Ovid's great model regarding *minima* and bodies' beginnings and endings, Lucretius's *De rerum natura*. Lucretius's poem builds what will become Ovid's allegorized questions into the description of matter itself. Here is how *De rerum natura* approaches the paradoxes of numerical and every other finitude (1.600–614):

> Then again since each of those ultimate particles that are beneath the ken of our senses has an extreme point, that point is evidently without parts and is the smallest existence; it never has had and never will be able to have an independent, separate existence, since it is itself a primary and unitary part of something else. Then rank upon rank of similar parts in close formation provide the ultimate particle with its full complement of substance and, since they cannot have an independent existence, they must cling so fast to the whole atom that they cannot by any means be wrenched apart from it. The primary elements are therefore solid and simple, being formed of smallest parts packed solid in a closely cohering mass; they are not compounded as a result of the assembly of those parts, but rather derive their power from their everlasting simplicity; nature does not allow anything to be torn away or subtracted from them and so preserves the seeds of things.[10]

With Epicurus, Lucretius says: Atoms, *a-tomos,* are precisely indivisible—they are *one*. But, Lucretius asks here, don't they have analogues of parts: orientation, upsideness, downsideness, and edges? For if it is finite, if it has an edge, an *apex* or even a *terminus,* then every atom has, at and as its end, a last part.[11] A part that can be part-ed from it? The crucial verse, *alterius quoniamst ipsum pars primaque et una,* "since it is itself a primary and unitary part of something else" (1.604), is obscure. Leonard has: "Since 'tis itself still parcel of another, / A first and single part."[12] Some time ago, Furley's careful *Indivisible Magnitudes* located "the difficulty . . . mainly in the words *pars primaque et una.*"[13] Just here, Furley notes, Lucretius distinguishes between parts-of-one

---

10. Translation by Smith (1969).
11. On the political philosophy entailed in *terminus* in Lucretius, see Lezra (2020, 40–73).
12. Leonard 2004, 18.
13. Furley 1967.

that *could* indeed be separated from the one and thus render it (or show it to have been) molecular rather than atomic; and *analogues to* parts-of-one that properly, indisseverably, and uniquely, belong-to each one: the lastness of its edge, its orientation. The formulation in Lucretius is paradoxical. Discrete bodies, which are aggregates of similarly discrete atomic bodies, begin and end at last; they can be counted as one, they can be one-body, just because the first- and last-ness of their edge is a "part" of them different in kind from the attributes and elements that make them up but can subsist parted from the discrete body: color; or the properties of duration and extension, which can be attributed to any discrete body.[14] What makes the discrete body *one* inasmuch as it is discrete, is the indisseverable, ordinal mark of first- and lastness that its edges bear. But this indisseverable ordinal mark is, *as it were,* the sign that the discrete object's edge belongs to something other, *alterum*: *alterius quoniamst ipsum pars primaque et una*. Furley throws up his hands: "I am unable to solve this problem, and can only say that somehow Lucretius believes it to be established that the minimum part cannot possibly exist in separation." In fact what Lucretius is maintaining is even less intuitively clear: that "the minimum part," the ordinally last part that marks out the edge of the one body, both is and is not wholly, only, an indisseverable "part" (in a different, analogic sense) *of* that body. The insult to the logic of identity is profound, and both addressed and performed in the poetical expression. Performed: between the ordinal *primus, pars prima,* and the cardinal attribute of being-one, *pars una,* Lucretius doubles his conjunctions, *-que, et*. The attributes of ordinal primacy and of cardinal numeration share conjuncts (*-que, et*) and substance (*pars*): the edge between them dissolves, as, if we follow Lambinus, does the difference between the first and the last, "*Id est, et prima atque ultima.*" Lucretius draws ordinal primacy and cardinal numeration, like firstness and lastness, into one common body. At the same time this common body, the mark of the edge of the other, of the condition of finitude, cleaves that one common body from within with, to, the failure of the conjunct of ordinality and cardinality, of *pars prima* or *pars ultima* and *pars una*.

The long and varied history of Niobe's grief doubles her figure, as if her statue were meant to hold together eternally each one child and every child that is the last, or the first, to die. She becomes the statue of a statue. Moralized, this means: she was already, *at first,* as hard, as stony, as a statue, and the gods—good sculptors—chip or shear from her, one child at a time, one edge at a time, all that was not marble about her, or all that hid her doubly marble form. She, too, has become *at last* truly *one,* one stony stone, a statue of her-

---

14. Lucretius, 1.647–55, 665–67.

self alone, the statue of the stone that she was at first. Niobe's grief is the first institution—ordinally, but also typologically. It is, like the altar that Henry James's Stransom erects in the forgotten chapel of "The Altar of the Dead," "the great original type, set up in a myriad temples, of the unapproachable shrine [I have] erected in [my] mind."[15] Mine? Ours? Niobe's grief, the first and universal institution, then helps me to understand an intellectual tradition and a group of institutions that seek to conjoin ordinality and cardinality, *pars prima* or *ultima* and *pars una,* and to do so in order to manage grief. The water that endlessly weeps from the stone is *another* matter—edgeless, it is what cannot be made *one* in either of our two senses (cardinal one, ordinal one) and marks what is left after the sculptural violence of institution has run its course. Does it count as one tradition and one group of institutions at all, I ask? I have in mind philosophical, theological, sociocultural institutions. How do Niobe's stories, the acts of instituting, and the institutions that her stories allegorize help me grieve for you, for you only?

I have before me Roberto Eposito's recent *Istituzione* (2021), an expansion of his important 2020 monograph *Instituting Thought: Three Paradigms of Political Ontology.*[16] Esposito enjoins his reader to abandon the "reactionary," "coercive interpretation" of institutions that conceives of them as "simultaneously the system of rules governing a community, and the power that constrains [members of the community] to respect them . . . beginning with the State, the strongest and most consolidated [institution]."

An institution, I said, is what we install: a stone, a statue, it is proof against time's passing. As classically imagined, institutions are phenomenological frames and formats (*Stiftungen*) that provide repeatability, recognition; schemes of inclusion and exclusion; protection; identities and analogies over time, even the time in which identity, coherence, and sufficient reason can take shape and *work*. On this description, institutions are objects that furnish objectality to other objects—give them recognizable and agreed edges, times, ordinal as well as cardinal qualities. For Esposito—who follows Mary Douglas and, more remotely, Max Weber—these objective and objectifying phenomenological formats coerce, regulate, and enforce. They arrest the living movement of bodies so as to give them force and duration. But today "the requirement that life be instituted returns to the fore in the double sense of bringing institutions to life and of restoring to life those instituting traits that push it beyond mere biological matter." This is achieved, he writes, by "mobilizing institutions, bringing them into movement, so they can once again find

---

15. "The Altar of the Dead," in James (1895, 212–13).
16. Esposito 2021 (my translation).

creative power." The task is framed conditionally, reflexively, and impersonally. Esposito offers a diagnosis and a path—but no clear sense of just *who* will act, or of *how* institutions "can once again find creative power": do these phenomenological frames and formats act upon themselves (instituting themselves, mobilizing themselves), or are they to be acted upon by impersonal forces, cold revengeful gods or unknown but beckoning political subjectivities (being instituted, being mobilized)? For the diagnosis and path to be right; for it to be the case that current societies have moved into "a biopolitical dimension that is irreducible to the paradigm of sovereignty," thus toward "the requirement that life be instituted" in the double sense that *Istituzione* proposes; for institutions to be mobilized and life instituted, the uncertainty whether the first and last movements are proper to the objects we call institutions, or are the marks of what is improper to them—what marks their edge, their *terminus*—must be maintained. And if institutions so (self-)mobilized cannot, then, be *one*—can the "life" they institute *be one,* one life, a conceptual object brought back to the fore, recovered, preserved, enforced?

Let us ask again, in Niobe's name: what is *one* life?

1.

Is it this? Borges imagines the last Saxon, dying alone, "casi a la sombra de la nueva iglesia de piedra," nearly in the shadow of the new stone church.

> Antes del alba morirá y con él morirán, y no volverán, las últimas imágenes inmediatas de los ritos paganos; el mundo será un poco más pobre cuando este sajón haya muerto.... Una cosa, o un número infinito de cosas, muere en cada agonía.... ¿Qué morirá conmigo cuando yo muera, qué forma patética o deleznable perderá el mundo? ¿La voz de Macedonio Fernández, la imagen de un caballo colorado en el baldío de Serrano y de Charcas, una barra de azufre en el cajón de un escritorio de caoba?[17]

Here is Andrew Hurley's translation:

> Before dawn he will be dead, and with him, the last eyewitness images of pagan rites will perish, never to be seen again. The world will be a little poorer when this Saxon man is dead.... One thing, or an infinite number of things, dies with every man's or woman's death.... What will die with me the

---

17. Borges 2000, 57.

day I die? What pathetic or frail image will be lost to the world? The voice of Macedonio Fernández, the image of a bay horse in a vacant lot on the corner of Serrano and Charcas, a bar of sulfur in the drawer of a mahogany desk?[18]

I imagine, with Borges, that what "dies with each man's last breath" may be a stubborn and unique collection of last *immediate* images, the ones I witnessed alone and alone recall: your touch, her voice, smells, my mother's face one day. A fragile set of perishing forms collected in my name and for me, of "One thing, or an infinite number of things," or as Norman Thomas di Giovanni's translation has it, "some thing—or an endless number of things." They are what counted for *one* life: what we *witness, that* is the one life we lead. What makes me—or anyone, or the "last Saxon"—both *one* and *unique* or *singular* is just the way one thing or event, or an infinite number of things or events, immediately relates to me (or anyone else, etc.), or bears my signature.

Borges's parable, approaching the definition from its other side, from some question asked after our eyes close on the last event we witnessed, makes sense intuitively (of course the image that I witnessed disappears when my memory of it does—the image *just is* my memory of it!). It rightly lays its stress on the signature, "Borges." It asks, what sort of thing is it that witnesses? Is it *like* the "one thing, or an infinite number of things, [that] dies with every man's or woman's death"? Is it just one of these things, one among many or one next to many things that I witnessed? Borges's parable asks: does "immediate" self-witnessing *also* "die"? Who or what witnesses, immediately, what dies with the dying witness? If this who or what that witnesses what dies is not a thing-among-things, then it is perhaps something like the mere this-ness that supports a name, or holds together a thing I point at, say, a stone. But this way too I find difficulty. "What is it in this stone," Duns Scotus asks—Scotus, whom Borges returns to again and again as "Erigena"—"by which as by a proximate foundation it is absolutely incompatible with the stone for it *to be divided into several parts each of which is this stone, the kind of division that is proper to a universal whole as divided into its subjective parts*?" (*Ordinatio* II, d. 3, p. 1. q. 2,

---

18. Borges (tr. Hurley) 1999, 311. Compare Hurley's translation with Norman Thomas di Giovanni's (2014, 47):

Before daybreak he will die, and with him will die—never to come back again—the final first-hand images of heathen rites. . . . Some thing—or an endless number of things—dies with each man's last breath . . . . What will die with me when I die, what poignant or worthless memory will be lost to the world? The voice of Macedonio Fernández, the image of a brown horse grazing in an empty lot at the corner of Serrano and Charcas, a sulphur candle in the drawer of a mahogany desk?

n. 48).[19] The immediate this-stoneness of what I point to supports it; makes it *one*, particular. And every one thing shares with the infinite number of things the quality of possessing this-ness. No thing is just one, entirely singular, for this reason: it shares, being one, in this universal. (And to this extent it can be likened to every other thing: it counts, like every other thing.) Not you, my friend, my father, and my last child, *et unam*.

This is perhaps too strong an argument. That every single thing—your one life among them—is a *haecceity* means that everything has, with every other thing, a common property, "being a haecceity." Does this not mean that no thing is *genuinely* singular, absolutely one? Or are we committing ourselves to too strict of a definition of "singularity": surely a *single* property, just one alone, *et unam*, can be universally shared without foreclosing the ethically preferable, romantically preferable, chaotic disunity of universal singularity and of the absolutely discernible? (Something like the converse of Max Black's "twin spheres" argument is entailed.)

Borges allows us to weaken the argument in three ways, but the price may be too high. In his Spanish, the qualifier "immediate" or "immediately," "las últimas imágenes inmediatas," bears a great deal of weight—so it is telling that both of Borges's translators, Hurley ("the last eyewitness images") and di Giovanni ("the final first-hand images"), sidestep the term.[20] It is, perhaps, too immediately philosophical a word for them; the register the translators seek is instead juridical: a "witness" at a trial, an eyewitness possessed of firsthand information, will at some point have the event or the image at hand or before his eyes, and will affirm so. I will swear to it: there, in the lot at the corner of Serrano and Charcas, a brown horse. (Or is it a bay? The Argentine is "colorado," which is also "red." Am I seeing a color? Do color names designate real things, or are they a matter of perspective: my red, your brown, her bay?) Your verdict depends on it.

Juridical, of course. But "El Testigo" is *also* concerned with "imágenes," "formas," "mediación," and "inmediatez" ("immediacy"); with "conjetura," "cosa," "uno," and "infinito," on a register that is not only juridical and not only colloquial. An "image" may "die"—phenomenologies are finite; we speak for instance of the persistence of vision, of afterimages; stone wears down with the flow of water, tears; I imagine that material supports fail, that my photographs of Sergio fade or lose their digital coherence to new platforms; and my memories of my mother will be lost. But can a "form," *forma*, "die"? Not in the same way as the "image" does, not if we attend to the philosophi-

---

19. John Duns Scotus, *Ordinatio* in Spade (1994, 69). Scotus is arguing against Henry of Ghent's theory of individuation.

20. Di Giovanni 1970, 47; Borges 1999, 311.

cal tenor of Borges's fable and despite the terms' apparent synonymy. Borges mentions the theosophists' conjecture that the universe has a memory, but "El Testigo's" conversation in 1960—like "Tlön, Uqbar, *Orbis Tertius*'s" (1940), and like the even earlier conversation behind the speculative *History of Eternity* (1936)—is with Platonism's "conjecture" that forms do *not* perish, no matter how fragile and passing the material, empirical instances that participate in them: their "imágenes." Here in 1960 the synonymous "forma" and "imagen" are also, if anything, antonyms; "forma" and "imagen" cannot be, in the same way, "patética o deleznable." The paradox that Ovid condenses in the figure of the endlessly weeping Niobe, stone impervious to wear, expresses the fantasy of achieving a *poetical* expression both immortal *and* transient; Borges's parable expresses the fantasy of finding a *philosophical* expression that permits the "form" of an object or a life, of a life-as-object, and the "image" of an object or a life to be synonyms *and* antonyms.

An object; *a* life. But Borges is not settled on how we are to count objects, things, or lives possessed of this poetical, philosophical paradox. Take these sentences: "¿Qué morirá conmigo cuando yo muera, qué forma patética o deleznable perderá el mundo?," "What will die with me the day I die?" For in every death, "en cada agonía," in every *one* death, he says, "una cosa, o un número infinito de cosas, muere." Hurley: "One thing, or an infinite number of things, dies with every man's or woman's death"; di Giovanni: "Some thing—or an endless number of things—dies with each man's last breath." We are invited to read Borges's "o," his "or," in the sense made possible, even likely, by works like "El Aleph," or "La biblioteca de Babel": conjunctively, expressing synonymy or equivalence or internal translation: "One thing, *that is; or; id est*, an infinite number of things." A world, of course, in a grain of sand; a word, an image, or a form in which all words are contained. In the *aleph* that the grieving Borges sees "in the heart of a stone" in the cellar of Beatriz Viterbo's house: "Cada cosa . . . era infinitas cosas, porque yo claramente la veía desde todos los puntos del universo," "Each thing . . . was infinite things, since I distinctly saw it from every angle of the universe."[21] Borges faces an impossible central problem in trying to describe the *aleph*: "What I want to do," di Giovanni translates, "is impossible, for any listing of an endless series is doomed to be infinitesimal." Borges has in mind a more specific formulation: "[El] problema central es irresoluble: la enumeración, siquiera parcial, de un conjunto infinito." Not a series but a *set*; not "endless" but "infinite"; not a "list," but an "enumeración," "enumeration." And no "doom" at all. When "una cosa" becomes syntactically synonymous (conjunctive "or") with "un número

---

21. "El Aleph," in Borges 1974, 625. The English is from di Giovanni (1970, 26–27).

infinito de cosas" in "El Testigo," Borges has in mind to give a bounded "one" the extension of an infinite set ("un conjunto infinito"): every "cosa" that dies with me is *aleph* in precisely the sense in which the word is used, as Borges recalls with regard to "The Aleph," in "Cantor's *Mengenlehre* . . . [:] the symbol of transfinite numbers, of which any part is as great as the whole." What I witnessed—ephemeral, unimportant: a horse in a lot; a sulphur bar—will turn out to be as great as the whole world of which it is just *one* part.

But Borges's "or" is not *only* conjunctive: it is also disjunctive. His "o" is not only Latin *aut* but also *vel*: a choice *must* be made. "*En cada agonía,*" in every *one* death, "una cosa, o un número infinito de cosas, muere." Not *one*, but an infinite number; not *id est* but the privative *vel*. One or the other. I think of it as a matter of attention, and maybe even of responsibility: to *this* event, or to *this* image, in itself: *haecceity*. *This* event or *this* image, not taken or experienced as *a part* or as a number counted alongside other numbers. There, in the lot at the corner of Serrano and Charcas, I saw a horse. An infinite number of images crowds the lot; the horse I saw is at the battle of Junín, Alexander rides it, El Cid, Don Quixote . . . it is, in short, no longer *this one thing* or event that I witness. (As the knots in Niobe's story will always lead me through others: through Ovid's verse and Lucretius's, through Borges's parables . . .) How will I affirm that what I saw, one afternoon in Buenos Aires, was this and not that, that I saw it then and not at another moment? The piece's juridical register may bend translations of "El Testigo" away from the work's philosophical commitment, but it cannot be discarded: justice requires my testimony; flowing from it, a verdict regarding what I witnessed. If *one thing* or one event is an infinite number of things or events, then the truth about this thing that I witnessed cannot be offered assuredly.

Synonymy *and* antinomy; conjunction *and* disjunction. I asked, with Niobe: what is *one life*? If I grieve for you, for what else and for whom else do I grieve? Who also grieves where I grieve?

2.

"Transience," Judith Butler explains, "exceeds moral causality. As a result, it may be that Niobe's tears provide a figure that allows us to understand the transition from mythic to divine violence. What would Niobe's expiation look like? Can we imagine? Would justice in this case require a conjecture, the opening up of the possibility of conjecture? We can imagine only that the rock would dissolve into water, and that her guilt would give way to endless tears."[22]

---

22. Butler 2012, 89.

Thus Butler, explaining in *Parting Ways* the enigmatic appearance of Niobe in Walter Benjamin's essay "Critique of Violence." She has in mind these lines. "Violence," Benjamin writes,

> therefore bursts upon Niobe from the uncertain, ambiguous sphere of fate. It is not actually destructive. Although it brings a cruel death to Niobe's children, it stops short of claiming the life of their mother, whom it leaves behind, more guilty than before through the death of the children, both as an eternally mute bearer of guilt and as a boundary stone on the frontier between men and gods ("als ewigen stummen Träger der Schuld wie auch als Markstein der Grenze zwischen Menschen und Göttern zurückläßt").[23]

How does Butler understand "the transition from mythic to divine violence"? By first imagining grief "giving way," so that the tears of Niobe may dissolve this "boundary stone," so that, her grief having cleared the way for tears, she may dissolve herself *as* boundary stone—as the *Markstein,* the *terminus,* the mark of the minimum of sociality entailed in recognizing that a border can be drawn and attested, instituted, between two fields or two properties (understood extensively).

Thus far it is possible to conform Butler's position with Esposito's. But in Butler the "transition" between Benjamin's figures of violence maps onto a psychic and an ethico-political project that does not square with Esposito's. If I grieve for one, for one that I could hold and possess, could count and touch and point to, for one, one, the first or the last—then I mark my borders, I install myself, steal from the object my permanence as the grieving figure, sculpt myself into stone: *Statuae statua, et ductum de marmore marmor.* Imagine this injunction, then: *give way,* dispossess yourself of the object, dissolve the one statue you have become. A therapeutic injunction. Its ethico-political correlate: the dissolution of socialities and institutions based on property and recognition, and tending to reproduce them.[24] Butler's argument, I take it, departs from Esposito's by enjoining us, in *giving way,* to move through and beyond a grievable life, and by enjoining us to imagine the uncountable institutions that may then come or may be established beyond *any* "biopolitical dimension," whether "irreducible to" or sustained by "the paradigm of sovereignty." Here's how this might be undertaken.

"Moral causality," I understand, restricts my guilt to what I can stand for—to those effects of my acts that follow, along a perspicuous or discoverable causal chain, from what I do. For instance, from my words comparing the

---

23. Benjamin [1921] 1986, 295; Benjamin 1999, 197.
24. A detailed reading of the Niobe-boundary-stone problem is in Ty (2019).

number of my children to yours. It is a discoverable and fateful path, and when you take life from me, one child at a time, chipping at my heart as a sculptor chips away at rock to reveal the rock that lay below, you are moralizing me according to my last word.

"Transience" here means: what I am guilty of cannot be calculated. It is not composed of fixed and discrete, countable acts, events, or consequences; borders move and can be moved, or fade, or mingle, or dissolve; disorder garbles what was first or last; what was one counts as one *and* no longer does. My last word *may* lead back to me, but not (except accidentally) by a single path that lies ahead or behind me. Justice, Butler says, exceeds "moral causality" because it holds my responsibility to the test of transience. It holds me to account without counting forward to or back from the event. Because I give way, I face justice rather than judgment based in "moral causality." Now the path of expiation opens before me, uncertain, endless, conjectural: it is the way of endless tears.

"It may be that Niobe's tears provide a figure that allows us to understand the transition from mythic to divine violence." It is a careful, tentative formulation; questions follow; even the requirement that may flow from our understanding—the possible requirement of "a conjecture"—is followed by a double modification: "the opening up of the possibility of conjecture," "conjecture" not just posited or instituted as a principle, but "opened up," its inside revealed, maybe taken to bits, analyzed, its internal edges themselves subject to inquiry and understanding; and "conjecture" installed under the wing of its modality, its mere *possibility*. Then an answer—the conjecture that justice, *in this case*, conjecturing, stands on the answer to the question "Can we imagine?"

Behind Butler's questions we recognize the critical scheme, shaped here around three faculties, each finding its limit in the other two: "transience" described as above makes it impossible to establish judgment on *causal* understanding; "moral causality" and the faculty associated with disclosing "moral causality" find their limit in the limit that "transience" imposes upon the understanding; and finally the "imagination" is enrolled to supply, but *only* conjecturally and *only* "in this case," what we cannot otherwise understand, and what our moral faculty cannot grasp, because it lies beyond the limit that "transience" sets to both.

Linger on the imagination. For Butler, understanding the "transition from mythic to divine violence" passes through what justice now "requires": first, that "to conjecture" be synonymous with "to imagine"; second, that what we imagine can "only" be as she imagines ("We can imagine only that the rock would dissolve into water, and that her guilt would give way to endless tears");

finally, that *this* case, Niobe's case, may allow us to understand and open up, *in this case,* the necessity of conjecture.

Is Niobe's case singular, or can it serve as an example? Does not the very singularity, the atrocity of Niobe's grief, set the single standard for general conjecture? If so, we will reckon our own grief by the unit she provides. (Ordinally, cardinally: always less, by a degree, by a number, for instance, one child, one death, one friend.) But is her figure *one*, the highest concept, the most extreme, the last point or part imaginable for human suffering? If so, she will mark the edge, the *apex,* the *terminus* where the concept, like dissolving stone, loses its at-one-ness to "something else." As Lucretius says, "[the last point] never has had and never will be able to have an independent, separate existence, since it is itself a primary and unitary part of something else."

On these questions Benjamin, too, is silent—but his position seems different. The boundary-stone, *Markstein,* stands. The inscription, the mark, it bears may not be (equally) legible from either side of the frontier it marks ("legibility" is historically determined—and as the boundary stone on one reading marks the limit between two asymmetrical relations-to-history, a human and a divine one, the historicity of the mark and thus its senses and readings will be different on either side of the boundary). Only if it *does not dissolve* or fade over time, only if we precisely do not *give way,* and give up the object, will the stone mark what is ideally at stake—its historicity.

Here is where I stand when I translate my grief at losing you, just you, just one: imagining, but not *only* imagining, life beyond what I count as one life. Now I imagine the institution of collective grief, of more-than-one life, to stand on and mark mute historicity, as in Benjamin, but also to mark and stand on ground that makes its objective disappearance—as "dissolving," as the wearing-into-water of stone—the condition of its effectiveness.

CHAPTER 15

~

"How Strangely Changed"
Finding Phillis Wheatley in Niobean Myth and Memory, an Essay in Verse

DREA BROWN

> By highlighting Niobe's rebellion against a totalizing power,
> Wheatley reclaims black motherhood as a site of resistance,
> not just vulnerability. . . . Niobe [transforms] from haughty
> and prideful . . . to rebellious and determined.
> —Nicole Spigner, "Phillis Wheatley's Niobean Poetics"

1. FRAMING MYTH: A MOTHER ENDS IN GRIEF

it begins this way: the daughter of a king, wife of another, a queen-mother
so besotted with the heft of her own golden brood that she was aggrieved
with Leto's divine two. left incense unlit in her temples, gave no praise
but to her own creations. a glorious lot, how she loved her children.
such a careless offense, sharpening rage and arrow of splendid gods
all else is tragedy. they aimed for her heart. showed no mercy.

one shot in her eldest's right eye, the next pierced two sweat-slicked backs,
skewering them. another silenced through the throat, blood like water-
falls rushed from mortal wounds. rivers in the cup of her horrified hands.
she watched as more of her sons were ripped and smashed into lifeless
things. Each daughter left upturned and twitching until every seizing breath
stopped, and all twelve, all six and six had died.
she had called them alive once, but what to name this kind of dying,
how to leave their bodies and listen for the holler of ghosts—*oh mother!*
she begged for resurrection, a righteous intervention, she wrung her hands
with the blood of her progeny, became banshee wail and wet-breath.
what to do with such guttural sorrow? they had killed all her children
still, there was nothing she would take back.

this was the consequence of her loving, slaughter and unimaginable grief.
should she become stone? jagged heart, soggy rock, salt watered
each
losslosslosslossloss
losslosslossloss
losslossloss
a dank prayer.

what could hold her weight but the earth full on their bloodied lives
she could fix to the soil's stink and weep, there was no other mercy.
besides, what would change should the rock cry out, *oh gods*.

2. ANOTHER MOTHER, "POURED OUT WATER BEFORE THE SUN AT HIS RISING"[1]

another mother is made into myth by men purporting to be gods.
she in a thimble of light, mouth full of the dead and them that do not die
a calabash raised, its full belly emptied over earth with gratitude and mercy
this is the memory told: mother water praise, each morning. all the child
claimed to know. long after she was brought across the black-blue back
of Atlantic. but before any of this—water praise dawn, the mother.

---

1. Margaretta Odell (in Wheatley 1995, 82). In her "memoir," Odell writes that "[Phillis] does not seem to have preserved any remembrance of the place of her nativity, or of her parents, excepting the simple circumstance that her mother poured out water before the sun at his rising—in reference, no doubt, to an ancient African custom." The "memoir" is questionable in reliability, but as Glatt (2020) observes, the "claim that Phillis's single memory of Africa was of her mother pouring out ritual libations before the rising sun may well be a faithful transcription of a source's testimony."

3. THIS TOO IS DYING, THE CHILDREN, ONE BY ONE

the body a vein for the living, flesh not thick enough to survive on grief
alone. this mother honored all faces of her god, every living prayer
that carried her blood. six sons six daughters, every one cherished alive
her mouth full of their names. sweet incense flower crowns, handfuls
of seeds ripening to fruit, the dreams of their juice kept on her breath.
hips spread with memories of bearing, swayed and steady as cool water
some mothers are rivers, determined and wide, coursing relentless waters.
the heart, a vehement swell, the thrilling surpassed only by god, who
some believe themselves to be. skinless men. tongues hanged backward
ineffable and violent. it was not personal. love is paltry to merciless
labor. an ambush of fervent unconsecrated men wrangled her children
like kinless beasts. chased into coffles, all of them refused to die.[2]

---

    2. This fracturing of family and attempt at erasure of humanity is another form of death: social, spiritual, psychic, emotional. Also, see Orlando Patterson's *Slavery and Social Death: A Comparative Study* (1982).

4. AND THE MOTHER TOO

some mothers are rivers. their children suns rippling with unbridled life.
when the eldest fell, then a row of brothers chained at the neck, grief
dragged her load across the ground. *dear god.* the only prayer.
she saw her daughters prodded and husked. watched their damned breaths
flounder. it was not personal. no one thought of this mother's
dreams of ripe life, sour in her cheeks, they simply bound her hands[3]

then the feet. she could not stand her own weight, could not handle
capture and carnage. who would claim the dead and call them by water's
first light? whose arm lay unattended reaching from the dirt *oh mercy!*
what fool-gods are men. what is this but the strangest death, what life
is left here? how stony her feet, how petrified the heart in a mother's
chest. what should she become: amorphous rock, heaping unmovable grief?
all around pried maws made mute, flesh wounds and flayed backsides
her own maddening sounds. *give them back. give me back my children.*
her tongue threatened to pop out or lodge in her throat. this was the prayer
she had left. give them back . . .
                  but nothing came. and the nothing was a dying
stacked and sweltering, lonely and cold. there were pretend gods
towing an infinite mouth of sea, the sodden moan of its salty breath.[4]

---

3. This resistance to powerful oppressive forces found in the mother's fierce loving is also passed to the children whose lives will soon be denied. I also view this "rebellious and determined" love as divine. In this there is a claim and consciousness of self, of the ancestral and sacred. One that is not arrogant but full of self-worth and value.

4. Niobe is not only made to watch but also suffers a "death" in the fracture of her family and the transition from human to cargo. In this rendition, she is entangled in both myth and transatlantic memory. What happens to Phillis Wheatley's mother is caught up in what Saidia Hartman calls in "Venus in Two Acts" (2008, 7) an "impossible story," of which the archive provides no narrative outside of death. In addition to Niobe, this mother may also be viewed as Venus, one of many Black women unnamed and lost in the maritime tragedy of the Middle Passage. As I craft *an impossible story,* I look to Hartman as I aim "to tell a story about degraded matter and dishonored life that doesn't delight and titillate, but instead ventures toward another mode of writing."

5. "THE MOTHERS RETURN TO THE MOTHER"[5]

haaaaaa aaaaaaah haaaaaa aaaaaaaaah
awwwwwwww awwwwwww awwwwwww
hooooooooo ooooooooooo
awwwwwwww awwwwwww awwwwwww

her body. a stinging thing made raw. clammy hands
pulling her parts. and *naaaaaaaaaw naaaaaaaaaw*
                                           she ached for a splinter of mercy
bile lurching from her gut she ached with torn and tethered lives
cawing beside her. they became a squall of conjure for their children
and *awwwwwwww awwwwwwwww* all aboard was thunderous grief.

they became unpredictable weather, bucking and boundless, their backs
aching for wings, a synchronous heave, a wreck of taffrails and yemoja's
refusal, then heavy curious birds. when they dropped, an empyreal dye
stunned the sea,[6] churned cobalt peacock and raven's wing, underwater
and alive. they became aqueous murmuring surf, a gathered force of god.[7]
they became part of her name—fishes and mer mamas bowed in praise.

---

5. Washington 2013, 216. In this overflowing essay Washington speaks of the potent reach of Yemoja, found in all fluid, mother of all things, protector of all things; of the many prolific testaments to Yemoja, Washington writes:

> Mother molded us to perfection in liquids that we carry in us and spontaneously replenish for life. Seventy percent of our being is Yemoja. She is the saliva that makes speech possible. She is the blood surging through our veins. She is the vehicle through which sperm travels. She is the album, of fertile eggs, blood, and milk. She is the vaginal fluid of the Earth that glistens between lips, flows through rock gardens, chuckles in creeks, and shimmies down streams. The dance of the river, the ocean's roar, the gold-laced milk of my breasts, the salt of your tears: Yemoja.

It is here where these Niobean mothers return to the Mother, in an act of resistance but also a desire to be held as they once held their children, and as the only means to possibly hold them again, carrying them across the Atlantic.

6. I draw on the tale of the Igbo people who, after arriving on St. Simon's Island (at Dunbar Creek, what is now called Igbo Landing), rather than be enslaved in a new world chose instead to walk into the water to go back home. I also look to the folktale of the flying Africans who, when the time came, flew from captivity back to Africa. Some versions suggest it was the Igbo who took to sky rather than water. Virginia Hamilton writes another version in *The People Who Could Fly: American Black Folktales* (1985).

7. Though all onboard did not call to Yemoja, I am offering that she was a familiar name at sea, that in grief and turmoil there was a call to higher forces.

devolving without end wading in waves on waves of loosed prayers[8]
how strangely changed, how beautiful in woe[9] their bubbling breaths.

---

8. Wheatley, "Ocean" (2001, 79, line 26). A reworking of the line "And waves on waves devolving without End."

9. Wheatley, "Niobe in Distress for Her Children Slain by Apollo" (2001, 176, line 58). While Wheatley signifies Niobe's transformation in grief, "how strangely changed" is somewhat ambiguous, and my intervention aims to step into the opening. The strange change speaks to the transformation from free to fettered, as well as the transformation of a collective of grieving mothers, whose tears return to another Mother—Yemoja, mother of all life. It is through Yemoja that these mothers reclaim their children who do not survive the Middle Passage; those thrown overboard or who surrender to waiting and watching arms. In this form, these mothers become more than a crying rock, they become the fluid itself—while the stone is emblematic of Niobe's punishment and grief, the water allows these mothers a kind of freedom taken from them in captivity. In these waters, grief, memory and the sacred coalesce. As M. Jacqui Alexander offers in *Pedagogies of Crossing: Meditations of Feminism, Sexual Politics, Memory, and the Sacred* (2005, 303), "water overflows with memory. Emotional memory. Bodily memory. Sacred memory."

6. "ONE ONLY DAUGHTER LIVES, AND SHE THE LEAST"[10]

we are many. small ones and biting women pitching forth never back
to wherever my mama. we are all gone. everything taken to water.
a body falls against my back, the back in front keeps flies, it is almost dead.
the dead are never quiet. something calls my name, gentle like my mama.
sometime sea is red and thrashing then gurgle and *plunk!* maybe grief
overboard grow a tail and swim away. mama's voice is foamy and alive.
i want to splash with her but flop into a fit of dream with blueface gods
when i wake i am a barnacle on milked breasts, we become one merciful
heart tremble and dry like salt meat. i think we float and mama's wet hands
carry us across. but who would believe the frenzy of a sea-wrought child

---

10. Wheatley, "Niobe" (2001, 59, line 217).

7. A MOTHER BECOMES MYTH, THE CHILD REMEMBERS AND WRITES ANOTHER

an impossible story to tell: being brought. bought. the ship on the child's
head. her mother a briny venus, the sea conflicted with maritime prey.
she saw their faces and blinking eyes the glory of black liquescent hands
waving. mellifluent ocean calling her name. what a salve—*'twas mercy*
she offered to satisfy, like sweet resin or lilies placed before a new god.
memory under tongue, how sacred the swallow, the ink of a versed life.

she mused on myth to remember. aurora neptune niobe, morning sea ndye
how distressed the mouth damming tide. how unspeakable the backflow
of maternal misery. they took her children, o sea, they left them all to die
a sable assembly of ghosts. what should this little one become, breath
transformed by cruel fate, how jailed the chain, the strained breasts of water
struck by fallen kin. lust for freedom springs from her pen, such filial grief.[11]

---

11. A nod to Phillis Wheatley's "To the Right and Honorable William, Earl of Dartmouth": "Should you my lord, while you peruse my song / wonder from whence my love of *Freedom* sprung" (2001, 40, lines 20–21) and "I, young in life, by seeming cruel fate / Was snatch'd from *Afric's* fancy'd happy seat" (40, lines 24–25).

8. CRISSCROSSING

here is a poet named for a tragic ship, named for a woman claimed by grief.
phillis on the shore restless in wait for her love, incessantly like a child
seeking a familiar face in the brine. nine times she returned. goddamn
empty sea thought, her heart hanged from an almond tree. my mama
is everywhere dreamt the child on a ship, even in terror-wrecked prayers.
the sea is full of flower fish she thought, readying for return to water

for the promise of print and mama-blossom. there was no going back.
no longer freight, a ruddy passenger venturing a free and published life.
there was something like sovereignty in the old stones, the handsome
cool of king's country, in breaking fog and almost easy breathing.
it was not her choice to stomach the tide again. the mistress dying
could not without her. goddam broken vow, what land is mercy?

9. AGAIN AND AGAIN NIOBE

truth be told the old myth repeats. in this telling may there be some mercy.
manumitted and married with persistent pen you become a mother of grief.
But first you are free black woman poet wheatley peters, your hands
are your hands. claim them before fate takes you, indigent winter prayer.
may morning rise in your face, may a bulbous glass yield grace and water
the earth. you keep a full mouth. dear girl, poet, foremother your mother
left to sea, you a wife of a man believed sturdy who took you back
to the place of his fettered life. in middleton he called you a lady of god
called you a nurse, how quiet you seem in the record of newlywed life.[12]
your man off on some business or griff, you bear soft-boned children
the flora of your flesh, what did you call those short seasons of breath—
vivian, laurel, pearly everlasting? tell me gardens thrive after their dying.

---

12. Dayton 2021.

10. ELEGY FOR THE CHILDREN PETERS, UNBORN AND SHORT-LIVED

where are the psalms for infants smelling of milk, clothed in soft death
may their cries reign on celestial horn, may sky bear witness and mercy
to a mother's fresh born gone. how many unaccounted or taken to water
for blood to come out in the wash? did you see the faces of your children
tenebrous and lovely? what miscarried elegy what petition in prayer
could bring them back, bring you back, bring your children? *oh god
seat of eternal mystery what lies beyond stained and wanting hands*
silence fills their space, no crumbled stone marks an irretrievable life.
tongue unlocked, open the hatch, console yourself in verses of grief
the tender meat swiftly snatched, the bitter marrow of a mother
pleading to keep the last. what to do with that flame of tiny breath
clasped to the chest then blown out that no kiss will bring back.

11. IT ENDS LIKE THIS

it is no secret what comes next, there is no going back
the course already laid. here is a black woman dying.
the body in ruins, freedom a precarious mercy.
go on, say this was not the work of men praying
to be more than men, tallying others' worth. few hands
are clean. a wonder before the wheezing last breath—
what could she become? everything given to god.
what to want except perhaps a sip of cool water
to soothe the throat and call to her children.
oh foul myth of mothers made stone in grief
oh miracle of crossing, poems that lived!
return to earth, to water, mourning, mother.

12. CODA: BUT IT IS NOT

if this were the final word on such a life, such an endemic myth, surely water would cry out a roaring juba of deep-sea hands and heads thrown back. should the children live beloved, the waters would greet the day, prayers merciful and succulent, everything black and flourishing. the old grief tired of itself, haints wearing flesh like a new coat, every ripe breath warm. but *aaww god naawww,* the myth is steeped in diabolic dye.[13]

---

13. Wheatley, "On Being Brought from Africa to America" (2001, 13, line 6). A nod to the line "their color is a diabolic dye" to further suggest continued assumptions and mythologies of Blackness.

BIBLIOGRAPHY

Adelman, J. 1992. *Suffocating Mothers: Fantasies of Maternal Origin in Shakespeare's Plays,* Hamlet to The Tempest. Routledge.

Agamben, G. 1998. Homo Sacer: *Sovereign Power and Bare Life.* Stanford UP.

———. 2000. *Means without End: Notes on Politics.* U of Minnesota P.

———. 2009. *The Signature of All Things: On Method.* Zone Books.

Ahmadi, A. 2015. "Benjamin's Niobe." In *Towards the Critique of Violence: Walter Benjamin and Giorgio Agamben,* ed. B. Moran and C. Salzani, 57–72. Bloomsbury.

Ahmed, S. 2014. *Willful Subjects.* Duke UP.

Ahmed, S., and M. Binyam. 2022. "You Pose a Problem: A Conversation with Sara Ahmed." *The Paris Review,* January 14, 2022. https://www.theparisreview.org/blog/2022/01/14/you-pose-a-problem-a-conversation-with-sara-ahmed/.

Alaimo, S. 2000. *Undomesticated Ground: Recasting Nature as Feminist Space.* Cornell UP.

———. 2008. "Trans-Corporeal Feminisms and the Ethical Space of Nature." In *Material Feminisms,* ed. S. Alaimo and S. Hekman, 237–64. U of Indiana P.

Alciato, A. ("Alciatus"). 1621. *Emblemata.* Petro Paulo Tozzi. https://www.emblems.arts.gla.ac.uk/alciato/emblem.php?id=A21a067.

Alexander, M. J. 2005. *Pedagogies of Crossing: Meditations on Feminism, Sexual Politics, Memory, and the Sacred.* Duke UP.

Alford, C. F. 2000. "Levinas and Winnicott: Motherhood and Responsibility." *American Imago* 57.3: 235–59.

Anderson, W. S., ed. 1972. *Ovid's* Metamorphoses, *Book 6–10.* U of Oklahoma P.

Arendt, H. 1958. *The Human Condition.* U of Chicago P.

———. 1969. "Reflections on Violence." *New York Review of Books* 12.4 (February 27, 1969). https://www.nybooks.com/articles/1969/02/27/a-special-supplement-reflections-on-violence/.

———. 1970. *On Violence*. Harcourt, Int.

Auden, W. H. 1960. *Homage to Clio*. Random House.

Badiou, A. 2008. *Conditions*. Trans. S. Corcoran. Continuum.

Baert, B. 2004. "El pensamiento petrificado. A propósito de la tercera dimensión en la teoría de la imagen medieval." In *El fruto de la fe*, 119–27. Fundacion Carlos Amberes.

———. 2013. "Nymphe (Wind). Der Raum zwischen Motiv und Affekt in der frühen Neuzeit (Zugleich ein Beitrag zur Aby Warburg-Forschung)." *Ars* 46.1: 16–42.

———. 2014. *Nymph: Motif, Phantom, Affect, I*. Peeters.

———. 2016a. *In Response to Echo*. Peeters.

———. 2016b. *Nymph: Motif, Phantom, Affect, II*. Peeters.

———. 2017. *About Stains or the Image as Residue*. Peeters.

———. 2018. *What about Enthusiasm? A Rehabilitation*. Peeters.

Bakhtin, M. 1995. *Rabelais and His World*. Trans. H. Iswolsky. Indiana UP.

Baracchi, C. 2020. *Amicizia*. Mursia Editore.

———. 2022. "Writing Life: Biography, Autobiography, and the Remainder." In *Rethinking Life: Italian Philosophy in Precarious Times*, ed. S. Benso, 203–16. SUNY P.

Baraitser, L. 2009. *Maternal Encounters: An Ethics of Interruption*. Routledge.

Barkan, L. 1993. "The Beholder's Tale: Ancient Sculpture, Renaissance Narratives." *Representations* 44: 133–66.

Barolsky, P. 2005. "Ovid, Bernini, and the Art of Petrification." *Arion* 13.2: 149–62.

Beaulieu, A. 2005. "Deleuze et les stoïciens." In *Gilles Deleuze: héritage philosophique*, ed. A. Beaulieu, 45–72. PUF.

Benjamin, A. 2012. "Hegel's Other Woman: The Figure of Niobe in Hegel's 'Lectures on Fine Art.'" In *Die Aktualität der Romantik*, ed. F.-J. Deiters, A. Fleithmann, B. Lang, A. Lewis, and C. Weller, 159–77. Rombach Verlag.

———. 2015. *Towards a Relational Ontology*. SUNY P.

———. 2016. *Virtue in Being: Towards an Ethics of the Unconditioned*. SUNY P.

———. 2019. "God and the Truth of Human Being." *Journal for Continental Philosophy of Religion* 1: 149–60.

———. 2020. "Potentiality, Relationality and the Problem of Actualisation." *Teoria* 40.1: 115–24.

———. 2024. *On Gesture: Classical and Renaissance Expressions*. Edinburgh UP.

Benjamin, W. [1921] 1986. "Critique of Violence." In *Reflections: Essays, Aphorisms, Autobiographical Writings*, ed. P. Demetz, 291–316. Schocken Books.

———. [1931] 1986. "The Destructive Character." In *Reflections: Essays, Aphorisms, Autobiographical Writings*, ed. P. Demetz, 317–19. Schocken Books.

———. 1968. *Illuminations: Essays and Reflections*. Ed. H. Arendt and trans. H. Zohn. Schocken Books.

———. 1998. *Origin of the German Tragic Drama*. Trans. J. Osborne. Verso.

———. 1999. *Gesammelte Schriften*, Vol. 2.1. Ed. R. Tiedemann and H. Schweppenhäuser. Suhrkamp Verlag.

———. 2021. *Toward the Critique of Violence: A Critical Edition.* Ed. P. Fenves and J. Ng. Stanford UP.

Bennett, M. 2015. "Cicero's *De Fato* in Deleuze's Logic of Sense." *Deleuze Studies* 9.1: 25–58.

Berlant, L. 2011. *Cruel Optimism.* Duke UP.

Bernard, J. 2021. *Les mots et les choses dans l'œuvre théâtrale d'Alberto Savinio: un théâtre de l'entre-deux.* Linguistique, Normandie Université.

Bernstein, J. 2003. "Love and Law: Hegel's Critique of Morality." *Social Research* 70.2: 393–432.

———. 2017. "Remembering Isaac: On the Impossibility and Immorality of Faith." In *The Insistence of Art: Aesthetic Philosophy after Early Modernity,* ed. P. A. Kottman, 257–88. Fordham UP.

Bernstein, R. J. 2011. "Hannah Arendt's Reflections on Violence and Power." *Iris* 3.5: 3–30.

Berrettoni, G. 1989. "Il dito rotto di Zenone." *Materiali e discussioni per l'analisi dei testi classici* 22: 23–36.

Bertolini, D. 2019. "Un mito, qualunque mito non ha un valore storico ma un valore di eternità. La favola di Niobe nella prima metà del novecento." In *Il mito di Niobe,* ed. A. Bruciati and M. Angle, 90–94. Silvana Editoriale.

Bettini, M. 2008. *The Portrait of the Lover.* Trans. L. Gibbs. U of California P.

Bianconi, L. 1987. *Music in the Seventeenth Century.* Cambridge UP.

Binczek, N. 2007. *Kontakt: Der Tastsinn in Texten der Aufklärung.* M. Niemeyer Verlag.

Blanchot, M. 1982. *The Space of Literature.* Trans. A. Smock. U of Nebraska P.

———. 1996. *Pour l'amitié.* Fourbis.

Bömer, P., ed. 1976. *P. Ovidius Naso: Metamorphosen.* Carl Winter.

Bordignon, G. 2012. "'L'unità organica della *sophrosyne* e dell'estasi': una proposta di lettura di Mnemosyne Atlas, Tavola 5." *Engramma* 100 (September/October 2012). http://www.engramma.it/eOS/index.php?id_articolo=1145.

Borges, J. L. 1974. *Obras completas, 1923–1972.* Emecé.

———. 1999. *Collected Fictions.* Trans. A. Hurley. Penguin.

———. 2000. *Nueva antología personal.* Siglo XXI.

Boyd, B. W. 2020. "Still, She Persisted: Materiality and Memory in Ovid's *Metamorphoses.*" *Dictynna* 17: 1–17.

Brett, J. 1978. "Hugo von Hofmannsthal: 'Letter of Lord Chandos'—the Writer's Relationship to His Language." *American Imago* 35.3: 238–58.

Brill, S. 2022. "Biopolitics and the 'Boundless People': An Iliadic Model." In *Biopolitics and Ancient Thought,* ed. J. Backman and A. Cimino, 15–37. Oxford UP.

Brower, V. W. 2021. "Biopolitics and Probability: Modifications on Life's Way." In *Agamben and the Existentialists,* ed. M. A. Norris and C. Dickinson, 46–64. Edinburgh UP.

Bruciati, A., and M. Angle, eds. 2019. *Il mito di Niobe.* Silvana Editoriale.

Bulfinch, T. 2007. *Bulfinch's Mythology.* NuVision Publications.

Burchill, L. 2006. "Re-situating the Feminine in Contemporary French Philosophy." In *Beliefs, Bodies, and Being: Feminist Reflections on Embodiment,* ed. D. Orr et al., 81–102. Rowman and Littlefield.

———. 2017. "Reconsidering *Chôra,* Architecture and 'Woman.'" *Field* 7.1: 191–202.

Butler, J. 1993. *Bodies That Matter.* Routledge.

———. 1997. *The Psychic Power of Life: Theories in Subjection.* Stanford UP.

———. 2000. *Antigone's Claim: Kinship between Life and Death.* Columbia UP.

———. 2006. "Critique, Coercion, and Sacred Life in Benjamin's 'Critique of Violence.'" In *Political Theologies: Public Religions in a Post-Secular World,* ed. H. de Vries and L. E. Sullivan, 201–19. Fordham UP.

———. 2009. "Critica, coercizione e vita sacra in *Per la critica della violenza* di Benjamin." *Aut-aut* 344: 65–100.

———. 2012. *Parting Ways: Jewishness and the Critique of Zionism.* Columbia UP.

Butler, S. 2015. *The Ancient Phonograph.* Zone Books.

Buxton, R. 2009. *Forms of Astonishments.* Oxford UP.

Campbell, D. A., ed. 1990. *Greek Lyric: Sappho and Alcaeus.* Harvard UP.

Cardano, N. 2020. "Niobe." In *Savinio, A–Z,* ed. E. Cohen, 269–70. Electa.

Carretta, V. 2011. *Phillis Wheatley: Biography of a Genius in Bondage.* U of Georgia P.

Cavarero, A. 2009. *Horrorism.* Trans. W. McCuaig. Columbia UP.

Cavell, S. 2022. *Here and There.* Harvard UP.

Centanni M., et al. 2000. "Madre della vita, madre della morte. Figure e *Pathosformeln.* Saggio interpretativo di Mnemosyne Atlas, Tavola 5." *Engramma* 1 (September 2000). http://www.engramma.it/eOS/index.php?id_articolo=2744.

Chejfec, S. 1994. *Los incompletos.* Alfaguara.

Chevalier, J., and J. Gheerbrant. 2002. "Pierre." In *Dictionnaire des Symboles,* 751–58. Laffont.

Chitwood, A. 2004. *Death by Philosophy: The Biographical Tradition in the Life and Death of Archaic Philosophers Empedocles, Heraclitus, and Democritus.* U of Michigan P.

Cirulli, F. 2015. *The Age of Figurative Theo-humanism: The Beauty of God and Man in German Aesthetics of Painting and Sculpture (1754–1828).* Springer.

Collobert, C. 2011. "Poetry as Flawed Reproduction: Possession and Mimesis." In *Plato and the Poets,* ed. P. Destrée and F.-G. Herrmann, 41–62. Brill.

Cook, R. M. 1964. *Niobe and Her Children: An Inaugural Lecture.* Cambridge UP.

Cornwell, H. 2017. Pax *and the Politics of Peace: Republic to Principate.* Oxford UP.

Critchley, S. 2009. *The Book of Dead Philosophers.* Penguin Random House.

Crompton, L. 2003. *Homosexuality and Civilization.* Harvard UP.

Csapo, E., and P. Wilson. 2009. "Timotheus the New Musician." In *The Cambridge Companion to Greek Lyric,* ed. F. Budelmann, 277–93. Cambridge UP.

Curinga, L. 2013. "'La mort de Niobé,' un mito disarmonizzato." In *Musiche e immagini dagli anni dieci,* ed. G. Salvetti, 1–20. SidM.

Dacier, A. 1716. *Homère défendu contre l'apologie du R. P. Hardouin, ou suite des causes de la corruption du Goust.* Jean Baptiste Coignard.

d'Angour, A. 2006. "The New Music—So What's New?" In *Rethinking Revolutions through Ancient Greece,* ed. S. Goldhill and R. Osborne, 264–83. Cambridge UP.

Dayton, C. H. 2021. "Lost Years Recovered: John Peters and Phillis Wheatley Peters in Middleton." *The New England Quarterly* 94.3: 309–51.

de Arguijo, Juan. 2011. *Sonetos.* Biblioteca Virtual Digital Miguel de Cervantes.

DeBlieu, J. 1998. *Wind.* Houghton Mifflin Harcourt.

de Castris, P. L. 2001. *Polidoro da Caravaggio.* Electa.

Deigh, J. 1996. *The Sources of Moral Agency: Essays in Moral Psychology and Freudian Theory.* Cambridge UP.

Deleuze, G. 1986. *Cinema 1: The Movement-Image*. Trans. H. Tomlinson and B. Habberjam. U of Minnesota P.

———. 1990. *The Logic of Sense*. Trans. M. Lester. Columbia UP.

———. 1991. *Masochism: Coldness and Cruelty*. Trans. J. McNeil. Zone Books.

———. 1995. "The Exhausted." *SubStance* 24.3: 3–28.

Deleuze, G., and F. Guattari. 1987. *A Thousand Plateaus*. Trans. B. Massumi. U of Minnesota P.

———. 1991. *What Is Philosophy?* Trans. H. Tomlinson. Columbia UP.

Derrida, J. 1989. *Memoires for Paul de Man*. Trans. C. Lindsay, J. Culler, E. Cadava, and P. Kamuf. Columbia UP.

———. 1991. "'Eating Well,' or the Calculation of the Subject: An Interview with Jacques Derrida." In *Who Comes after the Subject?*, ed. E. Cadava, P. Connor, and J.-L. Nancy, 96–116. Routledge.

———. 1992. "Force of Law: 'The Mystical Foundation of Authority.'" In *Deconstruction and the Possibility of Justice*, ed. D. Cornell, M. Rosenfeld, and D. G. Carlson, 3–67. Routledge.

———. 1997. *The Politics of Friendship*. Trans. G. Collins. Verso.

———. 2011. *The Beast and the Sovereign*. Vol. 2. Trans. G. Bennington. U of Chicago P.

———. 2020. *Life Death*. Trans. P.-A. Brault and M. Naas. U of Chicago P.

———. 2021. *Clang*. Trans. G. Bennington and D. Wills. U of Minnesota P.

Deuber-Mankowsky, A. 2016. "Rhythms of the Living, Conditions of Critique: On Judith Butler's Reading of Walter Benjamin's 'Critique of Violence.'" In *Walter Benjamin and Theology*, ed. C. Dickinson and S. Symons, 253–71. Fordham UP.

———. 2019. "Niobe and Korah, Different Orders of Time: A Commentary on Paragraphs 14–17 of Walter Benjamin's 'Toward the Critique of Violence.'" *Critical Times* 2.2: 295–305.

Di Cesare, D. 2020. "It Is Time for Philosophy to Return to the City." *The Journal of Continental Philosophy* 1.2: 201–16.

Didi-Huberman, G. 2001. "Dialektik des Monstrums: Aby Warburg and the Symptom Paradigm." *Art History* 24.5: 621–45.

———. 2010. "Hepatische Empathie." *Trivium* 2: 2–17.

———. 2012. "Warburg's Haunted House." *Common Knowledge* 18.1: 50–78.

———. 2013. "Science avec patience." *Images Revues* 4.1: 1–16.

di Giovanni, N. T., ed. 1970. *Jorge Luis Borges: The Aleph and Other Stories*. Dutton.

———, ed. 2014. *Jorge Luis Borges: The Maker (Prose Pieces 1934–1960)*. https://archive.org/details/themaker_201811/page/n13/mode/2up.

Dolar, M. 2006. *A Voice and Nothing More*. MIT P.

Donne, J. 1967. *The Satires, Epigrams, and Verse Letters*. Oxford UP.

Dover, K., ed. 1993. *Aristophanes: Frogs*. Oxford UP.

Edelman, L. 2004. *No Future: Queer Theory and the Death Drive*. Duke UP.

Englert, W. 2017. "*Fanum* and Philosophy: Cicero and the Death of Tullia." *Ciceroniana Online* 1.1: 41–66.

Emlyn-Jones, C., and W. Preddy, eds. *Plato V: Republic*. Harvard UP.

Enterline, L. 2000. *The Rhetoric of the Body from Ovid to Shakespeare*. Cambridge UP.

Erskine, A. 2000. "Zeno and the Beginning of Stoicism." *Classics Ireland* 7: 51–60.

Esposito, R. 2011. *Immunitas: The Protection and Negation of Life*. Trans. Z. Hanafi. Polity.

———. 2019. *Politics and Negation: For an Affirmative Philosophy*. Trans. Z. Hanafi. Polity.

———. 2020. *Instituting Thought: Three Paradigms of Political Ontology*. Trans. M. Epstein. Polity.

———. 2021. *Istituzione*. Il Mulino.

Fagiolo dell'Arco, M. 1983. "Biographical Notes on a Metaphysical Argonaut—Alberto Savinio." *Art Forum* 21.5: 46–53.

Falciani, C., and A. Natali. 2010. *Bronzino: Artist and Poet at the Court of the Medici*. Mandragora.

Fanon, F. 1961. *The Wretched of the Earth*. Grove Press.

Farbman, H. 2012. "From the Cold Earth." *Postmodern Culture* 23.1.

Feldherr, A. 2004–5. "Reconciling Niobe." *Hermathena* 177–78: 125–46.

———. 2010. *Playing Gods: Ovid's* Metamorphoses *and the Politics of Fiction*. Princeton UP.

Felson, N. 2002. "*Threptra* and Invincible Hands: The Father-Son Relationship in *Iliad* 24." *Arethusa* 35.1: 35–50.

Fenichel, O. 1937. "The Scopophilic Instinct and Identification." *International Journal of Psychoanalysis* 18: 6–34.

Forbes Irving, P. M. C. 1990. *Metamorphosis in Greek Myths*. Clarendon P.

Fox, D. 2009. *Cold World*. Zero Books.

Frécaut, J.-M. 1980. "La métamorphose de Niobé chez Ovide (*Met.* 6. 301–12)." *Latomus* 39: 129–43.

Freedberg, D. 1989. *The Power of Images*. U of Chicago P.

Freud, S. 1917. "Mourning and Melancholia." *SE* 14: 239–60.

———. 1920. *Beyond the Pleasure Principle*. *SE* 18: 1–64.

Frosh, S. 2015. "Endurance." *American Imago* 72.2: 157–75.

Furley, D. J. 1967. *Two Studies in the Greek Atomists*. 1. *Indivisible Magnitudes*. Princeton UP.

Gagarin, M. 1986. *Early Greek Law*. U of California P.

Galinsky, K. 1996. *Augustan Culture*. Princeton UP.

Galland-Szymkowiak, M. 2011. "Le rôle de l'existence à l'apogée de la philosophie de l'identité." In *Das Problem der Endlichkeit in der Philosophie Schellings*, ed. M. Galland-Szymkowiak, 267–83. Lit Verlag.

———. 2019. "Chaos als ästhetischer, mythologischer und metaphysischer Begriff bei Schelling." *Schelling-Studien* 7: 155–76.

Gandorfer, D., and Z. Ayub. 2020. "Introduction: Matterphorical." *Theory & Event* 24.1: 2–13.

Geller, S. M., and L. S. Greenberg. 2012. *Therapeutic Presence: A Mindful Approach to Effective Therapy*. American Psychological Association.

Gesell, B. D. 2013. *Pillars of Salt and Stone*. Pacifica Graduate Institute.

Gilby, D. M. 1996. *Weeping Rocks*. PhD diss. U of Wisconsin–Madison.

Gillespie, S. H., and S. R. Hill. 2019. "On Walter Benjamin's Legacy: A Correspondence between Hannah Arendt and Theodor Adorno." https://www.samantharosehill.com/writing-page/on-walter-benjamins-legacy-a-correspondence-between-hannah-arendt-and-theodor-adorno.

Girard, R. 2011. *Géometries du désir*. Editions de l'Herne.

Glatt, C. 2020. "'To Perpetuate Her Name': Appropriation and Autobiography in Margaretta Matilda Odell's Memoir of Phillis Wheatley." *Early American Literature* 55.1: 145–76.

Gnann, A. 1997. *Polidoro da Caravaggio (um 1499–1543): Die römischen Innendekorationen*. Scaneg.

Goldhill, S. 2001. "The Erotic Eye: Visual Stimulation and Cultural Conflict." In *Being Greek under Rome*, ed. S. Goldhill, 154–94. Cambridge UP.

Goldschmidt, V. 1979. *Le système stoïcien et l'idée de temps*. Vrin.

Grau, S. 2010. "How to Kill a Philosopher: The Narrating of Ancient Greek Philosophers' Deaths in Relation to Their Way of Living." *Ancient Philosophy* 30: 347–81.

Graver, M. 2002. *Cicero on the Emotions: Tusculan Disputations 3 & 4.* U of Chicago P.

Graves, R. 1955. *The Greek Myths*. Penguin Books.

Griffith, M., ed. 1999. *Sophocles* Antigone. Cambridge UP.

Groys, B. 2012. *Introduction to Antiphilosophy*. Verso.

Gummere, R. M., ed. 1883–1969. *Ad Lucilium Epistulae Morales*. Harvard UP.

Hamacher, W. 1991. "Afformative, Strike." *Cardozo Law Review* 13: 1133–58.

Hardouin, J. 1716. *Apologie d'Homère*. Rigaud.

Harris, O. 2013. "The Ethics of Metamorphosis or A Poet between Two Deaths." In *Classical Myth and Psychoanalysis,* ed. V. Zajko and E. O'Gorman, 251–64. Oxford UP.

Hartman, S. 2007. *Lose Your Mother: A Journey along the Atlantic Slave Route*. Farrar, Straus and Giroux.

———. 2008. "Venus in Two Acts." *Small Axe* 12.2: 1–14.

Haubold, J. 2000. *Homer's People*. Cambridge UP.

Heath, J. 2011–12. "Poetic Simultaneity and Genre in Ovid's *Metamorphoses*." *CJ* 107: 189–211.

Hegel, G. W. F. 1975a. *Hegel's Aesthetics: Lectures on Fine Art*. Trans. T. M. Knox. Oxford UP.

———. 1975b. *Early Theological Writings*. Trans. T. M. Knox. Pennsylvania UP.

Heidegger, M. 1991. *Nietzsche: Volumes One and Two*. Trans. D. Krell. HarperCollins.

———. 1993. "Building, Dwelling, Thinking." In *Basic Writings*, ed. David F. Krell, 347–63. HarperCollins.

———. 2000. "Bauen Wohnen Denken." In *Vorträge und Aufsätze*, Vol. 7, *Gesamtausgabe*, 145–64. Vittorio Klostermann.

Herman, J. 1992. *Trauma and Recovery*. Basic Books.

Hinds, S. 1985. "Booking the Return Trip: Ovid and *Tristia* 1." *Proceedings of the Cambridge Philological Society* 31: 13–32.

Hofmannsthal, H. von. 2005. *The Lord Chandos Letter and Other Writings*. Trans. J. Rotenberg. New York Review of Books.

Holmes, B. 2017. "Liquid Antiquity." In *Liquid Antiquity,* ed. B. Holmes and K. Marta, 18–59. Athens: ΔΕΣΤΕ.

Honig, B. 2013. *Antigone, Interrupted*. Cambridge UP.

Horowitz, G. M. 2001. *Sustaining Loss: Art and Mournful Life*. Stanford UP.

Hsu, E., and C. Low. 2008. *Wind, Life, Health*. Blackwell.

Huffer, L. 2017. "Foucault's Fossils." In *Anthropocene Feminism,* ed. R. Grusin, 65–88. U of Minnesota P.

Ingold, T. 2005. "The Eye of the Storm." *Visual Studies* 20.2: 97–104.

———. 2007. "Earth, Sky, Wind, and Weather." *Journal of the Royal Anthropological Institute* 13: 19–38.

———. 2011. *Being Alive*. Routledge.

James, H. 1895. *Terminations*. Heinemann.

Janan, M. 2009. *Reflections in a Serpent's Eye: Thebes in Ovid's* Metamorphoses. Oxford UP.

Jeffers, H. F. 2020. *The Age of Phillis*. Wesleyan UP.

Jervell, J. 1960. *Imago Dei: Gen. 1, 26 f. im Spätjudentum, in der Gnosis und in den paulinischen Briefen.* Vandenhoeck & Ruprecht.

Jordan, J. 2002. "The Difficult Miracle of Black Poetry in America, or Something Like a Sonnet for Phillis Wheatley." In *Some of Us Did Not Die: New and Selected Essays*, 174–86. Civitas Books.

Kant, I. 1956. *Critique of Practical Reason.* Trans. L. W. Beck. Liberal Arts Press.

———. 1987. *Critique of Judgment.* Trans. W. S. Pluhar. Hackett.

Kaufman, E. 2013. "The Mineralogy of Being." In *Architecture in the Anthropocene: Encounters among Design, Deep Time, Science and Philosophy*, ed. E. Turpin, 153–66. U of Michigan P.

Kemp, W. 1991. "Visual Narratives, Memory, and the Medieval Esprit du System." In *Images of Memory*, ed. S. Küchler and W. Melion, 87–108. Smithsonian Institution Press.

Kerényi, K. 1979. *Goddesses of Sun and Moon: Circe, Aphrodite, Medea, Niobe.* Trans. M. Stein. Spring Publications.

———. 2010. *Miti e misteri.* Trans. A. Brelich. Bollati Boringhieri.

Keuls, E. 1978. "Aeschylus's Niobe and Apulian Funerary Symbolism." *ZPE* 30: 41–68.

Kierkegaard, S. 1992. *Either/Or: A Fragment of Life.* Penguin.

Koestenbaum, W. 1989. *Double Talk: The Erotics of Male Literary Collaboration.* Routledge.

Kornarou, E. 2010. "The Mythological *Exemplum* of Niobe in Sophocles' *Antigone* 823–33." *Rivista di cultura classica e medioevale* 52.2: 263–78.

Kottman, P. A. 2020. "*Noli tangere*: On the Limits of Seeing and Touching in Hegel's Philosophy of Art." *Studi di estetica* 48: 41–66.

Kristeva, J. 1998. *The Severed Head.* Trans. J. Gladding. Columbia UP.

Kuen, E. 2019. *Politische Botschaft und ästhetische Inszenierung: Aspekte der Opernlibrettistik am Hofe Max II. Emanuels von Bayern 1685–1688.* Universitätsbibliothek der Ludwig-Maximilians-Universität.

Kurke, L. 2019. "Musical Animals, Choral Assemblages, and Choral Temporality in Sappho's Tithonus Poem (fr. 58)." *American Journal of Philology* 142.1: 1–39.

Labate, M. 1984. *L'arte di farsi amare.* Giardini.

Lacan, J. 1992. *The Ethics of Psychoanalysis, 1959–1960.* Ed. J. A. Miller and trans. D. Porter. W. W. Norton.

———. 1998. *On Feminine Sexuality, the Limits of Love and Knowledge, 1972–1973: The Seminar of Jacques Lacan, Book 20.* Ed. J.-A. Miller and trans. B. Fink. W. W. Norton.

Lane, D. 2011. "Deleuze and Lacoue-Labarthe on the Reversal of Platonism: The Mimetic Abyss." *SubStance* 40.2: 105–26.

La Rocca, E. 1985. *Amazzanomachia: Le sculture frontonali del tempio di Apollo Sosiano.* De Luca.

———. 1988. "Der Apollo-Sosianus-Tempel." In *Kaiser Augustus und die verlorene Republik*, 121–36. Philipp von Zabern.

Leonard, W. E., ed. 2004. *Lucretius: On the Nature of Things.* Dover.

Lesky, A. 1936. "Niobe." In *Paulys Realencyclopädie der classischen Altertumswissenschaft*, vol. 33, 643–706. Druckenmüller.

LeVen, P. 2011. "Timotheus' Eleven Strings: A New Approach (*PMG* 791.229–36)." *Classical Philology* 106.3: 245–54.

———. 2013. "Reading the Octopus: Authorships, Intertexts, and a Hellenistic Anecdote (Machon Fr. 9 Gow)." *American Journal of Philology* 134.1: 23–35.

Levi, P. 1966. *Survival in Auschwitz.* Trans. S. J. Woolf. Simon and Schuster.

Levinas, E. 1989. *The Levinas Reader.* Ed. Seán Hand. Basil Blackwell.

———. 1998. "Reality and Its Shadow." In *Collected Philosophical Papers,* trans. A. Lingis, 1–14. Duquesne UP.

Levine, P. A. 2010. *In an Unspoken Voice.* California UP.

Lezra, J. 2020. *República salvaje: De la naturaleza de las cosas.* Ediciones Macul.

Lin, Y. 2013. *The Intersubjectivity of Time: Levinas and Infinite Responsibility.* Duquesne UP.

Lista, M., et al. 2003. *L'œuvre d'art totale.* Gallimard.

Loh, M. H. 2011. "Outscreaming the Laocoön." *Oxford Art Journal* 34.3: 393–414.

Long, A., and D. Sedley, eds. 1987. *The Hellenistic Philosophers.* Cambridge UP.

Longuenesse, B. 2017. *I, Me, Mine: Back to Kant, and Back Again.* Oxford UP.

Lopez Levers, L., ed. 2012. *Trauma Counseling: Theories and Interventions.* Springer.

Luciano, D., and M. J. Chen. 2015. "Has the Queer Ever Been Human?" *GLQ* 21.2–3: 183–207.

Lynes, P. 2018. "The Posthuman Promise of the Earth." In *Eco-deconstruction: Derrida and Environmental Philosophy,* ed. M. Fritsch, P. Lynes, and D. Wood, 101–20. Fordham UP.

Lynn-George, M. 1988. Epos: *Word, Narrative and the* Iliad. Palgrave.

Maccari, E. 1876. *Graffiti e chiaroscuri.* Enrico Maccari.

Marquet, J.-F. 1973. *Liberté et existence. Essai sur la formation de la philosophie de Schelling.* Gallimard.

Martelli, F. K. A. 2013. *Ovid's Revisions.* Cambridge UP.

———. 2021. *Ovid.* Brill.

McAuley, M. 2016. *Reproducing Rome: Motherhood in Virgil, Ovid, Seneca and Statius.* Oxford UP.

Mbembe, A. 2019. *Necropolitics.* Duke UP.

McNulty, T. 2015. "Speculative Fetishism." *Konturen* 8: 99–132.

Meillassoux, Q. 2006. *After Finitude.* Trans. R. Braissier. Continuum.

———. 2014. *Time without Becoming.* Ed. A. Longo. Mimesis International.

Merleau-Ponty, M. 2003. *Nature: Course Notes from the Collège de France.* Trans. R. Vallier. Northwestern UP.

Mikkonen, K. 1996. "Theories of Metamorphosis: From Metatrope to Textual Revision." *Style* 30.2: 309–40.

Moran, B., and C. Salzani. 2015. "Introduction: On the Actuality of 'Critique of Violence.'" In *Towards the Critique of Violence: Walter Benjamin and Giorgio Agamben,* ed. B. Moran and C. Salzani, 1–18. Bloomsbury.

Morton, T. 2007. *Ecology without Nature.* Harvard UP.

Most, G. W. 2003. "Anger and Pity in Homer's *Iliad.*" In *Anger: Perspectives from Homer to Galen,* ed. G. W. Most and S. Braund, 50–75. Cambridge UP.

Moten, F. 2003. *In the Break: The Aesthetics of the Black Radical Tradition.* U of Minnesota P.

———. 2017. *Black and Blur: Consent Not to Be a Single Being.* Duke UP.

Mülder-Bach, I. 1998. *Im Zeichen Pygmalions.* W. Fink.

Murray, P. 2011. "Tragedy, Women and the Family in Plato's *Republic.*" In *Plato and the Poets,* ed. P. Destrée and F.-G. Herrmann, 175–94. Brill.

Musser, A. 2018. *Sensual Excess: Queer Femininity and Brown Jouissance.* NYU P.

Naddaff, R. 2002. *Exiling the Poets: The Production of Censorship in Plato's* Republic. U of Chicago P.

Nancy, J.-L. 1993. *The Sense of the World*. Trans. J. S. Librett. U of Minnesota P.

Narbonne, J.-M., and W. Hankey. 2006. *Levinas and the Greek Heritage and One Hundred Years of Neoplatonism in France: A Brief Philosophical History*. Peeters.

Nash, J. 2021. *Birthing Black Mothers*. Duke UP.

Neer, R. 2010. *The Emergence of Classical Style in Greek Sculpture*. U of Chicago P.

Neils, J. 2008. "Niobe (?) on the Portonaccio Temple at Veii." *Etruscan Studies* 11: 35–48.

Neri, C., ed. 2021. *Sappho: Testimonianze e frammenti*. De Gruyter.

Neusner, J., tr. 1991. *The Mishnah: A New Translation*. Yale UP.

Neyrat, F. 2018. "Eccentric Earth." *Diacritics* 45.3: 4–21.

Ngai, S. 2005. *Ugly Feelings*. Harvard UP.

Nietzsche, F. 1991. *Human, All Too Human*. Trans. R. J. Hollingdale. Cambridge UP.

Nixon, R. 2011. *Slow Violence and the Environmentalism of the Poor*. Verso.

Nooter, S. 2017. *The Mortal Voice in the Tragedies of Aeschylus*. Cambridge UP.

North, J. H. 2012. *Winckelmann's "Philosophy of Art."* Cambridge Scholars Press.

Nussbaum, M. 1987. "The Stoics on the Extirpation of the Passions." *Journal for Ancient Philosophy and Science* 20.2: 129–77.

Nyong'o, T. 2019. *Afro-Fabulations: The Queer Drama of Black Life*. NYU P.

Ohrt, R., and A. Heil, eds. 2020. *Aby Warburg: Bilderatlas Mnemosyne—the Original*. Hatje Cantz.

Oliensis, E. 1997. "Return to Sender." *Ramus* 26: 172–93.

———. 2004. "The Power of Image-Makers: Representation and Revenge in Ovid *Metamorphoses* 6 and *Tristia* 4." *Classical Antiquity* 23.2: 285–321.

———. 2019. *Loving Writing/Ovid's* Amores. Cambridge UP.

Olsen, S. 2017. "The Fantastic Phaeacians: Dance and Disruption in the *Odyssey*." *Classical Antiquity* 36.1: 1–36.

Orlandi, L., and A. Steffani. 1688. *Niobe, Regina di Tebe*. Johann Jäcklin.

Ostwald, M. 1969. Nomos *and the Beginnings of the Athenian Democracy*. Clarendon P.

Otis, B. 1966. *Ovid as an Epic Poet*. Cambridge UP.

Ozbek, L. 2015. "Sofocle e la rappresentazione della morte: il 'caso limite' della *Niobe*." In *Staging Ajax's Suicide*, ed. G. W. Most and L. Ozbek, 261–72. Edizioni della Normale.

Palmer, L. R. 1950. "The Indo-European Origins of Greek Justice." *Transactions of the Philological Society* 49.1: 149–68.

Pardo, M. 1991. "Memory, Imagination, Figuration: Leonardo da Vinci and the Painter's Mind." In *Images of Memory*, ed. S. Küchler and W. Melion, 47–73. Smithsonian Institution Press.

Pearce, T. 2008. "Homer, *Iliad* 24,614–17." *Rheinisches Museum für Philologie* 151.1: 13–25.

Pennesi, A., ed. 2008. *I frammenti della* Niobe *di Eschilo*. Hakkert.

Pietrobuono, S. 2019. "'Whose Tears Remain in Marble to Be Seen': immagini letterarie del mito di Niobe." In *Il mito di Niobe*, ed. A. Bruciati and M. Angle, 44–51. Silvana Editoriale.

Pinto, S. 2020. *Infamous Bodies: Early Black Women's Celebrity and the Afterlives of Black Feminist Thought*. Duke UP.

Polati, A. 2010. *Il cavalier Carlo Ridolfi (1594–1658)*. Editrice Veneta.

Poliziano, A. 2019. *Greek and Latin Poetry*. Ed. and trans. P. E. Knox. I Tatti Renaissance Library.

Povinelli, E. 2016. *Geontologies*. Duke UP.

Prins, Y. 1999. *Victorian Sappho*. Princeton UP.

Puar, J. 2017. *The Right to Maim: Debility, Capacity, Disability*. Duke UP.

Pulcini, E. 2020. *Tra cura e giustizia*. Bollati Boringhieri.

Quashie, K. 2004. *Black Women, Identity, and Cultural Theory: (Un)becoming the Subject*. Rutgers UP.

———. 2021. *Black Aliveness, or a Poetics of Being*. Duke UP.

Rabel, R. J. 1990. "Apollo as a Model for Achilles in the *Iliad*." *American Journal of Philology* 111.4: 429–40.

Ramírez, C. 2021. "Cuerpos en fuga: el afecto espinosista en la teoría de los devenires de Deleuze y Guattari." *Metafísica y Persona* 13.25: 11–34.

Rancière, J. 2004a. "Is There a Deleuzian Aesthetics?" *Qui Parle* 14: 1–14.

———. 2004b. *The Flesh of Words*. Trans. C. Mandell. Stanford UP.

———. 2010. *Dissensus: On Politics and Aesthetics*. Trans. S. Corcoran. Continuum.

———. 2011. *Mute Speech*. Trans. J. Swenson. Columbia UP.

Rebaudo, L. 2012. "Il tema di 'Niobe in lutto.'" *Engramma* 99 (August 2012): 56–90. http://www.engramma.it/eOS/index.php?id_articolo=835.

Redfield, J. 1975. *Nature and Culture in the* Iliad. U of Chicago P.

Richardson, N., ed. 1993. *The Iliad: A Commentary*. Vol. 6. Cambridge UP.

Richter, S. 1992. *Laocoön's Body and the Aesthetics of Pain*. Wayne State UP.

Riedlmayer, A. 2001. "Convivencia under Fire: Genocide and Book Burning in Bosnia." In *The Holocaust and the Book: Destruction and Preservation*, ed. J. Rose, 266–94. U of Massachusetts P.

Rimell, V. 2006. *Ovid's Lovers: Desire, Difference, and the Poetic Imagination*. Cambridge UP.

———. 2015. *Closure of Space in Roman Poetics*. Cambridge UP.

———. 2020. "The Intimacy of Wounds." *American Journal of Philology* 141.4: 537–74.

Robinson, K. 2009. *Deleuze, Whitehead, Bergson*. Palgrave.

Rogers, C. 1961. *On Becoming a Person*. Houghton Mifflin.

Rosand, E. 1991. *Opera in Seventeenth-Century Venice: The Creation of a Genre*. U of California P.

Rosati, G., ed. 2004. *Ovidio*, Metamorfosi. Vol. 3, *Libri V–VI*. Fondazione Valla.

Rose, J. 2018. *Mothers: An Essay on Love and Cruelty*. Farrar, Straus and Giroux.

Rumpf, E. 1985. *Eltern Kind-Beziehungen in der griechischen Mythologie*. P. Lang.

Savinio, M. 1987. *Con Savinio. Ricordi e lettere*. Palermo.

Scaer, R. 2014. *The Body Bears the Burden: Trauma, Dissociation and Disease*. Routledge.

Schelling, F. W. J. 1856–61. *Sämtliche Werke*. Ed. Karl Friedrich August Schelling. Cotta.

———. 1968. "Concerning the Relation of the Plastic Arts to Nature." Trans. M. Bullock. In H. Read, *The True Voice of Feeling*, 323–64. Faber & Faber.

———. 1976–. *Historisch-kritische Ausgabe*, im Auftrag der Schelling-Kommission der bayerischen Akademie der Wissenschaften. Frommann-Holzboog.

———. 1989. *The Philosophy of Art*. Ed. and trans. D. W. Stott. U of Minnesota P.

Schmidt, D. J. 2017. "Between Niobe and Mary." *Research in Phenomenology* 47.2: 241–49.

Schmitt, C. 2003. *The Nomos of the Earth in the International Law of the* Jus Publicum Europaeum. Trans. G. L. Ulmen. Telos Press.

Schmitz, H. 1981. *System der Philosophie.* Vol. 3. Bouvier.

Schumann, D. 2009. *Political Violence in the Weimar Republic, 1918–1933: Fight for the Streets and Fear of Civil War.* Berghahn.

Seaford, R. 2005. "Death and Wedding in Aeschylus's *Niobe*." In *Lost Dramas of Classical Athens,* ed. F. McHardy, J. Robson, and D. Harvey, 113–27. Exeter UP.

Sellars, J. 1999. "The Point of View of the Cosmos: Deleuze, Romanticism, Stoicism." *Pli* 8: 1–24.

———. 2006. "An Ethics of the Event." *Angelaki* 11.3: 157–71.

Semon, R. W. 1908. *Die Mnème.* W. Engelmann.

Sevieri, R. 2010. "La forma del dolore: le immagini vascolari apule relative al mito di Niobe." In *Le immagini nel testo, il testo nelle immagini,* ed. L. Belloni, A. Bonandini, G. Ieranó, and G. Moretti, 197–240. Labirinti.

Sidgwick, E. 2014. *From Flow to Face.* Peeters.

Smith, M. 1970. "On the Shape of God and the Humanity of Gentiles." In *Religion in Antiquity: Essays in Memory of Erwin Ramsdell Goodenough,* ed. J. Neusner, 315–426. Brill.

Smith, M. F., trans. 1969. *Lucretius:* On the Nature of Things. Hackett.

Sommerstein, A., ed. 2009. *Aeschylus: Fragments.* Harvard UP.

Sorel, G. [1908] 1999. *Reflections on Violence.* Ed. J. Jennings. Cambridge UP.

Spade, P. V., ed. 1994. *Five Texts on the Medieval Problem of Universals: Porphyry, Boethius, Abelard, Duns Status, Ockham.* Hackett.

Spaeth, B. S. 1994. "The Goddess Ceres in the Ara Pacis Augustae and the Carthage Relief." *American Journal of Archaeology* 98: 65–100.

Spigner, N. A. 2014. *Niobe Repeating.* PhD diss. Vanderbilt U.

———. 2021. "Phillis Wheatley's Niobean Poetics." In *Brill's Companion to Classics in the Early Americas,* ed. A. J. Goldwyn, M. Feile Tomes, and M. E. Duquès, 320–42. Brill.

Stark, K. B. 2022. *Niobe und die Niobiden in ihrer literarischen, künstlerischen und mythologischen Bedeutung.* Legare Street Press.

Steiner, D. T. 2001. *Images in Mind.* Princeton UP.

———. 2021. *Choral Constructions in Greek Culture.* Cambridge UP.

Steiner, G. 1984. *Antigones.* Yale UP.

Stergiopoulou, K. 2014. "Taking 'Nomos': Carl Schmitt's Philology Unbound." *October* 149: 95–122.

Stevens, B. 2009. "*Per Gestum Res Est Significanda Mihi*: Ovid and Language in Exile." *Classical Philology* 104: 162–83.

Stoichita, V. I. 2008. *The Pygmalion Effect.* U of Chicago P.

———. 2015. *The Self-Aware Image.* Brepols.

Strohm, R. 2007. "Die klassizistische Vision der Antike: Zur Münchner Hofoper unter den Kurfürsten Maximilian II. Emanuel und Karl Albrecht." *Archiv für Musikwissenschaft* 64.1: 1–22.

Swift, S. 2013. "Hannah Arendt, Violence, and Vitality." *The European Journal of Social Theory* 16.2: 357–76.

Taplin, O. 1972. "Aeschylean Silences and Silences in Aeschylus." *Harvard Studies in Classical Philology* 76: 57–97.

———. 2007. *Pots & Plays.* The J. Paul Getty Museum.

Telò, M. 2020. *Archive Feelings: A Theory of Greek Tragedy.* Ohio State UP.

———. 2023. *Greek Tragedy in a Global Crisis: Reading through Pandemic Times.* Bloomsbury.

Thorsrud, H. 2008. "Cicero's Adaptation of Stoic Psychotherapy." *Annaeus* 5: 171–88.

Thorton, J. 2008. "'All Beautiful in Woe': Gender, Nation, and Phillis Wheatley's 'Niobe.'" *Studies in Eighteenth-Century Culture* 37.1: 233–58.

Tilley, C. 2004. *The Materiality of Stone: Explorations in Landscape Phenomenology*. Routledge.

Timms, C. 2003. *Polymath of the Baroque: Agostino Steffani and His Music*. Oxford UP.

Toadvine, T. 2018. "Thinking after the World: Deconstruction and Last Things." In *Eco-deconstruction: Derrida and Environmental Philosophy*, ed. M. Fritsch, P. Lynes, and D. Wood, 50–80. Fordham UP.

Toscano, A. 2018. "Antiphysis/Antipraxis: Universal Exhaustion and the Tragedy of Materiality." *Mediations* 31.2: 125–44.

———. 2021. "George Sorel, from *Reflections on Violence*." In *Walter Benjamin: Toward the Critique of Violence*, ed. P. Fenves and J. Ng, 194–200. Stanford UP.

Trendall, A. D. 1972. "The Mourning Niobe." *Revue Archéologique* 2: 309–16.

Ty, M. 2019. "Benjamin on the Border." *Critical Times* 2.2: 306–19.

Unger, D. 2018. "Klassizität im Übergang. Zur besonderen Stellung der Niobe in Schellings Erörterung der Skulptur." *Schelling-Studien* 6: 163–73.

Van der Kolk, B. 2014. *The Body Keeps the Score: Brain, Mind and Body in the Healing of Trauma*. Penguin Books.

Vasari, G. 1853. *Le vite de' piu eccellenti pittori, scultori e architetti di Giorgio Vasari*. F. Le Monnier.

Verhaeghe, P. 2013. "Louise Bourgeois." In *For Your Pleasure?*, ed. M. De Kesel, S. Houppermans, and M. Kinet, 69–90. Garant.

Villegas Vélez, D. 2020. "Interruption—Intervention: On the Interval between Literature and Music in Jean-Luc Nancy's 'Myth Interrupted.'" *Performance Philosophy* 5.2: 183–202.

———. 2022. "Apparatus of Capture: Music and the Mimetic Construction of Social Reality in the Early Modern/Colonial Period." *CounterText* 8.1: 123–48.

Vogel, J. 2008. "Galatea unter Druck." *Das Magazin des Intituts für Theorie* 12–13: 96–102.

Voigt, E.-M., ed. 1971. *Sappho et Alcaeus. Fragmenta*. Polak and van Gennep.

Wahl, J. 2016. *Human Existence and Transcendence*. Trans. W. Hackett. U of Notre Dame P.

Walcot, P. 1987. "Plato's Mother and Other Terrible Women." *Greece & Rome* 134.1: 12–31.

Warburg, A. M. 1892. *Introduction to the Second Proof of the Doctorate on Sandro Botticelli (1445–1510)*. Warburg Institute Archive, III. 39. 6, 1. The Warburg Institute.

———. 1992. "Mnemosyne Atlas." In *Die Beredsamkeit des Leibes*, ed. I. Barta-Fliedl and C. Geismar, 156–73. Residenz.

———. 1999. *The Renewal of Pagan Antiquity*. Getty Research Institute.

———. 2010. *Werke in einem Band, auf der Grundlage der Manuskripte und Handexemplare*. Suhrkamp Verlag.

Washington, T. 2013. "The Sea Never Dies. Yemoja: The Infinite Flowing Mother Force in Africana Literature and Cinema." In *Yemoja: Gender, Sexuality and Creativity in the Afro-Atlantic Diasporas*, ed. S. Otero and T. Falola, 215–66. SUNY P.

Weigel, S. 1996. *Body- and Image-Space: Re-reading Walter Benjamin*. Routledge.

Weiser, C. 1998. *Pygmalion*. P. Lang.

Welcker, F. G. 1836. *Über die Gruppierung der Niobe und ihrer Kinder*. E. Weber.

Wheatley, P. 1988. *The Collected Works of Phillis Wheatley*. Edited by J. C. Shields. Oxford UP.

———. 1995. *Poems of Phillis Wheatley: A Native African and a Slave*. Applewood Books.

———. 2001. *Complete Writings*. Penguin.

———. 2020. *Poems on Various Subjects, Religious and Moral, and a Memoir of Phillis Wheatley, a Native African and a Slave*. Kemp House.

Whistler, D. 2013. *Schelling's Theory of Symbolic Language: Forming the System of Identity*. Oxford UP.

Wiemann, E. 1986. "Der Mythos von Niobe und ihren Kindern." In *Manuskripte zur Kunstwissenschaft* 8: 6–9. Wernersche Verlagsgesellschaft.

Williams, G. 1994. *Banished Voices*. Cambridge UP.

Winckelmann, J. J. 2006. *History of the Art of Antiquity*. Trans. Harry Francis Mallgrave. Getty Research Institute.

Yu, J. 2008. "Living with Nature: Stoicism and Daoism." *History of Philosophy Quarterly* 25.1: 1–19.

Zanker, P. 1983. "Der Apollontempel auf dem Palatin. Ausstattung und politische Sinnbezüge nach der Schlacht von Actium." *Analecta Romana Instituti Danici*, Supplementum 10: 21–40.

———. 1988. *The Power of Images in the Age of Augustus*. Trans. A. Shapiro. U of Michigan P.

Zartaloudis, T. 2020. *The Birth of Nomos*. Edinburgh UP.

Zeidler, P. 2018. "Die Tötung der Nioben." In *Göttliche Ungerechtigkeit?*, ed. F. Rumschreid, S. Schrenk, and K. Kressirer, 15–77. Imhof.

Zeuch, U. 2000. *Umkehr der Sinneshierarchie*. M. Niemeyer Verlag.

CONTRIBUTORS

BARBARA BAERT is Professor in Medieval Art, Iconology and Historiography at the KU Leuven. Her work links knowledge and questions from the history of ideas, cultural anthropology and philosophy, and shows great sensitivity to cultural archetypes and their symptoms in the visual arts. She has been honored with several awards, among which the most prestigious is the Francqui Prize for Human Sciences in 2016. Her recent books include *Signed PAN* (2020); *From Kairos to Occasio along Fortuna: Text / Image / Afterlife* (2021); and *Looking into the Rain: Magic-Moisture-Medium* (2022).

ANDREW BENJAMIN is an Honorary Professorial Fellow at the University of Melbourne. He has taught in universities in both Australia and the United Kingdom. His forthcoming book is *Gesture and Form: Classical and Renaissance Expressions* (2024).

DREA BROWN is the author of *dear girl: a reckoning* (2015) and coeditor of *Teaching Black: The Craft of Teaching on Black Life and Literature* (2021). Their writing has appeared in publications such as *Hypatia: A Journal of Feminist Philosophy*; *Stand Our Ground: Poems for Trayvon Martin and Marissa Alexander*; *About Place Journal*; *Smithsonian Magazine*; and *Zócalo Public Square*. drea is currently an assistant professor in the English Department at Texas State University.

ADRIANA CAVARERO is Honorary Professor at the University of Verona. Her writings focus on ancient philosophy, political theory, feminism, and literature. Among her books are *In Spite of Plato: A Feminist Rewriting of Ancient Philosophy* (1995);

Relating Narratives: Storytelling and Selfhood (2000); *Stately Bodies: Literature, Philosophy and the Question of Gender* (2002); *For More Than One Voice: Toward a Philosophy of Vocal Expression* (2005); *Horrorism: Naming Contemporary Violence* (2009); *Inclinations: A Critique of Rectitude* (2016); and *Surging Democracy: Notes on Hannah Arendt's Political Thought* (2021).

REBECCA COMAY teaches in the Philosophy Department and the Centre for Comparative Literature at the University of Toronto, where she is also affiliated with the German Department, the Centre for Jewish Studies, and the Program in Literature and Critical Theory. She works mainly on nineteenth- and twentieth-century Continental philosophy (especially Hegel, Marx, and critical theory), psychoanalysis, and contemporary art. Her books include *Mourning Sickness: Hegel and the French Revolution* (2010) and (cowritten with Frank Ruda) *The Dash—The Other Side of Absolute Knowing* (2018). She is currently working on a book on the temporality of deadlines and another book called *Dramaturgies of the Dialectic*.

MILDRED GALLAND-SZYMKOWIAK is director of research at the CNRS and a professor at the Ecole normale supérieure (Paris). She has taught at the Sorbonne (Paris IV), the University of Bremen and at Monash University (Melbourne). Her fields of research are German philosophy since the end of the eighteenth century and aesthetics. She is a specialist in Schelling, Hegel, and early German Romanticism and is particularly interested in the question of the symbol in the history of philosophical aesthetics. Among her publications are (ed.) *Le problème de la finitude dans la philosophie de Schelling / Das Problem der Endlichkeit in Schellings Philosophie* (2011); K. W. F. Solger, *Écrits philosophiques,* traduction et commentaire (2015); and *Dialogue et système: Schelling, Solger, Hegel* (2023).

JOHN T. HAMILTON is the William R. Kenan Professor of German and Comparative Literature at Harvard University. Publications include *Soliciting Darkness: Pindar, Obscurity, and the Classical Tradition* (2004); *Music, Madness, and the Unworking of Language* (2008); *Security* (2013); *Philology of the Flesh* (2018); *Complacency: The Displacement of Classics in Higher Education* (2021); and *France/Kafka: An Author in Theory* (2023). His current project is entitled *Culture of Convenience.*

PAUL A. KOTTMAN is Professor of Comparative Literature, Chair of Liberal Studies and codirector of the Institute for Philosophy and the New Humanities at the New School for Social Research. He is the author, most recently, of *The Insistence of Art: Aesthetic Philosophy after Early Modernity* (2017) and *Love as Human Freedom* (2018). He also edits the book series *Square One: First Order Questions in the Humanities* for Stanford University Press.

JACQUES LEZRA is Distinguished Professor of English and Hispanic Studies, University of California—Riverside, and 2022 Chaire Internationale de Philosophie Contemporaine, Université de Paris-8. His most recent books are *República salvaje: De la naturaleza de las cosas* (2020); *On the Nature of Marx's Things: Translation as Necrophilology* (2018); *Untranslating Machines: A Genealogy for the Ends of Global*

Thought (2017); *"Contra todos los fueros de la muerte": El suceso cervantino* (2016); and *Wild Materialism: The Ethic of Terror and the Modern Republic* (2010; Spanish translation 2012; Chinese translation 2013). He is the coeditor of *Dictionary of Untranslatables: A Philosophical Lexicon* (2014). His translations include Paul de Man, *Visión y ceguera*; Etienne Balibar, *Universales*; and Alain Badiou, *The One*.

ANDRES MATLOCK is assistant professor of Classics at the University of Georgia. His work focuses on philosophy in the Roman context and applies critical and comparative approaches to ancient thought. He has published articles on topics ranging from Alain Badiou's "event" in the poetry of Sappho to the "feral" in post-Platonic ideas about nature and is currently writing his first book, entitled *Anachronous Habits: The Experience of Time in Cicero's Late Philosophy*.

BEN RADCLIFFE is a lecturer in Classics at Loyola Marymount University. His research and teaching focuses on Homer, ancient Greek literature, ancient and modern political thought, utopianism, and aesthetic theory. His work has appeared in the *American Journal of Philology, Ramus,* and *Classical Antiquity,* and he co-organized a seminar on paranoia in Greek and Roman literature at the 2022 ACLA conference. He is currently working on a project about the aesthetics of surplus in archaic Greek epic.

VICTORIA RIMELL is Professor of Latin at the University of Warwick. Her research, which spans many different authors and genres, engages critically with major themes in Roman literature and culture and aims to promote dialogue between classical philology and modern philosophical and political thought. Her latest books are *The Closure of Space in Roman Poetics* (2015); *Ovidio,* Remedia Amoris: *Introduzione, Testo, Commento* (2022); and (ed. with Elena Giusti) *Vergil and the Feminine* (*Vergilius* special issue, 2022).

MARIO TELÒ is Professor of Rhetoric, Comparative Literature, and Ancient Greek and Roman Studies. He is the author of *Aristophanes and the Cloak of Comedy* (2016); *Archive Feelings: A Theory of Greek Tragedy* (2020); *Greek Tragedy in a Global Crisis: Reading through Pandemic Times* (2023); *Resistant Form: Aristophanes and the Comedy of Crisis* (2023); and *Reading Greek Tragedy with Judith Butler* (2024), as well as coeditor of *Greek Comedy and the Discourse of Genres* (2013); *The Materialities of Greek Tragedy* (2018); *Queer Euripides* (2022); *Radical Formalisms: Reading, Theory, and the Boundaries of the Classical* (2024); and *The Before and the After: Critical Asynchrony Now* (2024).

MATHURA UMACHANDRAN is a Lecturer in the Department of Classics, Ancient History, Religious Studies, and Theology at the University of Exeter, UK, and teaches Greek and Reception studies. They hold a PhD from the Department of Classics, Princeton University (2018), where they worked on the reception of German philhellenism in twentieth century thought. Forthcoming books include *The Case for Critical Ancient World Studies: Forgetting Classics,* coedited with Marchella Ward, due to appear in late 2023 with Routledge. Their writing has appeared or is forthcoming in *Classical Receptions Journal, Ramus, American Journal of Philology, New German Critique,* and *American Historical Review.* They also hold a BA in Literae Humaniores from Wadham College, Oxford (2009), and an MA in Reception of the Ancient World from University College London (2011).

DANIEL VILLEGAS VÉLEZ is a musicologist based in Tiohtià:ke/Montréal. He received his PhD in Musicology from the University of Pennsylvania (2016) and held postdoctoral fellowships at Rutgers University and the Institute of Philosophy, KU Leuven. His work on early modern/colonial aurality, Western music aesthetics, and the role of timbre and technology in popular and experimental music has appeared in the edited volumes *Sound and Affect: Voice, Music, World*; *The Routledge Companion to Affect and Gender*; and *The Oxford Handbook of Timbre*, as well as in the journals *Performance Philosophy* and *Tijdschrift voor Filosofie*. His book *Mimetologies: Mimesis and Music, 1600–1850* is forthcoming with Oxford University Press.

INDEX

Abraham, 161, 165, 167–70, 173

Abramović, Marina, 73–75

Achilles and Priam, 2–3, 19, 55–59, 61, 63, 65–66, 82, 109, 115

Adorno, Theodor, 52, 196n2

Aeschylus, 121; in Aristophanes, 3–4, 18–20, 42–43, 73–74, 76, 85–89, 94–97, 182; *Niobe,* 3–4, 6, 18–19, 116, 118–19, 217

aesthetics, 3, 7, 14, 20, 51, 65, 72, 126, 135–36; glacial, 85–97; Hegelian, 173–76; of the image/icon, 76–77, 117–21; Kantian, 160–64; of Schelling, 145–46, 152–56; and sovereignty, 21

affect, 1–2, 21, 87–89, 121, 123, 140, 153, 157, 201, 221

agency, 4, 83, 201, 206–7

Aguilar, Laura, 205

Alexandros of Athens, 211, 214

allegory, 37, 47–49, 52–53, 91, 117, 179, 188, 191, 204, 223–29

Amphion, 2, 9, 29, 70, 103, 105, 179, 187, 208, 216

Antigone, 83, 114; Kierkegaard on, 12–13; Lacan on, 93–94, 97n58; as semblant of Niobe in Sophocles, 3, 12–13, 25–26, 41–42, 54, 71, 74–77, 79, 93–94, 96, 181–83

Apollo: and Achilles and Priam, 55–62; as agent of slaughter, 2, 9, 26–27, 36, 38, 55–62, 79, 86, 107, 119, 225; in artworks, 32, 131, 132 fig. 8.1, 134, 139, 145, 151, 153–54, 211, 214, 217 fig. 13.1; and Dionysus, 129, 135, 137; in opera, 187, 191–92; temples of, 78, 136

Arachne, 28, 48, 81, 98, 102–3, 105, 108–10

Arendt, Hannah, 21, 195–201, 207, 210n6

Aristophanes: and Aeschylus in *Frogs,* 3–4, 18–20, 42–43, 73–74, 76, 85–89, 94–97, 116n11, 182

Aristotle, 7, 42, 95, 181–82, 211–12

art, 4, 14–18, 20, 74–76, 109–10, 179; Hegel on, 171–73; Platonism on, 117–19; of the Renaissance, 131–32; Schelling on, 145–50, 153–55. *See also* aesthetics; engraving; painting; sculpture

Artemis: and Achilles and Priam, 55–62; as agent of slaughter, 2, 32, 38, 55–62, 86, 119, 225; in artworks, 32, 152, 217 fig. 13.1; in opera, 187

Artemisia, 120–21

• 271 •

Athena, 28, 29, 83n47, 98, 101–3, 110, 218

Atlas, 105, 107

Auden, W. H., 175–77

Augustus, 78–79, 86, 88–91, 108, 111–12

autonomy, 159, 161–71, 174–75

Baroque: myth, 52; opera, 21, 178–79, 185, 191

Bauer, Johann Wilhelm, 219–20

Benjamin, Walter, 1, 47, 188; and Arendt, 195–98; on law and guilt, 3, 12–14, 17–19; on mythic vs. divine violence, 19–21, 49–53, 56, 59–66, 195–201, 204, 207, 224, 235, 237

Bernini, Gian Lorenzo, 134, 139

Bilderatlas (Warburg), 136, 140, 180

biopolitics. *See* politics: biopolitics

Boccaccio, Giovanni, 3, 131, 209

Borges, Jorge Luis, 230–34

boundaries, 2, 36, 116, 121; between gods and humans, 19, 25–28, 54–66, 178, 187, 190–92, 211–12, 224, 235, 237; law and, 17–19, 49–51, 60–66, 178–83, 190–92; ontological, 121, 204; petrification and, 14, 36, 49–51

boundary stone, 49–51, 61, 181, 192, 224, 235, 237

Butler, Judith, 2n3, 17n64, 71–72, 161n3, 162nn5–7, 164; on justice and violence, 21, 224, 234–36; on law and guilt, 3, 7, 12–13, 18n71

Caesar, Julius, 98–99, 108, 111, 113

care, 2, 10–11, 21, 213, 221–22

Cicero, 20, 48–49, 82–83, 116, 120, 125, 209, 219

comedy. *See* Aristophanes; Philemon

community. *See* sociality

Cybele, 25, 37, 137

Danaids, 47, 52

Dante, 48, 221

death: and beauty, 153–56; and frozenness, 147–51; and life, 4–5, 21, 79–81, 103, 147–50, 171–74, 219; and maternity, 34; of Niobids, 208–9; philosophers on, 121–23. *See also* death-drive

death-drive, 3, 13–14, 41–41, 69–72, 85–86, 93–95, 97

Deleuze, Gilles, 20, 85–86, 88–94, 96, 117, 123–26, 191

depression, 162–64, 169–71, 174, 176

Derrida, Jacques, 14n48, 49, 64, 92, 94n49, 125

desire, 39–43, 69, 71, 80–82, 93–94, 97, 133, 160–67

Deucalion. *See* Pyrrha

Diana. *See* Artemis

Dione, 89

Dionysus, 29, 42, 102, 129, 135, 137, 139

Donne, John, 208

drama. *See* Aeschylus; Aristophanes; Euripides; opera; Sophocles; tragedy

Echo, 20, 80, 130, 144

ecology, 6, 20, 65, 85–86, 92–97

Electra, 41

engraving, 52, 70–71, 219–20

epigram, 47, 74–75, 82, 208

Esposito, Roberto, 14, 229–30, 235

ethics, 2–3, 20, 47–48, 84, 235–36; melancholic, 92; Platonic and Stoic, 117–26; and politics, 235–36; and relationality, 21, 43, 70–74, 160–77. *See also* guilt; hubris; justice; punishment

Euripides, 29–30, 42, 73, 76, 86, 97, 224

Eustathius, 131

exempla, 3, 37, 41, 47–49, 55–58, 109, 115, 119

feminism, 4, 28–32, 47, 92, 135. *See also* misogyny

fertility. *See* maternity; reproduction

fetish, 52, 80, 85, 89–91, 95

Field, Michael, 8–11

Freud, Sigmund, 52, 73–74, 93, 139, 160–64, 170–71

friendship, 7–8, 20, 76, 117, 119, 124, 166–67, 170–71; between Niobe and Leto, 8, 70, 115–16, 125, 210–15. *See also* sociality

gender. *See* feminism; queerness

gesture, 58, 123, 131, 147, 152, 219–20
Girard, René, 142
gods: as agents of violence and punishment, 50–51, 80–83, 200, 207, 238–42; as bounded from mortals, 19, 25–28, 54–65, 178, 211–12, 224; in competition with mortals, 98–99, 101–10, 112–13, 215–17; Socrates on representation of, 118–19
Gorgon, 83, 99, 101, 106, 181–82
grief, 2–3, 12–13, 36, 40, 116, 120; articulation of, 181–82; calculation of, 223–29, 234–37; and community, 52–57; engagement with, 70–83, 87–89, 124–25, 157, 172–74, 176; inexhaustibility of, 19, 41–43, 88, 111; maternal, 6–7, 28, 33, 120, 129–31, 157, 209, 238–39, 241–51; and resistance, 48–49, 52–53
guilt: Benjamin on, 3, 12, 18, 49–53, 61, 64, 201, 204, 224, 234–35; Butler on, 3, 7, 235–36; and punishment, 49–51; and trauma, 83–84. *See also* punishment

Hamlet, 3, 49
Hartman, Saidiya, 5–6, 203, 242n4
Hegel, Georg W. F., 1–3, 20–21, 48, 62n18, 69, 72, 161, 163–74
Heidegger, Martin, 40, 218
Heraclitus, 212
Herodotus, 43
Hesiod, 26n2, 64n25, 104, 110
Homer, 1, 4, 26n2, 38, 54–66, 71, 115, 125, 130, 143, 182, 224. *See also* Achilles and Priam
hubris, 3, 33, 70–71, 80–81, 129–30, 159, 188, 223–24, 238; as arrogance toward the gods, 25–28, 47–48, 54, 98, 102–7, 209, 215; and maternity, 28–30

image: and aliveness, 11–12, 39–40, 111; Borges on, 230–34; of the limit, 71; petrification and, 97, 99, 130–31; Platonism on, 20, 117–20, 125; Schelling on, 146–53; self-referential, 132–35; Ur-image, 140–44; Warburg on, 135–40; withdrawal of, 2, 37–38. *See also* representation; sculpture

Juno, 106, 109
Jupiter. *See* Zeus

justice, 4, 21, 70, 74, 76–77; Butler on, 234–37; and care, 221–22; education and, 118–20; and (im)mediacy, 2, 209–14, 218

Kant, Immanuel, 20, 93, 160–65, 168, 172, 174–76
Kierkegaard, Søren, 4, 12–14
Korah, 50–51, 64

Lacan, Jacques, 47, 89; on the death-drive, 3, 13, 20, 85–86, 93–94, 97; on Niobe's petrification, 69–75, 77, 79–81, 85–86, 93–94
lament. *See* grief
Laocoon. See sculpture: *Laocoon* group
Latona. *See* Leto
law, 3, 21, 54, 89, 96, 181; constancy of, 210, 214–15; and mediation, 215–18; moral, 162–63, 165, 168–69; ordering function of, 178, 182–84, 191–92; and punishment, 12, 49, 118–20; and violence, 6, 18–19, 49–51, 59–65. *See also* punishment; violence
Leto: friendship with Niobe, 8–10, 70, 76, 115–16, 125, 210–14, 205n26, 209–14; rivalry with Niobe, 2, 26–29, 38, 54–59, 90, 98–99, 103–9, 114, 178, 180, 202, 238; vengeance on Niobe, 38, 47, 111–12, 209–10
Levinas, Emmanuel, 4, 16n55, 44, 117–19, 121
liquidity, 1, 13–14, 16, 20, 78, 80, 95, 111, 114, 116, 244n9, 246. *See also* movement; petrification
logos. See speech
loss, 12, 55, 80, 130, 162, 174, 223, 225; Mary's vs. Niobe's response to, 21, 170–71; maternal, 1, 5–6, 8, 21–22, 87–90, 116, 157, 170–71, 203, 239; self-loss, 6, 11
Lucretius, 227–28, 234, 237

Markstein. See boundary stone
Mary, 2n4, 3, 8, 21, 48, 69, 70, 76, 161, 170–74, 176
Marx, Karl, 198
maternity, 2, 4, 20, 69–70, 81, 108; and Black experience, 6–7, 22, 32–33, 202–4, 241–51; glacial, 85, 88–95; hypermaternity, 10–11, 15–17, 19, 25–34, 37, 47, 146–50;

and love, 8–11, 69–70, 157–59, 173; and nourishment, 115–20, 123–24. *See also* reproduction

matter, 2, 20, 74, 141, 201; and art, 13–18, 30–34, 134, 147–48, 153, 171; Lucretius on, 227–28; "matterphorical," 5–6, 13; and philosophy, 115–17, 120–22; resistance of, 96, 171

Medusa, 52, 72, 81, 83, 101, 130, 133

melancholy, 1–2, 12, 19–21, 42, 48, 52, 92, 161–63, 170–71, 174–77

Metamorphoses (Ovid). *See* Ovid

metamorphosis. *See* petrification

Minerva. *See* Athena

misogyny, 3, 11, 28–30, 47, 50, 210n5. *See also* feminism

monumentality, 1, 17, 48, 133, 139, 143, 181, 225; Augustan, 79, 90–91, 111–12; and law, 50, 189, 192; in Ovid, 100–101, 109–12; and sculpture, 15, 31, 34, 36–37, 131

mortality. *See* death

motherhood. *See* maternity

mourning. *See* grief

movement, 5, 78, 159, 206–7; and immobility, 2, 15–16, 31, 86–87, 94–97, 219–21; in *Metamorphoses*, 86–87, 100, 104–5, 111–12; of Niobe and nymphs, 55, 63, 65–66; toward death (*see also* death-drive), 13–14

mural. *See* painting

music, 16–18, 21, 148–49, 179–80, 184–85, 189–91. *See also* opera

myth, 28–31, 33–35, 47, 83, 109, 114, 133, 166; and *logos*, 20, 99, 104–5; and philosophy, 117–23; on the stage, 185–86, 191; and violence, 50–52, 58–64, 198–207

Narcissus, 20, 72, 80–81, 94n48, 144, 223

necropolitics. *See* politics: necropolitics

Nietzsche, Friedrich, 30, 86, 126, 174, 224

Niobe: connected with Cybele, 25, 37; as exemplum, 3, 37, 41, 47–49, 55–58, 109, 115, 119; genealogy of, 2, 27n4, 114; and motherhood (*see* maternity); reception of, 1, 56, 202, 209 (*see also* engraving; opera; painting; poetry; sculpture; *and names of individual authors and artists*);

relationship with Leto, 8–10, 70, 115–16, 125, 210–14

Niobe (Aeschylus). *See* Aeschylus: *Niobe*

Niobe, Regina di Tebe (Steffani and Orlandi), 179–80, 185–92

Noah, 165–67, 170

nomos. *See* law

Oedipus, 42, 80, 89, 187

ontology, 10, 17, 65, 85, 93–95, 115–17, 120–21, 126, 205

opera, 18, 21, 178–80, 185–92

Orestes, 119

Orlandi, Luigi, 179–80, 185–91

Orpheus, 137, 139, 178–80

Ovid, 1, 4, 54, 71, 76–91, 94, 97; on Arachne, 102–3; and Augustan politics, 78–79, 89–91, 98–99; exile poetry of, 80–84, 87–91, 152; influence on Steffani and Orlandi, 187–88, 190–1; influence on Wheatley, 31–33, 202; on Narcissus, 72; on Niobe, in *Metamorphoses*, 2, 12, 20, 26–29, 38–39, 47, 54, 69–70, 76–80, 82–83, 85–88, 98–116, 129–32, 148, 179–80, 208–9, 215–20, 223–27, 233

painting, 36, 39, 103, 112, 129, 148, 164, 181; by Aguilar, 205; Hegel on, 171–73; mural, 75–76, 76 fig. 4.1; Renaissance, 131–32, 132 fig. 8.1, 134–35, 179; by Savinio, 14–18, 15 fig. 0.1; vs. sculpture and music, 149; vase, 3nn10–11, 31, 44–46, 45 fig. 2.1, 46 fig. 2.2, 86, 219–20; wall, 211, 214

Palaephatos, 131

Pausanias, 35, 37, 72, 130, 141, 209n3

Perseus, 72, 99–101, 106

petrification, 1–6, 12–17, 114, 140–44, 228–29, 239, 242; and animation, 39–40; and boundaries, 49–51, 61; and community, 55–56, 63; and the death-drive, 71, 93–94; depicted in artifacts, 31–32, 43–46, 131–32, 134–35, 219–20; depicted in literature, 32–34, 48, 78–82, 86–87, 104, 107–11, 129–31, 219; depicted in opera, 179, 187, 189–90; and maternity, 30–31; and mythic violence, 48–53; and philosophy, 114, 117–20, 126; Schelling on, 146–56; and silence, 31, 44, 97, 119–20, 124, 133,

179–82; subjectivity after, 201–8; and/as violence, 49–52, 142, 204

Philemon, 131

Philomela, 20, 79, 81, 226

philosophy, 35, 51, 71, 146–48, 209n5, 213–14, 229; of art, 153–59; in Borges, 232–34; on desire, pleasure, and melancholia, 160–77; Niobe as a problem for, 77, 81, 115–26; on violence, 197–201. *See also* aesthetics; ethics; Hegel, Georg W. F.; Kant, Immanuel; ontology; Plato/Platonism; Schelling, Friedrich von; Stoicism

Pindar, 110, 181, 224

Plato/Platonism, 20, 31, 41, 85, 115–22, 125–26, 184, 233

pleasure principle, 20, 79, 94, 160–66, 172–77

Pliny the Elder, 78, 136

Plutarch, 92

Priam. *See* Achilles and Priam

poetry, 64, 77, 99, 101–4, 145, 148, 233; by brown, 238–51; and depiction of gods, 103–4, 119–20; and monumentality, 112; and the post-melancholic, 175–77. *See also* epigram; *and names of individual authors*

politics, 3–5, 212, 224; and aesthetics, 85–91; Augustan, 88–89; biopolitics, 11–14, 20, 210n5, 213, 230, 235; and collective action, 62–66, 195–207; early modern European, 185–89, 191–92; Esposito on, 229–30, 235; and the law, 20–21, 49–51, 59–65, 179–83, 189–92; necropolitics, 20, 95–97; revolutionary, 51–53, 59–61. *See also* justice; law; rebellion; resistance; violence

pottery. *See* painting: vase

pride. *See* hubris

psychoanalysis, 3, 20, 39, 71–75, 85–86, 89–90, 93–95, 130, 139, 162n6. *See also* Freud, Sigmund; Lacan, Jacques

psychology, 21, 85, 90–95, 125, 129, 150–52, 160–77

psychotherapy. *See* trauma: psychotherapy and

punishment, 4, 19, 21, 47–53, 82–84, 86, 117–18, 178–82, 192, 206, 209, 244n9; of Antigone, 181–82; of Arachne, 98; of Atlas, 105–6; and divine/human boundary, 58, 60–61, 110, 204; and guilt, 18, 49–51; and hubris, 25–28, 47, 70, 130, 133, 182; and law, 12, 49, 119, 121, 178, 215–16. *See also* guilt; law; politics; violence

Pygmalion, 110, 134–35

Pyrrha, 110, 166, 168

queerness, 10–11, 21, 92, 202, 204–6

Rancière, Jacques, 4, 85–86, 95–96

Raphaël, Antonietta, 2, 19, 34, 35 fig. 1.1

rebellion, 25–26, 48, 51–53, 59–61, 202, 238, 242n3

reception: of Niobe (*see* Niobe: reception of); of Ovid, 112–13

relationality. *See* sociality

Renaissance. *See* painting: Renaissance; sculpture: Renaissance

repetition, 19, 48–49, 91, 95, 106, 108, 149, 178, 184, 191, 217, 225, 229

representation, 2, 4, 37, 39, 99, 109; and Baroque opera, 185–86; imperatives of, 17, 20, 85, 96–97; Platonism on, 117–19; and politics, 85, 96–97; Schelling on, 129–46; Stoics on, 123–26. *See also* art; engraving; image; painting; sculpture

reproduction, 10–11, 25–30, 42, 47, 51–52, 88–91, 107, 147, 202–6. *See also* maternity

resistance, 4, 6n19, 17n64, 18n71, 19–21, 96, 119, 196, 198–202, 205–7

revolution. *See* rebellion

Sappho, 1, 4, 8, 10–11, 70, 77, 115–16, 125, 205n26, 211, 224

sarcophagus, in the Glyptothek, 216, 217 fig. 13.1

Savinio, Alberto, 4, 14–18

Schelling, Friedrich von, 4, 20, 145–59

sculpture, 31, 36–37, 43, 74, 77, 104, 112, 129, 147, 179, 228, 235; *Apollo and Daphne* (Bernini), 134, 139; *Apollo* of Belvedere, 145, 151, 153–54; in Dante, 48; on Glyptothek sarcophagus, 216, 217 fig. 13.1; Hegel on, 171–73; *Laocoon* group, 136, 145, 151; in Ovid, 39–40, 99, 134; by Raphaël, 2, 19, 34–35, 35 fig. 1.1; Renaissance, 131–32, 134–35; Roman, 34, 44, 78, 99n1, 136–39, 138 fig. 8.2, 145, 148–59, 216, 217 fig. 13.1, 221; in the Uffizi Gallery, 34, 44, 132 fig.

8.1, 134–39, 138 fig. 8.2, 145, 148–59, 221. *See also* art; monumentality

Seneca, 20, 39, 124–25

silence, 4, 19, 44, 74, 119–20, 123, 130, 133, 179–82, 201; in Aeschylus, 3, 6, 18, 31, 42–43, 73, 86, 89, 97; Cicero on, 116, 209; and guilt, 50, 72, 201; in opera, 21; in Ovid, 33, 78, 81–82, 86–90, 116n8, 180, 217–18

slavery, 4–7, 22, 32–33, 126, 200, 202–4, 212, 240, 242–51

sociality, 79–80, 208; and the divine, 62–66, 168–69, 215–16; and friendship, 210–13; and grief, 43, 54–58; in the *Iliad*, 54–58, 62–66; in Kantian and Hegelian ethics, 164–77; and *logos*, 181–82; and maternity, 11, 20, 115–16, 124, 173–74; and *nomos*, 182–85; and philosophy, 20, 115–17; and spatiality, 212–15, 217–18, 221–22. *See also* friendship

Socrates, 31, 44, 118–20

solitude, 2, 16, 36, 41, 54, 77

Sophocles, 3–4, 19, 25, 29, 41–42, 54, 71–72, 74–75, 77, 79, 86n3, 94, 96, 133n21, 133n23, 181, 183

sorrow. *See* grief

speech, 3, 20, 74, 94, 97, 116, 123, 148, 181–82, 184, 217–18

Statius, 39

statues. *See* sculpture

Steffani, Agostino, 179–80, 185–86, 188

Stoicism, 20, 115–17, 121–26

stone. *See* petrification

subjectivity, 2n4, 4–5, 10–13, 18, 50, 52, 80–83, 92–97, 160–69, 174–77, 201–7, 230

suicide, 3, 103, 122, 196, 208, 216

supplication, 56, 89

Symbolic, 3, 10, 11n34, 17, 30, 47, 81, 94, 119–21

Tantalus, 2, 27n4, 75, 105, 107, 114, 188, 219

temporality, 1, 12, 44, 66, 88–95, 107, 124, 204, 209; and ancestrality, 93–94; and Augustan futurism, 89–91, 112–13; of the image, 117–18; Kierkegaard on, 12–14; and law, 49–50; and relational ethics, 21, 217–18, 221–22

Theodoridas, 74

Timotheus, 122, 125, 179n1

Tiresias, 39, 80, 103, 187, 190–1

tragedy, 79, 82, 238; and aesthetics, 77, 85–86, 88, 97; Echo as tragic, 144; Kierkegaard on, 12; Niobe as tragic, 3, 40–43, 132, 143; Niobe as un-tragic, 159; and opera, 187–89; by Savinio, 16; Wheatley and, 33. *See also* Aeschylus; Euripides; Sophocles

trauma, 4, 7, 42–43, 54, 80–84, 115, 141, 176, 203; and exile, 88; Hegel on, 165–68, 170–72, 174; and mythic violence, 49–50; psychoanalysis and, 71–77; psychotherapy and, 82–83

Tzetzes, John, 131

Uffizi Gallery. *See* sculpture: in the Uffizi Gallery

uncanniness, 28–31, 33–34, 40, 52, 66

vase painting. *See* painting: vase

violence, 17, 114, 119, 184, 218, 229; Arendt on, 195, 197–200; and Atlantic slavery, 5, 203–4; Benjamin on, 12, 21, 49–51, 56, 59–66, 195–201, 204, 207, 224, 234–35; Butler on, 12–13; Girard on, 142; glacial, 95; in the *Iliad*, 55–59, 63–66; and law, 19–20, 49–51, 54–66; mythic vs. divine, 49–51, 59–66, 199–201, 204, 207, 224, 234–35. *See also* punishment; politics

Warburg, Aby, 4, 20, 129, 135–40, 142, 180

weaving, 26, 28, 98, 102–3, 108–9

Wheatley, Phillis, 1, 4–7, 19, 22, 32–33, 202, 238, 240n1, 242n4, 244n9, 246n11, 248, 251n13

Winckelmann, Johann, 136, 142, 145, 150–52, 154–55, 159

Zeno, 44, 121–23, 125

Zeus, 9, 29, 55–57, 63–64, 101–3, 105–6, 122n31, 119, 190

CLASSICAL MEMORIES/MODERN IDENTITIES
Paul Allen Miller and Richard H. Armstrong, Series Editors

Classical antiquity has bequeathed a body of values and a "cultural koine" that later Western cultures have appropriated and adapted as their own. However, the transmission of ancient culture was and remains a malleable and contested process. This series explores how the classical world has been variously interpreted, transformed, and appropriated to forge a usable past and a livable present. Books published in this series detail both the positive and negative aspects of classical reception and take an expansive view of the topic. Thus it includes works that examine the function of translations, adaptations, invocations, and classical scholarship in the formation of personal, cultural, national, sexual, and racial formations.

Niobes: Antiquity, Modernity, Critical Theory
EDITED BY MARIO TELÒ AND ANDREW BENJAMIN

Virginia Woolf's Mythic Method
AMY C. SMITH

Shadows of the Enlightenment: Tragic Drama during Europe's Age of Reason
EDITED BY BLAIR HOXBY

Modern Odysseys: Cavafy, Woolf, Césaire, and a Poetics of Indirection
MICHELLE ZERBA

Archive Feelings: A Theory of Greek Tragedy
MARIO TELÒ

The Ethics of Persuasion: Derrida's Rhetorical Legacies
BROOKE ROLLINS

Arms and the Woman: Classical Tradition and Women Writers in the Venetian Renaissance
FRANCESCA D'ALESSANDRO BEHR

Hip Sublime: Beat Writers and the Classical Tradition
EDITED BY SHEILA MURNAGHAN AND RALPH M. ROSEN

Ancient Sex: New Essays
EDITED BY RUBY BLONDELL AND KIRK ORMAND

Odyssean Identities in Modern Cultures: The Journey Home
EDITED BY HUNTER GARDNER AND SHEILA MURNAGHAN

Virginia Woolf, Jane Ellen Harrison, and the Spirit of Modernist Classicism
JEAN MILLS

Humanism and Classical Crisis: Anxiety, Intertexts, and the Miltonic Memory
JACOB BLEVINS

Tragic Effects: Ethics and Tragedy in the Age of Translation
THERESE AUGST

Reflections of Romanity: Discourses of Subjectivity in Imperial Rome
RICHARD ALSTON AND EFROSSINI SPENTZOU

Philology and Its Histories
EDITED BY SEAN GURD

Postmodern Spiritual Practices: The Construction of the Subject and the Reception of Plato in Lacan, Derrida, and Foucault
PAUL ALLEN MILLER